BOLOGNESE INSTRUMENTAL MUSIC, 1660–1710

To my parents,
Robert and Louise

Bolognese Instrumental Music, 1660–1710

Spiritual Comfort, Courtly Delight, and Commercial Triumph

GREGORY BARNETT
Rice University, USA

ASHGATE

Published by
Ashgate Publishing Limited
Gower House
Croft Road
Aldershot
Hampshire GU11 3HR
England

Ashgate Publishing Company
Suite 420
101 Cherry Street
Burlington, VT 05401-4405
USA

Ashgate website: http://www.ashgate.com

British Library Cataloguing in Publication Data
Barnett, Gregory Richard, 1964–
    Bologna and late seventeenth-century Italian instrumental music 1. Instrumental music – Italy – Bologna – History and criticism 2. Music patronage – Italy – Bologna – History – 17th century 3. Bologna (Italy) – Intellectual life – 17th century
    I. Title
    784'.094541'09032

Library of Congress Cataloging-in-Publication Data
Barnett, Gregory Richard, 1964–
    Bolognese instrumental music, 1660–1710 : spiritual comfort, courtly delight and commercial triumph / by Gregory Barnett.
        p. cm.
    Includes bibliographical references (p.   ).
    ISBN 978-0-7546-5871-9 (alk. paper)
  1. Instrumental music–Italy–Bologna–17th century–History and criticism. 2. Instrumental music–Italy–Bologna–17th century–Analysis, appreciation. 3. Instrumental music–Italy–Bologna–18th century–History and criticism. 4. Instrumental music–Italy–Bologna–18th century–Analysis, appreciation. 5. Music–Social aspects–Italy–Bologna–History–17th century. 6. Music–Social aspects–Italy–Bologna–History–18th century. I. Title.

    ML503.8.B65B37 2007
    784.0945'41–dc22

                                                        2007010308
ISBN 978 0 7546 5871 9

Printed and bound in Great Britain by
MPG Books Ltd, Bodmin, Cornwall.

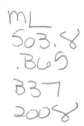
Contents

List of Figures

List of Tables

List of Music Examples

Acknowledgments

In the course of researching and writing this book, I have accumulated a great number of debts that I am pleased to acknowledge. Fellowships from the Italian Fulbright Commission and a summer stipend from the National Endowment for the Humanities helped me during the writing stage of this project, as did a grant from the Shepherd School of Music at Rice University. The staffs of several libraries and archives proved indispensible in the research of this book. In particular, the assistants at the Museo Internazionale e Biblioteca della Musica di Bologna and at the Biblioteca Estense Universitaria in Modena were uncommonly generous in helping me to track down and reproduce materials from their vast collections.

The book began years ago as a Ph.D. dissertation at Princeton University under the direction of the late Thomas Walker who introduced me to seventeenth-century Italy and its music. His rigorous standard of scholarly enquiry and deep understanding of Italian musical culture furnished me with essential tools as I began my research. The imposing intellect and boundless imagination of my foremost mentor at Princeton, the late Harold Powers, broadened my perspective and inspired me to pursue diverse questions that I could never have formulated on my own. One of those questions relates to tonal style. Jessie Ann Owens, a keen scholar of early tonal practices, encouraged me to continue that research while helping me to focus my ideas. Similarly, Michael Talbot, Jeffrey Kurtzman, and Anne Schnoebelen frequently and generously shared their views and spent significant amounts of time helping me with my own. Marc Vanscheeuwijck, expert on the music and musical practices of San Petronio in Bologna, and Carol Marsh, scholar and practitioner of Baroque dance, have on several occasions shared their abundant and detailed knowledge with me. Several colleagues—Lowell Lindgren, Andrew Dell'Antonio, Eleanor McCrickard, and John Suess—read various chapters and offered crucial advice that helped me to expand my findings or to hone my arguments. I hasten to add that the defects which remain here are my own stubborn doing.

My deepest appreciation is for my family. Stephen Kennamer, music critic and my uncle who knows music and knows writing, has stimulated and challenged me with his powers of observation, writerly acumen, and unmatched wit. Sylvia Ouellette, my wife, mother to our remarkable son Harry, and violinist extraordinaire, first made a musician out of me and then coaxed out my best ideas about music in our many conversations. And finally, Robert and Louise Barnett—my parents, my first and ongoing teachers, and excellent editors—have seen nearly all of my prose and have always improved it. I dedicate this book to them with love and gratitude.

List of Abbreviations

As used in *Répertoire international des Sources Musicales* (*RISM*)

GB-Lbl	British Museum, London
GB-Ob	Bodleian Library, Oxford
I-Baf	Accademia Filarmonica di Bologna
I-Bas	Archivio di Stato di Bologna
I-Bc	Museo Internazionale e Biblioteca della Musica di Bologna (formerly the Civico Museo Bibliografico Musicale)
I-Bca	Biblioteca Comunale dell'Archiginnasio di Bologna
I-Bsp	Archivio della Basilica di San Petronio, Bologna
I-Bu	Biblioteca Universitaria di Bologna
I-FEas	Archivio di Stato di Ferrara
I-FEca	Curia Arcivescovile di Ferrara e Comacchio, Archivio
I-MOas	Archivio di Stato di Modena
I-MOe	Biblioteca Estense Universitaria, Modena

Introduction

This book explores the instrumental music that flourished in the Bolognese region of north-central Italy during the late seventeenth century. During this time, dances, sonatas, and the emerging concerto figured prominently throughout Italy as part of elaborate church rituals, opulent public and private celebrations, and meetings of learned societies. This period also witnessed the heyday of Bolognese instrumental music publishing, whose success was due in large part to the abundance of sonatas and dances that were adaptable to various devotional, diversional, and even pedagogical uses. The seven chapters of this study thus detail a picture of the repertory and the broader milieu in which it was created. The aim here is to illustrate not only the historically significant and defining features of the music, but also the interaction between instrumental ensemble music, on the one hand, and aristocratic traditions, civic customs, and ecclesiastical institutions, on the other. In doing so, this book seeks to recapture the musical life that lay behind the surviving repertory while detailing much of its finest music.

The roughly 50-year period covered here—an extended late seventeenth century that begins in 1657 with the arrival of the prolific Maurizio Cazzati in Bologna and ends in 1709 with the death of Giuseppe Torelli—embraces the initial burst of compositional activity by Cazzati that inspired a younger generation of instrumentalist-composers and the crucial developments in the emerging Bolognese concerto. This period also encompasses the rise and fall of Bolognese music publishing, which surpassed the output of older Venetian firms from the 1660s on and then declined, like that of Venice, in the face of a market flooded with engraved prints (of often pirated music) produced in Amsterdam, London, and Paris.

Chapter 1, "Chronicles of Instrumentalists and Composers," examines the professional and personal circumstances of the musicians (instrumentalists, chapel-masters, dilettante musician-aristocrats) who composed sonatas in Bologna. The documents that detail musical careers originate in various sources: membership and pay records of musical institutions such as the Bolognese Concerto Palatino and the *cappella musicale* of San Petronio;[1] letters written to the influential Bentivoglio family of Ferrara;[2] the prescriptive *ordini* published by musical *accademie*; and the numerous prefatory letters and dedications included with the printed sonatas themselves.

---

1   Documents pertaining to the Concerto Palatino and to music at San Petronio are collected in two books by Osvaldo Gambassi: *Il Concerto Palatino della Signoria di Bologna: cinque secoli di vita musicale a corte (1250–1797)* (Florence: Olschki, 1984); and *La cappella musicale di S. Petronio: maestri, organisti, cantori, e strumentisti dal 1436 al 1920* (Florence: Olschki, 1987).

2   The Bentivoglio letters from 1646 to 1685 have been transcribed in Sergio Monaldini, ed., *L'Orto dell'Esperidi: musici, attori e artisti nel patrocinio della famiglia Bentivoglio (1646–1685)* (Lucca: Libreria Musicale Italiana, 2000).

The larger picture sketched by these sources is a familiar one: professional musicians were compelled to seek multiple positions in order to earn an adequate living. They did so despite the prohibitions against this by patron-employers whose interest lay in exerting control over a loyal and readily available stable of performers. The publications of these performers usually represented that which they modestly denied in their dedications: a means of ingratiating themselves with a patron and of attaining prestige in a competitive and uncertain field. The fascination here lies not only in the career and patronage patterns that emerge, but also in the particulars of individual cases—for instance, the supplications of a rank-and-file violist, Geminiano Bosi, who lost his position at S. Petronio, at least for a time, by trusting an improvident patron; the various entrepreneurial initiatives of cellist-composer Giovanni Battista Vitali as both performer and music printer; and the wranglings of Giovanni Battista Mazzaferrata with the pay-master of his Accademia della Morte di Ferrara, where even as maestro di cappella, Mazzaferrata was sometimes left unpaid for services and unreimbursed for expenses.

Whereas the opening chapter focuses on instrumentalists and composers, Chapter 2, "The Forms and Uses of the Sonata da Camera," directs attention toward their patrons by detailing the intersections between the late-*Seicento* aristocracy and the sonata da camera. The genre furnished music for their instruction as instrumentalists and dancers, their theatrical performances of ballets in the Jesuit Collegio de' Nobili, and their ostentatious celebrations in the frequent *feste da ballo* that comprised part or all of an evening's entertainment on signal occasions (a prominent wedding, the visit of a foreign dignitary, the elevation of a local aristocrat to the cardinalate, and the like).

On close examination, the sonata da camera is seen to subsume a wide variety of musical styles that reveal its origins in diverse circumstances: the rhythmically strict dances, marked *alla francese*, that satisfied the resurgent late-*Seicento* vogue of French courtly dance; the more varied Italian dances that fit with contemporary descriptions of a relatively free and less intricate Italian tradition of dancing (according to French and English observers, mere walking to a nearly superfluous musical accompaniment);[3] fugal and even canonic *balli*, along with various puzzle canons, that evidence a delight in contrapuntal games; and, from the 1680s, dances whose double-stops and passage-work for string players emphasize instrumental performance itself.

Chapter 3, "Bologna, Modena, and the Place of Virtuosity," introduces the large, unique, and, as argued here, German-influenced collection of music in manuscript from the Biblioteca Estense Universitaria in neighboring Modena.[4] This extraordinary repertory from the court of Duke Francesco II d'Este (1660–94) adds significantly to our perspective of Italian instrumental music because it contains pieces so different from the better-known printed repertory, despite the fact that many of the composers whose music was published in Bologna are also represented here. Numerous pieces

---

3   Irene Alm, "Operatic Ballroom Scenes and the Arrival of French Social Dance in Venice," *Studi musicali* 25 (1996): 345–71, includes detailed accounts of Venetians dancing as witnessed by French and English visitors.

4   Appendix B lists this repertory and other instrumental music in manuscript by Modenese composers.

from the ducal collection represent genres and scorings that are rarely or never found elsewhere and are technically demanding well beyond anything in print.

The chapter begins with a reconstruction of standard violin technique of the period as transmitted in treatises and assorted exercises. The basic skills as outlined in these sources are not far short of those required to perform the sonatas and dances from the Bolognese presses, which produced accessible pieces useful in various circumstances. By contrast, solo repertory in the Modenese manuscripts challenges violinists with intricate chordal playing, extremely high positions, and sophisticated bowings—techniques that are nearly or entirely absent from anything in print. The two repertories thus complement one another in style and function: the prints offer music designed for and marketed to a musically trained public; the manuscripts represent music of the professional soloist for concert use at the court of a major Italian prince.

Chapter 4, "*Da Chiesa* and *Da Camera*," addresses the long-troubling complications of sonata genres, performing venues (implicit and explicit), and musical style. Using the phenomenon described by linguists as markedness to study the pair of terms that occur regularly in the sonata repertory—"sonata" (unmarked) and "sonata da camera" (marked)—this chapter argues for the implicit suggestion of churchliness in the unmarked term "sonata." This reading is supported by Bolognese publishers' catalogs that detail terminology which links "sonata" and "sonata da chiesa" in meaning. This is reinforced by the testimony of composers, who, while making a distinction between styles appropriate to the church and the chamber and associating a churchly style with the unmarked sonata, emphasize that the actual performance of such sonatas was not restricted to any one venue. The sonata (*da chiesa*) may therefore be understood as conceived for use in church, while multipurpose in actual practice.

Looking at the broader picture, the codification of sonata genres as churchly or courtly follows clear functional distinctions already established at the beginning of the seventeenth century. However, the emergence of more detailed genre terminology in the latter half of the century occurs during a period in which publishers were focusing, with considerable commercial success, on single-genre prints—whether sonatas (church or chamber), cantatas, motets, or masses.

While Chapter 4 explicates the idea of the church sonata, Chapter 5, "Sacred Music, Musical *Topoi*, and the Sonata in Church," focuses on the stylistic profile of the genre and its evocations of the Catholic liturgy. The bulk of this chapter draws on sources of instrumental music for church use (Banchieri, Bottazzi, Frescobaldi, and others)[5] to show how commonly occurring movement types in the sonata repertory

---

5 Adriano Banchieri, *L'organo suonarino*, Op. 13 (Venice: Amadino, 1605; facsimile, Bologna: Forni, 1969); Amante Franzoni, *Apparato musicale di messa, sinfonie, canzoni, motetti, & letanie della Beata Vergine a otto voci, con la partitura de bassi*, Op. 5 (Venice: Amadino, 1613); Giovanni Battista Milanuzzi, *Armonia sacra* (Venice: Vincenti, 1622); Girolamo Frescobaldi, *Fiori musicali di diversi compositioni, toccate, kirie, canzoni, capricci, e ricercari*, Op. 12 (Venice: Vincenti, 1635; facsimile with an introduction by Luigi Ferdinando Tagliavini, Bologna: Forni, 2000); Giovanni Salvatore, *Ricercari a quattro voci, canzoni francesi, toccate, et versi per rispondere nelle messe con l'organo al choro* (Naples: Beltrano, 1641); Antonio Croci, *Frutti musicali di messe tre ecclesiastiche per rispondere alternatamente al choro ... con cinque canzoni & un ricercaro cromaticho,*

reflect musical *topoi* of the sacred liturgy (the *toccata d'intonazione*, Kyrie mottos, the *ricercar cromatico* for the Offertory, and *durezze e ligature* for the Elevation). The presence of these churchly *topoi* within the sonata lays bare its links with liturgical music, particularly that for the organ, and impresses upon it what was then perceived to be a sacred stylistic profile.

In light of the stylistic evidence discussed here, the final section of this chapter addresses two further issues: (1) the liturgical role of sonatas themselves; and (2) the appearance of dance-*topoi* as sonata finales. In its liturgical use, the sonata appears to have been adaptable to a maximum of different practices, from a movement-by-movement performance at points across an entire Mass or Vespers to the use of a complete sonata at a single moment of the ceremony. In these and other possibilities, dance-*topoi*—also used in Bolognese masses and motets as "alleluia" settings—evoked not secular dance but sacred jubilation.

Chapter 6, "Tonal Style, Modal Theory, and Church Tradition," shows the links between sonatas and the modes, which were a crucial article of Counter-Reformation faith and the typical means by which composers and musicians categorized different tonalities. In the latter half of the seventeenth century, two composers, Giovanni Maria Bononcini and Giulio Cesare Arresti, published collections of sonatas arranged according to modal criteria. Although their theories of a modal system differ markedly from one another, Bononcini and Arresti's common use of a particular set of eight tonalities—known since the early seventeenth century as *tuoni ecclesiastici* (church keys)—reveals a practice among sonata composers that extended well beyond the Bolognese orbit.

In this practice, the tonalities of numerous sonatas prints were ordered according to identical or similar sequences of tonics and key signatures as those of the *tuoni ecclesiastici*. Moreover, composers expanded the eight *tuoni* to greater numbers through transpositions, reflecting a practical conception of a core set plus its transpositions. These origins explain the unique tonal style of the Bolognese repertory (in particular a "Phrygian key" descended from the *quarto tuono* and a "plagal key" descended from the *ottavo tuono*) and the use of incomplete key signatures that have long puzzled scholars.

The final chapter of this book, "The Concerto Before the Concerto," focuses on the concerto idea in Bolognese music and the emergence of the musical features that would characterize the eighteenth-century concerto. Scholars from Arnold Schering (1905) to Richard Maunder (2004) have rightly focused on S. Petronio in Bologna as a critical venue in the emergence of the genre, but the origins of the musical features that Bolognese composers would eventually associate with the concerto genre have never been clearly sorted out. This chapter therefore traces the emergence of non-imitative and recapitulatory movement types back from Giuseppe Torelli's Op. 8 concertos (1709) to mid-century polychoral sonatas and other works for larger ensembles, and then to trumpet sonatas. This line of development, which often features *stile tromba* writing even when no trumpets were called for, stands apart from the Roman tradition of concerto grosso instrumentation, whose origins were first detailed by Owen Jander.[6]

Op. 4 (Venice: Vincenti, 1642); Giovanni Battista Fasolo, *Annuale che contiene tutto quello, che deve far un organista, per risponder al choro tutto l'anno*, Op. 8 (Venice: Vincenti, 1645).

6   Owen Jander, "Concerto Grosso Instrumentation in Rome in the 1660's and 1670's," *Journal of the American Musicological Society* 21 (1968), 168–80.

Instead, trends in Bologna lead to a different kind of concerto marked as much by formal characteristics as by scoring. Sources that document its performance in theaters, *palazzi*, and churches, moreover, enable us to envision both the function and spirit of this new genre and the musical effects that its composers strove to create.

This much outlines the chapters that follow. The remainder of this introduction traces the emergence of the instrumental repertory, presents its main genre, the sonata, and details the ensembles for which sonatas were written. But first, in order to picture the setting in which this music flourished, we turn to late-*Seicento* Bologna and its musical celebrations.

Festive Bologna

Richard Lassels, on visiting Bologna in the late seventeenth century, judged it "one of the greatest townes of Italy, and one of the hansomest."[7] According to the travelogue of Maximilian Misson, published in English translation in 1695, Bologna was "reckon'd to be somewhat greater and even richer than Florence, and to contain more Inhabitants by a third part."[8] Franciscus Schott, who traveled there earlier in the seventeenth century, but whose writings were published only in 1660, confirms the good opinion of these two writers in a detailed description. He begins by explaining the city's most famous epithet, *Bologna grassa*:

> That Bologna abounds with all things is known to all, whereby they give it the stile of Fatt: Its Fields are fair and large, producing all sorts of Corn, and Wines of the best sorts in Italy, with all kinds of Fruits, particularly Olives, so bigg and sweet, that they give not place to them of Spain; it hath also Woods for Foul, and Beasts of Chase, and notwithstanding there be few Lakes, yet tis plentifully served with fish from Comacchio and Argenta. Here (to maintain their Epithite of Bologna la grassa) they make those famous Salsages, which for their excellency are esteemed a costly dish through the World, as also a Conserve of Quince and Sugar called gelo or gelly, fit for the Table of a Prince. They here also work with great Art, Sheaths for Knives of boyled Leather, and fair Harquebuses, and Flacks or Bottels. They have great numbers of Silk-Worms, from whose labour they extract quantity of Silk, whereof they make Sarcenet, Velvet, and other Silks, in such plenty, as that they not only supply all Italy therewith, but England and the Low Countreys. Tis adorned with superb and spatious Edifices, as well for divine worship as private use.[9]

To judge from these writers and other visitors to Bologna during the seventeenth century, the city not only prospered among its fertile plains, but also exhibited its good fortune in its rich cuisine and thriving silk and other industries. Charles Thompson, who visited there some time in the first half of the eighteenth century, noted that Bologna's good situation stemmed in part from its advantageous relationship within

---

7   Richard Lassels, *The Voyage of Italy* (London: Strakey, 1670), 141.

8   Maximilian Misson, *A New Voyage to Italy*, 2 vols (London: Bently, 1695), vol, 2, 185. Originally published as *Nouveau voyage d'Italie* (The Hague: van Bulderen, 1691).

9   Franciscus Schott, *Italy in its Original Glory, Ruine, and Revival* (London: Griffin, 1660), 88.

the Papal States as a relatively autonomous city.[10] He also remarked on its flourishing artistic culture, including impressive musical performances: "the great Plenty of Provisions, the Politeness of the Inhabitants, the fine Paintings and Statues with which it abounds, and their frequent Concerts of Musick, Opera's, and Comedies, render it delightful to a Traveller, and afford him both Instruction and Amusement."[11]

The most famous such "Concert of Musick" took place during the liturgical celebration of the city's patron saint, S. Petronio, each year on October 4 at the enormous church named for him. Figure 0.1 reproduces a depiction of the feast-day celebrations from 1722, during the visit of James Stuart, the Catholic pretender to the English throne, and his wife Clementina Sobieski. Clearly shown are the church's two organs, and scores of singers and instrumentalists arrayed within a vast, two-tiered performing space, the *cantoria*, behind the main altar.[12] As one of the most solemn feasts of the Bolognese calendar, its observance included a Mass plus Te Deum hymn, and first and second Vespers performed by the full *cappella* of the church augmented by scores of extra musicians hired for the event. The resulting collection of performing forces was observed by Edward Wright during his 1721 visit, when he "heard a noble Concert of Musick, Vocal and Instrumental, in which the Performers were above a hundred and forty in number."[13]

---

10 Charles Thompson, *The Travels of the Late Charles Thompson, Esq.* (Reading: Newberry and Micklewright, 1744), 97: "We have already hinted, that Bologna threw itself under the Protection of the Pope about the Year 1278, and procur'd very advantagious Terms, and many Privileges, which it enjoys to this Day. These Advantages are the Cause of this City's flourishing beyond any other in the Pope's Dominions, who nevertheless draws more Taxes from this Place of Liberty, than from those where his Authority is unlimited and absolute, which are by that means almost dispeopled, whilst Bologna contains about eighty thousand Inhabitants. The Pope has his Legate here, who is a kind of Viceroy; and criminal Matters are determin'd by Judges of the Pope's appointing; but Crimes are only punishable in the Persons of those who commit them, and their Estates are not to be confiscated to the Government for any Offences whatsoever. In Civil Causes the Magistrates have the Power of Judicature; and the City is allow'd to appoint an Auditor to the Rota, and to have an Ambassador at Rome to take care of its Privileges."

11 Ibid.

12 This water-color rendition belongs to a series of commemorative paintings known as the *Insignia degli Anziani del comune*. They were commissioned to mark an important event that took place within each two-month term of the city's ruling consul of *Anziani* and chief magistrate (*Gonfaloniere*). These paintings are preserved in the Archivio degli Anziani of the Archivio di Stato di Bologna (I-Bas), and a catalog of the images is Giuseppe Plessi, ed. and introduction, *Le insignia degli anziani del comune dal 1530 al 1796: catalogo-inventario* (Rome: Ministero dell'Interno Pubblicazioni degli Archivi di Stato, 1954). Three studies have detailed the performance practices of the *cappella musicale* in S. Petronio: Anne Schnoebelen, "Performance Practices at S. Petronio in the Baroque," *Acta musicologica* 41 (1969): 37–55; Eugene Enrico, *The Orchestra at San Petronio in the Baroque Era* (Washington, DC: Smithsonian Institute Press, 1976); and Marc Vanscheeuwijck, "Musical Performance at San Petronio in Bologna: A Brief History," *Performance Practice Review* 8 (1995): 73–82. For a more recent and comprehensive study of S. Petronio during the late seventeenth century, see Vanscheeuwijck, *The Cappella Musicale of San Petronio in Bologna under Giovanni Paolo Colonna (1674–1695)* (Brussels and Rome: Institut Historique Belge de Rome, 2003).

13 Edward Wright, *Some Observations Made in Travelling through France, Italy, &c. in the Years 1720, 1721, and 1722*, 2 vols (London: Ward and Wicksteed, 1730), vol. 2, 440.

Figure 0.1   *Insignia degli Anziani*, vol. 13, 37/a: the feast of S. Petronio, 1722. Archivio di Stato di Bologna (I-Bas), Archivio degli Anziani

Wright's figure is no exaggeration. Anne Schnoebelen, in her study of performance practice at S. Petronio, has reconstructed the musical forces involved in several of these feast-day celebrations from surviving pay records in the archives of the basilica. The number of musicians paid for the performance shown in Figure 0.1 was 141, comprising 34 regular members of the *cappella musicale* and 107 supplemental musicians.[14] During the late seventeenth century the number of regular and imported musicians (*forestieri*) for the feast was smaller, but by no means small. Totals, according to Schnoebelen's reconstructions, are 86 (1663), 106 (1687), and 105 (1694).[15] The combination of such musical forces with a display of fireworks and artillery fire outside the church during the Te Deum attests to a level of extravagant celebration that distinguished the most prominent Italian cities during the seventeenth century.

Other public celebrations in Bologna reveal similar large-scale efforts. The Festa della Porchetta, the commemoration of the feast of S. Bartholomew (August 24) and of the Bolognese victory in 1249 at the Battle of Fossalta, involved the construction in the main square, the Piazza Maggiore, of a temporary theater for an elaborate entertainment with music, dance, and stage machinery. Figs. 0.2–0.4 show, respectively, the outdoor theater built in 1680 with singers and instrumentalists on top, undecorated machinery used in the celebration of 1683, and the decorated machinery from 1683 which features three enormous working fountains. Among those fountains are cypresses and—much smaller in size—groups of dancers in the guise of nymphs.[16] Also during the Festa della Porchetta, a ball with refreshments was held in the vast Sala d'Ercole of the Palazzo della Signoria, the seat of city government.[17] That room, which was used for other musical events as well as meetings on municipal business, is shown in Figure 0.5. Depicted in that image is the 1705 celebration of the Feast of the Annunciation, which features singers and instrumentalists on an enclosed and elevated stage.[18]

---

14 Schnoebelen, "Performance Practices," 39.

15 Schnoebelen, "Performance Practices," 43.

16 For a study of the Festa della Porchetta and its entertainments during the seventeenth century, see Elita Maule, "La 'Festa della Porchetta' a Bologna nel Seicento: indagine su una festa barocca," *Il carobbio* 7 (1980): 251–62. The 1683 feast is discussed briefly on p. 257.

17 Maule, "Festa della Porchetta."

18 I-Bas, Archivio degli Anziani, *Insignia*, vol. 11, 105b–106a (second bimester, 1705).

Figure 0.2   Collezione delle relazioni della Festa della Porchetta, vol. 1: illustration of the stage and scenery for the Festa della Porchetta of 1680. Biblioteca Comunale dell'Archiginnasio, Bologna (I-Bca), Gabinetto Disegni e Stampe

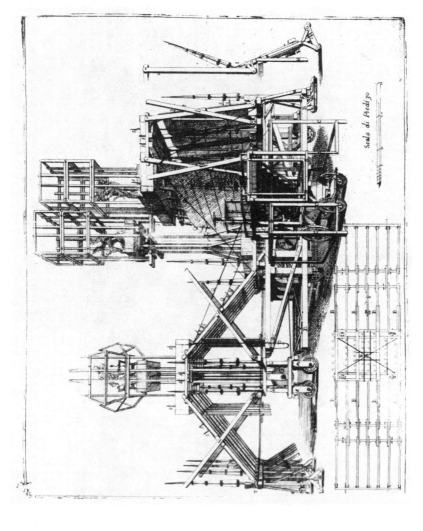

Scala di Piedi30

Figure 0.3   *Collezione delle relazioni della Festa della Porchetta*, vol. 1: undecorated machinery from *Prometeo liberato*, performed for the Festa della Porchetta of 1683. Biblioteca Comunale dell'Archiginnasio, Bologna (I-Bca), Gabinetto Disegni e Stampe

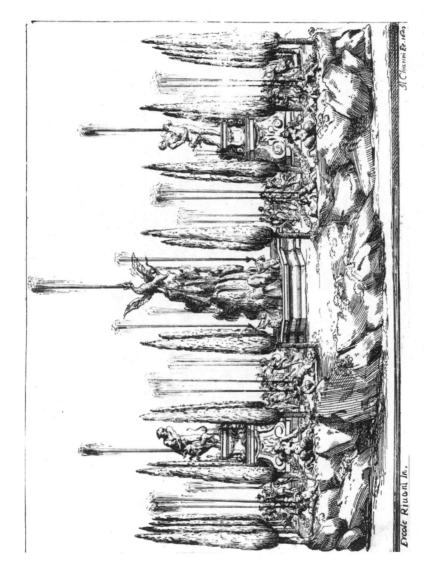

Figure 0.4   *Collezione delle relazioni della Festa della Porchetta*, vol. 1: nymphs dancing among fountains in *Prometeo liberato*, performed for the Festa della Porchetta of 1683. Biblioteca Comunale dell'Archiginnasio, Bologna (I-Bca), Gabinetto Disegni e Stampe

Figure 0.5   *Insignia degli Anziani*, vol. 11, 105b: musical celebration of the Feast of the Annunciation at the Palazzo della Signoria, Bologna, 1705. Archivio di Stato di Bologna (I-Bas), Archivio degli Anziani

Private functions were no less extravagant. An idea of Bolognese aristocratic celebrations comes from an engraving, Figure 0.6, showing an outdoor serenata that featured over 50 singers and instrumentalists, held in 1692 at the country home of one of Bologna's senatorial families. Likewise, a detailed description of a 1705 literary academy and ball hosted by Count Alamanno Isolani, a member of the Bolognese senate, gives us a sense of painstaking preparation, enormous expense, and sumptuous atmosphere.[19] According to the diarist who recorded it,

> The event could not have been more noble nor better received. It was done in the courtyard of the Luppari house, now of the Isolani. And in this annexed courtyard of irregular form but made octagonal by manufacture, having raised several arches over columns disposed in two rows on two levels (so well in agreement and so richly adorned that it seemed to have been the Palace of Apollo), all the capitals and bases of these columns, covered by gold-threaded crimson damask, were plated with gold. On the first floor, where the ladies were in the middle of the theater, there were steps from one column to the other covered with the finest carpets. And from the arches hung trellises made for the occasion held up by statues also plated with gold, two for each arch; the number of the arches of the first and second floors was twelve. Everything in its turn was decorated with the finest tapestries, placed between damask hangings also threaded with gold, paintings, and mirrors. This courtyard was covered with a ceiling of crimson interspersed with cloths of gold color; the trellises were similarly decorated. This great theater was illuminated by three large suns of 72 candles each, and by twelve crystal chandeliers, well distributed, as well as 50 silver candle-holders for the orchestra with three candles for each [musician].[20]

---

19 Antonio Francesco Ghiselli, *Memorie antiche manuscritte di Bologna raccolte et accresciute sino à tempi presenti dal canonico Antonio Francesco Ghiselli nobile bolognese*, MS, early eighteenth century, Bologna, Biblioteca Universitaria (I-Bu), ms. 770, vol 57, 3 ff. Quoted in Corrado Ricci, *I teatri di Bologna nei secoli XVII e XVIII* (Bologna: Successori Monti, 1888; facsimile, Bologna: Forni, 1965), 261–3.

20 Ghiselli, "L'accione non poteva riescire più nobile nè meglio intesa; fu fatta nella Corte di Casa Luppari, hora degl'Isolani, et a questa annessa Corte di forma irregolare, ma ridotta ottangola a forza di manifattura, havendovi alzato attorno alcuni archi sopra colonne disposte in due ordini a due piani, così bene intese e così ricche d'adornamenti che pareva la Regia d'Apollo; tutti i capitelli e Base di esse colonne, ch'erano coperte di damaschi cremisi trinati d'oro, erano posti a oro. Nel primo piano, ove stavano nel mezzo del Teatro le dame era circondato da una colonna all'altra di scalinate coperte di finissimi tapeti, e dagl'archi pendevano spalliere d'inventione sostenute da statue poste a oro, due per arco; il numero degli archi del primo e secondo piano erano dodici. Veniva poi tutto addobato a torno di finissimi arazzi, framezzati di Damaschi pure trinati d'oro, di quadri e di specchi. Era coperta questa Corte d'un cielo di cendado cremesino tramezzato con teli di color d'oro, come pure erano guernite le spalliere suddette. Illuminavano questo gran Teatro tre gran soli di settantadue candele per ciascheduno, e di dodici lumiere di cristallo benissimo compartite, oltre ciò da cinquanta candelieri d'argento per l'orchestra con tre candele per ciascheduno."

Figure 0.6   Serenata held in the courtyard of the Albergati estate outside Bologna, 1692. Biblioteca Comunale dell'Archiginnasio, Bologna (I-Bca), Gabinetto Disegni e Stampe, Raccolta Gozzadini

A depiction of the Isolani academy is shown in Figure 0.7. In it we see five sides of the octagonal space described above. According to an accompanying engraving and a libretto that record the event, three singers representing Venus, Juno, and Minerva in that evening's cantata are seated underneath the central arch of the picture, with accompanying instrumentalists, 29 in all, flanking the singers.[21] Still further to the sides and in the gallery above are seated the scores of citizens and foreigners in attendance. At ground level and closest to the viewer are some 30 members of the Accademia de' Gelati, "each one at a table with lighted candles where he recited his compositions."[22] Also in attendance were dukes and princes from Modena, Mirandola, and Brunswick, as well as the principal figures in Bolognese society—the ruling legate, vice-legate, *Gonfaloniere*, and *Anziani*—all of whom sat in specially placed seats facing the singers and academicians.

From such recollections and images we gain a sense of Bologna's prosperity and her musical patronage.[23] That patronage, in turn, nurtured the local population of instrumentalist-composers who created the sonatas and concertos for which the city is remembered. As we shall see, the instrumental repertory was the fruit not only of local musicians, but also of the entrepreneurial initiatives of music publishers working in the favorable climate of Bologna *grassa*.

* * *

21 The libretto, *Introduzione ed intramezzi per musica nell'Accademia de' Signori Gelati* (Bologna: Pisarri, 1705), reproduces the verses that were sung and describes order of events. An engraving showing a bird's-eye view of the room with a description of the seating is found in the Raccolta Gozzadini (Cartella 2, No. 72) of the Gabinetto Disegni e Stampe, Biblioteca dell'Archiginnasio, Bologna (I-Bca). According to this drawing, the number of musicians appears to be 29, but Ghiselli mentions there being 40 (see Chapter 2, p. 89).

22 I-Bca, Gabinetto Disegni e Stampe, Raccolta Gozzadini, Cartella 2, No. 72. The caption describing the academicians reads as follows: "Luoghi degl'Ill.mi SS.ri Accademici Gelati con tavole e candelieri accesi ove ogn'uno recitò le sue compositioni, come nel loro libretto, che dispensavano si puol vedere."

23 A collection of essays on festive spectacle and music is *Musica in torneo nell'Italia del Seicento*, ed. Paolo Fabbri (Lucca: Libreria Musicale Italiana, 1999). Within that volume, the essay that focuses on Bologna is Sergio Monaldini, "'La montagna fulminata': Giostre e tornei a Bologna nel Seicento," 103–33.

Figure 0.7   Festa of the Accademia de' Gelati at the Palazzo Isolani, 1705. Biblioteca Comunale dell'Archiginnasio, Bologna (I-Bca), Gabinetto Disegni e Stampe, Raccolta Gozzadini

Beginning in the 1660s, musicians from Bologna and surrounding regions of north-central Italy began to compose and publish music for ensembles of strings and continuo in unprecedented quantities. A repertory for all occasions, instrumental genres served as embellishment of the sacred liturgy, as accompaniment to the frequent balls (*feste da ballo*) held by the local aristocracy, as music for the diversion of instrumentalists in private academies, and as repertory for young nobles learning to dance and to play instruments. Ghiselli and other chroniclers of the period detail the indispensable contribution of instrumental ensembles within this festive milieu.[24] At the masquerades held as part of the 1710 carnival celebrations a "clamorous [strepitosa] sinfonia" was played by "all of the virtuosos of this city, that is, of the violin, contrabass, oboe, and trumpet." For a visit by the King of Denmark there were "celebrations and the most solemn music" that included, at the entrance to the *palazzo* of the Ranuzzi family, "a harmonious consort of trumpets and oboes positioned along the balustrade of the stairway" and then, during his meal there, was heard "a great sinfonia of the choicest instruments that surrounded the large hall in two choirs."[25] A "sinfonia so sweet that it carried away one's spirits" began the *gran festa* held at the house of the Albergati family to honor the Prince of Piombino.

The sudden rise to prominence of instrumental music within the Bolognese milieu was the result of several converging factors: the arrival of Maurizio Cazzati in 1657 as maestro di cappella at S. Petronio; the founding in 1666 of the Accademia Filarmonica; and, perhaps most important, the aggressive marketing of instrumental music by Bolognese publishers from the 1660s on. Cazzati was already an experienced church musician who had held prestigious positions in Mantua, Ferrara, and Bergamo when he was appointed maestro di cappella at S. Petronio, the principal church in Bologna. A zealous reformer who expanded the personnel of the *cappella musicale* and significantly elevated its musical profile,[26] Cazzati was also a prolific composer whose output included numerous collections of sonatas and dances for ensembles of strings and continuo. Following his example, composers from Bologna and surrounding regions produced works in the same genres: thus in the 1660s, G. B.Vitali (Cazzati's student), Francesco Prattichista, Gioseffo Placuzzi,

---

24 Ricci, *I teatri di Bologna*, transmits brief excerpts from these chroniclers in his exhaustive survey of entertainments in Bolognese theaters, private and public, during the seventeenth and eighteenth centuries. The accounts quoted here are found in Ricci, 396–407.

25 The performers described here are most likely members of the Concerto Palatino della Signoria di Bologna, whose duty it was to perform during functions of the municipal government. One of these was to play during the midday meal of the ruling *Gonfaloniero* and *Anziani*. For a documentary history of the ensemble, see Gambassi, *Il Concerto Palatino*.

26 Cazzati's tenure at S. Petronio was marked by controversy. His status as an outsider to Bologna, reforming zeal, and desire for unprecedented control over the administration of the *cappella musicale* inspired much enmity, which led to a polemic over his competency as a composer. The circumstances of his stormy tenure are detailed in Anne Schnoebelen, "Cazzati vs. Bologna 1657–1671," *Musical Quarterly* 57 (1971): 26–39. The details of the polemic itself are the subject of a thorough study with transcribed and translated documents by Ursula Brett, *Music and Ideas in Seventeenth-Century Italy: The Cazzati–Arresti Polemic*, 2 vols (New York: Garland, 1989).

G. M. Bononcini, and Giuseppe Colombi began sending instrumental music to the presses in Bologna. More and more composers joined them in the following decades, so that Bologna surpassed her main rival, Venice, as the leading publisher of sonatas and dances, and became the foremost center in Italy for the dissemination of instrumental music.

At this same time, the concentration of local talent and patronage facilitated the creation of the Bolognese Accademia Filarmonica, an organization of professional musicians—admitted as composers, singers, or instrumentalists—whose weekly meetings provided a stimulating forum for the performance and discussion of members' latest compositions. Their annual Mass and Vespers in honor of the academy's patron saint, S. Anthony, became an event to rival the ceremony for S. Petronio in grandeur and fame. Already in the early years of the Accademia Filarmonica its annual celebration was praised "for both the variety and exquisiteness of the compositions that were heard and for the gathering of more than the usual great number of academicians, among whom many foreign composers and singers brought off their virtues to particular applause."[27] The Bolognese milieu was expanded, moreover, through its frequent exchange of musicians with the nearby cities of Modena and Ferrara. In Modena, the patronage of Duke Francesco II d'Este (1660–94), a violinist himself and an eager supporter of music, provided a further catalyst to instrumentalist-composers. From 1674, the year that Francesco assumed power after his mother's regency, he dramatically expanded the personnel in his *cappella* from eight to 22 musicians.[28] He also amassed a large manuscript collection of virtuoso repertory for violin and for cello, by Giuseppe Colombi, G. B. Vitali, G. B. Degli Antonii, Domenico Gabrielli, and others.[29] In Ferrara, the late seventeenth century coincided with the height of activities of its two musical academies, the Accademia dello Spirito Santo and the Accademia della Morte.[30] Each was associated with a confraternity of the same name and kept a maestro di cappella and organist on its permanent payroll. Both, however, regularly hired singers and instrumentalists

---

27 *Gazzetta di Bologna*, July 2, 1687, transcribed in Osvaldo Gambassi, *L'Accademia Filarmonica di Bologna: fondazione, statute e aggregazione* (Florence: Olschki, 1992), 339: "riuscì tal funzione al maggior segno decorosa, sì per la varietà, e squisitezza delle composizioni, che furono udite, come anche per il concorso più del solito numeroso de Signori Accademici stessi, fra quali alcuni signori compositori, e cantori forastieri fecero spiccare la lor virtù con applauso particolare."

28 Victor Crowther, *The Oratorio in Modena* (Oxford: Clarendon Press, and New York: Oxford University Press, 1992), 5.

29 Appendix B, a list of instrumental music from Bologna and Modena in manuscript, shows the predominance of manuscripts from the Biblioteca Estense, originally the music collection of Duke Francesco II. Other composers represented in the Modenese collection of instrumental music are Domenico Galli, Antonio Gianotti, Carl'Ambrogio Lonati, Luigi Mancia, Evilmerodach Milanta, Giuseppe Pozzatti, Pietro Soresina, and Alessandro Stradella.

30 Studies devoted to these institutions are, respectively, Giovanni Pierluigi Calessi, *Ricerche sull'Accademia della Morte di Ferrara* (Bologna: Antiquae Musicae Italicae Studiosi, 1976); and Donato Mele, *L'Accademia dello Spirito Santo: un istituzione musicale ferrarese del secolo XVII* (Ferrara: Liberty House, 1990).

for important feast days, and from surviving personnel records of the Accademia della Morte we know that it drew on singers and instrumentalists from the Veneto as well as cities throughout Emilia and Romagna.[31]

Bolognese Music Publishing

Central to the rising prominence of Italian instrumental music and Bologna's part in it was music publishing in the city. We may perceive the significance of the years around 1660 as a turning point by examining the printed output in Bologna of instrumental genres from that time. The number of prints, decade by decade, furnishes the most succinct and compelling testimony on the emergence of instrumental music in Bologna (Table 0.1). In the 1650s, Bologna produced just a single print of instrumental music: the 1659 reprint of Maurizio Cazzati's *Sonate a due violini col suo basso continuo*, Op. 18.[32] These sonatas had originally been published in Venice, which produced some 16 instrumental prints during the 1650s. The reprint of Cazzati's sonatas in Bologna marked a tentative beginning, probably inspired by Cazzati's arrival, in 1657, as maestro di cappella of S. Petronio.[33]

Table 0.1   Instrumental prints in Bologna and other Italian cities

Year	Bologna	Modena	Venice	Rome	Other
1650			I	I	II
1651			II	I	I
1652			I	I	
1653					I
1654			I	I	
1655			IIII		
1656			IIII	I	I
1657			I	II	
1658			I		I
1659	I		I		
1660	I		I		II
1661					
1662	I				
1663	I	I	II		
1664			II	I	
1665	I		IIII	I	
1666	II		I		
1667	IIIII		III		I
1668	III		II		III

31 Calessi, 73–4.
32 The work was first published in Venice in 1656 by Francesco Magni.
33 This edition of Cazzati's Op. 18 sonatas, published by Benacci, features a frontispiece depicting Bologna's patron saint, San Petronio, holding a miniature representation of the city.

Year	Bologna	Modena	Venice	Rome	Other
1669	IIIIIII			I	I
1670	III		II	I	
1671	IIIIIII				
1672			I		II
1673	IIIIII		IIII		
1674	IIIII			I	II
1675	II				I
1676	II				I
1677	IIIII		III	II	II
1678	III		II	I	I
1679	II		III		I
1680	III		II		
1681	I		I	II	III
1682	IIII	I	IIII	I	
1683	III	I	III	I	I
1684	III	I	II		I
1685	IIIIII	III	II	IIII	III
1686	IIIII		I		I
1687	IIIIIII	I	II		I
1688	IIIIII			II	II
1690	IIIII		II		
1691	III		II	II	II
1692	II	I	IIIII	I	III
1693	IIIII	III	II	I	I
1694	II		II	I	
1695	IIIIII	I	II	II	III
1696	II	I	III	I	II
1697	IIII	III	IIIII	I	II
1698	I	I	II		IIIIII
1699		I	I	I	I

The 1660s, by contrast, saw a marked change in output: in that decade Bolognese instrumental prints amounted to 21; those of every other Italian city combined amounted only to 25. In the 1670s, Bologna's output easily outpaced that of all other cities. After that point, other cities began to produce more instrumental prints, and although Bologna continued to lead through the end of the century, the surge in printed instrumental music was now spread throughout Italy. Modena, for example, began to follow Bologna's lead in the early 1680s, due to the initiative of a transplanted Bolognese composer, G. B. Vitali.[34] In that decade Venice and Rome—

---

34 Vitali's career is summarized in Chapter 1. A study of the documents connected with Vitali's efforts at music publishing is Carlo Vitali, "Giovanni Battista Vitali editore di musica fra realizzazione artistica e insuccesso imprenditoriale," *Nuova rivista musicale italiana* 27 (1993): 359–74.

partly on the strength of Arcangelo Corelli's trio sonatas, and partly because the Bolognese output was now split between Bologna and Modena—sent slightly more instrumental music to the presses.

The relative importance of published instrumental music compared to other genres can be gauged by looking at the catalogs of the leading Bolognese printer, Giacomo Monti. Under the heading of *suonate, correnti, e balletti* (i.e., sonatas and dances), Monti's 1682 catalog lists some 32 items.[35] The same catalog lists 25 motet collections and 15 of *canzonette* (a category that includes all genres of secular vocal music: cantatas, madrigals, canzonas). By the early eighteenth century, Monti's successor, Marino Silvani, lists 71 instrumental works, 33 motet collections, and 38 collections of secular vocal pieces, mostly cantatas. In sum, the publication of instrumental works for sale had, by 1707, equaled motets and cantatas combined.

Before all other factors, the enterprises of the publishers themselves contributed vitally to the creation of this repertory. Marino Silvani, before he took over the Monti presses in 1702, had worked in Bologna from 1665 as a bookseller and, it seems, as a commissioning agent. His efforts in collecting music for publication (and republication) and in finding a patron to subvent the costs of printing is revealed in the letters of dedication that he wrote. The Op. 15 *Correnti e balletti* of Cazzati, as Silvani explains in the 1667 dedication of their second printing, "proved to be so precious to the world that presently one necessarily weeps for them, even though a very great number was produced by the presses. I, with the consent of the author, have resolved to bring them to light once again in order to satisfy the public desire of the connoisseurs."[36]

Writing the 1684 dedication of Domenico Gabrielli's Op. 1 dances to a Bolognese count, one Giuseppe Filippo Calderini,[37] Silvani recounts that

> Having heard the practising of various *balli da camera* by the masterly bow of Sig. Domenico Gabrielli, I prevailed upon him to allow me the liberty of transmitting them in print; he, as one who has never felt the pricking of such a Glory's spur, rendered vain my desires with a negative [response]. But in hearing that I had in mind imprinting on the cover the name of your illustrious lordship (who has a very generous spirit and a dilettante's feeling for such beautiful harmony), he gave me free rein to send them to the presses.[38]

---

35 This information may be found in Oscar Mischiati, ed., *Indici, cataloghi e avvisi degli editori e librai musicali italiani dal 1591 al 1798.* (Florence: Olschki, 1984), which is a collection of catalogs by Italian music publishers of the seventeenth and eighteenth centuries.

36 Marino Silvani, dedication to Maurizio Cazzati, *Correnti e balletti a cinque, alla francese, et all'italiana, con alcune sonate à 5. 6. 7. e 8*, Op. 15 (Bologna, Monti, 1667): "riuscirono così pretiosi al Mondo, che di presente se ne piange necessitoso, benche in grandissimo numero si fossero dati alle Stampe. Io, considerata la brama de' Virtuosi, risolsi col beneplacito del proprio Autore, di bel nuovo darle alla luce, per sodisfare al publico desiderio de gl'Intendenti." Cazzati's dances were first published in 1654.

37 The Calderini family is among the 100 most prominent families as listed in Pompeo Scipione Dolfi, *Cronologia delle famiglie nobili di Bologna, con le loro insignie, e nel fine i cimieri* (Bologna: Ferroni, 1670; facsimile, Bologna: Forni, 1990), 226.

38 Marino Silvani, dedication from Domenico Gabrielli, *Balletti, gighe, correnti, alemande, e sarabande, à violino, e violone*, Op. 1 (Bologna: Monti, 1684): "Avendo udito

A third example tells a similar story from the composer's perspective. In his note to the reader, Count Pirro Albergati, a Bolognese noble as well as composer, protests that his compositions are too flawed for the presses. And yet "friend printer's sweet persuasion so violently pushed me that it was necessary for me to see to his repeated solicitations."[39]

The geographical reach of Bolognese music publishers extended well beyond the city itself, and composers who sent their music to its presses hailed from all parts of Italy.[40] In 1680, Monti published an anthology of sonatas by selected composers (Table 0.2), which, except for its inclusion of Roman and Venetian works, gives us a sense of the wider "Bolognese" orbit as defined by the reach of its publishers. In addition to publishing composers from the length and breadth of Emilia and Romagna (this would encompass Modena, Parma, Ferrara, Forlì, and Ravenna), Monti and other Bolognese publishers drew on music from Lombard cities (Milan, Brescia, Cremona, and Mantua) and, to a lesser degree, on Vercelli and Turin in Savoy, Verona in the Veneto, and Florence in Tuscany.

Table 0.2   Composers published in the *Scielta delle suonate* (Bologna, 1680) and their city of activity

Giovanni Battista Bassani	Mirandola, maestro di cappella at the ducal court
Giovanni Francalanza	Parma, Madonna della Steccata
Petronio Franceschini	Bologna, maestro di cappella, S. Maria della Morte
Andrea Grossi	Mantua, "musico e sonatore di violino" at the ducal court
Pietro Degli Antonii	Bologna, maestro di cappella, S. Maria Maggiore
Alessandro Stradella	Rome (in Genoa from 1678)
Giovanni Maria Bononcini	Modena, maestro di cappella at the cathedral (d. 1678)
Giovanni Appiano	Milan, maestro di cappella, S. Simpliciano

esercitar più volte dall'Arco Maestro del Sig. Domenico Gabrielli varij Balli da Camera, l'hò pregato a darmi la libertà di trasmetterli alle Stampe, & egli come quello che non si è mai sentito pungere dallo sprone di sì fatta Gloria, hà reso vano con la negativa il mio desiderio. Ma al sentire, ch'io avevo in pensiero d'improntarli in fronte il pregiatissimo Nome di V. S. Illustrissima, c'hà un animo tanto generoso, e un'Idea dilettante di sì vaghe armonie, subito hà felicitato le mie brame, e mi hà dato libero il Campo di mandarli sotto à Torchij."

39 Pirro Albergati, *Balletti, correnti, sarabande, e gighe à violino e violone, con il secondo violino à beneplacito*, Op. 1 (Bologna: Monti, 1682), "L'autore al benigno sonatore: una dolce persuasione dell'amico Stampatore, si violentemente hammi spinto à farlo, che mi hà necessitato ad accudire alle sue replicate istanze."

40 Other late seventeenth- and early eighteenth-century music publishers in Bologna are Gioseffo Micheletti, Carlo Maria Fagnani, Antonio Pisarri, Fratelli Peri, Eredi del Benacci, Giovanni Battista Ferroni, and Eredi del Dozza. Although a few of these produced several prints of instrumental music, none came close to the output of Monti and Silvani. For a history of Bolognese publishing, see Albano Sorbelli, *Storia della stampa in Bologna* (Bologna: Zanichelli, 1929; facsimile, Bologna: Forni, 2003).

n.n. Romano	Rome
n.n. Romano	Rome
n.n. Veneziano	Venice
Giacinto Pestalozza	Milan (1679 dances published there with a Milanese dedicatee)

Largely excluded are Venetians and, with the exception of a couple of composers active in Verona, anyone from the Veneto. The sonatas and dances of composers active in Venice or published by the Venetian presses during the late seventeenth and early eighteenth centuries were not published in Bologna.[41] An exception is Giovanni Legrenzi, a reprint of whose Op. 8 sonatas was brought out by Monti in 1671, quite possibly in connection with the composer's candidacy for the job of maestro di cappella at S. Petronio in 1671.[42] Roman composers, too, were not published in Bologna, with the towering exception of Arcangelo Corelli. But Corelli had connections to Bologna: he was a native of Fusignano, a small town in Romagna equidistant from Bologna and Ravenna, and spent his early years in Bologna, joining the Accademia Filarmonica in 1670 before moving to Rome around 1675. Although he began publishing sonatas only later in 1681, he bore the epithet "Il Bolognese" in his first two opuses, having studied violin and possibly composition in that city.[43]

The full scope of the Bolognese orbit, then, was north-central Italy, a region dominated by the vast plain that follows the course of the Po River, encompassing parts of Savoy, Lombardy, Emilia, and Romagna. Within that larger area, however, a more cohesive musical region is defined by the career paths of the majority of instrumental composers that linked Bologna, Modena, and Ferrara. Representative cases are easily found. For instance, Giovanni Battista Bassani, a native of Padua, was from the late 1660s organist to the Accademia della Morte in Ferrara. In 1677, the year he published his Op. 1 collection of dances, he was admitted to the Bolognese Accademia Filarmonica at the rank of *compositore*.

---

41 Composers active in Venice or the Veneto of the late seventeenth and early eighteenth centuries would include Antonio Caldara, Domenico Dalla Bella, Carlo Fedeli, Giorgio Gentili, Giovanni Legrenzi, Giovanni Reali, Giovanni Maria Ruggieri, Bernardo Tonini, Alessandro Ziani, Pietro Andrea Ziani, and Giovanni de' Zotti. Eleanor Selfridge-Field, *Venetian Instrumental Music from Gabrieli to Vivaldi*, 3rd ed. (New York: Dover, 1994), provides an excellent survey of seventeenth- and early eighteenth-century instrumental repertory of San Marco and elsewhere.

42 Monti reprinted Legrenzi's *Sonate a due, trè, cinque, e sei stromenti*, Op. 8 in 1671 with a new dedication to Lorenzo Perti, who was a member of the S. Petronio chapter, written by Marino Silvani. Legrenzi's prior association with institutions within the Bolognese orbit was his service as maestro di cappella at the Accademia dello Spirito Santo in Ferrara from 1656 to 1665.

43 Little about Corelli's early life is known with any certainty. Hawkins asserted that he studied composition with G. B. Bassani. Martini named Giovanni Benvenuti and Leonardo Brugnoli as his violin teachers. Neither claim can be verified with supporting evidence. Michael Talbot, "Pistocchi Sketches Corelli (and Others)," in *Studi corelliani* V, ed. Stefano La Via (Florence: Olschki, 1996), 441–3, published a sketch from the late 1660s or early 1670s showing "Archangelo" playing the violin among other Bolognese musicians, confirming Corelli's musical beginnings there (see Figure 0.8).

Figure 0.8 Sketch by the violinist Giovanni Pistocchi made on the inside cover of
the first violin part of G. M. Bononcini, *Varii fiori del giardino musicale*,
Op. 3 (Bologna: Monti, 1669). It shows Pistocchi himself (labeled
"Padre"), his son Francesco Antonio ("Pistocchino"), Arcangelo
Corelli ("Archangelo"), Giovanni Battista or Antonio Bonini ("Bonino
dala tiorba"), and Giovanni Maria Bononcini ("Bononcini"). Museo
Internazionale e Biblioteca della Musica di Bologna (I-Bc)

In the early 1680s, he held positions in the Modenese town of Finale and in Mirandola before his 1682 election to a leadership position in the Accademia Filarmonica as *principe*. His professional duties then took him back to Ferrara, where he became maestro di cappella for the Accademia della Morte (1683) and then of the cathedral (1686). As a composer of opera and oratorio, he produced most of his work for Ferrara, although he had several premieres in Modena and Bologna.

Giovanni Battista Vitali, to give another example, followed a career path that took him from his native Bologna to Modena. His first professional position, starting in 1658, was as *suonatore di violone da brazzo* (that is, a player of the bass violin) in the *cappella musicale* of S. Petronio. He was a founding member of the Accademia Filarmonica in 1666, the year of his first musical publication, and in 1673 he went on to become maestro di cappella at the church of S. Rosario in Bologna, by which time he had produced five collections of instrumental music. The following year, he took a position in Modena in the ducal *cappella* of Francesco II d'Este as vice-maestro. His son, Tomaso Antonio, made his career in Modena as a violinist in the ducal *cappella*, working there many years from 1675 until shortly before his death in 1745. During that time, however, Tomaso Antonio took on Girolamo Nicolò Laurenti and Luca Antonio Predieri, both members of Bolognese musical families, as students, and he was admitted to the Accademia Filarmonica, first at the rank of *suonatore* (instrumentalist) in 1703 and then as *compositore* three years later.

One further case of musical exchange between Bologna and Modena is seen in a sketch, Figure 0.8, representing musicians from the two cities playing together in an ensemble ideally suited the late-*Seicento* sonata: two violins, violoncello (in this case played horizontally at chest level),[44] and theorbo. According to Michael Talbot, who has identified the musicians shown, the drawing is the work of Giovanni Pistocchi, violinist and father of the singer Francesco Antonio Pistocchi (shown in his father's arms).[45] It also depicts Giovanni Maria Bononcini, a violinist for the Duke of Modena, with musicians from Bologna: the elder Pistocchi, Giovanni Battista or Antonio Bonini, and the young Arcangelo Corelli before his transfer to Rome.

---

44 Gregory Barnett, "The Violoncello da Spalla: Shouldering the Cello in the Baroque Era," *Journal of the American Musical Instrument Society* 24 (1998): 81–106.

45 Talbot, "Pistocchi Sketches Corelli (and Others)," *Studi corelliani* V, 441–3.

Suited to the Church

According to period conceptions of genre, the broad distinctions among instrumental compositions were made according to venue, church (*da chiesa*) and chamber (*da camera*), connoting music suited to one or the other place. The history of the sonata da chiesa through the late seventeenth century follows a path back to the late Renaissance *canzon francese per sonare*.[46] Mile-posts along that path from canzona to sonata include the transition, during the last decades of the sixteenth century, from transcriptions of French (actually Netherlander) chansons to original compositions in the lively polyphonic chanson style; the incorporation of contrasting movements in triple meter and of slow cadential or transitional sections in the early years of the seventeenth century (both shown in excerpts from a Frescobaldi canzona, "La Lipparella," Example 0.1);[47] a gradually increasing specificity of performing media (Frescobaldi's ensemble canzonas from the early *Seicento* are "to be played on any type of instrument");[48] the emergence of the *stile moderno* sonata in the 1620s with its mercurial virtuosity and strong contrasts of tempo and affect over the course of the piece;[49] and the late-century trend toward longer movements and an accompanying decline in recapitulated sections over the course of a piece.[50]

---

46 Various terms found in printed titles for the Renaissance instrumental genre based on the chanson are: *canzoni da sonare* (Florentio Maschera, 1584), *canzoni per sonar* (Alessandro Vincenti [ed.], 1588), *canzoni francese* (Sperindio Bertoldo, 1591), *canzoni alla francese* (Adriano Banchieri, 1596), *canzonette alla francese* (Giuseppe Guami, 1601), *canzon in aria francese* (Adriano Banchieri, 1607), *canzonette d'aria francese* (Tarquinio Merula, 1615; in the dedication), and even *aria di canzon francese per sonare* (Lodovico Viadana, 1590).

47 Frescobaldi's canzona exists in two versions. The first was published in 1628 in *Il primo libro delle canzoni, ad una, due, trè, e quattro voci* by Bartolomeo Grassi in score and by G. B. Robletti in partbooks, both in Rome. It was then published by Alessandro Vincenti in *Canzoni da sonare a una due tre et quattro con il basso continuo* (Venice, 1634) in a revised version with the addition of the tempo designations shown in Examples 0.1a and 0.1b.

48 The 1628 Grassi edition specifies "per sonare con ogni sorte di stromenti"; the Robletti, "accomodate per sonare ogni sorte de stromenti." The definitive study of the instrumental canzona of the early seventeenth century is still Eunice C. Crocker, "An Introductory Study of the Italian Canzona for Instrumental Ensembles and its Influence upon the Baroque Sonata," Ph.D. dissertation, Radcliffe College, 1943. For a comparative study of the different editions of Frescobaldi's canzonas, see John Harper, "Frescobaldi's Reworked Ensemble Canzonas," 269–83 in *Frescobaldi Studies*, Alexander Silbiger, ed. (Durham, NC: Duke University Press, 1987).

49 For an in-depth study of style and structure in the *stile moderno* sonata, see Andrew Dell'Antonio, *Syntax, Form and Genre in Sonatas and Canzonas: 1621–1635* (Lucca: Libreria Musicale Italiana, 1997).

50 The evolution of the canzona/sonata is surveyed in John Suess, "The Ensemble Sonatas of Maurizio Cazzati," *Analecta musicologica* 19 (1979): 146–85.

Example 0.1a   G. Frescobaldi, *Canzoni da sonare*, bk. 1 (1634), Canzona a 2,
                  canto e basso, detta "La Lipparella"

Example 0.1b   "La Lipparella" (1634), cont'd

By the 1660s, the term "sonata" (literally, a "sounded thing")—or "sinfonia" in several cases—had replaced "canzona" to designate a multi-movement instrumental composition in Italian prints. The late-*Seicento* sonata's debt to the canzona lay in its spirited contrapuntal style; its debt to the *stile moderno* sonata lay in its sharply differentiated movements, idiomatic writing for the violin, including the occasional use of double-stops and scordatura, rapid string-crossings, and tremolo effects. Virtuosity, however, was not a hallmark of the Bolognese repertory, most of which, for example, was playable in the violin's first position for the left hand.[51]

---

51 Chapter 3, which studies the virtuoso repertory of Modenese manuscripts, focuses on the particular place of virtuosity and its relative absence from published instrumental music.

Two contrasted movement types, both descended from the main sections of the early seventeenth-century instrumental canzona, such as Examples 0.1a–b, form the core of a typical late-*Seicento* sonata: the first, fugal and often in duple meter; and the second, in a lighter texture, often in triple meter. A sonata might have more than one each of these movement types, particularly the fugue; and connecting movements, usually slow, add further contrast and fill out the whole composition. Introductory slow movements, typically marked grave, were an option that became more and more common toward the end of the century. Examples 0.2a–c contain excerpts from the second of G. B. Vitali's Op. 2 sonatas (1667), representing sonatas from the 1660s with their canzona-like features. The piece begins with its fugue (Example 0.2a), featuring a canzona-style repeated-note subject seen in the Frescobaldi (cf. Example 0.1a). At 22 measures it is the longest movement of the piece. Example 0.2b demonstrates the relatively lighter triple-time movement of the sonata, comparable to Example 0.1b of the Frescobaldi. Imitative but not fugal, its texture features short motifs traded in the violins. The slow movement that follows, Example 0.2c, is really an eight-measure section that connects without break to another allegro. Over the course of the sonata's 84 measures there are seven changes of tempo or meter, but just four double bars, including the final. The resulting sectional continuity is another feature that recalls the earlier canzona.

Sonata composers experimented not only with the sequence of tempos and number of movements (or sections), but also with their length, and the degree of continuity over the course of the complete piece, generally working away from brief sections and toward longer and more discrete movements. Vestiges of what is known as the variation canzona, in which sections or movements are thematically linked, also occur in Vitali, although not his Op. 2, No. 2, but this feature is rare by the 1660s and almost unique to Vitali when he was still practicing it in his Op. 9 sonatas (1684).[52] Instead, late-*Seicento* sonata movements were most often independent of one another in terms of thematic material and overall affect.

---

52 For a study of subtler thematic relationships between movements within a sonata, see Dennis Libby, "Interrelationships in Corelli," *Journal of the American Musicological Society* 26 (1973): 263–87.

Example 0.2a   G. B. Vitali, Op. 2, No. 2 (1667)

Example 0.2b   cont'd

iii. (mm. 1–10)

Example 0.2c   cont'd

iv. Grave (complete)

For comparison, Examples 0.3a–c show excerpts from a sonata of the early 1690s by Vitali's son, Tomaso Antonio. The younger Vitali's composition, the first sonata from his Op. 1 (1693), begins with a slow movement (not shown here) and includes a fugue of 42 measures (Example 0.3a) whose subject and overall length nearly double those of the older Vitali's fugue. The slow third movement (Example 0.3b) is comparable to the grave of the older Vitali's sonata (Example 0.2c), as a relatively brief, tonally open link between two faster movements. The final movement (Example 0.3c), marked in cut time for a quick tempo and featuring a concertato cello line beneath the playful counterpoint in the violins, furnishes the lighter-textured contrast to the fugue, comparable to the 9/8 section of Example 0.2b. At the core of both sonatas, the father's and the son's, are movement types that may be traced back to the multi-sectioned canzona of the early seventeenth century. Their differences reflect the preference toward the end of the seventeenth century for a longer overall composition more clearly divided up into discrete movements.[53] In the next century, composers would regularize the number and sequence of movement types, popularizing the familiar slow–fast–slow–fast pattern of the late-Baroque trio sonata.

---

[53] A thorough examination of the concept of movement and section within both the church and chamber sonata of the seventeenth century is John Daverio, "Formal Design and Terminology in the Pre-Corellian 'Sonata' and Related Instrumental Forms in the Printed Sources," Ph.D. dissertation, Boston University, 1983.

Example 0.3a   T. A. Vitali, Op. 1, No. 1 (1693)

Example 0.3b   cont'd

iii. Grave (complete)

Example 0.3c   cont'd

iv. (mm. 1–9)

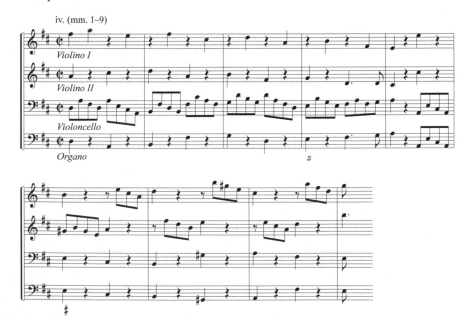

Suited to the Chamber

Over the course of the seventeenth century, the selection of courtly dances written for instrumental ensemble changed and broadened: the balletto and corrente replaced the ubiquitous pavan and gagliarda of the late Renaissance as the primary duple- and triple-meter dances of the latter half of the seventeenth century. By the 1660s composers frequently included the allemanda, sarabanda, and giga as well. Beginning in that same decade, the spread of French courtly culture throughout northern Italy introduced, first, the general qualifier *alla francese* or *in stil francese*, usually applied to the corrente, and second, more recent dances of French provenance, such as the gavotta, borea, and minuetto (in their Italian appellations). Variation sets were also material for the sonata da camera, although the early seventeenth-century delight in variations over diverse ostinatos—Ruggiero, Romanesca, Bergamasca, Ballo del Granduca, La Monica—was less pronounced later in the century, with only occasional, if sometimes impressive, variations on the folia, chaconne, and passacaglia included among collections of dances.

"Sonata da camera," the generic term consistently associated with dances for instrumental ensemble, connotes the action of instrumental playing in the secular and relatively private sphere of the household chamber, as opposed to the more public church or theater. Especially in the 1660s and 70s, composers often omitted the genre term from title pages and simply listed the dance types contained in a print. In other cases, they employed more descriptive or colorful alternatives to "sonata," such as *trattenimento, divertimento, allettamento, concerto* or *concertino*, and even *bizzarria*; *da camera*, meaning "for the chamber," was nonetheless added to all of these to signify the inclusion of dance movements.[54] The musical composition embodied by the term "sonata da camera," however, was changing in the late seventeenth century, referring at first to an individual dance and later to a suite of them. The most explicit use of "sonata da camera" to mean a single dance occurs in Oratio Polaroli's Op. 1 collection (1673): *Correnti, balletti, gighe, allemande, arie, etc. overo suonate da camera à trè* [Correnti, balletti ... otherwise chamber sonatas *a 3*]. The same is implied in G. M. Bononcini, *Varii fiori del giardino musicale, overo sonate da camera* [Various flowers of the musical garden, otherwise chamber sonatas], Op. 3 (1669), which contains individually numbered dances.[55] The use of the term to refer to suites is seen in the many prints after the mid 1680s whose tables of contents list ten or twelve sonatas da camera and whose pages reveal individual dance movements within each.

---

54 This changed later in the century when Pirro Albergati, Op. 5 (1687), Giuseppe Jacchini, Op. 2 (1695), and Antonio Veracini, Op. 2 (c.1696) published contrapuntally simplified, multi-movement works without dance movements as sonatas da camera.

55 Much in this discussion of the evolving sonata da camera, including the use of Polaroli, Op. 1 and G. M. Bononcini, Op. 3, draws upon Michael Talbot's expert survey of the issue in "The Taiheg, the Pira and Other Curiosities of Benedetto Vinaccesi's 'Suonate da camera a tre', Op. I," *Music & Letters* 75 (1994): 344–64. Bononcini also includes two multi-movement pieces, each titled "sonata da camera," that contain no dance movements. Relative to his church sonatas, these are modest in scale and complexity and reflect his idea of a multi-movement chamber analog to the church sonata.

This shift in the meaning of the genre term reflects a change in how composers presented their dances within a publication, that is: singly, in pairs, in suites of several dances, or, from the 1680s on, in suites of dances intermingled with non-dance or abstract movements. In sum, we may observe the dance-suite idea taking hold in Italian music for instrumental ensemble between the 1660s and 1690s. Why it took hold has been a matter of some speculation: in an article on the origins of the sonata da camera, John Daverio suggested the specific influence of German tradition transmitted by Georg Muffat to Arcangelo Corelli in Rome in the early 1680s.[56] Although it has generated debate,[57] Daverio's theory has never been disproved, and it neatly explains two sudden changes in Italian instrumental music of the mid 1680s: (1) the change in meaning of "sonata da camera," first seen in Corelli's *Sonate da camera*, Op. 2 (1685), to refer to a collection of related movements rather than an individual dance; and (2) the fashion of adding preludes and other, usually slow, non-dance movements to create something more than a grouping of just dances. Taken together, both church and chamber sonata reflect a uniform trend in the evolution of a "sonata idea" during the seventeenth century from single-movement origins (albeit divided into continuous sections in the canzona) toward a multi-movement composition comprising discrete and contrasting movements.[58]

Excerpts from three prints (Examples 0.4–0.6) give a sense of this development within the sonata da camera and, in one case, of French influences in the later Bolognese dance repertory. Typically, this is music on a small scale, meant to divert performer, dancer, and listener alike with attractive tunes, clear-cut phrases, uncomplicated textures, and occasional unexpected twists. Example 0.4, a stand-alone corrente from Francesco Prattichista's *Concerti armonici di correnti, e balletti*, Op. 1 (1666), exemplifies the Italian form of that dance in its flowing rhythms and use of hemiola, especially at cadences. The piece also includes a tease for the performers, who are instructed to maintain a single unhurried tempo through its four different meters. The balletto and corrente (Example 0.5)—the pairing designated by the possessive: *sua* corrente—of Pietro Degli Antonii's, *Balletti, correnti, & arie diverse … per camera*, Op. 3 (1671), are linked only by tonality and not by shared theme or motif, as is typical of each of the dance

---

56 John Daverio, "In Search of the Sonata da Camera before Corelli," *Acta musicologica* 57 (1985): 195–214.

57 Arguments against Daverio's theory have been advanced by Sandra Mangsen, "The 'sonata da camera' before Corelli: A Renewed Search," *Music & Letters* 76 (1995): 19–31; and Peter Allsop, "*Da camera e da ballo—alla francese et all'italiana*. Functional and National Distinctions in Corelli's *sonate da camera*," *Early Music* 26 (1998): 87–96. In support of Daverio is Talbot, "The Taiheg, the Pira and Other Curiosities."

58 Talbot, "The Taiheg, the Pira and Other Curiosities," 350, summarizes the process by which the two genres of sonata arrived at this point: "Both types originated as single movements, but whereas the mature church sonata consisting of several discrete movements was the product of a fission process occurring within the original movement, the chamber sonata was the product of a fusion process binding together movements that were formerly independent."

pairings in Degli Antonii's collection and of the repertory on the whole.[59] The violin's cadential flourishes in mm. 2 and 4 and the dotted runs of the second strain give us a glimpse of performed embellishments. French influence is advertised in the corrente from the eighth suite (balletto, grave, and corrente) of Giuseppe Jacchini's, *Concerti per camera*, Op. 3 (1697) (Example 0.6). Jacchini specifies *Allegro alla Francese* in this corrente, and the French influence is further evident in the rhythms of this dance. First, the preponderance of dotted rhythms was the Italian manner of (literally) rendering the *pointé* style.[60] Second, the regular shift of accent from the first to the second beat in alternating measures is a hallmark of the French courante that creates a sense of 3/2 meter (continuous hemiola) against the notated 3/4.[61]

---

59 As far as I know, only one composer represented in the late seventeenth-century Bolognese repertory used a procedure akin to the variation suite: Andrea Grossi, whose first two publications comprise dance suites in which the individual dances are related by a common motif.

60 Examples from the Bolognese repertory of written-out dotted rhythms to mimic the French *pointé* are: Domenico Gabrielli, *Balletti, gighe, correnti, alemande, e sarabande à violino e violone, con il secondo violino à beneplacito*, Op. 1 (Bologna: Monti, 1684), Balletto alla francese (twelfth suite); Carlo Andrea Mazzolini, *Sonate per camera à trè, due violini, e clavicembalo ò tiorba*, Op. 1 (Bologna: Micheletti, 1687), Balletto alla francese (third suite); Giuseppe Torelli, *Sinfonie à tre e concerti à quattro*, Op. 5 (Bologna: Gioseffo Micheletti, 1692), Concerto primo à 4 in stile francese; Bartolomeo Bernardi, *Sonate da camera a trè, due violini, e violoncello col violone, ò cimbalo*, Op. 1 (Bologna: Monti, 1692), Corrente alla francese (seventh suite).

61 This characteristic is familiar to those acquainted with J. S. Bach's dance music. For a study of the relationship between courante rhythms and dance-steps, see Wendy Hilton, "A Dance for Kings: The 17th-Century French *Courante*," *Early Music* 5 (1977): 161–72.

Example 0.4   F. Prattichista, Op. 1 (1666), [Corrente] "La Fava"

Si averte, che le mutanze delle tripole non mutano
il tempo, e non si fa molto in fretta.

Example 0.5   P. Degli Antonii, Op. 3, No. 5 (1671)

Example 0.5   cont'd

Example 0.6   G. Jacchini, Op. 3, No. 8 (1697)

Example 0.6   cont'd

Instrumental Ensembles

A large majority of the Bolognese prints—*da chiesa* and *da camera*—call for some form of trio ensemble, that is, two violins and different combinations of instruments to play a bass line—an ideal ensemble requiring just a few performers but enough to bring off contrapuntal and even fugal textures. A sizable minority of prints also call for just one violin; others, for larger ensembles that might include more than two violins, alto and tenor violas, and even trumpets.[62] The number-designations used in Italian prints to categorize the different ensemble types—sonata *a 2*, sonata *a 3*, and so forth—were mostly but not entirely consistent in counting the number of parts in addition to the basso continuo. That interpretation holds up well for the church sonata, but not well for the chamber sonata, whose details of scoring are discussed below. In the pair of prints used above to illustrate the church sonata (Examples 0.2 and 0.3), there are three partbooks to G. B. Vitali's *Sonate a due* [2] *violini col suo basso continuo per l'organo*: violino primo, violino secondo, and organo. Adding a cello to the ensemble makes four partbooks in Tomaso Antonio Vitali's *Sonate a trè* [3], *doi violini, e violoncello, col basso per l'organo*: violino primo, violino secondo, violoncello, and organo. In both cases, the number-designation is one fewer than the number of partbooks. These two ensemble types—*a 2* and *a 3*, both of which are described as trios among Anglophone musicians and scholars—are the most frequently occurring in late-*Seicento* instrumental music as seen in Table 0.3, a handlist of sonata ensembles in the Bolognese repertory.

---

62 In only one case, Maurizio Cazzati's *Sonate a due istromenti, cioè violino, e violone*, Op. 55 (1670), is any alternative to the violin given, in this case the cornetto. In some prints that call for the trumpet, violins are allowed as substitutes.

Table 0.3   Sonata scoring, selected examples

Composer (year)	Title page: instrumentation	Partbooks
Cazzati (1663)	*a tre, due violini è violone, con il suo basso continuo*	violino 1—[violino 2]—violone—basso continuo
Arresti (1665)	*a 2 & a tre, con la parte del violoncello a beneplacido*	violino 1—violino 2—violoncello—basso continuo
Cazzati (1665)	*à due, tre, quattro, e cinque, con alcune per tromba*	violino 1—violino 2—alto viola—tenor viola—violone—tiorba o contrabasso—organo
G. M. Bononcini (1666)	*a due violini*	violino 1—violino 2—basso continuo
Placuzzi (1667)	*a duoi, à trè, à quattro, à cinque, & otto instromenti*	violino [1] primo choro—violino 2/alto primo choro—alto/ tenore viola primo choro—violoncello primo choro—violino 1 secondo choro—violino [2]/alto secondo choro—alto/tenore viola secondo choro—violoncello secondo choro—organo
G. B. Vitali (1667)	*a due violini, col suo basso continuo per l'organo*	violino 1—violino 2—organo
G. B. Vitali (1669)	*a due, trè, quattro, e cinque stromenti*	violino 1—violino 2—[alto & tenore] viola—violone—organo
Cazzati (1670)	*a due istromenti, cioè violino e violone*	violino o cornetto—violone—organo o tiorba
G. M. Bononcini (1672)	*a due violini*	violino 1—violino 2—basso continuo
Colombi (1673)	*à due violini, col suo basso continuo*	violino 1—violino 2—organo
Mazzaferrata (1674)	*a due violini, con un bassetto viola se piace*	violino 1—violino 2—bassetto viola—basso continuo
Colombi (1676)	*a due violini, con un bassetto viola se piace*	violino 1—violino 2—bassetto viola—basso continuo
P. Degli Antonii (1676)	*a violino solo*	violino—basso
Anthology (1680)	*a due violini, con il basso continuo per l'organo*	violino 1—violino 2—organo
A. Grossi (1682)	*a due, trè, quattro, e cinque instromenti*	violino 1—violino 2—viola—bassetto—tromba—organo
Bassani (1683)	*a due, e trè instromenti, con il basso continuo per l'organo*	violino 1—violino 2—violoncello—organo
Albergati (1683)	*a due violini, col suo basso continuo per l'organo, & un'altro à beneplacito per tiorba ò violoncello*	violino 1—violino 2—tiorba o violoncello—organo

Table 0.3   cont'd

Composer (year)	Title page: instrumentation	Partbooks
G. Bononcini (1685)	a 5. 6. 7. e 8. istromenti, con alcune à una e due trombe, servendo ancora per violini	violino 1—violino 2—violin 3—violin 4—alto viola—tenore viola—violoncello 1—violoncello 2—tromba 1 ò violino—tromba 2 ò violino—violone ò tiorba—organo
A. Grossi (1685)	a trè, due violini e violone, con il basso continuo	violino 1—violino 2—bassetto—basso continuo
Torelli (1686)	à tre stromenti, con il basso continuo	violino 1—violino 2—violoncello—tiorba o violone—organo
P. Degli Antonii (1686)	a violino solo, col basso continuo per l'organo	score
G. Bononcini (1686)	a trè istromenti, col basso per l'organo	violino 1—violino 2—violoncello—violone ò tiorba—organo
Torelli (1687)	à 2. 3. 4. istromenti	violino 1—violino 2—alto viola—violoncello—organo
G. Bononcini (1687)	a quattro, cioè due violini, alto viola, e violoncello obligato	violino 1—violino 2—alto viola—violoncello—organo
G. Bononcini (1687)	a due strumenti, violino e violoncello, col basso continuo per l'organo	violino—violoncello—organo
Vannini (1691)	a tre, due violini e violoncello, col suo basso continuo e la violetta ad libitum	violino 1—violino 2—violetta—violoncello—organo
Torelli (1692)	sinfonie à tre e concerti à quattro	violino 1—violino 2—alto viola—violoncello—tiorba o violone—organo
T. A. Vitali (1693a)	a trè, doi violini e violoncello, col basso per l'organo	violino 1—violino 2—violoncello—organo
T. A. Vitali (1693b)	à doi violini, col basso per l'organo	violino 1—violino 2—organo
Bernardi (1696)	à trè, due violini e violoncello, con il basso per l'organo	violino 1—violino 2—tiorba o violoncello—organo
Aldrovandini (1703)	a due, violino e violoncello o tiorba	violino—violoncello ò tiorba—basso continuo
Anthology (1706)	a tre, due violini e violoncello, col basso per l'organo	violino 1—violino 2—violoncello—organo

Many composers wrote for both ensemble types, and *a 2* versus *a 3* in some cases amounts to a distinction without a difference in contrapuntal style.[63] The elder Vitali's fugue, for instance, features three contrapuntal parts because the continuo line shares in the imitation; the younger Vitali's fugue, although scored for four players, is also a fugue for three voices because the continuo essentially doubles the cello throughout. Beyond these two basic ensemble types, composers employed others, as mentioned above, but to a lesser degree. Sonatas *a 4*, *a 5*, *a 6*, and *a 7* feature ever-greater numbers of contrapuntal parts (plus continuo); number-designations of *a 8* and beyond reflect composition for two or more choirs of instruments.

Further details of scoring concern the bass instruments of the ensemble. Numerous prints advertise ad libitum substitutions among the bass instruments of the church sonata: while the keyboard instrument is almost invariably the organ,[64] the bowed bass (violone, violoncello, or even *contrabasso*) and plucked bass (theorbo) are interchangeable (Table 0.3: Cazzati, 1665; Albergati, 1683; G. Bononcini, 1685; etc.). In a few cases, a bowed bass might be designated *a beneplacito* (i.e., optional) (Table 0.3: Arresti, 1665; Mazzaferrata, 1674; Colombi, 1676), but the majority of sonata prints require the support of two bass instruments, and a few call for even more bass reinforcement. Cazzati (1665), which contains sonatas *a 5* with trumpets, and Torelli (1692), which recommends reinforcing the violin parts to perform the concertos, have partbooks for three bass instruments: violone, tiorba o contrabasso, and organo (Cazzati); violoncello, tiorba o violone, and organo (Torelli).

Sonata da camera scoring, by contrast, often calls for just one bass instrument; furthermore, that instrument need not be chord-playing (see Table 0.4). Rather, the violone and harpsichord (or spinet) are frequently interchangeable, with the violone as the preferred instrument. The late seventeenth-century sonata da camera, in fact, often calls for string trio without continuo, that is, two violins and violone. And through the mid 1680s, the second violin of this string trio is frequently an optional part (Table 0.4: G. B. Vitali, 1668; P. Degli Antonii, 1670; Bassani, 1677; etc.). In other examples, composers simply wrote violin-and-bass duets without the optional inner voice (P. Degli Antonii, 1671; Torelli, 1688; Jacchini, 1697; etc.). Penna (1673) and G. M. Bononcini (1673), moreover, offer the choice of performing their dances on the unaccompanied solo violin.[65]

---

63 Peter Allsop, *The Italian "Trio" Sonata: From its Origins until Corelli* (Oxford: Clarendon Press, and New York: Oxford University Press, 1992), 24–6, asserts that the term "trio sonata" is a misleading simplification because, he argues, the *a 2* and *a 3* scorings amount to stylistically distinct genres of sonata. His argument, however, hinges on the "non-thematic" nature of the continuo in the *a 2* scoring and on the equal participation of the melodic bass line in the *a 3* scoring, neither of which can be assumed.

64 Cazzati's Op. 55 (1670) offers a choice of harmonic bass on the organ or theorbo. For a book-length study on the instrumentation and performance practice of the basso continuo, see Tharald Borgir, *The Performance of the Basso Continuo in Italian Baroque Music* (Ann Arbor, MI: U.M.I, 1987).

65 G. M. Bononcini, *Ariette, correnti, gighe, allemande, e sarabande; le quali ponno suonarsi a violino solo; a due, violino e violone; a tre, due violini e violone; & a quattro, due violini, viola e violone* [Ariette, correnti … which can be played by the violin alone, *a 2* (violin and violone), *a 3* (two violins and violone), and *a 4* (two violins, viola, and violone)], Op. 7 (Bologna: Monti, 1673).

Table 0.4   *Sonata da camera* scoring, selected examples

Composer (Year)	Title Page: Instrumentation	Partbooks
Cazzati (1660)	*à due violini e violone, se piace*	violino 1—violino 2—violone o tiorba—spinetta
Cazzati (1662)	*per sonare nella spinetta, leuto, ò tiorba; overo violino e violone, col secondo violino à beneplacito*	[violino 1]—violino 2—[violone] & in score
G. B. Vitali (1666)	*a due violini, col suo basso continuo per spinetta ò violone*	violino 1—violino 2—spinetta o violone
Prattichista (1666)	*a tre, cioè due violini, e basso*	violino 1—violino 2—spinetta ò violone
G. B. Vitali (1668)	*à violino e violone ò spinetta con il secondo violino a beneplacito*	violino 1—violino 2—violone o spinetta
P. Degli Antonii (1670)	*a violino e violone ò spinetta, con il secondo violino à beneplacito*	violino 1—violino 2—violone o spinetta
G. M. Bononcini (1671a)	*a violino e violone over spinetta*	violino—violone o spinetta
G. M. Bononcini (1671b)	*a 5 e 6, col suo basso continuo; et aggiunta d'una sinfonia à quattro*	violino 1—violino 2—alto/canto viola—tenore viola—violone—basso continuo
P. Degli Antonii (1671)	*à violino e violone per camera, & anco per suonare nella spinetta, & altri instromenti*	in score
Penna (1673)	*a quattro, cioè due violini, violetta, e violone, con il basso continuo per il clavicembalo; Aviso [on back page]: Che può suonarsi ogni cosa à Violino solo, à due. Violino Primo, e Violone, à due Violini, & à trè, Violino Primo, Violino Secondo, e Violone.*	violino 1—violino 2—violetta—violone—clavicembalo ò tiorba
G. M. Bononcini (1673)	*ponno suonarsi à violino solo; a due, violino e violone; a trè, due violini e violone; a quattro, due violini, viola, e violone*	violino 1—violino 2—alto viola—violone o spinetta
Bassani (1677)	*à violino e violone overo spinetta, con il secondo violino à beneplacito*	violino 1—violino 2—violone o spinetta
G. M. Bononcini (1678)	*a trè, due violini e violone*	violino 1—violino 2—violoncello
Albergati (1682)	*à violino e violone, con il secondo violino à beneplacito*	violino 1—violino 2—violone o spinetta
Gabrielli (1684)	*à violino e violone, con il secondo violino à beneplacito*	violino 1—violino 2—violone o spinetta
G. B. Vitali (1684)	*à sei stromenti*	violino 1—violino 2—violin 3—alto viola—tenore viola—spinetta o violone

Table 0.4   cont'd

G. B. Vitali (1685)	à cinque stromenti	violino 1—violino 2—alto viola—tenore viola—violone ò spinetta
Torelli (1686)	à due violini e basso	violino 1—violino 2—violone—clavicembalo
Mazzolini (1687)	à trè, due violini e clavicembalo ò tiorba	violino 1—violino 2—clavicembalo o tiorba
Torelli (1687/88)	a violino e violoncello	violino—violoncello
Colombi (1689)	a tre strumenti, due violini e violone ò cimbalo	violino 1—violino 2—violone ò cimbalo
Belisi (1691)	à due violini e violoncello, con il suo basso continuo	violino 1—violino 2—violoncello—clavicembalo
Bernardi (1692)	a trè, due violini e violoncello, col violone ò cimbalo	violino 1—violino 2—violoncello—cimbalo
G. B. Vitali (1692)	a trè, due violini e violone	violino 1—violino 2—violone
T. A. Vitali (1695)	a trè, due violini e violone	violino 1—violino 2—violone
Jacchini (1697)	à violino e violoncello solo, e nel fine due sonate à violoncello solo col basso	violino—violoncello/basso
Pegolotti (1698)	à violino solo e violoncello	violino—violoncello
Cattaneo (1700)	a trè istromenti, due violini e violoncello ò cembalo	violino 1—violino 2—basso
Albergati (1702)	a tre, quattro e cinque	violino 1—violino 2—alto viola—tenore viola—violoncello—cembalo
Manfredini (1704)	a violino e violoncello, o tiorba	violino—violoncello ò tiorba
Bergonzi (1705)	a trè, due violini ò [recte e] arcileuto	violino 1—violino 2—cembalo

To summarize, church sonata scorings preserve the contrapuntal textures of the genre while offering options to increase bass sonority; chamber sonata scorings lighten the bass and frequently reduce the music to a treble-and-bass framework, or, in Penna and Bononcini, a single line. And while the two genres of sonata, church and chamber, sometimes overlap in the kinds of movements they contain, they are cleanly and consistently distinguished in terms of timbre and sonority in a manner fitting to the designations of venue themselves. The rooms of most any household, even the ballroom of an aristocratic *palazzo*, will constitute a smaller space than most church naves. Thus, the instrumental ensemble of the chamber sonata is smaller and quieter than that of the church sonata.

All of this requires the caveat that we are dealing with the specifications of the printed title pages and not with documented performance practices. The two could and did diverge from one another. Nonetheless, the prints do reflect some of the realities of historical performances. In her study of performance practice at S. Petronio, Schnoebelen discovered a preponderance of bass instruments among the ensembles used within that largest of performing spaces.[66] Furthermore, the acoustic distinctions between music appropriate for one or the other venue reflects a longer tradition of giving quieter performances in chambers than in churches. The church sonority, according to Nicola Vicentino, writing about singing in 1555, is louder and fuller than that of the chamber: "in churches one sings with full voices and with many singers, but in chamber music ... one sings softly."[67] For Gioseffo Zarlino, writing a few years later in 1558, the distinction in singing styles also reflects public and private spaces: "One sings in one way in churches and public chapels and in another in private chambers, such that there [in church] one sings with a full voice and in chambers one sings in a sweeter more subdued fashion without any shouting."[68]

The difference between church and chamber sonatas thus represents an inherited tradition of performance practice and is as much, and sometimes more, an acoustic distinction as stylistic, setting apart the sonorities of public and private music making. And music emanating from the largest of public venues, say, S. Petronio, might further amplify the bass beyond the usual. Cazzati's *Sonate à due, trè, quattro, e cinque, con alcune per tromba* (1665) are distinguished as containing the first published sonatas with trumpet; they inaugurated an illustrious period in which trumpet music was written for the resonant acoustics of Bologna's enormous church. Torelli's *Sinfonie à tre e concerti à quattro* (1692), the music of a S. Petronio musician of the next generation, introduces the performance practice of multiple

---

66　Schnoebelen, "Performance Practices," 44–9.

67　Nicola Vicentino, *L'antica musica ridotta alla moderna pratica* (Rome: Barre, 1555; facsimile, Kassel & New York: Bärenreiter, 1959), bk. 4, ch. 29, "nelle chiese ... si canterà con le voci piene, & con moltitudine de cantanti ... ma nella musica da camera ... si cantera piano." Quoted in David Fallows, "The Performing Ensembles in Josquin's Sacred Music," *Tijdschrift van de Vereniging voor Nederlandse Muziekgeschiedenis* 35 (1985): 32–66, p. 64.

68　Gioseffo Zarlino, *Le istitutioni harmoniche* (Venice: Franceschi, 1558; facsimile, New York: Broude, 1965), bk. 3, ch. 45, "Ad altro modo si canta nelle chiese & nelle capelle publiche, & ad altro modo nelle private camere: imperoche ivi si canta a piena voce ... & nelle camere si canta con voce piu sommessa & soave, senza fare alcun strepito." Quoted in Fallows, "Josquin's Sacred Music," 64.

players on a part in the concertos. In both prints, composers and their publishers took the time and expense to include a third partbook for bass instruments. As we shall see in the final chapter of this study, the desire for larger ensembles and experiments of scoring for them lays bare the early history of the Bolognese concerto, which emerged only in the 1690s but consolidated earlier developments in church sonatas written for more parts than the typical *a 2* or *a 3*.

Chapter One

Chronicles of Instrumentalists and Composers

During the late seventeenth century, from the rank-and-file instrumentalist to the maestro di cappella, nearly every kind of musician composed sonatas and dances. Individual profiles, however, reveal multiple appointments and activities, such that the ensemble instrumentalist and maestro sometimes came together in a single person who might have had other duties as well. Nor were published sonata composers necessarily professional musicians: young students of counterpoint (i.e., composition) and dilettante instrumentalists also contributed to the repertory.

The profile of Giuseppe Matteo Alberti (1685–1751), composer of a well-regarded set of concertos and of solo sonatas for the violin, is typical of the period.[1] From 1709, he was violinist at S. Petronio. At different times over the course of his career, he also played violin in the church of S. Paolo Maggiore,[2] directed concerts at the house of Count Orazio Bargellini (probably including duties as personnel manager of the musicians who participated),[3] taught violin at the Bolognese Collegio de' Nobili, and served as maestro di cappella at S. Giovanni in Monte and S. Domenico.[4] He was therefore violinist, violin teacher, instrumental ensemble leader, and church music director. To give another example, Bartolomeo Bernardi (c.1660–1732), who published a collection each of church and chamber sonatas in the 1690s, pursued

---

1   *Concerti per chiesa, e per camera ad uso dell'accademia eretta nella sala del sig. co. Orazio Leonardo Bargellini, nobile patrizio Bolognese*, Op. 1 (Bologna: Silvani, 1713); *Sonate a violino e basso*, Op. 2 (Bologna: n.p., 1721).

2   The personnel lists of S. Paolo Maggiore of the 1740s and 50s, albeit of a later period, show significant overlap with those of S. Petronio. See Paolo da Col, "Cronache di musica e storia degli organi nella Basilica di S. Paolo Maggiore di Bologna," *Rivista internazionale di musica sacra*, 12 (1991): 145–57, which transcribes the personnel lists of the church from the 1740s (pp. 152–3). Similarly, Giovanni Battista Martini, *Serie cronologica de' principi dell'Accademia Filarmonica di Bologna* (Bologna, 1776; facsimile, Bologna: Forni, 1970), 17–18, recounts of Girolamo Nicolò Laurenti, "divenne uno de' più celebri sonatori del suo tempo. Servì per capo d'orchestra la Cap. di S. Petronio, e tutte le altre Chiese per molti anni."

3   Corrado Ricci, *I teatri di Bologna nei secoli XVII e XVIII* (Bologna: Successori Monti, 1888; facsimile, Bologna: Forni, 1965), 248–9, reports on the concert of music given under the directorship of Alberti at Bargellini's *palazzo* on August 5, 1713.

4   An English-language biography of Alberti is given in Michael Talbot, "A Thematic Catalogue of the Orchestral Works of Giuseppe Matteo Alberti (1685–1751)," *Royal Musical Association Research Chronicle*, 13 (1976): 1–26, p. 2.

the single activity of church violinist, but did so in numerous places.[5] According to the biographical entry for Bernardi in the *Catalogo degli aggregati della Accademia Filarmonica*, "he became by his musical virtues an instrumentalist in the illustrious *cappella* of S. Petronio and of S. Lucia and other churches. He also made himself heard in various important cities of Italy, clearly possessing a style that was serious and suitable to the church."[6]

The likely reason why these two violinists worked as many jobs as they did is hinted in the pay records from S. Petronio.[7] Laurenti was hired in 1669 at 8 *lire* (£) per month as the third violinist in the *cappella musicale* during Maurizio Cazzati's tenure as maestro. In 1682, Laurenti was receiving £11.15 per month.[8] By 1695, after 26 years' service, he was earning £15, but the musical ensemble was disbanded in order to pay for repairs to the roof of the church.[9] Over the next six years, he was hired on a per-service basis, earning, for example, £4.10 for the 1696 Mass and Vespers of All Saints' Day and the Mass for All Souls' Day.[10] If he hadn't already been doing so by this point, Laurenti must have started playing in other Bolognese churches and elsewhere outside of the city. Even after the musical ensemble of

---

5   *Sonate da camera a trè, due violini, e violoncello col violone, ò cimbalo*, Op. 1 (Bologna: Monti, 1692); *Sonate à trè, due violini, e violoncello, con il basso per l'organo*, Op. 2 (Bologna: Fagnani, 1696).

6   The *Catalogo degli aggregati della Accademia Filarmonica di Bologna*, MS, c.1736; facsimile with foreword by Anne Schnoebelen (Bologna: n.p., 1973), was originally thought to have been the work of G. B. Martini, but may have been compiled by Olivo Penna (d. 1754) with additions and reworkings by Martini (see Chapter 4, n. 14 for bibliography on the authorship of the *Catalogo*). Its more than 600 entries are numbered and indexed. The original Italian in the entry on Bernardi (N° 298) reads as follows: "divenne per la sua virtù della musica suonatore di questa insigne Cappella di S. Petronio, come di S. Lucia e di altre chiese. Si fece ancora udire in varie città cospicue d'Italia, possedendo francamente lo stile serio e da chiesa."

7   Osvaldo Gambassi, *La cappella musicale di S. Petronio: maestri, organisti, cantori, e strumentisti dal 1436 al 1920* (Florence: Olschki, 1987) is a detailed sourcebook on music at S. Petronio that contains (pp. 51–286) annual personnel lists (*organici annuali*), including salaries where they are available.

8   The main unit of currency in Bologna was the *lira*, which was divided into *baiocchi* (also called *bolognini* or *soldi*) at 20 *baiocchi* per *lira*. Laurenti's £11.15, as listed in the pay records, represents not a decimal system, but rather 11 *lire* and 15 *baiocchi*, which is actually close to twelve *lire*. Sometimes a third figure (e.g., £11.15.8) is used to represent an even smaller unit, the *denaro*, in which 12 *denari* = 1 *baiocco*. For information on currency in the Papal States and elsewhere in Italy, see Ronald Edward Zupko, *Italian Weights and Measures from the Middle Ages to the Nineteenth Century* (Philadelphia: American Philosophical Society, 1981). See also the entry under "Papal Mint" at the online *Catholic Encyclopedia* www.newadvent.org/cathen/index.html.

9   For an excellent study of S. Petronio and its *cappella musicale* during the late seventeenth century, see Marc Vanscheeuwijck, *The Cappella Musicale of San Petronio in Bologna under Giovanni Paolo Colonna (1674–1695)* (Brussels and Rome: Institut Historique Belge de Rome, 2003). On the disbanding of the *cappella*, see pp. 90–91.

10   Vanscheeuwijck, *Cappella Musicale of San Petronio*, 266, transcribes the pay records for these services.

S. Petronio was reconstituted in 1701, he would have needed to continue outside work because his new salary was £5.15, a little over a third of his income in 1695 and less even than his beginning salary in 1669. Laurenti retired from S. Petronio in 1706 on the relatively fortunate terms of keeping that same £5.15 per month for life. However, to put those terms into further perspective, the maestro di cappella at that time, Giacomo Perti, was earning £50. Perti's predecessor, Giovanni Paolo Colonna, earned around £75, and both of these salaries pale in comparison to the £120 per month earned by Cazzati, who preceded Colonna.

Alberti's starting salary as violinist in 1709 is not recorded, but in 1715 it was £4, and during his time as violinist at S. Petronio until 1750 it never rose above £7. Salaries at S. Petronio were generally lower in the eighteenth century than they had been during the latter part of the seventeenth century, but even during the better-paying years, violinists rarely earned a lucrative sum. In addition to these musicians who had regular positions in a famous *cappella musicale*, others pursued less steady careers that are harder to reconstruct because they took place largely outside of institutions whose records survive. Domenico Marcheselli (d. 1703), a native of Bologna and member of the Accademia Filarmonica from 1681, was remembered as "skilled at balls while he was head violinist at the most sumptuous celebrations. He competed with the most diligent of his time."[11] Antonio Grimandi (d. 1731), also a Bolognese violinist and, from 1684, member of the Accademia Filarmonica, "was heard in the principal cities of Italy in both ecclesiastical and theatrical functions.... He also had various violin students, in both Bologna and Ferrara, who praise him."[12] Both performed in S. Petronio as *sopranumerari* (i.e., extra musicians for its larger feast-day ceremonies), receiving one *lira* per service, and both competed for a regular position there, but as far as is known, they made do in freelance careers that included teaching the violin, composing a few sonatas, and playing at churches, theaters, or balls in Bologna and elsewhere.

A handful of sonata composers were students or members of the nobility, or otherwise worked outside the musical profession. Tomaso Pegolotti, the author of a set of suites, described himself as "vicesegretario e cancelliere" (assistant secretary and chancellor) to Foresto d'Este, Marquis of Scandiano.[13] Artemio Motta, a priest and member of a good family according to the historian Nestore Pelicelli,[14] reveals nothing of himself in his published *Concerti a cinque* (1701), save that he was a native of Parma and, with a dedication in verse, that he wrote poetry. Francesco Giuseppe De Castro was a student at the Collegio de' Nobili in Brescia when he published his Op. 1 dance suites, or as he characterizes them, the "first works, I would say, not of

---

11 *Catalogo degli aggregati*, No. 210: "pratico del Ballo, mentre nelle feste più sontuose esso ne era Capo sonatore di Violino. Gareggiò coi più studiosi di quel tempo."

12 *Catalogo degli aggregati*, No. 232: "si fece udire nelle cospicue Città d'Italia tanto nelle funzioni ecclesiastiche, che Teatrali.... Fece anch'egli diversi allievi nel suono del Violino tanto in Bologna che in Ferrara, i quali ne fanno il suo Encomio."

13 Pegolotti, *Trattenimenti armonici da camera*, Op. 1 (Modena: Rosati, 1698). Foresto d'Este (1652–1725) was a distant cousin to the Dukes of Modena, descended, as they were, from Alfonso II, the last Duke of Ferrara.

14 Nestore Pelicelli, "Musicisti in Parma nel secolo XVII," *Note d'archivio per la storia musicale* 10 (1933): 32–43, 116–26, 233–48, 314–25.

my study, but of my respite from the more rigorous and severe occupation of other studies."[15] Music, then, was a sideline to his principal studies. De Castro describes the priorities of his dedicatee, Gaetano Giovanelli, a Venetian count and fellow *convittore* at the Brescian *collegio*, in similar terms: "To him ... wholly intent on the seriousness of philosophical studies and on the amenities of literature, the offering of a harmonic diversion, perhaps unseasoned, might seem an audacious importunity."[16] According to the plan of studies instituted in the Jesuit-run schools for the nobility, music, although diligently cultivated, amounted to a gentlemanly refinement outside the main curriculum of philosophy and literature.[17] De Castro's sonatas are thus a reflection of activities fostered as aristocratic diversions. The works of Pegolotti, an official under an important noble, and Motta, a cleric who delighted in writing in verse, may also represent the fruits of a gentleman's extracurricular pursuits.

Less obscure and of higher social rank than these three composers is Pirro Albergati, who bore the title of count and belonged to one of Bologna's senatorial families (see Figure 0.6, which shows a grand serenata held at their country estate).[18] This may have afforded him a certain marketable cachet, at least in the eyes of Giacomo Monti, the music publisher, and Marino Silvani, Monti's selling-agent. As mentioned in the introduction, Albergati's first publication, a collection of dances printed in 1682, was the result of the publisher's persuasions. And his second, an assortment of church sonatas, was printed the following year at the expense of (*a spese di*) Silvani.[19] Was Albergati a marketable quantity at least partly because of his good social standing? Possibly. His Op. 1 dances would sell well enough to merit reprinting in a few years' time, but his Op. 2 sonatas demonstrate an inconsistent talent. Albergati's Op. 2, No. 5, for example, begins with a movement (Adagio, adagio) of inspired pathos (Example 1.1a), perhaps anticipating his later activity composing for the theater, but that conspicuous opening is followed by easily the most tedious movement in the Bolognese repertory—a lengthy Allegro in concertato style that comprises little more than a series of overextended sequences (Example 1.1b). The other non-professionals reveal a range of musical sophistication, from the simple-but-competent dance movements by De Castro (shown in Chapter 2 as Examples 2.2c and 2.2d) to the impressive violin suite in double-stops by Pegolotti (Chapter 2, Example 2.8b), so that it would be untenable to link professional standing with musical quality. Nonetheless, the inclusion of various non-professional as well as professional composers points up the music publishers' efforts in building up a catalog of instrumental music by drawing on all available sources.

---

15 De Castro, *Trattenimenti armonici da camera a trè*, Op. 1 (Bologna: Monti, 1695), dedication: "Eccoglielo in questi pochi fogli di Trattenimenti Musicali, primizie del mio non dirò studio mà sollievo dalla più rigorosa e severa occupazione d'altri studij."

16 Ibid., "A chi ... tutto intento alla serietà de studij Filosofici, ed all'amenità delle belle Lettere, porgere un divertimento d'Armonie, forse incondite, sembra una importunità d'audacia."

17 See Chapter 2 for a discussion of the Jesuit schools for the nobility.

18 Victor Crowther, *The Oratorio in Bologna, 1650–1730* (Oxford and New York: Oxford University Press, 1999), 14–18, gives a biography of Albergati and includes detailed information and translated documents centering on his musical patronage.

19 Albergati, *Suonate a due violini col suo basso continuo per l'organo, & un'altro à beneplacito per tiorba, ò violoncello*, Op. 2 (Bologna: Monti, 1683).

Example 1.1a   P. Albergati, Op. 2, No. 5 (1683)

Example 1.1b   P. Albergati, Op. 2, No. 5 (1683)

Instrumentalists and Patrons

The Bolognese market thus saw prints by composers from two broad classes of musician: the professional instrumentalist who pursued, often by financial necessity, a multifaceted career, and produced sonatas and dances as a byproduct of his playing circumstances; and the composer by avocation whose music for instrumental ensemble reflects the pursuits appropriate to a gentleman of the period. Among the professionals, music was often a family occupation, and in several cases blood relations were invoked in petitions for employment. Giulio Cesare Arresti, the son of a lutenist in the Concerto Palatino of Bologna, followed in his father's footsteps there, beginning as a *sopranumerario di liutista* at the tender age of nine.[20] He later won a position as organist at S. Petronio and had been first organist there for many years when he petitioned the vestry-board to name his own son, Floriano, as his replacement in the early 1690s:

> Giulio Cesare Arresti, Bolognese citizen and most humble servant of Your Most Illustrious Lordships, reverently expresses to you that for nearly sixty years he has enjoyed the honor of serving as organist in the illustrious Collegiata of S. Petronio and now, being of a very advanced age—but, with the help of God, in perfect health—and having a son among others by the name of Floriano Maria who currently exercises the same profession of organist and composer ... dares to request the infinite goodness of Your Most Illustrious Lordships for the substitution of this son in the above-named position of organist, and this so that the petitioner may have the consolation before he dies of seeing his son honored with the position that his father currently enjoys.[21]

Despite his father's letter, Floriano never got the job,[22] but other petitions on behalf of family members were successful. Nor was it unusual for a son, sometimes at a remarkably early age, to take up a position his father had just vacated. A father and two sons of the Degli Antonii family—Giovanni, Giovanni Battista, and Pietro—worked as musicians in the Concerto Palatino for several decades in the mid seventeenth century.

---

20 Osvaldo Gambassi, *Il Concerto Palatino della Signoria di Bologna: cinque secoli di vita musicale a corte (1250–1797)* (Florence: Olschki, 1984), a collection of source materials on the Concerto Palatino, includes over 1,400 transcribed documents. Doc. No. 392 (p. 209) records the hiring of "Giulio Cesare figliolo di Ms. Innocenzo" on February 29, 1628.

21 Ibid., 462, Doc. No. 26: "Giulio Cesare Aresti [sic] cittadino di Bologna et humilissimo servitore delle Signorie Vostre Ill.me riverentemente gli espone essere da circa sessanta anni che gode l'honore di servire per organista nell'Insigne Collegiata di S. Petronio et essendo hora in età molto avanzata, ma però con l'aiuto di Dio di perfetta salute, et havendo un figliuolo tra gli altri per nome Floriano Maria quale presentemente esercita in Roma la stessa professione d'organista e compositore di musica ... ardisce supplicare la bontà infinita delle Signorie Vostre Ill.me per la sostitutione di questo suo figlio nel posto predetto d'organista, e ciò per havere l'oratore questa consolatione prima del suo morire di vedere il figlio honorato del posto che presentemente gode il padre."

22 The personnel records of the *cappella* do not include the younger Arresti for any year of the late seventeenth and early eighteenth centuries, and the *Catalogo degli aggregati*, No. 217, records that Floriano Arresti instead became organist at the cathedral of S. Pietro nella Metropolitana and in other churches.

In 1650, Giovanni Battista, age thirteen, was admitted as *sopranumerario* trombonist just after his father's retirement as *ordinario* on that instrument, the son having performed an audition with the ensemble (from which his father recused himself) on recorder and trombone.[23] Five years later Pietro, the younger son, joined as *sopranumerario* "after having been heard to play diverse instruments with every perfection and excellence."[24] He was sixteen at the time. Giovanni Battista Bassani was maestro di cappella at the Accademia della Morte in Ferrara when his son Paolo Antonio became organist there in 1691;[25] Pietro Paolo Laurenti joined his father, Bartolomeo, as violinist at S. Petronio in 1692; and later, in 1707, Girolamo Nicolò Laurenti, another son of Bartolomeo, was also admitted as violinist there in the year his father retired from that job;[26] and G. B. Vitali was vice-maestro di cappella at the court of Francesco II d'Este when his son, Tomaso Antonio, joined as a violinist in 1675 at no more than twelve years of age.[27]

The principal musical employers within the Bolognese orbit—that is, Bologna, Modena, and Ferrara—encompassed church, court, and civic institutions. In Bologna, the *cappella musicale* of S. Petronio regularly employed around a dozen instrumentalists (2–4 violins, 1–3 violas, violoncello, violone, 1–2 theorbos, 1–2 trombones, 2 organs) after Maurizio Cazzati's arrival in 1657.[28] The Concerto Palatino typically featured eight trumpets, eight *piffari* (cornetts and trombones), a harpist, lutenist, and drummer for its civic functions.[29] In Ferrara, the competing Accademia dello Spirito Santo and Accademia della Morte each kept a salaried maestro di cappella and organist, and hired singers and instrumentalists, mostly strings, on a per-service basis for feast-day performances throughout the liturgical year.[30] And in Modena, the *cappella musicale* of the cathedral and the ducal *cappella* of the Este court, with more than a dozen instrumentalists during the reign of Francesco II, were the largest musical employers in that city.[31] That much accounts

23 Gambassi, *Il Concerto Palatino*, 231–2, Doc. No. 459, dated February 10, 1650. G. B. Degli Antonii was born June 24, 1636.

24 Gambassi, *Il Concerto Palatino*, 240, Doc. No. 486, dated September 20, 1655. Pietro Degli Antonii was born May 16, 1639.

25 Giovanni Pierluigi Calessi, *Ricerche sull'Accademia della Morte di Ferrara* (Bologna: Antiquae Musicae Italicae Studiosi, 1976), 42. Paolo Antonio played there for just a short time, June through December, 1691, receiving 1 *scudo* (£4) per month.

26 Gambassi, *S. Petronio*, organici annuali, 154 and 160–61.

27 Carlo Vitali, "Giovanni Battista Vitali editore di musica fra realizzazione artistica e insuccesso imprenditoriale," *Nuova rivista di musicologia italiana* 27 (1993): 359–74, p. 371, reproduces the father's petition on behalf of his son.

28 For studies on performance practice at S. Petronio, see Anne Schnoebelen, "Performance Practices at S. Petronio in the Baroque," *Acta musicologica* 41 (1969): 37–55; Eugene Enrico, *The Orchestra at San Petronio in the Baroque Era* (Washington, DC: Smithsonian Institute Press, 1976); and Vanscheeuwijck, *Cappella Musicale of San Petronio*.

29 Gambassi, *Il Concerto Palatino*, 9.

30 Studies devoted to these institutions are: Calessi, *Ricerche sull'Accademia della Morte*; and Donato Mele, *L'Accademia dello Spirito Santo: un istituzione musicale ferrarese del secolo XVII* (Ferrara: Liberty House, 1990).

31 Studies on music and musical patronage in late-*Seicento* Modena include Gino Roncaglia, *La cappella musicale del duomo di Modena* (Florence: Olschki, 1957); William

for most of the steady work, to which we may add seasonal theater work (opera and oratorio) and occasional performances for private *accademie* and *feste* patronized by the numerous local nobility.

Employment in this milieu was obtained with the support of that nobility. In Modena, the centralized ducal court meant that the Este duke himself was the principal patron of the arts, exercising direct control over the musical personnel working at his court and also having a strong influence over personnel decisions at the cathedral.[32] Not coincidentally, Francesco II and members of the Este family were frequent dedicatees of works by composers in Modena and nearby Bologna. Bologna and Ferrara, as cities within the Papal States, had no ruling family and no central court. Each was instead home to a collection of well-established noble families who patronized musical activity through the governing boards of the principal musical institutions and, as mentioned above, through frequently held private functions. The two musical *accademie* of Ferrara were administered by an elected *principe* chosen from members of the local nobility.[33] The *cappella musicale* of S. Petronio was governed by its vestry-board whose members (a *presidente* and *fabbricieri*) were drawn from the Bolognese senate.[34] The Concerto Palatino of Bologna, which furnished music to accompany functions of city government, was administered

---

Klenz, *Giovanni Maria Bononcini of Modena: A Chapter in Baroque Instrumental Music* (Durham, NC: Duke University Press, 1962), especially pp. 14–19; Victor Crowther, *The Oratorio in Modena* (Oxford: Clarendon Press, and New York: Oxford University Press, 1992), especially 3–6; and Crowther, "A Case-Study in the Power of the Purse: The Management of the Ducal Cappella in Modena in the Reign of Francesco II d'Este," *Journal of the Royal Musical Association* 115: 2 (1990): 207–19.

32 Francesco II, born in 1660, became Duke two years later on the early death of his father, Alfonso IV. His mother, Laura Martinozzi, acted as regent until 1674, and it was to her that G. M. Bononcini, turned in 1673 for support in his bid to become maestro di cappella at the cathedral of Modena. The young Duke, however, recommended a rival, Giuseppe Colombi, but too late: the Chapter of Canons had already voted to install Bononcini. Francesco, on hearing this, reacted tactfully, saying that he had "recommended, not commanded" Colombi's appointment. This event is reported with relevant documents translated into English by Klenz, 7–8.

33 The Accademia dello Spirito Santo was founded in 1597 by the Marquis Guido Bentivoglio, and for much of the seventeenth century its *principe* was a member of that family. The Accademia della Morte, traces its origins to the late fifteenth century. From the middle of the seventeenth century, a different *principe* is listed sometimes each year and sometimes every third or fourth year (see Calessi, 29–45).

34 Examples of composers who (1) dedicated a work to the entire senate or to the *Gonfaloniero* and *Anziani* or (2) crafted mini-dedications to different patrons for each piece within a collection are not uncommon during the late seventeenth century. On the origins of this latter practice, see Claudio Sartori, "Une pratique des musiciens lombards (1582–1639): l'hommage des chansons instrumentales aux familles d'une ville," in *La musique instrumentale de la Renaissance*, ed. Jean Jacquot (Paris: Éditions du Centre national de la Recherche Scientifique, 1955), 305–12.

directly by its highest legislative body, the *Gonfaloniere di Giustizia* and eight *Anziani*, whose members were drawn, again, from the Bolognese senate.[35]

Hardships

Musicians in search of employment in this milieu thus looked to the nobles in charge and made their petitions in the ornate and effusive epistolary style of the period, often intensifying the tone of their petition with a mention of hardships endured. In December of 1679, for example, a violinist of the Ferrarese Accademia dello Spirito Santo, known only as Desiderio, made the following request to the *principe* of the academy, Count Antonio Mosti, in order to gain some theater work in addition to his position with the Spirito Santo:

> Desiderio, instrumentalist in the Accademia of the most illustrious *Signori Cavalieri*, most humble servant of Your Most Illustrious Lordship, presents himself before Your indescribable gentility and inexplicable generosity with every reverent supplicating deference so that through Your powerful patronage he might petition for the position of playing the violin in the *Teatro delle Comedie* for this year, so that with this help he may alleviate himself of the not few miseries that oppress him.[36]

Even by standards of the seventeenth century, the language is extravagant, but for good reason: a musical career depended on negotiations carried out by individual supplications for work, for a pay raise, for release from work, for a pension, and other benefits of a patronage system.

Requests also ran in the other direction, from noble to musician, and in the language of the time these were known as commands. In one instance, we see that Carlo Francesco Casanova, a player on an unspecified instrument handling a "command" he cannot fulfill, maintains the characteristic tone of extravagant humility in spite of his non-compliance. In his letter, dated April 13, 1660, to the Marchese Ippolito Bentivoglio, an earlier *principe* of the same Accademia dello Spirito Santo, Casanova writes that

> The opinion that Your Excellency has formed of me, your servant, has perhaps caused me to receive the honor of Your commands, which would normally be followed punctually.

---

35 The Bolognese *Anziani* served two-month terms under the *Gonfaloniere di Giustizia*, also a two-month appointment. Senators were drawn, one member each, from Bologna's 50 most prominent families of senatorial rank. See Vanscheeuwijck, *Cappella Musicale of San Petronio*, 25–31, for a summary of Bolognese governance.

36 Archivio di Stato di Ferrara (I-FEas), Serie Bentivoglio, Lettere Sciolte, Busta 365, cc. 435–6. Letters to the Bentivoglio family from the years 1646–85 are transcribed with annotations in Sergio Monaldini, ed., *L'Orto dell'Esperidi: musici, attori e artisti nel patrocinio della famiglia Bentivoglio (1646–1685)* (Lucca: Libreria Musicale Italiana, 2000). The letter cited here is No. 179 within the year 1679 (p. 412): "Desiderio sonatore dell'Accademia delli Ill.mi sig.ri Cavalieri, humilis[si]mo servo di V. S. Ill.ma con ogni riverente osequio, suplichevole, si presenta avanti la di lei indicibile gentilezza, et inesplicabile generosità, acciò, mediante il suo potente patrocinio, si degni impetrarli il luoco di suonare con il violino nell teatro delle comedie di q[ues]to anno, per potere con q[ues]to aiutto solevarsi da non pocche miserie che lo tengono opresso."

It displeases me only that because of my weaknesses in the business of playing I will not be able to meet with your expectations. I console myself, however, by considering that a *Cavaliere* of such generosity as Your Excellency has already wished to raise me up beyond my own merits to a favor so great as to serve you.[37]

The precariousness of a musical career is evidenced by the vagaries of the musical ensemble at S. Petronio during the latter half of the century. In 1657, Maurizio Cazzati, newly appointed as maestro di cappella and filled with a reformer's zeal, summarily dismissed the entire *cappella* in order to reaudition each member. As part of his reformation, he instituted a stricter set of guidelines concerning, among other particulars, attendance, which limited members' much-needed opportunities to work outside of the church. In 1695, as mentioned above, the *fabbriceria* disbanded the musical ensemble, except for the maestro di cappella and one organist, in order to set aside funds for needed repairs to the roof of the church.[38] Less drastic, but nonetheless a hardship, was the decrease in 1682 of all salaries by three *bolognini* for every *lira* earned (i.e., 15%).[39]

Individual petitions heighten our awareness of the sometimes desperate circumstances of musicians in this environment. For example, the petition of Geminiano Bosi, predecessor to Giuseppe Torelli on the tenor viola, to the vestry-board of S. Petronio is arresting:

> *Gieminiano Bosi*, poor and unhappy Bolognese citizen and musician, age 52, most humble servant and supplicant of the Most Illustrious Lordships, and with most profound reverence humbly expresses himself to have served previously in your church … as singer, and as instrumentalist on the viola and violin for nearly 30 years continuously, with every punctuality and exact fidelity. It was necessary some years ago to absent himself from your service, renouncing his cloak and key, not being able to continue his monthly duties on account of the magnificent Elisabetta Martij Giugliani, his supposed protectress. The wretched supplicant repents having made such a renunciation and leaving his position. Owing to the great hardships that he has undergone and undergoes daily and desirous that

---

37 Ibid., Busta 331, cc. 406 (Monaldini, No. 13 in 1660, p. 147): "Il Concetto, che V. E. hà formato d'un suo servitore mi haverà forse fatto ricevere l'honore de' suoi comandi, i quali saranno da me pontualmente esequiti. Mi dispiace solo, che per la mia debolezza nell'esercitio di suonare non potrò corrispondere alla sua aspettativa. Mi consolo però il considerare, che un Cavagliere di tanta generosità come V. E., già che hà voluto sollevarmi contro ogni mio merito ad un favor cosi grande, di poterla servire.

38 Vanscheeuwijck, *Cappella Musicale of San Petronio*, 90–91.

39 That decrease may be seen in Gambassi, *S. Petronio*, 147–8, by comparing the salaries of 1682 with those of 1681. The specific act of reducing the salaries is mentioned in a petition for a raise written in 1691 (ibid., 464, Doc. No. 34): "Giacomo Maria Bergamini cittadino bolognese humilissimo oratore di Vostra Signoria Ill.ma l'espone come l'anno 1675 fu admesso per musico trombone in questa basilica di S. Petronio con la mercede di lire sei il mese[,] et l'anno 1682 gli Ill.mi Signori Fabricieri pro tempore fecero un callo generale a tutti li musici di bolognini tre per lira si che il sudetto oratore restò con mercee di lire cinque et bolognini due il mese; l'anno 1690 ricorse alla innata bontà di Vostra Signoria Ill.ma con suplicarlo di augmento."

he be newly admitted among the musicians of the *cappella* and to die in that position, he begs the full clemency and pious goodness of the Most Illustrious Lordships.[40]

The official record goes on to mention that Bosi was living by fishing at the time of his request, and that a Signora Boschetti supported his petition. Further details of Bosi's misfortunes do not survive, but his luck changed, and he regained his position with the musicians of S. Petronio, serving there, according to his expressed wish, until his death.

This is not to argue a Dickensian existence for all composer-instrumentalists of late-*Seicento* Italy. Rather, some enjoyed esteem and generous remuneration for their talents, enabling them to act with greater self-assurance. An incident in the annals of the Concerto Palatino from November 21, 1656 reveals even ill-tempered and haughty behavior on the part of a violinist:

> Ercole Gaibara, one of the musicians under the deacon … this past Sunday morning … was commanded by order of the *Signoria* to play the violin in concert with other musicians (who played, respectively, trombones, violins, and flutes) … not only did he not wish to do as he was commanded, but after having responded with the most ill-mannered sermon and impertinent words … he went off saying that he had always wanted only to play the instrument he preferred and not to be commanded by the *Signori Anziani*.[41]

The context appears to have been the music that accompanies the midday meal of the *Gonfaloniero* and *Anziani*. The deacon in this context was the ranking member of the ensemble. The record goes on to report that Gaibara was summarily and unanimously dismissed. Clearly, he was confident of his own worth and decided he could do better than the bidding of the *Anziani*. He was, in fact, Bologna's most prominent string player who taught many of the professional violinists in the city,

---

40 Ibid., 467–8, Doc. No. 45: "*Gieminiano Bosi*, povero ed infelice cittadino bolognese musico, in età d'anni 52 humilissimo servitore et oratore delle Signorie loro Ill.me, con atto di proffonda riverenza humilmente gl'espone haver servito altre volte nella loro chiesa … per cantore, sonatore di violetta et violino per il spazio d'anni 30 continovi in circa, con ogni puntualità et esatta fedeltà. Fu necessitato alcuni anni sono absentarsi dal loro servitio rinuntiando la di lui cotta et chiave per non poter conseguire le di lui mensuali provigioni a causa della Magnifica Elisabetta Martij Giugliani di lui pretesa creditrice. Dal che pentito detto meschino oratore d'haver fatto simil rinuntia et essersi absentato, stante il grande detrimento ch'egli ha sopportato e sopporta quotidianamente doppo la di lui absenza et dessideroso d'essere nuovamente agregato nel numero di Signori musici di detta Perinsigne Collegiata et in esso morire, supplica perciò la somma clemenza e pia benignità delle Signorie loro Ill.me."

41 Ibid., 243, Doc. No. 496 (November 21, 1655): "il Priore … espose come Ercole Gaibara, uno de musici … al quale del decano di detti musici domenico mattina prossima passata che fu alli 19 del corrente mese di novembre … di ordine di Sua Signoria … fu commandato che sonasse il violino in concerto con gli altri musici che rispettivamente sonavano tromboni, violini, e flauti, non solo non volle fare quanto gli era stasto commandato, ma dopo haver risposto con cattivissimo sermone et parole impertinenti al sudetto decano, se n'andò via dicendo che sempre voleva sonare quell'istromento che li pareva e che non voleva commando de gli Sig.ri Antiani."

and he also held a regular position at S. Petronio.[42] Simply put, he was secure enough to indulge in a fit of temper.

Gaibara excepted, most musicians were concerned over problems of income. Even relatively prominent composers suffered distressing financial hardship. The family of Giulio Cesare Arresti, longtime organist at S. Petronio, was fortunate to be granted the sum of £100 after his decease, in recognition of his many years of service and "the poverty of his family."[43] In some cases, just getting paid was a problem. Giovanni Battista Mazzaferrata, writing in 1673 as maestro di cappella of the Accademia della Morte in Ferrara, found himself pleading with the academy's *commissario* to be reimbursed for expenses related to the copying of music for three feasts:

> I find myself without a penny [*baiocco*]; you who have a family know what that means … if you would have the grace to make me an order of payment for these [compositions], you may rest completely certain that every service will be performed that should be, as is my usual habit … I pray that in one manner or another you favor this bill today … so that tomorrow I not do without that which is necessary for the maintenance of my household.[44]

The fact that even positions of prestige, such as a maestro di cappella, did not guarantee a comfortable or even steady income further explains why musicians sought to augment their income by taking on work outside of the regular positions they held. And yet, for as low-paying as most positions were, they bore the requirement of a solid commitment on the part of the musician-employee to be present at all functions. Thus, in 1658, when the vestry-board of S. Petronio published a reformed set of regulations for music and musical personnel, the *Ordini per la musica dell'insigne Collegiata di S. Petronio*, drawn up as part of Cazzati's reforms, an attendance policy within the *cappella* was a major point of concern. The *Ordini* set forth rules on which musicians were expected to perform at which services and on the penalties

---

42 Marc Pincherle, *Corelli: His Life, his Work*, trans. Hubert E. M. Russell (New York: W. W. Norton, 1956), 20, describes Gaibara as "the true founder of the Bolognese School of the violin." He was the teacher of many violinists of north-central Italy, including Giovanni Benvenuti and Leonardo Brugnoli, both of whom Pincherle lists as the teachers of Corelli.

43 Archivio della Fabbriceria di S. Petronio (I-Bsp), *Decreta Congregationis*, Libro VII, fol. 175a.

44 Curia Arcivescovile di Ferrara e Comacchio, Archivo (I-FEca), Fondo Morte ed Orazione, Busta 16 bis. This collection contains payment requests and receipts for musical services undertaken at the Accademia della Confraternità della Morte during the years 1651–84. The complete letter to Cesare Quatteri, the *commissario* of the Accademia della Morte, reads: "Io mi trovo senza un Baioco, Lei che há familia sá cosa vuol dire. V.S. sá che nello creditore di tutte le compositioni delle tre feste passate, quando peró le habbi consegnate il chi sara ad ogni suo cenno, se V.S. mi puó far gratia di farmi un mandato aconto della spesa di quelle puó restar certissima che ad ogni candidezza si praticherà quello li devo come fú sempre mio solito, e resterà tanto meno il deb.o professandomi oltre di piú obligat.mo del favore, quando V.S. non voglia gratiarmi di quello mi honori di farmi il mandato d'una mezza doppia che mi paga la compagnia per l'olio e sapone che per quest'anno mi chiameró sodisfato la prego o in una o l'altra maniera favorirmi del mandato per oggi per poter andare intorno per non restar domatina sprovisto di quello bisogno per il sostenamento di mia casa."

for absenteeism. Depending on the importance of the service, differing numbers of performers were required. Among the instrumentalists, cornettists, trombonists, and violonists (i.e., players of the bass violin) were always required during "solemnities and feasts, such as Saturday evenings for the litanies or a motet for the Madonna."[45] On more important occasions, those instrumentalists plus violinists, violists (alto and tenor), and theorbists were required "quando si canterà sù gli organi" (that is, when certain singers, positioned near the organs, were accompanied by all of the instruments in the *cappella*,[46] implying the use of concerted music).

In either case, the penalties for missed services were as follows:

> Those found absent from either all or part of a service without legitimate reason or without permission to do so will forfeit a *lira* for the first time, two *lire* for the second, [and] a month's salary the third time; and those who reach a fourth [absence] shall be understood to be completely excluded from the musical performances.[47]

The regulations go on to specify that these fines apply to those whose monthly salary was £10 or less. For those earning more, the fines were doubled. During the most important feasts observed at S. Petronio (that is, during Holy Week, Rogation Days, and the feast of Bologna's patron saint, S. Petronio), the presence of every member of the ensemble—singer and instrumentalist—was required, and the regulations decreed the harsher penalty of automatic expulsion for any absence whatsoever on those occasions: "[t]hose who are absent from service when the entire *cappella* is required shall be understood to be completely excluded from musical performances."[48]

Absenteeism was an ongoing problem not only in the *cappella musicale* of S. Petronio, but also in the Concerto Palatino because musicians from each organization sought to earn extra income by performing with the other. Thus the 1658 *Ordini* of S. Petronio included a clause forbidding that very practice,[49] and a few years later, in 1662, the *Anziani* who governed the Concerto Palatino drew

---

45 *Ordini per la musica dell'insigne Collegiata di S. Petronio, reformate d'ordine de gl'illustrissimi signori Presidente, e Fabbricieri della reverenda Fabbrica di essa* (Bologna: n.p., 1658), 6: "solennità, e feste, come né Sabati la sera per le Litanie, ò Mottetto alla Madonna." Vanscheeuwijck, *Cappella Musicale di San Petronio*, 114–32, offers a detailed study of performance practice at S. Petronio in the context of the feasts of the liturgical year.

46 "All of the instruments" does not necessarily mean every instrumentalist, but sources on S. Petronio performance practice are unclear on this point.

47 *Ordini*, 8: "Chi mancherà ò à tutto un servigio, ò à parte d'esso senza causa legittima, ò senza licenza perda la prima volta lire una, la seconda volta lire due, la terza tutto il salario del Mese, e chi arriverà alla quarta s'intenda escluso affatto dalla Musica."

48 *Ordini*, 9: "Chi mancherà al servitio quando si fà Cappella s'intenda escluso affatto dalla Musica."

49 *Ordini*, 12: "quel Cantore, ò Sonatore, che entrarà Mansionario, ò Musico di Palazzo subito sia escluso affatto dalla Musica di S. Petronio [it is declared that any singer or instrumentalist who takes on duties or enters as *Musico* in the service of the *Palazzo* (i.e., the Concerto Palatino) will be immediately and irrevocably dismissed from the ensemble of S. Petronio]." Cazzati began as maestro di cappella in 1657, and the *ordini* of San Petronio, published a year later, were a result of his reforming initiative.

up a reciprocal decree, complaining particularly about the impact of the feast of S. Petronio. The palatine musicians, the decree states,

> assume authority without permission of their lordships [the *Anziani*] to go serve in various places and in various functions, in particular for the vigil and feast of the glorious S. Petronio, and this against the orders and decrees of the *Signori Anziani*. Concerning these decrees, [the *Anziani*] order and expressly command that any said musician in this organization dare not go henceforth either in the church of S. Petronio or in any other place to serve on any occasion even under pretext of obligation or of being salaried any time that it impedes the service of their lordships, unless with express permission from the *Signori Anziani*.[50]

A similar state of affairs plagued the two *accademie* in Ferrara, each of which drew up detailed regulations concerning musicians who might serve at outside functions: the rules of the Accademia dello Spirito Santo required that permission be obtained from the *principe* in all such cases,[51] whereas those of the Accademia della Morte specifically prohibited admitting musicians who performed with the Accademia dello Spirito Santo.[52] In both Bologna and Ferrara, the regulations of the main musical ensembles betray an almost jealous attitude of administrators over their musical personnel, each guarding its members from the incursions of any other employer. Herein lay a fundamental conflict between individual musician and employing institution: for reasons of financial need, professional advancement, or simply opportunity, musicians sought outside work that might conflict with the duties of their main employment; for reasons of institutional prestige and the desire for reliable service, employers prohibited them from doing so.

But the field of opportunities was enticingly rich. Outside the sphere of ecclesiastical music, surviving librettos attest not only to the number of instrumentalist-composers who fulfilled commissions to write for the theater, but also to a steady number of performing occasions: every opera, oratorio, *festa da ballo*, and *accademia* of

---

50 Gambassi, *Concerto Palatino*, 253, Doc. No. 528 (October 31, 1662): "si pigliano authorità, senza licenza d'essi Sig.ri, di andare a servire in diversi luoghi et a diverse funtioni in particolare nella vigilia del glorioso S. Petronio et di lui festa, et questo contro gli ordini et decreti di detti Sig.ri Antiani, inherendo a detti decreti ordinano et espressamente comandano che alcuno di detti musici di sua famiglia per l'havenire non habbi ardire di andare tanto in detta Chiesa di S. Petronio quanto in qualsivoglia luogo per servire in qualsivoglia occasione anche sotto pretesto d'obligo, o essere salariato, ogni volta che impediscano il servicio delle Sig.rie Loro, se non con espressa licenza di detti Sig.ri Antiani."

51 The *Oblighi de signori mastro di cappella, e musici dell'Accademia dello Spirito Santo di Ferrara* (Ferrara: Stampatore Episcopale, 1677) is wholly devoted to matters of attendance and discipline, imposing fines, for example, for absence and tardiness.

52 *Ordini stabiliti per lo buon governo dell'Accademia della Compagnia della Morte* (Ferrara: Gironi, 1648), 23: "si comanda, che niun Musico, che serva all'erudita Accademia dello Spirito Santo, non possa proporsi, ne accettarsi allo servitio dell'Accademia della Morte [It is commanded that no musician who serves in the learned Accademia dello Spirito Santo may be proposed or accepted for service in the Accademia della Morte]."

musical concerts demanded the services of accompanying instrumentalists.[53] And the same aristocratic circles that patronized such performances also provided teaching opportunities at the several schools for the nobility in Bologna—among them, the Collegio de' Nobili di S. Francesco Saverio, the Accademia degli Ardenti, and the Collegio di S. Luigi Gonzaga—where young males of the nobility pursued not only a classical education, but also the refinements of their class: fencing, horsemanship, music (singing and playing), and dance. Librettos of performances within the Collegio de' Nobili list directors of music and instructors of various instruments, and these include sonata composers.[54]

It is also worth mentioning that much within the regulations was open to negotiation. Domenico Gabrielli, for instance, successfully tested the rules at S. Petronio for absenteeism in 1687, notifying the president of the *fabbriceria*, the Marquis Girolamo Albergati, that an opera performance in Crema, a Lombard town near Milan, would take him away from Bologna during the patronal feast.[55] A letter written by one Pietro Francesco Maccarini to Giovanni Paolo Colonna, maestro di cappella, implies that Gabrielli thought Colonna might intercede on his behalf:

> you are desired particularly by Signor Domenico Gabrielli who wishes you to speak to the *padroni* on the matter I raised with you.... He goes to Crema to play in the opera, so that he will not be in Bologna for S. Petronio, as is also the case with Sig.r Rinaldino [the soprano Rinaldo Gherardini]. Gabrielli has told me that the Marchese Albergati does not wish to grant him leave, so he says, and he says he has written him because leave for the feast of S. Petronio is not given.[56]

---

53 A complete catalog of librettos to all manner of Bolognese performances is Laura Callegari, Gabriella Sartini, and Gabriele Bersani Berselli, eds., *La librettistica bolognese nei secoli XVII e XVIII: catalogo ed indici* (Rome: Torre d'Orfeo, 1989). Librettos typically do not list the instrumentalists accompanying a performance, but the sheer number of operas, oratorios, ballets, and other staged entertainments with music that took place in Bologna attests to the favorable circumstances for local instrumentalists. 439 librettos of such entertainments held in Bologna survive from the period between 1660 and 1710. Decade by decade, their number increased during that time: 1660s (58); 1670s (84); 1680s (83); 1690s (92); 1700s (118).

54 G. M. Alberti, as mentioned above, taught the violin and served as maestro di cappella in the Collegio de' Nobili. Giuseppe Jacchini taught the violoncello, and Bartolomeo taught the trumpet marine and violin.

55 This incident and the relevant documents are found in Vanscheeuwijck, *Cappella Musicale of San Petronio*, 157, 240, and 275.

56 This letter, dated June 19, 1687, is found in the correspondence of G. P. Colonna that is preserved in the Museo Internazionale e Biblioteca della Musica di Bologna (I-Bc), shelf-mark P.142, No. 129. The complete letter reads: "Dimatina Venerdi à hore 12 si fà la congregatione in S. Petronio sopra la musica, et ella è desiderata particolarmente dal sig.r Domenico Gabrielli quale voria che lei parlasse ai Padroni sopra l'interesse che io le accenai, non parendole bene il parlar lui, esse non fosse hoggi alla musica di S. Gervasio saria venuta à pregarla di persona. Lò stesso và à sonar à Crema per l'Opera si che non sarà à Bologna per S. Petronio come pure il sig.r Rinaldino m'a detto sig.r Gabrielli non vorria che il sig.r Marchese Albergati le dasse licenza, così mi dice e dice haver scritto collà che per la festa di S. Petronio non li dà licenza. Il sig.r Giovanardi si risolve poi andare hieri alla musica del Bassani, mà non già il Mozzi per la pretensione del mezzo ducatone. Si vede caminare per Bologna quello dalle

Colonna's action on this matter is unknown, but the vestry-board's response is preserved in the archival records: Gabrielli, Gherardini, and also Giovanni Battista Bonini, a theorbo player who went along with them, were dismissed for their absence.[57] Gabrielli, however, did not suffer. He was readmitted to the *cappella* in March of the following year, just after the premieres of two of his operas in Venice in January and February. In short, Gabrielli's employers in Bologna accommodated him nicely, rules notwithstanding, and his readmission at S. Petronio is testimony of his worth there as a virtuoso cellist.[58] Perhaps not surprisingly, he stayed put for less than a year. In November of 1688 he was lured away to Modena, joining the court musicians of Duke Francesco II. In the pay records of the Modenese court he is listed, uniquely among the Duke's musicians, as "virtuoso," and he was paid a hefty salary of 330 Modenese *lire* a month (much more, for instance, than the maestro di cappella).[59] This was money well spent: the Duke's collection of music manuscripts, now in the Biblioteca Estense Universitaria in Modena, includes two outstanding sonatas for cello and continuo and a fine set of ricercars for one and two cellos without continuo by Gabrielli (see Appendix B). These pieces, the legacy of his time as a virtuoso performer at the ducal court, are discussed in Chapter 3.

The Ambitions of G. B. Vitali and G. M. Bononcini

The most enterprising among instrumentalist-composers in cobbling together a living out of diverse activities was Giovanni Battista Vitali, composer, bass violinist, maestro di cappella, and music printer. Midway through his career, Vitali, along with eight other string players (some, like him, employed at S. Petronio),[60] took advantage of the reformist Cazzati's departure in 1671 to do precisely what the 1658 *ordini* forbade: apply for work with the Concerto Palatino. The nature of the petition made by Vitali and his colleagues was not the ordinary request to fill an open position because none was available; rather, their idea was to create a new string

---

delizie rogie si che non è ---orato. Altre novità non possò darle solo che si starà attendendo per dimatina per godere del fresco che dà là Città, et la riverisco."

57 The dismissal is recorded in the annals of the vestry-board preserved in the Archivio della Fabbriceria di S. Petronio (I-Bsp), *Decreta congregationis,* Libro VII, fol. 83b.

58 For a recent biographical sketch of Gabrielli, see Marc Vanscheeuwijck, Preface to *Ricercari per violoncello solo; Canone a due violoncelli; Sonate per violoncello e basso continuo* (Bologna: Forni, 1998).

59 The record of Gabrielli's appointment is found in the Archivio di Stato of Modena (I-MOas), Salariati, 185, fol. 126r. I would like to thank Professor Hendrik Schulze for bringing this information to my attention.

60 Along with Vitali, the petitioners were Antonio Maria Filippi (violin), Leonardo Brugnoli (violin), Antonio Maria Zambonini (violone), Bartolomeo Laurenti (violin), Gulielmo Elementi (violin), Francesco Gitti (enrolled as a tenor in the Accademia Filarmonica), Giovanni Francesco Padovani (a tenor singer as member of the Accademia Filarmonica), and, as supernumerary, Guido Borghesi (trombone). At the time of their application to the Concerto Palatino, Vitali, Filippi, Brugnoli, Laurenti, and Borghesi were members of the *cappella* of S. Petronio, and all of them were members of the Accademia Filarmonica.

ensemble (*banda di viole*) for use of the *Anziani*.[61] The *Anziani* happily took them on by splitting the duties and salaries of the current *musici da fiato* (wind players, that is, the *concerto* of cornettists and trombonists) with the newly hired *musici da arco* (string players). That decree, dated October 29, 1671, is worth recording here because the duties it describes give an idea of the routine uses of instrumental music by the municipal government in Bologna. The *Anziani* stipulated

> that the wind players must always play at the nine o'clock hour and after the regiments have finished [before sunset] from the balcony [of the municipal palace above the Piazza Maggiore] as is usual;[62] that the string players must always play at the table of the Signori *Anziani*, that is, on all those days during which the wind players usually played; that on occasions [in which the *Anziani*] go outside the palace, either to Mass or to any other function in which the musicians must play or go, one month must be played by the wind players and the following month, in alternation, by the string players, the string players needing to appear and serve in the same retinue as have the wind players ... and finally that the string players must be subject to and fulfill all the functions, obligations, burdens, and performance of services as those to which the wind players were subject and obligated. Beyond these obligations they must be particularly ready and serve without pay on the occasion of any festivities of dancing and every other event that occurs in the palace.[63]

---

61 Current information on this event in Vitali's life is the result of researches on the Concerto Palatino conducted by Osvaldo Gambassi, first reported in "Origine, statuti e ordinamenti del Concerto Palatino della Signoria di Bologna," *Nuova rivista musicale italiana* 18 (1984): 261–83 and 469–502. My summary is indebted to that work.

62 Gambassi, *Concerto Palatino*, 261, Doc. No. 555, records an article from the *Capitoli et ordini da oservarsi*, dated August 6, 1668, which sets forth the regular morning and evening practice: "Debbi avertire che li musici e trombetti che sono otto per ciascheduno si trovino tutti a sonare in Palazzo [della Signoria] dopo nona et la sera alla ringhiera di piazza [maggiore] e mancando qualcheduno senza licenza si tratenga la parte né gli la possa restituire sin che dalli Signori non si sarà ordinato [It must be noted that the musicians and trumpeters, who are each eight in number, must all be in place to play in the palace after nine [in the morning] and in the evening on the balcony above the piazza, and anyone being absent without permission will have a part [of his salary] withheld without possibility of restitution unless by order of the Signori]."

63 Gambassi, *Concerto Palatino*, 266–7, Doc. No. 567: "che i musici da fiato [Giacomo Predieri, Giovanni Battista Degli Antonij, Matheo Canetoli, Pietro Maria Minelli, Gioseffo Vanti, Stefano Prandi, Angelo Michele Loli] debbano sonar sempre al hora di nona e doppo finiti li Regimenti, et alla ringhiera conforme il solito; che i musici da arco debbano sonar sempre alla tavola delli Sig.ri Antiani, et cioè in tutti quelli giorni, ne quali esser soliti li musici da fiato a sonare, che in occasione d'andar fuori di Palazzo o a Messa o a qualsivoglia altra fontione nella quale i musici dovessero sonare o andare si debba alternativamente sonare un mese da musici da fiato e l'altro mese seguente da musici da arco, dovendo i musici da arco far il medesimo corteggio, e servire come facevano quelli da fiato ... e finalmente dovrano i musici da arco sogiacere, et adempire a tutte quelle funzioni, oblighi, pesi, e prestationi di servigio a quali erano e sono soggetti et obligati i musici da fiato, oltre i quali oblighi dovrano in specie esser pronti, e servire gratis in occasione di qual si voglia festa si da ballo come d'ogni altra sorte che si facesse in Palazzo."

The *Anziani* logically used the string players for playing *alla tavola* (at the table, indoors) and the wind players, *alla ringhiera* (on the balcony, outdoors), and decreed that the strings be on call for gratis performances at dances and other social functions held in the municipal palace. The salary increase for the string players offered by the additional work was substantial: Vitali, for instance, earned £15 per month at S. Petronio, and his new arrangement added £8.7.9 to that income.[64] The duties, however, were not light. Indeed, the last obligation of being on call was by itself no small burden: an entry from January 1, 1669 records that the musicians were expected to be on hand for the arrival of a cardinal, but that many were lacking because of the cardinal's late arrival. In response, "the *Anziani* ordered their bread and usual provisions be suspended."[65]

Predictably, the cornettists and trombonists of the Concerto Palatino vigorously protested the introduction of a string ensemble and the halving of their salaries. The *Anziani*, not having extra funds to maintain extra personnel and previous salaries, surrendered the attractive idea of a *banda di viole* after just a few months.[66] For his part, Vitali remained at S. Petronio for two more years before taking a position as maestro di cappella at the Bolognese church of S. Rosario. He stayed there just a year before joining the court *cappella* of Francesco II as vice-maestro in 1674. During this time, instrumental music that he had published in Bologna during the 1660s began to sell. From 1670 to 1680, his published dances for small ensembles of strings and continuo were reprinted multiple times: three times for his Opp. 1 and 3, and four for his Op. 4. His sonatas—Opp. 2 and 5—also did well, with one reprint of each during the 1670s. Before Corelli's phenomenal success in the 1680s, Vitali's instrumental music sold better than any other composer's. None of this, however, did him any financial good. Composers were paid a flat fee, if anything, when they submitted their works to the presses, and the profits from reprinted editions usually accrued to the publisher only.[67]

What Vitali did next and how he fared are detailed in a petition he made to Francesco II sometime in 1684:[68]

> Giovanni Battista Vitali, current servant of Your Most Serene Highness, makes known his having introduced the profession of music printing to the city of Modena, by means of which he has printed three of his own works [Opp. 7, 8, and 10] and is preparing the fourth [Op. 11]. But because these works have been reprinted in Bologna and Venice without permission of the author, compromising their marketability, he is most notably harmed.

---

64 To be precise, £8.7.9 is 8 *lire*, 7 *bolognini* (@ 20 per *lira*) and 9 *denari* (@ 12 *denari* per *bolognino*).

65 Ibid., 262, Doc. No. 558.

66 These musicians were: Giacomo Predieri (cornetto), Giovanni Battista Degli Antonii (cornetto), Matteo Canetoli (trombone), Pietro Maria Minelli (cornetto), Gioseffo Vanti (trombone), Stefano Prandi (cornetto), Angelo Michele Loli (trombone).

67 On the commissioning and financing of single-author prints, albeit in sixteenth-century Venice, see Jane Bernstein, *Print Culture and Music in Sixteenth-Century Venice* (Oxford and New York: Oxford University Press, 2001), 74–83.

68 Research on this phase of Vitali's life is reported in Carlo Vitali, "Giovanni Battista Vitali editore di musica."

For this reason he requests Your Highness to be pleased to expressly prohibit the printers in both Bologna and Venice from reprinting the works that Vitali published in Modena so that they may only sell those works that will have been consigned by the author to his own presses.[69]

Between the years 1682 and 1685, Vitali produced six collections of music in Modena: four of dances (Opp. 7, 8, 11, and 12), one of church sonatas (Op. 9), and one of hymns (Op. 10). Vitali's mention of four printed collections (three already published and a fourth in press) in his letter to Francesco II would exclude his Op. 9 church sonatas because they were brought out by an Amsterdam publisher, Johann Philipp Heus, and his Op. 12 dances because they probably postdated the letter. The facts of publication of Vitali's music and his letter suggest that having seen the marketability of his instrumental music, particularly the dances, Vitali stockpiled his compositions during the 1670s while making plans to print them himself. This he started to do in 1682, but by 1684, the year in which he wrote his letter to Francesco II, his Opp. 7 and 8 had been pirated by other publishers. His letter to stop this was only partly successful: the printing firm of Giacomo Monti in Bologna made no further reprints of the works Vitali had published in Modena, but the Venetian firm of Francesco Magni made a further reprint of his Op. 8, and Giuseppe Sala (also in Venice) made one of his Op. 12 dances. For a second time, Vitali was unable to realize his plans for a better living, and the consequences ultimately fell on his widow. Vitali died in 1692; at some point around 1695, his widow was reduced to petitioning Duke Rinaldo I d'Este for charity:

Catterina, widow of Giovanni Battista Vitali who was maestro di cappella of the late Duke [Francesco II], was left on the loss of her husband deprived of any human subsidy, and after the frequent illnesses she has had during her widowhood she is reduced to such a state as not having the resources even to feed herself.[70]

A different but equally arduous career path, that of G. M. Bononcini, reveals a musician engaged in a sustained effort to show off his talents. Financial pressures weighed heavily on him. Several years after Bononcini's death, his son Giovanni recounted the family's poverty in a letter of grateful dedication to G. P. Colonna:

---

69 Carlo Vitali, "Giovanni Battista Vitali attuale servitore di Vostra Altezza Serenissima espone haver introdotto nella Città di Modena la proffessione della stampa di musica, cò la quale sin hora stampato trè opere sue, et è attorno alla quarta ; mà p[er]che d[ett]e opere sono state ristampate in Bologna, et in Venezia senza licenza dell'Autore, pregiudicandoli all'esitatione delle sue, gli riesce di danno notabiliss.[i]mo, p[er]ciò supplica l'A.V. compiacersi di fare espressam.[en]te proibire tanto allo stampatore di Bologna, come à quelli di Venezia, di non ristampare le opere del Vitali stampate in mod.[en]a; ma che solam.[en]te vendano le sud.[ett]e opere che dall'autore nella propria stampa consegnate le saranno."

70 Cattarina's request is transcribed in Carlo Vitali, "Giovanni Battista Vitali," 373. The complete letter reads: "La Catterina Vedova di Gio: Batta Vitali, che era mastro di Capella del Ser.mo defonto, restò con la perdita del marito anche priva d'ogni sussidio humano, e doppo le frequenti malatie havute nel stato vedovile è ridotta in tale necessità, che non hà con che cibarsi. Supplica per tanto l'O[rat]rice l'A.V.S. à fargli qualche Carità, che per ciò non mancherà mai di pregare S.D.M. per i felici successi di V.A.S."

"from my parents I had only as much of life as was enough to introduce me to misery, while they, upon dying, abandoned me, still a babe in arms, to poverty."[71] We may trace the cause of the elder Bononcini's situation to his circumstances at the Este court in Modena where he was *musico di violino* in the ducal Concerto degli Strumenti (instrumental consort). Not being a favorite of Duke Francesco II, he received a pittance for his service at court, a situation mitigated only by income from a second position as maestro di cappella at the cathedral of Modena from 1673.[72] In these circumstances, Bononcini appears to have sought greater notoriety for himself, hoping perhaps to catch the attention of a more generous patron.

His first mark of distinction lay in the publishing of canonic sections within sonatas and dances, and then numerous independent canons. His *Varii fiori del giardino musicale, overo sonate da camera*, Op. 3 (1669) marks the height of these efforts, containing no fewer than twelve "canoni studiosi & osservati."[73] Although the Modenese violinist Marco Uccellini had set a precedent for adding a few canons or other musical bizarrerie to instrumental collections, the number and variety in Bononcini's Op. 3 was unprecedented. After this point, he demonstrated his learning with modal composition in the *Sonate da chiesa*, Op. 6 (1672), studied here in Chapter 6. According to Bononcini, the unusual modal designations he added to each sonata, including specifics of transposition, would demonstrate concepts to be explained in a forthcoming treatise on musical composition.[74]

The treatise, his *Musico prattico*, Op. 8 (1673), established Bononcini's credentials as a theorist and pedagogue. He further distinguished himself by publishing a collection of madrigals, his Op. 11 (1678), also composed according to twelve-mode theory and all the more impressive for its final madrigal composed in all twelve modes.[75] The canons, modal sonatas and madrigals, and composition

---

71 Giovanni Bononcini, *Sinfonie a 5. 6. 7. e 8. istromenti, con alcune à una e due trombe, servendo ancora per violini*, Op. 3 (Bologna: Monti, 1685), Dedication: "da i genitori hebbi quel tanto di vita, come bastò per produrmi alle miserie, mentr'essi, morendo, m'abbandonarono Fanciullo ancora in braccio alla povertà."

72 Crowther, "Case-Study," 213–14, summarizes G. M. Bononcini's professional fortunes in Modena. See also Crowther, *Oratorio in Modena*, 5.

73 Giovanni Maria Bononcini, *Varii fiori del giardino musicale, overo sonate da camera a 2. 3. e 4. col suo basso continuo*, Op. 3 (Bologna: Monti, 1669).

74 Bononcini, *Sonate da chiesa a due violini*, Op. 6 (Venice: Magni, 1672), Al lettore: "In questa mia fatica ritroverai (oltre il modo di contessere le Consonanze, è Dissonanze, e diversi inditij del Tempo, che nello stile concertato si può praticare) che hò nominati gli Tuoni fuor dell'uso comune, e ciò perche habbia à valere per maggiore esplicazione di quanto vedrai descritto sù questo particolare nel mio Trattato di Musica, che già ti hò promesso, è'l quale sebene è compito, ne resta più che di metterlo sotto 'l Torchio [In this work of mine you will find—beyond ways of weaving consonances and dissonances as well as diverse tempo indications which may be practiced in the *stile concertato*—that I have designated the *tuoni* outside of common practice. I have done so because this will most effectively demonstrate that which you will see described on this matter in my *Trattato di Musica*, which I have already promised and which, although finished, remains to be printed]."

75 Bononcini, *Partitura di madrigali a cinque voci sopra i dodici tuoni, ò modi di canto figurato*, Op. 11 (Bologna: Monti, 1678), A gl'Intendenti, e Professori di Musica: "Non faccio poi alcuna spiegazione del Madrigale Non più guerra sopra tutti i dodici Tuoni, o Modi, poiche

treatise constitute a unique body of work among violinist-composers. On the one hand, they reflect Bononcini's predilection for contrapuntal complexities, and, on the other, they reveal his keen desire to be noticed outside his immediate circle. Worth noting in that regard is the dedicatee of the Op. 8 treatise and Op. 11 madrigals: the Holy Roman Emperor Leopold I. In short, Bononcini appears to have harbored aspirations well beyond his unhappy situation in Modena, meaning to conquer a larger musical world through his learning. In one respect, his strategy would pay off: the treatise was reprinted twice before the end of the century and translated into German in 1702. From the early eighteenth century onward Bononcini would stand prominently among Italian theorists after the Renaissance.[76] It did him little good: he died poor in Modena, 36 years old, in 1678, the year his Op. 11 madrigals were published.

The Accademia dei Filarmonici di Bologna

Low pay, restrictive decrees of employers, fickle patrons, and the piracy of publishers seem an almost overwhelming array of challenges inherent in the music profession. But there was also considerable generosity among music-loving patrons and support within the community of musicians: the activities of the Accademia Filarmonica, a defining feature of the Bolognese musical landscape, fill out this portrait of musical life for the composer-instrumentalists, illustrating an innovative resource for Bolognese musicians.[77] The Accademia Filarmonica was neither a performing ensemble, like the Ferrarese Accademia della Morte, nor a learned society of non-professionals, like the Bolognese Accademia de' Gelati, but rather an organization of professional musicians devoted equally to the welfare of its members and to the perfection of musical composition. The early workings of the academy, founded in 1666 and held in the house of its founding patron, count Vincenzo Maria Carrati, stressed the benefit of its members, as much as their talents. In its earliest statutes, the *Capitoli della Academia de SS.ri Filarmonici*, a fund was established to pay for

---

facilmente si può comprendere il mio pensiero da quanto hò detto nell'accennato Musico Prattico in questo particolare [I give no explanation of the madrigal 'Non più guerra' in all twelve tones or modes because one can easily comprehend my thinking from what I have said on this matter in the already-mentioned *Musico prattico*]."

76 The eighteenth-century historian Giuseppe Ottavio Pitoni, *Notitia de' contrapuntisti e compositori di musica*, MS, c.1725, modern ed. by Cesarino Ruini (Florence: Olschki, 1988), 317, had high praise for Bononcini on account of his treatise, writing, "in materia dottrinale e discorsiva, è riuscita la migliore e la più facile che oggi vada in giro per apprendere il contrapunto e per il gradimento ristampata più volte."

77 Studies devoted to the Accademia Filarmonica are Nestore Morini, *La R. Accademia Filarmonica di Bologna: monografia storica* (Bologna: Cappelli, 1930; reprint, Bologna: Tamari, 1966); John Suess, "Observations on the Accademia Filarmonica of Bologna in the Seventeenth Century and the Rise of a Local Tradition of Instrumental Music," *Quadrivium* 8 (1967): 51–62; Laura Callegari-Hill, *L'Accademia Filarmonica di Bologna, 1666–1800* (Bologna: Antiquae Musicae Italicae Studiosi, 1991); and Osvaldo Gambassi, *L'Accademia Filarmonica di Bologna: fondazione, statuti e aggregazioni* (Florence: Olschki, 1992).

the funeral rites of deceased members.[78] Accademicians were asked to pay 20 *soldi* (the equivalent of a *lira*) on the occasion of a death in the academy. The fund was soon expanded to render aid to financially stricken or infirm members.[79]

The musical activities of the academy from its earliest years centered on its weekly *esercizi* that featured not only the performance and discussion of members' compositions, but included, as recalled by one of its founding members, Pietro Degli Antonii, "a reception with comestibles constituting sweets and fruits according to the season and exquisite wine, white and red, and such things."[80] The atmosphere of the *esercizi*, moreover, was to be strictly positive, as spelled out in the statutes of the academy: "because every respect must be paid to a civil and decorous meeting such as ours, he that seeks in this Academy to mock, ridicule, or tease either the person or any virtuous action of a fellow academician will be immediately excluded from these gatherings."[81]

The largest and most public event undertaken by the academicians was their annual celebration of the feast of S. Anthony of Padua, the institution's patron saint. Compositions for the occasion, written by members and performed gratis (with the help of additional paid performers), comprised a Mass and Vespers ceremony, which was performed publicly in the Bolognese church of S. Giovanni in Monte. After these performances, according to Degli Antonii,

> one went to the academy where, in the room in which the *esercizi* were and are still held, a great table was prepared with a lavish reception that consisted of cheeses, *mortadella*, pie, cake, fruits and fennel according to the season, exquisite white and red wine, and all of this in such abundance that it was superabundant for all hundred or so. And then in the adjoining room that looks on the public street, a platter of sweets was prepared for each and every individual who participated in the celebration, according to their rank, the platter consisted of *zuccherini*, cookies, confections of quince jam and other kinds, with two *bracciatelle* for all.[82]

---

78 Callegari-Hill, 339.

79 Ibid., 345; and Gambassi, *Accademia Filarmonica*, 68–9.

80 Ibid., 10: "un rinfresco di commestibili, consistente in dulciari, et altri frutti, secondo la corrente stagione, e vino esquisito bianco, e nero, e cose tali."

81 *Ricordi per li signori compositori dell'Accademia de' Signori Filarmonici* (Bologna: Pisarri, 1689), 12: "perche ad un sì civile, e decoroso congresso, quale è il nostro, si deve ogni rispetto; perciò, chi ardira in Accademia beffegiare, motteggiare, ò burlare nella Persona, & in qualsivoglia attione virtuosa il Coaccademico, s'intenda subito escluso da questa radunanza."

82 Gambassi, *Accademia Filarmonica*, 10: "si andava alla detta Accademia, ove, nella sala dove si facevano e si fanno gli esercizi, stava preparata una gran tavola nella quale stava preparato un ben lauto rinfresco, consistente in formaggio di forma, mortadella, torta, offelle, frutti, e finocchi, secondo la corrente stagione, vino bianco, e nero esquisito, e la detta robba era in tale abbondanza, che era sovrabbondante per tutti al numero di circa a cento; e doppoi nella stanza contigua che guarda nella via pubblica stava preparata una piatanza di dulciari per ciascheduno, che singolarmente si dava a tutti quelli che avevano operato in detta festa, secondo il loro grado, la quale piatanza consisteva in zuccherini, biscottini, scattole di cotognata, et altri con due bracciatele per ciascheduno." *Zuccherini* is a generic term for sugar sweets, perhaps sugar-plums or something similar; *bracciatelle* are soft, ring-shaped cakes.

The nature of this academy, far from a gathering of dilettantes to pursue theoretical or aesthetic questions, was oriented toward the needs and activities of its professional members. Within this society of mutual benefit, its members refined their craft at its weekly exercises, after which they enjoyed offerings fit for nobility at the expense of Carrati and, later, his successors. The only expenses borne by the *accademici* themselves went toward the fund for the assistance and death benefits of fellow members.

In the context of the unpredictable and arduous professional life of late-*Seicento* composer-instrumentalists, the Accademia Filarmonica stands out as a benign exception. Its immediate success reflects both the need for such an organization and the heavy concentration of musical talent in and around Bologna. Its membership quickly spread beyond Bolognese environs and, ultimately, beyond Italy, but the early years of the Accademia Filarmonica coincide with the dynamic period of musical patronage, instrumental composition, and music publishing that distinguished Bologna's musical culture.

Chapter Two

The Forms and Uses of the
Sonata da Camera

Two movements by two composers, father and son, illustrate the curiosities and complexities that typify the dances of the late seventeenth-century sonata da camera. Example 2.1a shows a corrente from a suite *in stil francese* by the father, Giovanni Maria Bononcini, within a collection he entitled *Trattenimenti musicali* (1675). The layout of that collection, his Op. 9, is shown in Table 2.1. Multi-movement church sonatas precede paired allemande and correnti (designated *suonate da camera*), and the French-style dances conclude the print. For comparison with the opening example, a corrente from the paired dances of the same print is shown as Example 2.1b. Aside from binary form, a common feature of the two dances is syncopation within compound meter. Otherwise, they differ markedly: while the French-style corrente (Example 2.1a) suggests dancer's music because of its regular pattern of accents in a homophonic texture, the other (Example 2.1b) almost certainly precludes dancing to its rhythms, which obscure its meter with unceasing and unpredictable syncopation.

Table 2.1   G. M. Bononcini, *Trattenimenti musicali à trè & à quattro stromenti*, Op. 9 (Bologna, 1675), contents

Suonate da chiesa a trè	Suonate da camera a trè	Suonate à 4 in stil francese
Sonata prima	Allemanda prima	Brando
	Corrente prima	Gavotta
Sonata seconda		Corrente prima
	Allemanda seconda	Balletto primo
Sonata terza	Corrente seconda	Gagliarda
		Corrente seconda
Sonata quarta	Allemanda terza	
	Corrente terza	
Sonata quinta		
	Allemanda quarta	
	Corrente quarta	

Example 2.1a   G. M. Bononcini, Op. 9 (1675), Corrente prima in stil francese

A third corrente (Example 2.1c) furnishes music by the younger Bononcini, Giovanni, who is best remembered as an opera composer and Handel's rival in 1720s London. He began his composing career in 1685 with a set of dances tidily organized into twelve four-movement suites (see Table 2.2) and published as *Trattenimenti da camera*, Op. 1. Drawn from the fifth of these suites, Example 2.1c offers music so simple, rhythmically and harmonically, that it seems a beginner's etude. And, according to the composer, his *Trattenimenti* were just that. As he writes in an accompanying note to the reader, his dances are "children of one little more than 13 years of age [he was actually 15], of practice in playing little more than three, and of a study of counterpoint little more than one."[1]

---

1 Giovanni Bononcini, *Trattenimenti da camera a trè, due violini e violone, con il basso continuo per il cembalo*, Op. 1 (Bologna: Monti, 1685), "Dilettante cortese. Lascierei di avvisarti, che la seguente Opera, insieme con un'altra, che stà sotto il Torchio, sono figliuole d'un età di poco più di tredici anni, d'un esercizio nel suono di poco più di trè, e d'uno studio nel Contrapunto di poco più d'uno."

Example 2.1b   G. M. Bononcini, Op. 9 (1675), Corrente prima da camera

Example 2.1c   G. Bononcini, Op. 1, No. 5 (1685), Corrente

Table 2.2   G. Bononcini, *Trattenimenti da camera a trè*, Op. 1 (Bologna, 1685), contents

Trattenimento primo	Trattenimento quinto	Trattenimento nono
Adagio	Adagio	Adagio
Balletto, Allegro	Balletto, Allegro	Balletto, Allegro
Giga, Vivace	Corrente, Largo	Corrente, Vivace
Sarabanda, Prestissimo	Sarabanda, Allegro	Sarabanda, Allegro
Trattenimento secondo	**Trattenimento sesto**	**Trattenimento decimo**
Adagio	Adagio	Adagio
Balletto, Allegro	Balletto, Allegro	Balletto, Allegro
Corrente, Largo	Corrente, Largo	Giga, ——
Sarabanda, Presto	Sarabanda, Allegro	Sarabanda, Allegro
Trattenimento terzo	**Trattenimento settimo**	**Trattenimento undecimo**
Adagio	Adagio	Adagio
Balletto, Allegro	Balletto, Allegro	Balletto, Allegro
Giga, Largo	Giga, Vivace	Giga, Allegro
Sarabanda, Allegro	Sarabanda, Allegro	Sarabanda, Allegro
Trattenimento quarto	**Trattenimento ottavo**	**Trattenimento duodecimo**
Adagio	Adagio	Adagio
Balletto, Allegro	Balletto, Allegro	Balletto, Allegro
Giga, Allegro	Corrente, Largo	Giga, Largo
Sarabanda, Largo	Sarabanda, Allegro	Sarabanda, Allegro

These examples illustrate, first, two stages in the emerging conception of the sonata da camera as a suite of dances and other movements, rather than a single dance, and second, the wide range of styles found among the dances for instrumental ensemble. Much has been written about the evolution of the "suite idea" in late seventeenth-century Italian instrumental music, specifically on how dances were presented in published collections.[2] A less-explored topic is the diversity of styles and possible originating contexts of the dances, which is the focus of this chapter. Between father and son, writing just ten years apart, are three distinct styles of corrente that suggest just as many uses of the music—that is, dance accompaniment (Example 2.1a), diversional chamber music (Example 2.1b), and compositional etude (Example 2.1c).

Further examples covering an assortment of dance types divide along similar lines of musical style and likely function. Example 2.2a, a sarabanda from Carlo Andrea Mazzolini's *Sonate per camera*, Op. 1 (1687), illustrates the typical features of the dance in the seventeenth century: triple meter in a fast tempo and phrases consistently of four bars, often concluding with a metrically unaccented, or feminine, cadence. (A slow tempo and an accented second beat are characteristics of the French form of this dance, but not the Italian.) Mazzolini uses the opening phrase to introduce the main motif imitatively, but the dance otherwise features the homophony and regular phrasing of a danced sarabanda. By contrast, Example 2.2b, taken from Bartolomeo Laurenti's *Suonate per camera* (1691), is music for the diversion of the instrumentalists and their listeners with its ever-lengthening phrases (two measures, then three, then four-and-a-half) and its virtuoso cello part. The two minuets for violins in unison (Examples 2.2c and 2.2d), taken from the *Trattenimenti armonici per camera* (1695) by Francesco Giuseppe De Castro, in turn demonstrate a novice's strict adherence to a simple formula: in the first half of both dances, the opening phrase is varied in order to cadence on the fifth degree; in the second half, sequential motion over falling fifths in the bass leads to the final phrase, in which the tonal center is re-established. A glance at De Castro's prefatory note to the reader confirms our impression of his beginner's status. "Know that I have not resorted to the presses out of ambition to be noticed, but merely to satisfy my natural taste and delight, conceived in the practice of handling the bow on a few strings, which I have undertaken for a few years now for my own diversion."[3]

---

2   John Daverio, "In Search of the Sonata da Camera before Corelli," *Acta musicologica* 57 (1985): 195–214. Arguments against Daverio's theory have been advanced by Sandra Mangsen, "The 'Sonata da Camera' before Corelli: A Renewed Search," *Music & Letters* 76 (1995): 19–31; and Peter Allsop, "*Da camera e da ballo—alla francese et all'italiana*: Functional and National Distinctions in Corelli's *sonate da camera*," *Early Music* 26 (1998): 87–96. In support of Daverio is Michael Talbot, "The Taiheg, the Pira and Other Curiosities of Benedetto Vinaccesi's 'Suonate da camera a tre,' Op. I," *Music & Letters* 75 (1994): 344–64.

3   De Castro, *Trattenimenti armonici da camera*, Op. 1 (Bologna: Monti, 1695): "Sappiate, ch'io non sono ricorso alla Stampa, per ambizione di comparire; mà per soddisfare meramente ad un mio naturale genio, e diletto conceputo nell'esercizio, che per mio divertimento intrapresi pochi anni sono, di maneggiar l'arco sù poche corde." De Castro's status as a student-composer is briefly discussed in the previous chapter (pp. 53–4).

Example 2.2a   C. A. Mazzolini, Op. 1, No. 4 (1687), Sarabanda

Example 2.2b   B. Laurenti, Op. 1, No. 3 (1691), Ballo

Example 2.2c   F. G. De Castro, Op. 1, No. 1 (1695), Minuet all'unisono

Example 2.2d   F. G. De Castro, Op. 1, No. 4 (1695), Minuet all'unisono

To examine just a few movements from the vast repertory of chamber sonatas published in late-*Seicento* Bologna is to appreciate an eclecticism that suggests various uses and diverse originating circumstances. The aim here is to explore such uses and origins by surveying assorted testimony on dancing and other contexts in which dance music was performed. Sources that reveal the uses of dance music in various events and activities are scattered piecemeal among librettos, diaries, and illustrations, as well as among a few titles, prefaces, and dedications from the prints themselves. These sundry bits of evidence sketch the musical culture whose surviving trace is the published repertory of dances. That culture, as we shall see, centers on the habits of Italian nobles who made use of instrumental dances in their roles as lavish patrons of the *festa da ballo*, as dilettante performers in the musical *accademia*, and even as students of courtly deportment in the *esercizio cavalleresco*.

Bologna and Dance

These three categories of context and function—*festa, accademia*, and *esercizio*—provide the broad outline followed here. That there might be any connection between the published sonatas and prior recorded events is evidenced by Maurizio Cazzati's *Trattenimenti per camera*, published in 1660 (Table 2.3). This collection of short ballets stands out because of the curious designations given to each, such as *ballo de matacini, ballo delle ombre*, and *ballo de satiri* (that is, ballets of clowns, ghosts, and satyrs). The titles refer to what seem to have been pantomimes for theatrical performance, and a survey of Bolognese librettos raises specific possibilities. One, entitled *Applausi nuzziali* and published the year before Cazzati's *Trattenimenti*, commemorates the wedding of Count Antonio Orsi and Orintia Bolognetti, which was celebrated with a theatrical performance.[4] As noted in the concluding pages, "the arrangement of the scenes, the scenery, and the music was by Maurizio Cazzati, maestro di cappella of S. Petronio."[5] The Orsi–Bolognetti wedding is, however, just one of two possibilities suggested by surviving librettos; the other is an earlier musical *applauso* composed by Cazzati in 1658 in honor of the visiting "ambassador extraordinary" of the Emperor Leopold I, Don Gaspare de Brachamonte.[6]

---

4 The title, description, and facts of publication for this libretto are as follows: *Applausi nuzziali: nel felicissimo sposalizio de gl'illustrissimi signori conte Antonio Orsi e signora contessa Orintia Bolognetti* (Bologna: Monti, 1659). A bibliographic listing of this libretto may be found in Claudio Sartori, *I libretti italiani a stampa dalle origini al 1800*, 7 vols (Cuneo: Bertola and Locatelli, 1990–94), No. 2303.

5 *Applausi nuzziali*, 28.

6 *Le gare de'fiumi: applauso per musica, all'illustriss. ed eccellentiss. sig. D. Gaspare de Brachamonte Co. di Pignoranda ... ambasciatore straordinario alla maestà di Cesare* (Bologna: Monti 1658). The listing in Sartori, *Libretti*, is No. 11247, which includes from the libretto, "Parole del sig. dottor Gio. Battista Pellicani, e musica del sig. D. Mauritio Cazzati."

Table 2.3   M. Cazzati, *Trattenimenti per camera* (Bologna, 1660), contents

Aria prima parte	Ballo de Tadeschi	Brando
Aria seconda parte	sua corrente	
Aria terza parte		Brando
Ballo dell'aria	Ballo de satiri	
sua corrente	sua corrente	Passacaglio
Ballo delle dame	Ballo de Matacini	Ciaccona
sua corrente	sua corrente	
		Capriccio sopra 12 note
Ballo de' cavalieri	Ballo delle ombre	
sua corrente	sua corrente	
Ballo de contadini	Ballo delle ninfe	
sua corrente	sua corrente	

On the basis of Cazzati's dance titles and his involvement with the two theatrical performances of 1658 and 1659, we might wonder whether the published collection of 1660 originated in the one, the other, or both. A well-known precedent for a composer's later publication of music, originally composed and performed for one or more signal events, is Lorenzo Allegri's *Primo libro delle musiche* of 1618 (Table 2.4).[7] Allegri culled his eight published *balli* from several Medici court entertainments of the previous ten years that are traceable in part because of the information he included about them.[8] By comparison, Cazzati gives us no information about originating circumstances, but provides many more dances in his printed output. After his *Trattenimenti* of 1660, he sent two more collections to the presses in the same decade, although neither with pantomimic titles.[9] Moreover, a third libretto—in this case recording "festivities of [military] arms and of dance" from 1662—also attributes music to Cazzati.[10]

---

7   Two other such precedents can also be identified: Filiberto Laurenzi, *Concerti et arie* (Venice: Vincenti, 1641) includes a "serenata à 5 fatta nelle feste dell'Ill.mo & Ecc.mo Procurator Giovanni de Pesaro" that contains passacaglie and correnti, both danced and sung; and Antonio Brunelli, *Scherzi, arie, canzonette, e madrigali* (Venice: Vincenti, 1616) contains a half-dozen *balli*, also danced and sung, from Tuscan court entertainments.

8   See Federico Ghisi, "Ballet Entertainments in Pitti Palace, Florence, 1608–1625," *The Musical Quarterly* 25 (1949): 421–36.

9   These are: *Correnti, e balletti per sonare nella spinetta, leuto, ò tiorba; overo violino, e violone, col secondo violino à beneplacito*, Op. 30 (Bologna: Pisarri, 1662); and *Varii, e diversi capricci per camera, e per chiesa, da sonare con diversi instromenti, a uno, due, e tre*, Op. 50 (Bologna: n.p., 1669). This latter print, despite the mention of church use, as well as chamber, is dominated by binary-form courtly dances, such as correnti, gighe, sarabande, and the like.

10   *Le gare d'Amore e di Marte: festa d'armi e di ballo rappresentata in palazzo il Carnovale del 1662 alla presenza dell'Eminentiss. e Reverendiss. Sig. Cardinale Farnese*

Table 2.4   L. Allegri, *Il primo libro delle musiche* (Venice, 1618), contents

Sinfonia

"Spirto del ciel'" [madrigal] *Poesie del Signor Ferdinando Saracinelli fatte in musica da Lorenzo Allegri, cantate e sonate da i Signori Paggi all'A.A. Serenissime*

Primo ballo *della Notte d'Amore danzato nelle nozze dell'A.A. Serenissime da Paggi, e dame*
Gagliarda seconda parte
Corrente terza & ultima parte

Secondo ballo *detto la Serena, danzato dall'A.A. Serenissimi Principi, cavallieri, e dame sotto l'habito di Deità Marittime*
Seconda parte
Gagliarda terza parte
Corrente quarta & ultima parte

Terzo ballo *detto Alta Maria danzato dalle SS.re Principesse*
Gagliarda seconda & ultima parte

Quarto ballo *detto i Campi Elisij danzato da cavallieri armati all'A.A. Serenissime*
Brando seconda parte
Gagliarda terza & ultima parte

Quinto ballo *detto le Ninfe di Senna danzato da SS.ri Paggi dell'A.A. Serenissime nelle nozze dell'Ill.mo & Ecc.mo Duca d'Onano, e Conte di Sancta Fiore, e dell'Ill.ma & Ecc.ma Sig.ra Arinea di Loreno*
Canario seconda parte
Gavotta terza parte
Corrente quarta & ultima parte

Sexto ballo *danzato da Signori Paggi dell'A.A. Serenissime nella venuta dell'Illustrissimo & Eccellentissimo Signor Francesco Orsino Marchese di Trinello, Imbasciator di Francia*
Grave seconda parte
Gagliarda terza & ultima parte

Settimo ballo *danzato da Sig.ri Paggi dell'A.A. Ser.me nella venuta del Ser.mo Principe d'Urbino*
Grave seconda parte
Corrente terza & ultima parte

Ottavo ballo *detto L'Iride danzato da Paggi, e dame nella festa particulare fatta dalla Serenissima Archiduchessa, e Granduchessa di Toscana*
Gagliarda seconda parte
Brando terza parte
Gagliarda quarta parte
Corrente quinta & ultima parte

---

legato di Bologna (Bologna: Monti, 1662), 40: "La Musica fù del Sig. D. Maurizio Cacciati [*recte* Cazzati] Mastro di capella di S. Petronio." The listing in Sartori, *Libretti*, is No. 11245.

None of these librettos names specific dances, so that a definitive connection between a published collection of dances and an event recorded by a libretto cannot be made. To give an example of the information they do furnish, the 1662 libretto—entitled *Le gare d'Amore e di Marte* and performed for the Papal Legate in honor of the birthday of Pope Alexander VII—presents an allegorical contest between Cupid and Mars that is resolved by Peace (whose patron and inspiration is the Pope). In the introduction, Cupid commands his followers, the Contented Ones, to express their enjoyment in dance, whereupon

> Ready for the dance, the Contented Ones immediately lit upon the stage. These were represented by twelve youths of the nobility, all richly dressed ... all of whom, at the same time that they moved their feet to the dance, invited the spirits to rejoice. Seeing their groupings varied so well and the figures [of the dance] so gracefully woven, one could perhaps imagine the regulation of the rotating spheres to be less perfect than their steps.[11]

We thus know the place of this dance within the larger allegory of Cupid and Mars and that Cazzati composed the music, but nothing that could link the events described to specific pieces from his published dances.

Nevertheless, this and other librettos reveal the festive circumstances for which Cazzati and others in Bologna composed dances. The entertainments for which he was commissioned to provide music—given to celebrate an aristocratic wedding, the reception of a visiting dignitary, and a pope's birthday—illustrate a few of the contexts for dancing. And there are others, most notable of which was the civic celebration known as the Festa della Porchetta. As the commemoration of both the Bolognese victory over the forces of Frederick II at the Battle of Fossalta in 1249 and the feast of S. Bartholomew (August 24), the Festa della Porchetta evolved into a large-scale theatrical event over the centuries, often involving choreographed dances.[12] An image of dancing at one of these celebrations, seen in Figure 2.1, depicts the 1671 performance of an allegory of *Marte, Pallade e Furore*.[13]

---

11 *Le gare d'Amore e di Marte*, 15: "Pronti al Ballo scesero subito nel Teatro i Contenti. Questi venivano rappresentati da dodici Nobili Giovinetti, guerniti di spoglie tutte riccamente. Erano Il Sig. Antonio Tortorelli. Il Sig. Angelo Maria Turini. Il Sig. Bartolomeo Fioravanti. Il Sig. Carlo Gessi. Il Sig. Camillo Palmieri. Il Sig. Francesco Maria Palmieri. Il Sig. Fabrizio Maria Fontana. Il Sig. Giulio Antonio Landini. Il Sig. Gio. Battista Palmieri. Il Sig. Giacomo Dondini. Il Sig. Lorenzo Tubertini, & il Sig. Marco Antonio Luppari. I quali nel medesimo tempo, che muovevano il piede alle danze, invitavano gli animi al gioire. Vedevansi variare così bene i gruppi, e sì leggiadramente intrecciar le figure, che meno perfetti de loro passi forse potevansi immaginare i regolamenti delle Sfere rotanti."

12 On the origins of this feast, see Lorena Bianconi, *Alle origini della festa bolognese della Porchetta* (Bologna: Clueb, 2005). Elita Maule, "La 'Festa della Porchetta' a Bologna nel Seicento: indagine su una festa barocca," *Il carrobbio* 6 (1980): 251–62, p. 251, examines the seventeenth-century entertainments of this large-scale celebration. A survey of Bolognese spectacle over several centuries is Marina Calore, *Bologna a teatro: vita di una città attraverso i suoi spettacoli, 1400–1800* (Bologna: Giudicini e Rosa Editori, 1981).

13 The image is headed "Disegno del teatro costruito in occasione della festa del 1671" in the *Collezione delle relazioni della Festa della Porchetta*, vol. 1, Gabinetto Disegni e Stampe,

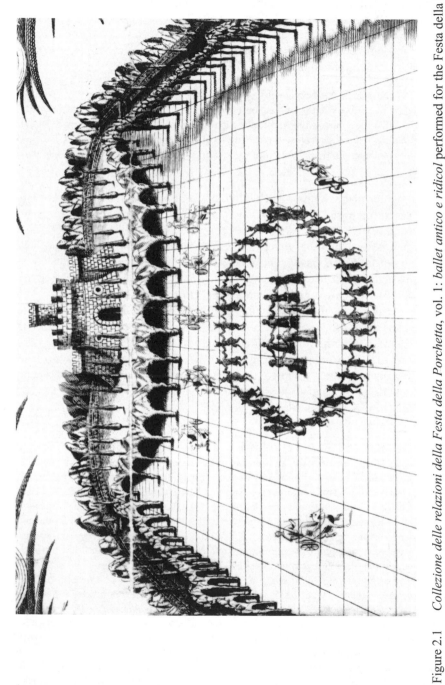

Figure 2.1　*Collezione delle relazioni della Festa della Porchetta*, vol. 1: *ballet antico e ridicol* performed for the Festa della Porchetta of 1671. Biblioteca Comunale dell'Archiginnasio, Bologna (I-Bca), Gabinetto Disegni e Stampe

The inner ring of seven dancing ladies (Hippodamia and her ladies-in-waiting) and surrounding ring of more than 30 satyr-like figures give an idea of staged ballet in Bologna from roughly the same time as Cazzati's commissions.[14]

The librettos that mention him, however, reflect more private entertainments, and they raise the issue of the involvement of local nobles, not only as patrons, but also as performers. Another performance, a 1658 ballet entitled *La gara delle Stagioni*, underscores this point in its opening remarks:

> Bolognese *cavalieri*, as those who well know that idleness in any *cavaliere* is the cause of odious vileness, never allow themselves to be conquered by it ... for this purpose, this year, with an invention of the four Seasons of the year accompanied by all of their Months, several *cavalieri* presented themselves in the *sala* of the Marquis Francesco Maria Angelelli in the presence of the most eminent Legate of Bologna and of all the most noble ladies of this city in order to show the vigor, valor, and spirit of the *cavaliere* both by means of a combat of arms and by means of the motions of their feet.[15]

In the entertainment of dancing and swordplay that follows, the Seasons (each a *virtuossisimo musico* who sings) and the Months (each a *cavaliero nobilissimo* who dances) act out a contest that is eventually resolved through the intervention of Cupid. The Seasons then sing a canzonetta of peace and contentment, after which the Months perform a final dance comprising nine figures, the first two of which are shown in diagram from a page of the libretto (Figure 2.2).

Biblioteca Comunale dell'Archiginnasio di Bologna (I-Bca). The libretto of this performance is *Marte Pallade e Furore. Lettera di ragguaglio della festa popolare della Porchetta fatta quest'anno 1671* (Bologna: Manolessi, 1671). Sartori, *Libretti*, No. 14184.

14 *Marte Pallade e Furore*, 3–4, briefly describes this opening scene of the performance, in which Hippodamia, bride of Pirithous, plus six ladies who serve her and "24 other personages diversely costumed" dance an ancient and comic dance.

15 *La gara delle stagioni: ballo rappresentato in casa dell'Illustriss. Sig. Marchese Francesco Angelelli, senatore, il dì 2 marzo 1658* (Bologna: Monti, 1658), 3–4: "I Cavaglieri Bolognesi, come quegli, che benissimo sanno l'Ozio in ogni Cavagliere esser cagione d'odiosa viltà, mai non si lasciano vincere da esso ... quest'Anno per l'appunto, con l'Invenzione delle Quattro Stagioni dell'Anno, accompagnate tutte da proprij Mesi, s'introdussero alcuni Cavaglieri nella Sala del Sig. Marchese Francesco Maria Angelelli, alla presenza dell'Eminentissimo Legato di Bologna, e di tutte le Dame nobilissime di questa Città, per mostrar, si frà l'abbattimento dell'Armi, come ne' moti del piede il vigore, il valore, & il brio Cavalleresco." The listing in Sartori, *Libretti*, is No. 11224.

Serui, omai con bella vſanza
Ne l' Impero
La tenzon cangiate in danza
Di quel Dio, che doma il tutto
Pronto il gioir ſempr' è maturo il frutto.

Cantando i ſudetti verſi, ſtauano nella
ſotto deſcritta figura le Stagioni, & i Meſi, poſcia con Amore vnitamente ſi partiro-
no le Stagioni, e reſtarono i Meſi al Ballo,
che quì pure ſi deſcriue nelle ſue figure.

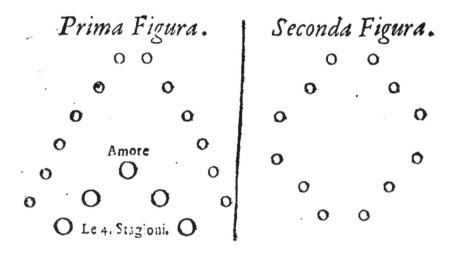

Figure 2.2 Libretto of *Le gare d'Amore e di Marte: festa d'armi e di ballo*
     (Bologna: Monti, 1658), 15. Biblioteca Comunale dell'Archiginnasio,
     Bologna (I-Bca)

Festa da Ballo

As we shall see, the participation of the local nobility is a persistent element in each of the performing contexts investigated here. And their part in theatrical ballets reflects just one of the two main contexts for dancing. The other was social dancing at the *festa da ballo*, which was often held as the culminating event of a festive occasion. For instance, in his history of Bolognese theaters, Corrado Ricci surveys performances of operas and oratorios in private theaters of the local nobility, after which, according to the sources he cites, a *rinfresco* (reception) and *festa da ballo* often followed.[16] A description by the diarist Antonio Francesco Ghiselli of a literary *accademia* with sung intermezzi gives an idea of an evening's entertainment ending with a ball.[17] Ghiselli's description of the sumptuous setting was quoted on p. 13 of the Introduction (see also Figure 0.7). On the function itself, the diarist is no less detailed:

> Alamanno Isolani, Senator and Count, [also] being *principe* of the Accademia de' Gelati and having arranged the wedding of his sister to Count Alessandro Pepoli, son of Count Cornelio, held a most noble academy of *belle lettere* in his own house with the attendance of the entire nobility (both ladies and gentlemen), the [Papal] Legate, the Vice-Legate, the Confaloniero, and the *Anziani*. And after the literary function there was held a *festa da ballo*.... There were 40 of the city's best instrumentalists, and three female virtuosos sang the musical introduction and intermezzi. There were two academic discourses [and] a most noble reception. Afterwards one saw a most beautiful apartment with a quantity of lights, tables for games, and site for the dance.[18]

Ghiselli mentions neither a composer nor specific pieces, but we can connect another aristocratic wedding to published dances from the Bolognese repertory. In 1673, Lorenzo Penna, maestro di cappella of the church of the Carmine in Parma, published his collection of 25 *Correnti francesi*, dances then in vogue in Parma and

---

16 Corrado Ricci, *I teatri di Bologna nei secoli XVII e XVIII* (Bologna: Successori Monti, 1888; facsimile, Bologna: Forni, 1965), 406–7, 413, and 415.

17 The libretto for this event survives as *Introduzione et intramezzi per musica. Nell'accademia de signori Gelati avutasi sotto il principato dell'illustrissimo signor conte e senatore Alemano Isolani il dì IV genajo 1705* (Bologna: Pisarri, 1705). Sartori, *Libretti*, No. 13516.

18 Antonio Francesco Ghiselli, *Memorie antiche manuscritte di Bologna raccolte et accresciute sino à tempi presenti dal canonico Antonio Francesco Ghiselli nobile bolognese*, MS, early eighteenth century, Bologna, Biblioteca Universitaria (I-Bu), ms. 770, vol. 58, 3–ff: "Essendo Principe dell'Accademia de' Gelati il Senatore Conte Alamanno Isolani, et havendo fatto sposa la sorella, come detto abbiamo, del conte Alessandro Pepoli del conte Cornelio, fece in casa propria una nobilissima Accademia di Belle lettere, con il concorso di tutta la Nobiltà, Dame e Cavalieri, il Legato, Vicelegato, Confaloniero et Antiani, e doppo la funzione letteraria si fece festa da ballo.... Vi si trovarono quaranta instrumenti de' più celebri della Città e tre virtuose cantarono la introduzione ed intermezzi per musica. Vi furono duoi discorsi accademici, un nobilissimo rinfresco. Indi si vidde un bellissimo apartamento, con quantità di lumi, tavolini da giuocare, e sito per il ballo."

other Francophile cities in Italy.[19] With the subtitle *Nuptial Applauses* and, as he writes, "with the sole intention of applauding in sound your most worthy joining," Penna dedicated the correnti to the newlywed Parmigiano couple Count Alessandro Sanvitali and Paula Simonetta.[20] Examples 2.3a and 2.3b show excerpts from the first two dances (those named for the Count and Countess), whose homophonic texture and accent pattern match that of Example 2.1a, Bononcini's corrente from his dances *in stil francese*. All three examples, in four-part texture associated with the French style rather than the Italianate trio texture,[21] exemplify the French courante rhythm in which accented first, third, and fifth beats of a two-measure pattern in 3/4 meter or of a single measure in 6/4 create a subtle but persistent hemiola. Because of surviving step-instructions on French dances from the early eighteenth century, including notated examples, dance historians have been able to match courante steps to this rhythmic trait that Italian composers reliably applied to their *correnti francesi*.[22] In sum, the original function of these pieces as accompaniment to festive dancing is unmistakable, and, as Penna intended it, the Sanvitali–Simonetta wedding provided the context.

---

19 The vogue for French dance would spread throughout Italy in the latter half of the seventeenth century. Leading this trend were the Francophile cities of Parma and Modena, which had political ties to the French royal court. Attesting to the popularity of French courantes in Parma is the title of Marco Uccellini's Op. 9 (Venice: Magni, 1667): *Sinfonici concerti ... con brandi, è coreti alla francese, è balletti al Italiana, giusta l'uso aprovatissimo della corte di Parma* [Symphonic concertos ... with French branles and courantes, and Italian balletti, exact to the most approved use of the court of Parma].

20 The full title of Penna's print reads: *Correnti francesi a quattro cioè due violini, violetta, e violone con il basso continuo per il clavicembalo, ò tiorba: applausi nozziali di Lorenzo Penna da Bologna maestro di capella del Carmine di Parma, e fra gli Accademici Filaschisi, e Risoluti, l'Indefesso, offerti a gl'illustrissimi signori novelli sposi Co. Allessandro Sanvitali Conte di Fontanelato e di Noceto Marchese di Belfort &c. e Contessa Paula Simonetti* (Bologna: Monti, 1673).

21 Of the 20 suites found in Jules Ecorcheville, ed., *Vingt suites d'orchestre du XVIIe siècle français*, 2 vols (Paris and Berlin, 1906; facsimile, New York: Broude, 1970), 16 use a four-part texture of *dessus, haute-contre, taille,* and *basse.* The remaining four add a fifth part (*quinte*), but none use the Italian trio texture. The violetta part of Penna's *Correnti francesi* seems to have given him trouble, as if he were converting trios into quartets with its insertion. By including it he introduced parallels in both of the examples reproduced here: Example 2.3a, between the second violin and violetta in the second and third bars after the repeat; and Example 2.3b, between the violetta and bass line in the first two beats of the third complete measure. Apart from these surprising solecisms (Penna had published a treatise in the previous year), the violetta part seems an afterthought because of its clashes with the other parts, as if Penna were comfortable writing for the trio texture but noticeably uncomfortable expanding it to four parts.

22 An analysis of the courante's musical characteristics in the context of its notated dance steps is given in Wendy Hilton, "A Dance for Kings: The 17th-Century French *Courante*," *Early Music* 5 (1977): 161–72. See also Meredith Little and Natalie Jenne, *Dance and the Music of J. S. Bach* (Bloomington, IN: Indiana University Press, 1991; expanded ed., 2001).

Example 2.3a   L. Penna, Op. 7 (1673), Corrente prima "La Sanvitali"

Example 2.3b   L. Penna, Op. 7 (1673), Corrente seconda "La Simonetta"

Similar examples of wedding music later sent to the presses can be identified by remarks culled from dedications. Dances by Giovanni Battista Vitali for the 1692 wedding of Duke Francesco II d'Este to his cousin Margherita Farnese are preserved as the composer's *Sonate da camera a trè*, Op. 14 (1692). The dedication to the new bride, written two months after Vitali's death by his son, Tomaso Antonio, recalls that "these harmonic notes came out of the pen of Giovanni Battista Vitali to make a concerto of the people's applauses during the wedding of Your most Serene Highness."[23] But dedications and prefaces tend not to mention originating circumstances, possibly because the dedicatee usually had no connection to those events. The great number and unadorned appearance of Bolognese prints also remind us that they were created not to commemorate important events, but to sell music. This may have motivated composers and publishers to omit or suppress the details of origins so as to point up the idea of repertory that was useful on any occasion and for whatever purpose.

Two illustrations capture the milieu of the *festa da ballo* during the Baroque era and further attest French influence in Italian social dancing. Figure 2.3 gives an idea of the *sala* (or ballroom) in which such an event took place and of the arrangement of its participants.

---

23 "Uscivano dalla penna di Gio. Battista Vitali queste armoniche note per far concerto à gl'applausi de' Popoli nelle gloriose nozze di V. A. Serenissima."

Figure 2.3   *Insignia degli Anziani*, vol. 12, 67b: ball at the *palazzo* of the Fibbia family, 1716. Archivio di Stato di Bologna (I-Bas), Archivio degli Anziani

Figure 2.4   *Insignia degli Anziani*, vol. 13, 125a: ball at the *palazzo* of the Fibbia family, 1737. Archivio di Stato di Bologna (I-Bas), Archivio degli Anziani

The occasion, in this case, is a ball given at the home of Bologna's prominent Fibbia family in 1716 to honor the visiting Archbishop of Milan.[24] In the illustration, the Archbishop is seated and a single couple, possibly the hosts, dances before him. The musicians are shown in the upper left-hand corner of the illustration. A later *festa* from 1737, held in the same household, is captured in another painting (Figure 2.4), which shows essentially the same arrangement: the hosts initiate the dance (and here we can see the dancers' feet turned out in the French style), ladies and gentlemen of the Bolognese nobility surround the dancing couple, and musicians play from a balcony overlooking the ballroom.[25] The Italian imitation of French dance practice is worth a further comment here. Social dancing in France after the early eighteenth century would more likely have featured several couples simultaneously dancing a contredanse. The depictions shown here instead demonstrate the continued Italian emulation of an older and more intricate style of French dancing from the time of Louis XIV.

Esercizio Cavalleresco

The settings in which dancing took place give us a glimpse into Baroque-era theatrical and social dancing in Bologna, but this by no means suggests a dance culture exclusive to that city. Rather, dance music was also published in Venice and, most likely, unpublished repertory from other parts of Italy was used in similar circumstances. A noteworthy concentration of chamber sonatas published in Bologna but written by Brescian composers illustrates this very point while introducing yet another originating context: the *esercizio cavalleresco* within the Jesuit *collegi de' nobili*, or schools for the nobility. Here the role of the sonata da camera is didactic, playing a part in the inculcation of refinements that marked a person of quality.

Links between Italian dance music and some instructional purpose are readily found in *Seicento* instrument treatises. For example, Girolamo Fantini's 1638 trumpet manual is dominated by dances, and Gasparo Zannetti's 1645 violin tutor is wholly comprised of them.[26] In a similar vein is the case of Giorgio Buoni, Bolognese priest, teacher of counterpoint at his own music school, and editor of three collections of sonatas (two for the chamber).[27] From the dedications and prefaces of these collections, we learn that Buoni's music students performed as the Concerto de' Putti (Consort of Boys) in different cities of northern and central Italy—Milan, Cremona,

---

24 I-Bas, Archivio degli Anziani, *Insignia degli Anziani del commune*, vol. 12, 67b–68a (Jan.–Feb., 1716).

25 I-Bas, Archivio degli Anziani, *Insignia*, vol. 13, 125a (May–June, 1737).

26 Fantini, *Modo per imparare a sonare di tromba* (Frankfurt: Vuatsch, 1638; facsimile with trans. by Edward Tarr, Nashville, TN: Brass Press, 1978); Zannetti, *Il scolaro per imparar a suonare di violino* (Milan: Camagno, 1645; facsimile, Florence: Studio per Edizioni Scelte, 1984).

27 The three prints, all issued in 1693 under Buoni's name and published by Pier-Maria Monti in Bologna, are the *Divertimenti per camera, a due violini, e violoncello*, Op. 1; *Suonate a due violini, e violoncello, col basso per l'organo*, Op. 2; and *Allettamenti per camera a due violini, e basso*, Op. 3.

Prato, and Lucca. The sonatas themselves are the students' compositions, written in the course of their study of counterpoint and instrumental performance, corrected by Buoni, and then sent to the presses with dedications to those who had hosted touring performances of the Concerto de' Putti.

The presence of the sonata da camera in the Jesuit schools is attested by the minuets of F. G. De Castro cited at the beginning of this chapter to illustrate student works (Examples 2.2c–d). De Castro is briefly profiled in chapter 1 because of his student-composer status. We return to him here to consider the origins and possible uses of his chamber sonatas. As he tells us in the preface to his dances, "[t]hese few sonatas are the employment of the time for recreation that is conceded to me in this place that I find myself, and for interruption of the labors in the study of the *belle lettere* and philosophy."[28] The place in which he found himself was the Collegio de' Nobili in Brescia, one of many Jesuit-run schools for the aristocracy.[29] During his time there, De Castro studied music with the school's maestro di cappella, Paris Francesco Alghisi, the fruits of which are his collection of dances. His main pursuit, however, was the noble's broader course of study with extra-curricular activities, including music as one of the so-called *arti cavalleresche*.[30] According to the English diarist William Bromley, who toured France and Italy in 1691, students at the Jesuit college for the nobility in Parma

> are generally received young, which is desired by the Fathers, that so they may have the training them up, and make the first Impressions, while they are *udum & molle lutum*. Here they be instructed in Grammar, Humanity, Rhetorick, Philosophy, Mathematicks, Geography, Theology, and Law, and the Duke furnishes them with Horses out of his own Stable to ride. They have also Masters that teach to write, cast Account, Musick,

---

28 Francesco De Castro, *Trattenimenti armonici da camera a trè, due violini, violoncello, ò cembalo* (Bologna: Monti, 1695): "Sappiate, ch'io non sono ricorso alla Stampa, per ambizione di comparire; mà per soddisfare meramente ad un mio naturale genio, e diletto concepuato nell'esercizio, che per mio divertimento intrapresi pochi anno sono, di maneggiar l'arco sù poche corde. Queste poche Suonate sono l'impiego del tempo, che nel luogo, ove mi trovo mi è conceduto per ricreazione, e per interrompimento dalla fatica dello studio delle belle lettere, e di Filosofia."

29 My discussion of the Jesuit Collegio de Nobili and its connections to the sonata da camera is indebted to Marco Bizzarini, "Diffusione della sonata a tre nella Brescia di fine Seicento: il ruolo del Collegio de' Nobili," in *Barocco Padano I: atti del IX Convegno Internazionale sulla Musica Sacra nei Secoli XVII–XVIII*, ed. Alberto Colzani, Andrea Luppi, and Maurizio Padoan (Como: Antiquae Musicae Italicae Studiosi, 2002), 279–309, which explores the links between published instrumental music and the Collegio de' Nobili in Brescia.

30 The major work on the Jesuit *collegi* and the early modern Italian aristocracy is Gian Paolo Brizzi, *La formazione della classe dirigente nel Sei–Settecento* (Bologna: Mulino, 1976). Stefano Lorenzetti, "'Per animare agli esercizi nobili': esperienza musicale e identità nobiliare nei collegi di educazione," *Quaderni storici* 95 (1997): 435–60, focuses on the role of music in these schools.

Singing, Dancing, as well after the French, as Italian Mode, to exercise their Arms, Vault, Fortification, Perspective, and Painting.[31]

A classical education and training in musical and athletic activities molded students of the Jesuit colleges as nobles according to an ideal of learning and deportment most famously articulated in Castiglione's *Il corteggiano*. By the late *Seicento*, this training had been institutionalized for more than a century, so that, under "Arti cavalleresche" in the 1695 handbook of the Bolognese Accademia degli Ardenti for nobles, we read that

> The cultivation of the *cavaliere*'s spirit has in the academy all that can be imagined for courteously adorning it. Fencing, dance, drawing, horsemanship, flag and pike sports, all in turn have their day distributed to them. [There is] the handling of horses for the biggest [students], as well as elective lessons in playing instruments, the French language, geography, painting, etc.—study not being compromised by any of these occupations their being allotted to hours of recreation and holidays.[32]

Thus, outside of their principal studies, students in the Jesuit *collegi* took lessons in music and other refinements. And they demonstrated their accomplishments in regular *esercizi* that included singing, dancing, and instrumental performance, the most important of which were given publicly once or twice during the academic year. For example, on the occasion of the visit of Cardinal Flavio Chigi in April 1673, students of the Bolognese Collegio de' Nobili performed *La gara delle Muse* (Figure 2.5), described in the surviving libretto as an *accademia d'esercizi di lettere, e cavallereschi* (academy of literary and gentlemanly exercises).[33] The performance, a paean to the Cardinal, begins with a welcoming speech in Latin followed by "a most gentle sinfonia." Then follow a learned oration, a duet between the Muses of Peace and War, a ballet, more instrumental music to symbolize the "pure equity" of the Cardinal, a recitation, another ballet, and so forth. In sum, these *esercizi* might include poetic recitations, orations, plays, displays of swordsmanship, and feats of vaulting, as well as a heavy representation of dancing and instrumental performance.

---

31 William Bromley, *Remarks Made in Travels through France & Italy: with many publick inscriptions lately taken by a person of quality* (London: Bassett, 1692), 109.

32 *Ristretto et informazione de' requisiti e cose più necessarie a giovani cavalieri nel loro ingresso in Accademia de' Signori Ardenti di Bologna* (Bologna: n.p., 1695), "Arti cavalleresche. La coltura dello spirito cavalleresco ha nell'Accademia tutto quel di beninteso possa immaginarsi per compitamente adornarlo. La Scherma, il Ballo, il Dissegno, gli Essercizi di Cavalletto, di Bandiera, di Picca tutti hanno à vicenda i loro giorni distribuiti. Il Maneggio de' Cavalli per i più grandi, oltre le lezioni arbitrarie di Suono, di Lingua Francese, di Geografia, di Pittura, & altro, non pregiudicando alcuno di questi impieghi allo studio, per essere compartiti in hore di ricreatione, & in giorni Festivi."

33 *La gara delle Muse: accademia d'essercizi di lettere, e cavallereschi, rappresentata da' signori convittori del Collegio de' Nobili di S. Francesco Saverio nel ricevimento in detto Collegio dell'Eminentissimo Sig. Cardinale Flavio Chigi li 11 d'Aprile dell'anno 1673* (Bologna: n.p., 1673).

LA GARA DELLE MVSE

ACCADEMIA D'ESERCIZI
Di Lettere, e Caualiereſchi,

RAPPRESENTATA

Da' Signori Conuittori del Collegio de' Nobili
di S. Franceſco Sauerio

Nel riceuimento in detto Collegio dell' Eminentiſsimo
Sig. Cardinale FLAVIO CHIGI
li 11. d'Aprile dell' Anno 1673.

DEDICATA

All'Eminentiſſ. e Reuerendiſſ. Sig Card.

GIROLAMO BONCOMPAGNI
Arciueſcouo di Bologna, e Principe.

Figure 2.5   Libretto from *La gara delle Muse* (Bologna, n.p., 1673), title page.
              Biblioteca Comunale dell'Archiginnasio, Bologna (I-Bca)

The utility of dance repertory within the *collegi* for training in dance and instrumental performance therefore needs little stressing. And the specific links of several composers of chamber sonatas—Bartolomeo Laurenti, Giuseppe Jacchini, Giacomo Cattaneo, Giulio and Luigi Taglietti, and, not least, De Castro and his teacher Alghisi—to the *collegi* only reinforces the connections between the dances they published and the activities of these schools.[34] De Castro offers, on the one hand, a representative case in demonstrating how the sonata da camera, beyond mere accompaniment to aristocratic pastimes, was used in the very creation of late-*Seicento* aristocratic identity. On the other hand, he is exceptional for having composed suites of dances beyond merely playing them or dancing to them.[35] However, by glimpsing the institutional nature of aristocratic education and the place of the sonata da camera within it through De Castro's example, we begin to understand the import of the genre within the courtly culture of the Italian Baroque.

Example 2.4a   M. Cazzati, Op. 22 (1660), "Corrente delle dame"

---

34 For instruments taught at the Collegio de' Nobili in Bologna, see Lorenzetti, "Per animare," 447–8.

35 De Castro is exceptional, but not unique: two other aristocrat-composers of dances are Marieta Morosina Priuli, described as a *nobile veneta* in her *Balletti et correnti a due violini, et violone, agionta la spineta* (Venice, 1665), and the Bolognese Count Pirro Albergati, who published five collections for instrumental ensemble during the late seventeenth and early eighteenth centuries.

Example 2.4b   M. Cazzati, Op. 22 (1660), "Corrente de' cavalieri"

Italian Dancing

If I am correct in connecting the sonata da camera to recorded dancing of the period, we may observe that there is little to distinguish the music of theatrical and social dancing. Examples 2.4a and 2.4b show excerpts of two correnti from Cazzati's *Trattenimenti* for the stage, one from the *Ballo delle dame*, the other from the *Ballo de' cavalieri*. Both demonstrate the same musical features as those of the now well-represented *corrente francese* seen in Penna's collection for the ballroom. The same musical features support dancing in the two different contexts.

The greater share of the Bolognese repertory, by virtue of clear-cut phrases, homophonic texture, and unambiguous accent patterns, similarly points to dancer's music of either staged ballets or social dances. Beyond these generalities, it is not yet possible to analyze how the music might have complemented actual dancing because Italian dance-steps of the late seventeenth century are almost entirely unknown. No

Italian dance treatises survive from the period between the late-Renaissance heyday of the gagliarde, pavane, and saltarello, on the one hand, and the early eighteenth-century dominance of the French *danse noble*, on the other.[36] Moreover, the best-known descriptions of Italian dancing that we have come from foreign visitors, mostly French, and what elicited the most comment among these observers was the free promenade-style of dance.[37] For instance, an account in the *Mercure galant* of March, 1681 of a party in Vicenza compares the dances of different nations and praises the Italian promenade as a positive reflection of good national character:

> In France branles, courantes, and figural dances are beloved. Sarabandes are to the taste of the Spanish. The dances of Germany are more impetuous, which is not to say military, each nation retaining for itself some character of its inclination in that which gives its pleasures. Italian dance is nothing other than a kind of promenade during which the gentleman and lady, who hold one another's hand, converse about that which they please within two rows of spectators who are ordinarily seated. One could consider it a consequence of the good judgment of the country. One sees all without effort. One makes oneself seen without affectation. One promenades without fatigue. One talks freely without suspicion and, finally, one is not obliged to subject one's pleasure to the cadence of the instruments, there being no measured steps that one learns with much time without any considerable usefulness.[38]

However, according to Saint-Didier's *La ville et république de Venise* (1680), the dancing that took place after a Venetian wedding also included figured dances,[39]

---

36 Surviving Italian dance treatises closest to the late seventeenth century are: Fabritio Caroso, *Nobiltà di dame* (Venice: Muschio, 1600; 2nd ed., 1605; 3rd ed., as *Raccolta di varij balli*, Rome: Facciotti, 1630); Cesare Negri, *Le gratie d'amore* (Milan: Pontio and Piccaglia, 1602; 2nd ed., as *Nuove inventioni di balli*, Milan: Bordone, 1604); Livio Lupi, *Mutanze di gagliarda, tordiglione, passo è mezzo, canari, è passeggi* (Palermo: Carrara, 1600; 2nd ed., 1607); Felippo Degli Alessandri da Narni, *Discorso sopra il ballo et le buone creanze necessarie ad un gentil huomo e ad una gentildonna* (Terni: Guerrieri, 1620); Giovanni Battista Dufort, *Trattato del ballo nobile* (Naples: Mosca, 1728).

37 An informative study of ballroom scenes in Venetian opera that includes a survey of foreigners' testimony on Venetian dancing is Irene Alm, "Operatic Ballroom Scenes and the Arrival of French Social Dance in Venice," *Studi musicali* 25 (1996): 345–71.

38 *Mercure galant* (March, 1681): 104–7, "En France on aime les Branles, les Courantes, & les Dances figurées. Les Sarabandes sont au goust des Espagnols. Les Dances d'Allemagne sont plus impétueuses, pour ne pas dire militaires, chaque Nation retenant, mesme dans ce qui fait ses plaisirs, quelque caractere de son inclination. La Dance Italienne n'est proprement qu'une maniere de promenade, pendant la quelle le Cavalier & la Dame qui se tiennent par la main, s'entretiennent de ce que bon leur semble entre deux rangs de Spéctateurs, qui sont d'ordinaire assis. On peut la considérer comme une suite de la prudence du Païs. On voit tout sans peine. On se fait voir sans affectation. On se promene sans lassitude. On cause librement sans soupcon, & enfin on n'y est pas obligé d'assujetir son plaisir à la cadence des Instrumens, ny des Pas mesurez qu'on n'apprend qu'avec beaucoup de temps sans aucune utilité considérable."

39 The precise meaning of "figured dances" is open to interpretation. In French usage, *danses figurées* were sometimes contrasted with *danses simples*; for example, a *courante figurée* and a *courante simple* appear in the third suite of Ecorcheville, ed., *Vingt suites*. In the

and in the French style, but done so badly and to such unfamiliar music that he could not be sure:

> After this ceremony, as the violins begin to play, they make room in the middle of the crowd, and the young bride dances all alone two or three kinds of figured courantes, and a few bourrées in the local style. I believe, however, that they imagine this to be dancing in the French style, but it is no less difficult to recognize the airs than the steps, and the disposition of the body there seems so removed from the freedom and grace that is had in France, that a person had to have been born in Venice and never left there to give, as they do, public applause for the little leaps and shoulder movements, with which these young ladies accompany their uncadenced steps. Nevertheless, everyone assembled usually exclaims, *hà balato divinamente* [she danced divinely].[40]

Saint-Didier's scathing remarks do not end there; he goes on to criticize the ensuing Italian promenade-style dancing, performed, as he says, "without observing either Measure or Cadence," and the accompanying music as "more proper to Inspire a desire of sleeping, than that of Mirth."[41] Nor did he have kind words for the entr'acte ballets at opera performances, describing them as "generally so pittiful, that they

---

opinion of dance historian Carol Marsh as communicated to me, the term "figured" refers to those dances whose carefully prescribed steps trace specific a pattern (or figure) on the floor. Such patterns are most clearly seen in the notated examples of French dance.

40 Alexandre-Toussaint de Limojon, Sier de Saint-Didier, *La ville et la république de Venise* (Paris: Louis Billaine, 1680), 472–3: "Aprés cette ceremonie, les Violons commencent à jouër, l'on fait faire place au milieu de la foule, & la jeune mariée y danse toute seule deux ou trois especes de courante figurées, & quelque bourrée à la mode du païs. Je crois pourtant que l'on s'imagine de danse à la Françoise; mais il n'est pas moins difficile d'en renconnoistre les airs, que les pas, & la disposition du corps y paroist si éloignée de la liberté & de la grace qu'on a en France, qu'il faut estre né à Venise, & n'en estre jamais sorti, pour donner, comme ils sont, de applaudissemens publics aux petits sauts, & aux mouvemens des épaules, dont ces Demoiselles accompagnent leur pas sans cadence: cependant toute l'assemblée s'écrie ordinairement, *hà balato divinamente*." Quoted in Alm, "Operatic Ballroom Scenes," 349.

41 Ibid., 100. Similar if less pointed testimony may be found in the diaries of other visitors to Venice, which also describe the ambience of the ball. Bromley, *Remarks*, 88: "I saw a Ball at the Palace of Mocenigo, a Noble Venetian, to entertain the Grand Prince of Tuscany. The Rooms were all open, richly furnished with Hangings and Pictures, and well filled with Company. In most of them were Consorts of Musick, playing, while the Gentlemen and Ladies, according to the dancing of the Countrey, walk'd hand in hand out of one Room into another, holding conversations together as they walked." Casimir Freschot, *Nouvelle relation de la ville & république de Venise* (Utrecht: Guilaume van Poolsum, 1709), 405: "There are balls in Venice, but without any figured dance, all consisting of the gentleman and the lady promenading and conversing together during some turn around the hall, or from one room to the other, although the players who are there play some airs for dancing interspersed with some symphonies [Il y a des bals à Venise, mais sans aucune dance figurée, tout y consistant entre le Cavalier & la Dame à se promener & s'entretenir ensemble pendant quelques tour de sale, ou d'une chambre à l'autre, quoi qaue le Joueurs qui y sont joüent des airs à dancer entremelés de quelques simphonies]."

would be much better omitted; for one would imagine these Dancers wore Lead in their Shoes."[42]

Despite his tone, Saint-Didier, along with the author of the *Mercure* article, does confirm that both Italian and French styles of dancing coexisted in late-*Seicento* Italy, lending support to the hypothesis of the dance historian Barbara Sparti that late Baroque dance was not solely French.[43] We may also infer that the Italian style was relaxed in comparison with the newer and more intricate French style, then beginning to take hold among the Italian nobility. To the French, accomplished in the complex steps of the *danse noble*, the Italian style must have seemed indifferent to the accompanying music, but it was likely more sophisticated than they cared to recognize. The dance types represented in the sonata repertory tell us that Italians were dancing in a variety of styles—Italian and French, old and new. The gagliarda, representing the oldest continuing tradition, persists into the 1680s. The balletto and corrente, also of long standing, were by far the most frequently occurring in the chamber sonata repertory and remained popular well into the eighteenth century. Newer dances represent French influence: apart from any designated *alla francese* or *in stile francese*, which occur in collections over most of the seventeenth century,[44] dance types such as the minuetto and borea (bourrée), appearing in Italian prints from the 1680s on, show the ever-growing inclination toward French practice.

Perhaps the best evidence of the late-*Seicento* intermingling of distinct styles of dancing comes from the librettos and reports of Jesuit college performances. From around 1700, when these sources begin to list the individual teachers of the various disciplines, we see separate *maestri* of French and Italian dancing, confirming the coexistence of the two traditions among the Italian nobility.[45] Descriptions of performed dances within the *collegio* librettos paint an even more detailed

---

42 Ibid., 61.

43 Barbara Sparti, "La 'danza barocca' è soltanto francese?," *Studi musicali* 25 (1996): 283–302.

44 Martino Pesenti published three collections of *correnti alla francese* for keyboard from c1619 through 1641. Other early-to-mid-century publications of dances *alla francese* include Stefano Pesori, *Lo scrigno armonico, ove si rinchiudono vaghissime danze, & ariette al modo italiano, spagnolo, e francese*, Op. 2 (Mantua?, c. 1650), for the guitar; Giovanni Battista Piazza, *Correnti e balletti alla francese* (Venice, 1620s–30s?); Francesco Boccella, *Primavera di vaghi fiori musicali, overo canzonette ad una, due, e tre voci, con diverse corrente, sarabande, e balletti alla francese*, no opus (Ancona, 1653); Cazzati, *Correnti e balletti a cinque, alla francese, et all'italiana*, Op. 15 (1654), and Salvador Gandini, *Corenti et balletti alla francese, et all'italiana*, Op. 4 (Venice, 1655), for strings and continuo.

45 A year-end publication of the Collegio de' Nobili, the *Foglio laureato dispensato da l'Onore Araldo di Pallade* (Bologna: Sarti, 1700), 12, records the *maestri* of the various extra-curricular pursuits, listing Sig. Antonio Fabri as *maestro di ballo italiano* and Monsieur Gio. Battista Coinde, Lionese, as *maestro di ballo francese*. The *Foglio laureato* also lists the students who attained proficiency in each discipline over the 1699–1700 academic year, recording almost equal numbers of students studying Italian dance (60) and French dance (62). In the early eighteenth century, the balance of interest shifted toward the French style. In its libretto to a 1713 performance of *Giasone*, the Collegio de' Nobili lists two *maestri* of French dance (Monsieur Antonio Ollaniè, Lionese, and Monsieur Giacomo Legerò da Parigi) and one of Italian (Sig. Francesco Barilli, Bolognese), who was also *maestro di bandiera* and *picca*.

picture. Table 2.5 lists the dances mentioned in five selected librettos from *collegio* performances of the late seventeenth century. These, too, underscore the coexisting French and Italian styles, along with the Spanish-style chaconne and the possibility of hybrids. They also reveal representational design in the choreographed figures of a star's rays (*Gara delle Muse*, 1673), evoking the Chigi coat of arms, and of the flight of the winds (*Rombi protettori*, 1678). And some idea of the diversity of steps in Italian dancing—probably both the intricate steps of the *danse noble* and the leaps of the Italian Renaissance tradition—is conveyed by the above-mentioned *Gara delle Muse* libretto in its description of the final ballet:

> Here at last the *accademia* ended with the dance of the *cavalieri*, combining interlacing figures, capers, steps that were heavy, light, swift, and slow, all regulated by sounding measure, in which seemed summarized the most beautiful flower of this art.[46]

Table 2.5   Dances from selected late-*Seicento* Bolognese *collegio* performances

---

1673   *La Gara delle Muse, Accademia d'essercizi di lettere, e cavallereschi:*

un ballo misto di Francese e d'Italiano ... maestoso del pari ne passeggi, ch'agile nelle caprivole	a dance of mixed French and Italian [styles] ... majestic in the evenness of steps as agile in the leaps
un ballo congegnato allo stile Italiano	a dance devised in the Italian style
una Ciaccona Spagnuola ballata con le naccare	a Spanish chaconne danced with castanets
un'artificioso balletto, nel fine del quale coll'unire de' raggi figurando una bellissima Stella	an artful little dance at the end of which with the uniting of its rays depicts a most beautiful star
ballo Francese figurato	a figured French dance
ballo de' Cavallieri ... misto di figure d'intrecci, di caprivole, di passeggi gravi, e leggiadri, veloci, e lenti	a dance of *cavalieri* ... intermingling woven figures, leaps, steps both grave and graceful, quick and slow

---

1678   *I Rombi protettori in cielo, e in terra della nave d'Argo, Accademia mista d'esercitii letterarii, e cavallereschi:*

un ballo in aria	a dance-song
Balli alla Francese [e] una Chiaccona Spagnola	dances in the French style and a Spanish chaconne
un Ballo in aria, intrecciato alle cadenze con spesse fughe, che figuravano le fughe de' Venti	a dance-song, interwoven in its cadences with frequent flights that depicted the flights of the winds

---

46 *La gara delle Muse*, 17: "Qui finalmente terminò l'Accademia col ballo de' Cavallieri, così misto di figure d'intrecci, di caprivole, di passeggi gravi, e leggiadri, veloci, e lenti, in tutto regolatissimo alle misure del suono, che in esso parve epilogato il più bel fior di quest'arte."

1699   *Il Tamerlano tragedia rappresentata dagl'illustrissimi signori accademici sotto la direzione de padri Somaschi nelle vacanze del corrente anno:*

Primo Intermezzo: Ballo in cinque all'Italiana	First Intermezzo: a dance for five in the Italian style
Secondo Intermezzo: Minuetto in due	Second Intermezzo: a minuet for two
Terzo Intermezzo: Minuetto del Delfino	Third Intermezzo: the Dauphin's minuet
Quarto Intermezzo: Ciaccona Spagnuola	Fourth Intermezzo: a Spanish chaconne

1700   *Foglio Laureato dispensato da l'Onore araldo di Pallade:*

Capriccioso intreccio di Ballo, e di Spade ... ballando all'Italiana, e poi alla Francese	whimsical weaving of dance and swordplay ... dancing first in the Italian style and then in the French
una vaga Sarabanda	a pretty sarabande
il Minuetto Delfino	the Dauphin's minuet
Ballo della Borea di Merlino	dance of the blackbird's bourrée

As before, none of these can be identified as corresponding to a specific dance movement from the sonata repertory, but we at least glimpse the rich tradition of courtly and theatrical dancing, both eclectic and refined, that counters Saint-Didier's prejudiced account and accords well with the varied selection of dances preserved in the sonata da camera.

Accademia Musicale

In some cases, however, the dances of the sonata da camera were designed with uses other than dance accompaniment in mind. The most famous and most explicit example is Roman: Arcangelo Corelli's Op. 4 dance suites, entitled *Sonate à tre composte per l'Accademia dell'Em.mo e Rev.mo Sig.r Cardinale Otthoboni* (Sonatas *a 3* composed for the *accademia* [and not *ballo*] of his most eminent and reverend Signor Cardinal Ottoboni), published in Rome and Bologna in 1694. Well before Corelli's Op. 4, however, titles from the published repertory reinforce this distinction: Giovanni Battista Vitali's *Balletti ... per ballare; balletti ... da camera* (1667) and G. M. Bononcini's *Sonate da camera e da ballo* (1667) both divide dances for dancing from those more generally designated "for the chamber."[47] Peter Allsop

---

47 The full titles are: Bononcini, *Sonate da camera, e da ballo a 1. 2. 3. è 4*, Op. 2 (Venice: Magni, 1667; facsimile, Bologna: Antiquae Musicae Italicae Studiosi, 1971); and Vitali, *Balletti, correnti alla francese, gagliarde, e brando per ballare. Balletti, correnti e sinfonie da camera à quattro stromenti*, Op. 3 (Bologna: Monti, 1667).

has argued that the balletti and correnti designated *da camera* (in contradistinction to *da ballo*) show evidence not only of undanceable phrase structure, but also of more dissonant harmonies and contrapuntal interest.[48] Dances in this vein would have served the interests of a patron such as Count Obizzo Guidoni, the dedicatee of Bononcini's *Arie, correnti, sarabande, & allemande*, Op. 4 (1671), whom the composer describes as

> not at all lacking in virtuous acts and all the more in the enjoyment of music, particularly that for instruments [as performed] by many *cavalieri* in his most noble house, [and who] also knows quite well, merely for his own taste and recreation, how to offer great delight to anyone who has occasion to hear him play the violone with no ordinary agility and mastery.[49]

Guidoni, then, was host to what were known as *accademie* in his household—that is, soirée performances—of instrumental music in which he also participated. Examples 2.5a and 2.5b demonstrate the nature of the dances that were written, as Bononcini reveals, "to serve and satisfy … [Guidoni's] taste and admirable talent."[50] Example 2.5a, an allemanda ("La Fogliana"), emphasizes imitation and motivic exchange;[51] Example 2.5b, a corrente ("La Buffalina"), furnishes a rare case of written-out melodic embellishment. Here, the changes of tempo between adagio and presto, the subdivided rhythms of mm. 33–7, and effusive cadential embellishments reflect instrumentalist's music—that is, dances *per camera*.[52]

Throughout his career, Bononcini, whose erudition is detailed in Chapter 1, was fond of incorporating contrapuntal intricacy into his dances. Examples 2.6a and 2.6b show excerpts from another allemanda and corrente, but from different prints.

---

48 Allsop, "*Da camera e da ballo*," 89.

49 Bononcini, *Arie, correnti, sarabande, gighe, & allemande a violino, e violone, over spinetta, con alcune intavolate per diverse accordature*, Op. 4. (Bologna: Monti, 1671), "A V. S. Illustrissima, che non degenerando punto nelle attioni virtuose, e più in dilettarsi della Musica, ed ispecie di Strumenti, da molti Cavalieri della sua nobilissima Casa, sà anche così bene per mero gusto suo, e ricreamento porgere gran diletto à chi può tal volta sentirla, suonando con non ordinaria agilità, e maestria il Violone; hò io da ciò preso motivo di dedicare le presenti mie Compositioni, fatte appunto, se non di espresso suo commando, per servire, e sodisfare almeno al suo genio, & ammirabile talento, in testimonio verace della singolarissima, & immutabile divotione che le professo."

50 Bononcini, *Arie, correnti, sarabande, & allemande* Op. 4, dedication.

51 In French dancing, there is some doubt as to whether the allemande was danced at all during the latter half of the seventeenth century. Contemporary sources implicitly cast doubt on the idea. Sébastien de Brossard, *Dictionnaire de musique*, 3rd ed. (Paris, c. 1708; facsimile, Geneva: Minkoff, 1992), "Allemande," for example, describes it as a "symphonie grave" and not as a dance. In Italy, by contrast, testimony from both before and after the late-*Seicento* lacuna in dance treatises indicate that the allemanda was danced. Degli Alessandri in his *Discorso sopra il ballo*, 217–18, lists the *alemanna* and the *alemana d'amore* along with the *correnta* as dances that were current in Italian practice. Little more than a century later, Giambattista Dufort, *Trattato del ballo nobile*, 22–3, mentions the *alamanda* among duple-meter dances that were to be danced quickly.

52 Two other seventeenth-century collections of dances that make the distinction between dances for dancers and dances for listeners are Nicola Matteis, *Ayres for the Violin*, parts 3 & 4 (London, 1685); and, before him, Johann Hermann Schein, *Banchetto musicale* (Leipzig, 1617).

Example 2.5a   G. M. Bononcini, Op. 4 (1671), Allemanda "La Fogliana"

Example 2.5b   G. M. Bononcini, Op. 4 (1671), Corrente "La Buffalina"

Example 2.6a   G. M. Bononcini, Op. 7 (1673), Allemanda obligata à 4

Example 2.6b   G. M. Bononcini, Op. 1 (1666), Corrente quarta

Example 2.6b   cont'd

Example 2.6a, the first strain of the allemanda, is a small essay in invertible counterpoint, in which the interweaving of the two subjects (a descending motif in half notes and a rising motif in quarters) precludes either the predictable accents or clear-cut phrases of dances *per ballare*. Example 2.6b, the corrente, is more ambitious. The opening bars sound its two main subjects. The first, introduced by the first violin, returns just once in m. 15 (second violin), but supplies a related motif that recurs frequently (cf. m. 9, second violin; mm. 10–11, basso continuo). The second motif, which begins with a descending minor triad, behaves more like a proper fugue subject, appearing in all three voices successively (second violin, first violin, and continuo). The corrente plays with these ideas through m. 42, at which point they are combined and treated, remarkably, in canon for the remainder of this virtuoso piece.

Dance movements by other composers similarly incorporate imitative textures: Oratio Polaroli crafts a fugal approach for the fifth corrente of his Op. 1 dances (Example 2.7a); Giuseppe Torelli, creating a binary-form fugue among his Op. 2 *Concerti da camera* (Example 2.7b), spins a complete allemanda out of a single subject; and he follows a similar but more relaxed binary-fugal procedure for violin and violoncello in a corrente from his Op. 4 *Concertino per camera* (Example 2.7c).

Example 2.7a   O. Polaroli, Op. 1 (1673), Corrente quinta

This last piece also introduces a degree of virtuosity with its multiple stops for the violin that lead us to further examples of double-stopping among the few engraved prints in the repertory, such as Torelli's Op. 4 ballo (Example 2.8a) and a balletto by Tomaso Pegolotti (Example 2.8b).[53] Other dance movements that draw our attention to the exertions of the instrumentalist are the *moto perpetuo*-style examples of Giacomo Cattaneo's corrente (Example 2.9a) and allemanda (Example 2.9b), and Laurenti's "Aria di gavotta" (Gavotte tune) (Example 2.9c).[54]

---

53 Example 2.8b shows the single violin part in its two versions, one with double-stops (*à doppie corde*) and one without, hence the three lines of music for a violin and violoncello duo.

54 The qualifiers *aria di* and the more common *tempo di* are used occasionally in the dance repertory (Mazzolini, Op. 1, De Castro, Op. 1, Torelli, Op. 4, and Alghisi, Op. 1, to name a few), but have no consistent implications for the intended function of a dance. Corelli's designation of *tempo di sarabanda*, for example, occurs over versions of the dance that comprise either four-bar phrases and homorhythmic texture perfectly suited to dancing, or ambitious counterpoint with unpredictable rhythms and phrases seemingly unsuited to dancing.

Example 2.7b   G. Torelli, Op. 2, No. 11 (1686), Allemanda

Example 2.7c   G. Torelli, Op. 4, No. 10 (1687/88), Corrente

Example 2.8a   G. Torelli, Op. 4, No. 7 (1687/88), Ballo

Example 2.8b   T. Pegolotti, Op. 1, No. 12 (1698), Balletto

Example 2.9a   G. Cattaneo, Op. 1, No. 11 (1700), Corrente

Example 2.9b   G. Cattaneo, Op. 1, No. 4 (1700), Allemanda

Example 2.9c   B. Laurenti, Op. 1, No. 9 (1691), Aria di Gavotta

Contrapuntal technique and performing virtuosity reflect an interest in music more for the diversion of listeners and performers than dancers. And yet, if these last examples direct our attention away from dancers to the performing instrumentalists, the technique required to perform them hardly represented the limits of technique on their instruments. Only Bononcini's corrente with canonic imitation requires the violinist to shift out of the first left-hand position (Example 2.6b, mm. 16–20).[55] Pegolotti's balletto, the most challenging of the examples shown here, offers a version of his suite without double-stops.[56] And nothing in this repertory places demands on the violinist as challenging as, say, some of the early *stile moderno* bizarreries in Carlo Farina's *Capriccio stravagante* (1627) or the more recent *Scherzi da violino* (1676) of Johann Jacob Walther, which was known in Italy. The examples introduced here instead display a restrained virtuosity suited originally to the abilities of noble patrons and then, when ultimately published, to a broader market of consumers. Bononcini's Op. 4, for example, offers musically interesting duets whose bass parts—designed for Count Guidoni, who was likely more aristocrat than violone player—are anything but virtuosic. Nor is the violinist confronted with formidable music: the part stays mostly within the first left-hand position, bowings are relatively uncomplicated (the greatest difficulty being string crossings to effect compound melodies), and double-stopping facilitated by scordatura occurs in only a few examples from the end of the print.

This attention to the dilettante instrumentalist's easy diversion in performance is underscored by collections of dances to which late-*Seicento* composers added witty canons and other *bizzarrie*. Figure 2.6 reproduces the first of three canons from the end of Giovanni Battista Bassani's *Balletti, correnti, gighe, e sarabande*, Op. 1 (1677), along with the composer's description—entertaining as much as erudite. The translated descriptions read as follows:

---

55 Late-*Seicento* violin technique and, in particular, the use of a single left-hand position are explored in Chapter 3.

56 The handful of prints that were produced by engraving rather than the predominant technology of movable type offer exceptions that prove the rule of the genteel virtuosity of the late-*Seicento* Bolognese prints: only a few were produced, and, with the exception of Pegolotti (who, as mentioned, offers the double-stop version as an alternative), they represent the initiative of a single engraver-musician in Bologna, Carlo Buffagnotti. Chapter 3 takes up the special niche of engravings in the course of comparing surviving manuscripts to prints of Italian instrumental music.

[1] infinite canon for six basses requiring the pitch *lychanos hypaton*, which can also be sung in inverted form, noting that MI is changed into FA and FA into MI; [2] infinite canon for four voices; [3] canon in which an answer in the alto is discerned after a double rest in the soprano subject, taken at the lower fifth, as is another answer in the bass subject—that is, the cantus firmus after a double rest, also at the lower fifth.[57]

To give another example (this one more clearly a spoof of abstruse musical learning), Figure 2.7 shows the canon that decorates the frontispiece of G. M. Bononcini's Op. 3 chamber sonatas (1669). Both Bassani's and Bononcini's canons are entertaining caprices rather than virtuoso demonstrations,[58] and the same can be said of the scordatura compositions that Bononcini included with his Op. 2 dances. The spirit of a giga from that collection, archly designated *Discordia concors* (Figure 2.8),[59] is a clever diversion in which the tuning is used not to create new possibilities for chord-playing on the violin, but instead to tease the performer with another puzzle to decipher.

---

57 Much in Bassani's instructions for the realization of his canon is unnecessary: the "obligatione della corda *lychanos hypaton*" is an ostentatiously clever reference to the pitch D as named in the Greater Perfect System of the ancient Greeks; and the note explaining that "il MI si muta in FA, & il FA in MI" is merely a consequence of inverting the *soggetto* for the second solution to the canon.

58 Other prints that contain canons are Uccellini, *Sinfonici concerti*, Op. 9; and Giovanni Maria Ruggieri, *Bizzarie armoniche esposte in dieci suonate da camera a due, cioè violino, e leuto o tiorba col suo basso per il violone, ò spinetta*, Op. 1 (Venice: Sala, 1689). Both of these prints includes two canons. Bononcini is a prolific exception, adding canons to his Opp. 3, 4, and 5 dances. His Op. 3 stands out among these with its dozen canons of various kinds.

59 Bononcini does use scordatura for the purpose of facilitating double-stops in three dances (an allemanda and two correnti) at the end of his Op. 4. Other examples of scordatura in the chamber sonata repertory, both for violoncello, reflect what may have been an alternate tuning of that instrument in which, relative to the standard tuning, the top string is tuned down a whole-step. This tuning is found in Giuseppe Jacchini's, sonata for violoncello solo from the *Sonate a tre di vari autori* (n.p., engraved by Buffagnotti?, n.d. [c.1700]) and Giacomo Cattaneo's sonata for violoncello solo, from his *Trattenimenti armonici da camera a trè istromenti, due violini e violoncello, ò cembalo con due brevi cantate à soprano solo, e una sonata per violoncello*, Op. 1 (Modena: Rosati, 1700).

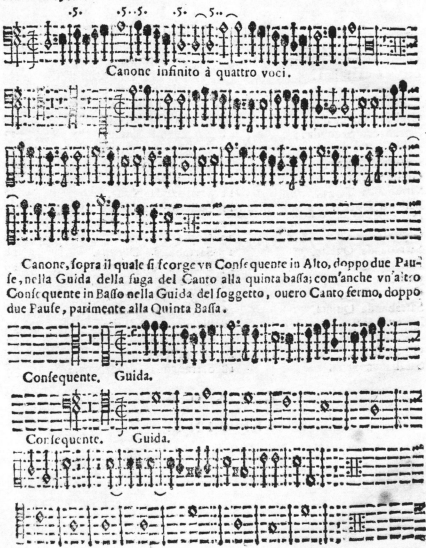

Figure 2.6   G. B. Bassani, *Balletti, correnti, gighe, e sarabande*, Op. 1 (Bologna: Monti, 1677), three canons. Museo Internazionale e Biblioteca della Musica di Bologna (I-Bc)

Violino Primo;

VARII FIORI
DEL
GIARDINO MVSICALE,

Ouero Sonate da Camera a 2. 3. e 4. col suo Basso continuo,
& aggiunta d'alcuni Canoni studiosi, & osseruati.

OPERA TERZA
DI GIO. MARIA BONONCINI MODONESE
DEDICATA
ALL' ILLVSTRISS. SIG. CONTE
BARTOLOMEO SCAPINELLI.

Canon a 2592. Voci dopo vn mezo sospiro dall' vna all' altra diuise in 648. Chori,
e volendo vscir fuori dell' ordine Musicale, cioè di far valer la Massima più di
quello, che nella Musica hà il suo termine, si può procedere in infinito.

Segno del tempo perfetto,
della prolazione perfetta, e
del modo maggior perfetto.

In Bologna, per Giacomo Monti. 1669. Con licenza de' Superiori.

Figure 2.7   G. M. Bononcini, *Varii fiori del giardino musicale*, Op. 3 (Bologna:
Monti, 1669): canon for 2,592 voices, an eighth note rest from one
to the other [and] divided into 648 choirs. And should one wish to
go outside of musical order—that is, to make the maxima worth
more than its limit in music—one can proceed ad infinitum. Museo
Internazionale e Biblioteca della Musica di Bologna (I-Bc)

Figure 2.8 G. M. Bononcini, *Sonate da camera, e da ballo*, Op. 2 (Venice: Magni, 1667), No. 8: Giga in scordatura, *Discordia concors* (violino primo). Archivio dell'Accademia Filarmonica di Bologna (I-Baf)

* * *

This survey of late-*Seicento* dance music and its uses in dancing and in instrumental performance offers an introduction to the circumstances in which the repertory originated prior to its publication, post hoc, by Bolognese music printers. This much enables us to appreciate what was still a courtly culture among north-central Italy's lesser nobility. The connecting thread among those circumstances is the performing aristocrat as dancer or instrumentalist in the diverse contexts of the *festa*, *esercizio*, and *accademia*—that is, commemorative celebration, perfection and display of "gentlemanly arts," and sophisticated diversion. Further details of dance practices on stage, in the ballroom, and within the *collegi* are to be had in a systematic examination of Bolognese librettos that record important events of late-*Seicento* aristocratic life there and in a study of the musical patronage connected with such events. Short of that, the uses of dance music and the multiple roles of the musical noble at least begin to account for a repertory that dominated the published output of Italian instrumentalist-composers during this period.

Chapter Three

Bologna, Modena, and the
Place of Virtuosity

The two largest collections of late-*Seicento* instrumental music are found in the Museo Internazionale e Biblioteca della Musica di Bologna and the Biblioteca Estense Universitaria in Modena.[1] The holdings of the Museo Internazionale comprise almost entirely printed music while those of the Biblioteca Estense are mostly manuscript.[2] Taken together, the two collections account for much of the known repertory of instrumental music from late seventeenth-century Italy. The prints and manuscripts are in many ways complementary, differing sometimes markedly in terms of musical style and in the techniques they require of the performer. The conspicuous contrast between the two repertories is illustrated even in the output of individual composers represented in both. Giuseppe Colombi, who spent his career serving at the Este court, produced five opuses with the Bolognese presses and also contributed a large body of manuscript works to the Este collection, which is in fact dominated by his music. Two fugues illustrate the disparity between his published and unpublished work. A passage taken from his *Sinfonie à due violini*, Op. 2, No. 8 (1673), offers a typical treatment (Example 3.1a): imitation in three parts on a common repeated-note theme comparable to that of G. B. Vitali's Op. 2, No. 2 (1667) seen in the introduction (Example 0.2a). Neither violin part of Colombi's sinfonia offers anything difficult to play; they stay comfortably in one left-hand position, avoid multiple stopping, and require no complex bowings or bow strokes. Rather, the interest lies in the frequent reappearances of the bouncy subject within the counterpoint. A similar subject appears in Example 3.1b, but here the work of two violins is given to a single performer who plays double-stops throughout to create the effect of two lines in imitation. The music, moreover, well exceeds the violin's first left-hand position; later on in the movement the performer must use higher positions, reaching a full octave above the open E string while continuing to play chords. The Este manuscripts likewise challenge the cellist, and published versus manuscript

---

1   The music studied here comes almost exclusively from these two libraries, whose international sigla are I-Bc and I-MOe, respectively. Apart from other smaller Bolognese libraries (the Archivio dell'Accademia Filarmonica [I-Baf] and the Archivio di San Petronio [I-Bsp]), the Oxford Bodleian Library (GB-Ob) and the British Museum (GB-Lbl) also house significant collections of Italian instrumental music.

2   Appendix B gives a bibliographic listing of manuscripts of instrumental works in the Biblioteca Estense that date from the reign of Francesco II d'Este, 1662–94, or shortly after. For a study of the musical holdings of Duke Francesco II, see Elisabetta Luin, "Repertorio dei libri musicali di S. A. S. Francesco II d'Este nell'Archivio di Stato di Modena," *Bibliofilia* 38 (1936): 418–45.

works of a single composer, Domenico Gabrielli in this case, make the point. In one instance (Example 3.2a), a sarabanda from Gabrielli's *Balletti*, Op. 1 (1684), shows a running bass he constructed for the dance. It is one of the more interesting bass lines from the collection, but offers less of a challenge than his unaccompanied ricercar, a work from the Este manscripts (Example 3.2b). In the ricercar, he extends the range of the instrument up to g and creates the effect of two competing lines, low versus high, by virtue of the large skips that frequently require the bow to cross over three or all four strings.

Example 3.1a   G. Colombi, Op. 2, No. 8 (1673)

i. (mm. 1-13)

Example 3.1b   G. Colombi, MS, I-MOe, Mus.F.280, No. 5

Example 3.1b   cont'd

Example 3.2a   D. Gabrielli, Op. 1, No. 5 (1684), Sarabanda

Allegro (mm. 1-8)

Example 3.2b   D. Gabrielli, Ricercaro quinto, MS, I-MOe, Mus.G.79

(mm. 1-8)

Example 3.2b   cont'd

(mm. 25-36)

Violoncello

Both the print and manuscript collections originate in the same period and the same region of Italy, and several composers are represented in both; but despite these similarities, they differ remarkably. Not only do the manuscript examples present the greater challenge in the examples seen here, but the different scorings in them—solo as opposed to trio—reveal the virtuosity of solo performers at the Modenese court.

Late-*Seicento* String Technique

These comparisons underscore a point made in the previous chapter: the published instrumental repertory largely shuns virtuosity. Even the more showy pieces among the Bolognese prints seem designed for dilettantes by comparison with works in the Este collection. The two repertories thus contrast basic versus virtuoso technique and ensemble player versus soloist. Indeed, the published repertory appears tailored to a set of basic skills that may be reconstructed in the few treatises and etudes for string players that survive from the mid and late seventeenth century. The only Italian writer of this period to discuss violin technique is Bartolomeo Bismantova, who sets forth the rudiments of bowing and fingering in his *Compendio musicale* (1677–94).[3]

---

3   Bartolomeo Bismantova, *Compendio musicale*, MS, Ferrara, 1677; expanded, 1694 (facsimile, Florence: Studio per Edizioni Scelte, 1978). Georg Muffat, *Florilegium secundum* (Passau, 1698) is chronologically the closest printed source that also discusses Italian violin playing. Muffat's prefaces to his published works, in which he draws on his first-hand knowledge of both French and Italian practices, are some of the most informative sources of the period on performance practice. These are collected in *Georg Muffat on Performance Practice*, ed. and trans. David K. Wilson (Bloomington and Indianapolis: Indiana University Press, 2001).

In addition to Bismantova's treatise, there is an earlier volume on string playing by Gasparo Zannetti, entitled *Il scolaro* (1645).[4] *Il scolaro* comprises a series of dances in both regular notation and tablature to show the fingerings used to play them. Apart from Bismantova and Zannetti, there are manuscript exercises for the violin preserved in the Museo Internazionale in Bologna (I-Bc), consisting of scales and other melodic patterns designed to improve left-hand facility.[5]

Bismantova's instructions on bowing include several music examples with bowings added and short discussions of the basic principles of each (see Example 3.3).[6] The underlying rule here—the so-called "rule of the downbow"—coordinates the downbow with accented or metrically stronger beats while the upbow is used for unaccented or weaker beats.[7] In cases where the rhythm or meter does not correspond to a simple alternation of bow strokes, up and down, he shows how repeated upbows or downbows enable the performer to coordinate a downbow with the first beat of each measure or for the first note of recurring rhythmic patterns such as triplets. Examples from printed partbooks of the period from which we can deduce intended bowings both reinforce and creatively expand upon Bismantova's instructions. The excerpts shown in Example 3.4, taken from three gigas by G. M. Bononcini and G. B. Vitali, show that while composers organized bowings to match repeated rhythms with consistent strokes, they also varied their bowings in order to suit the character of the melody at hand (see, in particular, the third excerpt).

---

4   Zannetti, *Il scolaro per imparar a suonare di violino, et altri stromenti* (Milan: Camagno, 1645; facsimile, Florence: Studio per Edizioni Scelte, 1984).

5   MS, I-Bc, AA.360. This item has the look of a music student's notebook: the violin exercises are scales, which bear marginal notes and are found in the midst of various musical sketches.

6   Bismantova, *Compendio*, 112–17, places a dot beneath the note to indicate downbow and above the note to indicate upbow.

7   David D. Boyden, *The History of Violin Playing from its Origins to 1761* (Oxford Clarendon Press, 1965), refers to this style of playing at several points in his history, giving a complete explanation on pp. 157–63.

Example 3.3   B. Bismantova, *Compendio musicale* (1677–94)

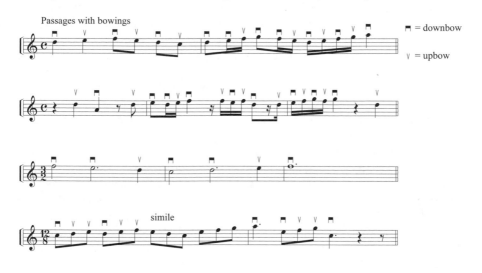

Example 3.4a   G. M. Bononcini, Op. 2 (1667), Giga

Example 3.4b   G. B. Vitali, Op. 4 (1668), Giga

Example 3.4c   G. B. Vitali, Op. 4 (1668), Giga

Such slurs account for the greater share of bowing instructions, most of which required only the basic level of technique outlined by Bismantova. Performers could certainly have executed their bow strokes with varying degrees of refinement, but the notated instructions themselves were relatively limited. Apart from the tremolo, a verbal indication that accompanied slurred eighth notes on the same pitch, other marks of articulation were rare in printed music.[8] Only toward the end of the century did composers begin to mark staccato articulations with dots or vertical slashes over noteheads, sometimes also writing *stacco*, *staccato*, or *spicco* in the part as well.[9]

Bismantova's instructions on bow technique are accompanied by an equally straightforward teaching of left-hand fingering technique that also serves well for much of the printed repertory.[10] In the brief sections devoted to string instruments— violino, violoncello da spalla, and contrabasso—he describes a left-hand technique based on a single hand position using diatonic fingerings that matches the range of modern-day first position in the case of the violin.[11] According to Bismantova, the range of each instrument is that covered in the single left-hand position, from the lowest open string to the highest string stopped with the fourth finger. Therefore, as he shows in his diagrams, reproduced in Examples 3.5a and 3.5b, the violin covers g to b^2 and the violoncello covers C (or D) to e^1. Seventeenth-century manuscript exercises from the Museo Internazionale cover the same range, as seen in

---

8   In tremolo passages, the string player must move the bow in the same direction for each of the slurred eighths, articulating each note with slight pauses in the motion of the bow. Stewart Carter, "The String Tremolo in the Seventeenth Century," *Early Music* 19 (1991): 43–59, provides a history of this technique on string instruments. Its origins, as elucidated by Carter, lie in the imitation of the organ tremolo's pulsing sound.

9   Giuseppe Jacchini, *Trattenimenti per camera*, Op. 5 (Bologna: Silvani, 1703); and Jacchini, *Concerti per camera*, Op. 4 (Bologna: Silvani, 1701), bear these indications prominently.

10   Bismantova's treatise discussed only the violin in its first draft of 1677. Later, in the 1694 additions, he included instructions for playing the violoncello and the contrabass. The charts shown here pertain to the violin and cello.

11   Numbered left-hand positions were not introduced in pedagogical treatises until the mid eighteenth century. Therefore, even though Bismantova describes first position on the violin, it was not yet known as such. The cello is a more complicated case since the instrument itself—and, therefore, the technique used to play it—was evolving more rapidly during the late *Seicento*. The fingering chart provided by Bismantova for the cello does not coincide with modern-day first position on the instrument. Instead, with its whole-steps between the second, third, and fourth fingers on the highest string, Bismantova's cello fingering resembles an extended position in modern cello technique. (In the modern unextended hand position, the fingers are separated by semitones.) In fact, his left-hand cello technique is simply transferred from the violin: on both instruments the fingers cover the diatonic notes between open strings tuned at fifths. On the shoulder-held position, playing technique, and possible repertory for the violoncello (or viola) da spalla, see Brent Wissick, "The Cello Music of Antonio Bononcini: Violone, Violoncello da Spalla, and the Cello 'Schools' of Bologna and Rome," *Journal of Seventeenth-Century Music* 12/1 (2006) (http://sscm-jscm.press.uiuc.edu/v12/no1/wissick. html), and Gregory Barnett, "The Violoncello da Spalla: Shouldering the Cello in the Baroque Era," *Journal of the American Musical Instrument Society* 24 (1998): 81–106.

Examples 3.6a–3.6d.[12] Zannetti supplies further corroboration and makes explicit in his tablature what we might have assumed on the basis of Bismantova's chart: pitches inflected up or down by accidentals require a similar adjustment of a finger within the stable hand position.[13] Figure 3.1, a Modenese woodcut from 1697, like similar iconographic evidence from the seventeenth century, illustrates why violinists usually played with a fixed left hand.[14] It shows the common "off-the-chin" position of the instrument on the performer's body, in which the left hand helped to hold it in place. With the violin loosely held in this manner, shifting the hand along the neck of instrument was a delicate maneuver and not within the repertory of basic techniques.

Example 3.5a   B. Bismantova, left-hand fingering chart for the violin, *Compendio musicale* (1677–94)

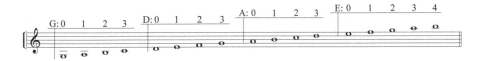

Example 3.5b   B. Bismantova, left-hand fingering chart for the violoncello, *Compendio musicale* (1677–94)

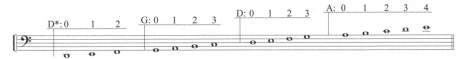

* Bismantova indicates that this string may be tuned down a whole-step to C.

---

12 MS, I-Bc, AA.360 (latter half of the seventeenth century). Three dates occur in this manuscript notebook of various dances and other pieces: 1661, 1671, and 1681. The musical handwriting is that of different authors so that it is probable that this notebook was in the possession of several musicians (possibly music students) of the latter half of the seventeenth century. Interestingly, these "scales" also give an idea of where violinist-composers may have found the inspiration for the extended sequences that decorate most of their fugal movements.

13 In Zannetti's tablatures for string instruments, flats and sharps are placed immediately in front of or below the number that indicates which finger is to be used.

14 This woodcut comes from the frontispiece of Giuseppe Jacchini, *Concerti per camera à violino, e violoncello*, Op. 3 (Modena: Rosati, 1697). This illustration, sometimes paired with the figure of a cellist, is used by the Modenese publisher Fortuniano Rosati in at least two other prints: Tomaso Pegolotti, *Trattenimenti armonici da camera à violino solo, e violoncello*, Op. 1 (Modena: Rosati, 1698); and, where the figure of the cellist appears alone in the *cimbalo* part, Antonio Veracini, *Sonate da camera a violino solo*, Op. 2 (Modena: Rosati, n.d.). For further iconographic evidence of off-the-chin playing positions, see Boyden, *The History of Violin Playing*, plates 12, 13, and 20–23.

Example 3.6a   Scala per il violino, MS, I-Bc, AA360 (late 17th century)

Example 3.6b   Altra scala per il violino, MS, I-Bc, AA360 (late 17th century)

Example 3.6c   Scaletta di contrappunto per il violino, MS, I-Bc, AA360 (late 17th century)

Example 3.6d   Scaletta all'incontrario di contrappunto, MS, I-Bc, AA360 (late 17th century)

Figure 3.1   G. Jacchini, *Concerti per camera*, Op. 3 (Modena: Rosati, 1697), violin partbook, detail from the title page. Museo Internazionale e Biblioteca della Musica di Bologna (I-Bc)

The use of a single hand position and of simple bowings as taught by Bismantova, Zannetti, and the manuscript etudes represents a level of string technique attainable by any player. According to Bismantova, his treatise offers instruction to beginners (*principianti*); Zannetti's string tablatures, he asserts, offer a method by which "any person can learn to play on his own" (*qual si voglia persona da se stesso potrà imparare à suonare*). It is this level of technique attainable by "any person" that appears to fit the Bolognese repertory. The composer Maurizio Cazzati, for example, rarely wrote notes for the violin higher than c^3, which lies just a half-step above the highest first-position note, b^2. The same is true of G. M. Bononcini, a violinist, and G. B. Vitali, a cellist, both of whom were even more conservative than Cazzati in their use of notes above b^2. The highest notes are typically $b\flat^2$, b^2, and c^3; and to reach c^3 (and even $c\sharp^3$) above b^2 on the violin required, not a shift of hand position, but only an extension of the fourth finger. For the bass violin,[15] Bolognese prints occasionally contain parts that range up to e^1 (the highest note in Bismantova's chart of notes on the violoncello) and, more rarely, to f^1. On smaller versions of the bass violin, such as the violoncello da spalla, these parts stay almost entirely within the single hand position. On other forms of bass violin, the part-writing seen in the printed repertory stays well within the range of notes played on the neck of the instrument, that is, never requiring left-hand positions beyond its shoulders.[16]

A further glance at prints of instrumental music shows that until the 1680s, the decade of Corelli's first three publications, composers rarely exceeded the range of the violinist's single hand position. From the 1680s onward, that range was extended, but only infrequently. And with the exception of engraved prints, chordal writing is almost entirely absent from the Bolognese repertory. Sophisticated bowing techniques, such as bariolage, slurred staccato, and arpeggiando, are not required.[17]

---

15 The bass member of the violin family presents an organological complexity because several possibilities are involved concerning the actual instrument used, terminology employed, and method of playing (see n. 11 in this chapter). A safe generic term for the bowed bass of late-*Seicento* Italian instrumental music is, with only few exceptions, the bass violin, or *basso*. More specific terms from the period are: *violone* and *violone da braccio*, usually an instrument with the tuning of the modern violoncello or a whole-step lower, but sometimes of larger proportions; *violoncello* (or *violoncino*, *violonlino*, and other variants), the instrument we recognize today and possibly distinguished then by its use of metal-wound strings; *violoncello da spalla*, a smaller bass violin, played horizontally at chest level or on the lap; and *bassetto viola* and even *viola*, terms more common in the Veneto for some form of bass violin. In general, I will use "bass violin" for this class of instruments; in specific cases, I will draw on the composer's term, when available.

16 Since the violoncello had more than one tuning, we should not take Bismantova's as wholly representative. Apart from the variable tuning of the lowest string, Bolognese cellists are also thought to have tuned the highest string to g as an alternative to a. I would like to thank Professor Brent Wissick for bringing this to my attention. Whatever tuning was used, the issue of shifting the left hand on the cello is unproblematic on the cello because the instrument either rested on the floor or was held firmly between the player's knees, except in the case of the violoncello da spalla.

17 As far as I know, there is one exception to the absence of double-stops in printed music of the late *Seicento*: Giovanni Maria Bononcini, *Arie, correnti, sarabande, & allemande*, Op. 4 (Bologna: Monti, 1671). The three last dances of this print do feature double-stops; these pieces are discussed below in detail.

Manuscripts of the Este Court

The manuscripts of the Este court in Modena, as shown earlier, contain something altogether different, offering challenges well beyond the basic string techniques of the period outlined here. The Este manuscripts include the music of numerous composers, but the bulk of the collection represents the work of the composer-violinist Giuseppe Colombi, who made his career at the ducal court in Modena. The quantity of his compositions in manuscript is enormous, comprising some 22 *libri* that range from 17 to a staggering 106 folios of music apiece, plus another five multi-author collections that include contributions by Colombi.[18] His music includes sonatas (or sinfonias), chaconnes and other variation forms, scordaturas, toccatas, *trombe* (that is, imitations of trumpet effects) for unaccompanied violin and unaccompanied bass violin, and over 1,100 dance (or dance-like) movements, most written for violin and bass duo, or a trio of two violins and bass.

Much of the instrumental music in the Este collection, that of Colombi and others,[19] can be dated to the latter half of the seventeenth century—more specifically, to the reign of Francesco II d'Este.[20] That reign began officially in 1662 on the death of his father, Alfonso IV; but until 1674, Francesco II, born only in 1660, was only titular duke while his mother, Laura Martinozzi, was regent. The few known facts of Colombi's biography allow for a broad span of time—between the late 1660s and 1694, the year he died—during which he could have written his virtuoso solos. His recorded employment at the ducal court in Modena began in 1671, three years after he had published his first collection of instrumental music with a dedication to Francesco. During that time, he may already have been violin teacher to the young duke because, in the dedication of his 1689 chamber sonatas, Colombi mentions

---

18 For a provisional works-list, see John Suess, "The Instrumental Music Manuscripts of Giuseppe Colombi of Modena: A Preliminary Report on the Non-Dance Music for Solo Violin or Violone," in *Seicento inesplorato: l'evento musicale tra prassi e stile—un modello di interdipendenza*, ed. Alberto Colzani, Andrea Luppi, and Maurizio Padoan (Como: Antiquae Musicae Italicae Studiosi, 1993), 387–409, pp. 395–7. See also Suess, "Giuseppe Colombi's Dance Music for the Este Court of Duke Francesco II of Modena," in *Marco Uccellini: atti del convegno "Marco Uccellini da Forlimpopoli e la sua musica" (Forlimpopoli, 26–7 ottobre 1996)*, ed. Maria Caraci Vela and Marina Toffetti (Lucca: Libreria Editrice Musicale, 1999), 141–62.

19 These include G. B. and Pietro Degli Antonii, Domenico Gabrielli, Carl'Ambrogio Lonati, Alessandro Stradella, and G. B. and Tomaso Antonio Vitali. Lesser-known composers with assorted pieces in the collection are: Giovanni Battista Gigli, Angelo Maria Fiorè, Domenico Galli, Antonio Giannottini, Luigi Mancia, Evilmerodach Millanta, Giuseppe Pozzati, and Pietro Sorosina. There are, moreover, a number of unidentified pieces listed.

20 Only a few compositions in the Este collection of instrumental music bear dates. These are Mus.G.238, an anthology of dances, *Ballet du roy, dansé a Fontainebleau*, 1664; Mus. F.122, G. B. Borri, *Sinfonie a trè*, 1687 (published a year later in Bologna by Giacomo Monti); and Mus.C.81, Domenico Galli, *Trattenimento musicale sopra il violoncello a solo*, 1691. Numerous concordances between the Modenese manuscript repertory and printed sources confirm that the bulk of the manuscripts preserve music from the reign of Francesco II.

having taught him "in his earliest years."[21] From that point, Colombi's progress was steady: by 1673, he was "capo de gl'istrumentisti del Serenissimo di Modana" (head of the court instrumental ensemble); in 1674 (the year in which Francesco began to rule in his own right after his mother's regency), Colombi added the duties of vice-maestro di cappella at the ducal court; and in 1678, on the death of G. M. Bononcini, he became maestro di cappella at the cathedral of Modena.

Colombi's sonatas for solo violin and continuo are central to this discussion of musical style as transmitted in manuscript sources: they significantly alter our perspective of instrumental technique and style in Italy during the decades preceding the landmark violin sonatas of Corelli's Op. 5 (1700).[22] For instance, bowings not found in Italian prints occur in Colombi's sonatas, such as the arpeggiando bowing applied to written triple-stops designated "arpeggio" (Example 3.7a). Another indication found in Colombi's manuscript sonatas is a slurred staccato (Example 3.7b). Left-hand technique in violin playing is similarly expanded in comparison to what we know from Bismantova's treatise and printed sources. Example 3.7c shows the extent to which Colombi pushed the violin range upward with a passage that reaches a full octave above the highest note of first position, from b^2 to b^3.

---

21 Giuseppe Colombi, *Sonate da camera a tre strumenti*, Op. 5 (Bologna: Monti, 1689), dedication: "Sia gloria eterna della rozza mia mano negli anni più teneri dell'A.V.S. ... l'haver sortito l'honore d'avanzare la di lei destra nata a gli Scetri à trattare pacificamente l'arco sonoro [May the glory be eternal of my own crude hand that had the honor of advancing your right hand (destined for the scepter) toward the peaceful handling of the sonorous bow in the earliest years of Your Majesty]."

22 Neither Boyden's *History of Violin Playing* nor Walter Kolneder's *The Amadeus Book of the Violin*, trans. and ed. by Reinhard Pauly (Portland, OR: Amadeus Press, 1998) mentions the Este repertory. Instead, the limited attention given to it has been that of specialists of seventeenth-century Italian violin music, such as Peter Allsop (see n. 29 below) and John Suess (see n. 18 above), whose articles about Colombi's contributions have been published in Italian journals or conference proceedings.

Example 3.7a   G. Colombi, MS, I-MOe, Mus.F.280, No. 6

Example 3.7b   G. Colombi, MS, I-MOe, Mus.F.280, No. 5

Example 3.7c   G. Colombi, MS, I-MOe, Mus.F.280, No. 2

i. (mm. 10-16)

A few of Colombi's sonatas are ideal for the study of violin technique because they exist in multiple versions that differ only in terms of technical difficulty.[23] First-movement excerpts from the two existing versions of a Sinfonia à violino solo by Colombi show differences that are representative of the versions of his other sonatas (Examples 3.8a–3.8c). The more difficult version reaches b[3] twice; the easier version of the same sonata, however, transposes passages with notes above the first-position range down an octave so that the piece is entirely playable using a fixed hand position. The high-reaching passages of the more difficult versions are particularly noteworthy because they are in no way tentative departures from first position: the last excerpt, for example, shows arpeggiated patterns that leap by thirds and fourths from one pattern to the next. In the second movement of this same sonata (Example 3.9), the two versions of the piece again differ in terms of left-hand technique: double-stops in the more challenging version are removed from the simplified version, which uses only the upper of the two lines found in the more difficult version. In the latter, moreover, the double-stops cover every diatonic interval from the second to the octave, and their deployment often creates counterpoint as well as block chords between two lines on the solo violin. Because Colombi served as violin teacher to Francesco, the different versions of these sonatas suggest modifications made for the duke's benefit. The versions would thus illustrate the distinct levels of technical facility appropriate to the student aristocrat and the professional virtuoso.

---

23 Each of the three sonatas by Colombi and their differing versions that are discussed here are contained in Mus.F.280. The first and second pieces contained in Mus.F.280 are two versions of one sonata; the fourth, fifth, and eighth pieces of the manuscript are similarly all versions of another; and the sixth and seventh are versions of yet one more.

Example 3.8a   G. Colombi, MS, I-MOe, Mus.F.280, No. 2 vs. G. Colombi, MS,
I-MOe, Mus.F.280, No. 1 (simplified version of No. 2)

Example 3.8b   G. Colombi, MS, I-MOe, Mus.F.280, No. 2 vs. G. Colombi, MS, I-MOe, Mus.F.280, No. 1 (simplified version of No. 2)

Example 3.8c   G. Colombi, MS, I-MOe, Mus.F.280, No. 2 vs. G. Colombi, MS, I-MOe, Mus.F.280, No. 1 (simplified of version No. 2)

Example 3.9   G. Colombi, MS, I-MOe, Mus.F.280, No. 2 vs. G. Colombi, MS, I-MOe, Mus.F.280, No. 1 (simplified version of No. 2)

Beyond the perspective they offer us on instrumental technique, style, and social function, the Modenese manuscripts also yield valuable evidence on violin embellishing practices from the late seventeenth century, both melodic and harmonic. In the case of melodic embellishment, the same two sonatas by Colombi discussed immediately above illustrate unembellished (Example 3.10a) and embellished (Example 3.10b) writing for the violin in their respective opening movements.

A technique of harmonic embellishment is also demonstrated in Colombi's slow movements in which the rhythmic pulse is steady and an entire line of music is added to the solo instrument by substituting double-stops for single notes. The existence of two versions of the Largo from Colombi's Sonata à violino solo (Example 3.11a)— one in double-stops and the other not—suggests just such a practice, in which accomplished violinists may have added thirds, sixths, and octaves that were not printed or otherwise written down. Along similar lines, two slow tremolo movements by Colombi—Example 3.11b, from his published sonatas, and Example 3.11c, from his unpublished sonatas—demonstrate how this type of movement was particularly receptive to harmonic embellishment.

Example 3.10a   G. Colombi, MS, I-MOe, Mus.F.280, No. 5

Example 3.10b   G. Colombi, MS, I-MOe, Mus.F.280, No. 7

Example 3.11a   G. Colombi, MS, I-Moe, Mus.F.280, No. 5 vs. G. Colombi, MS,
                  I-MOe, Mus.F.280, No. 4 (simplified version of No. 5)

Example 3.11b   G. Colombi, Op. 4, No. 3 (1676)

iv. Adagio (mm. 7-13)

Example 3.11c   G. Colombi, MS, I-MOe, Mus.F.280, No. 7

v. Grave (mm. 7-end)

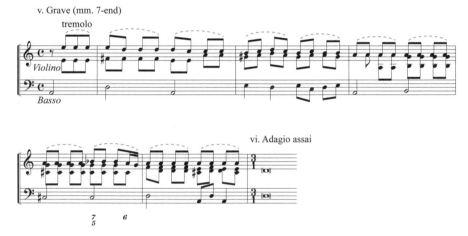

Music for the bass violin in the Modenese repertory, as contributed by Domenico Gabrielli, who served briefly at the Este court in the late 1680s, exhibits a similar profile of soloistic virtuosity.[24] His *Ricercari*, for example, present a striking picture of cello playing from the period, as seen earlier in Example 3.2b. Gabrielli wrote five ricercars for unaccompanied cello; a sixth is to be played by two cellos in canon. Three more pieces from the same manuscript (Mus.G.79) bear continuo

---

24 Gabrielli was, in fact, a highly paid "virtuoso" at the Modenese court hired in November of 1688 (he died shortly after in July of 1690). See Chapter 1, pp. 65–6, for a discussion of Gabrielli's brief career as a cello virtuoso.

accompaniment and are similarly identified as ricercars,[25] but they also exist in slightly different versions as movements within a sonata for cello and continuo in another Este manuscript (Mus.F.416). That sonata is one of two by Gabrielli among the Este manuscripts, both of which exhibit some of the same advanced techniques as those seen in Colombi's violin sonatas (see Example 3.12): double- and triple-stops, a higher range of pitches, and evidence of written-out melodic and harmonic embellishment.

Example 3.12   D. Gabrielli, MS, I-MOe, Mus.F.416, No. 2

---

25 The full title of the collection is *Ricercari per violoncello solo, con un canone a due violoncelli e alcuni ricercari per v.llo e B.C.* On the title page, the author Gabrielli is also called, in dialect, "Mingain dal Viulunzeel." A facsimile edition of both Mus.G.79 and Mus.F.416, which contains two sonatas for cello and continuo by Gabrielli, is *Ricercari per violoncello solo; Canone a due violoncelli; Sonate per violoncello e basso continuo,* ed. Marc Vanscheeuwijck (Bologna: Forni, 1998). As Vanscheeuwijck points out (pp. 7–8), the contents of Mus.G.79 are five ricercars for unaccompanied cello, one canon for two cellos, a slightly later piece, and three pieces, also numbered among the ricercars, that overlap with movements from the first sonata of two sonatas in Mus.F.416.

Bizarrerie

Apart from evidence of virtuoso playing techniques, unaccompanied compositions for both violin and bass violin in the Este collection further distinguish the manuscript repertory. Some also stand out as curiosities, bearing such titles as tromba and scordatura. In excerpts from Colombi's chaconnes for unaccompanied violin and for unaccompanied bass violin, the ground is the usual four measures in length, beginning on the second beat in 3/4 time (Examples 3.13a and 3.13b). Within each cycle, however, Colombi varies the implied harmonies. The "basso" upon which Example 3.13b was played uses a tuning associated with the early bass violin that persisted into the late seventeenth century: $B\flat^1$, F, c, g (a whole-step below that of the violoncello).[26] Only in that tuning can the performer manage the chords toward the end of the piece. The music of Colombi's Tromba à basso solo (Example 3.14), written for the same low tuning, is typical of its genre, featuring extended arpeggiation figures in vigorous rhythms that recall the trumpet and its fanfares. The two excerpts of Example 3.14 illustrate that Colombi's tromba, a showpiece for the soloist, makes liberal use of chords and rapid passages. Two other unaccompanied genres among Colombi's works are the toccata and the scordatura. The toccatas have the appearance of etudes, combining scale-patterns, arpeggios, and other figures, all in different rhythms and running on for many pages of manuscript. They are virtuosic principally because of the stamina required to play them, if indeed they were performed from beginning to end. The works in scordatura have the character of effects pieces, making three- and four-note chords easily played by tuning the open strings to the pitches of G- or C-major chords (Example 3.15). Otherwise, they pose fewer technical challenges than do the sonatas.

---

26 I am grateful to John Moran, cellist and expert on early cello repertory, for pointing this out to me. In Italian treatises, this tuning is cited by Lodovico Zacconi, *Prattica di musica*, Part I (1592) and Pietro Cerone, *El melopeo y maestro* (1613). It is also assumed by Zannetti in his tablatures for the "basso" part in his *Il scolaro* (1645).

Example 3.13a   G. Colombi, Chiacona à violino solo, MS, I-MOe, Mus.F.280, No. 10

Example 3.13b   G. Colombi, Chiacona à basso solo, MS, I-Moe, Mus.E.350

Example 3.13b,   Colombi, Chiacona, cont'd

(mm. 49-69)

Example 3.14   G. Colombi, Tromba à basso solo, MS, I-MOe, Mus.F.280, No. 14

(mm. 1-14)

Example 3.14   cont'd

(mm. 29-41)

Example 3.15   G. Colombi, Scordatura à violino solo, MS, I-MOe, Mus.F.283, No. 1, as written

Example 3.15   as sounded

Colombi's chaconne and tromba, along with Gabrielli's ricercars, stand out as some of the earliest unaccompanied music written for the bass violin. And to these we may add Domenico Galli's *Trattenimento musicale sopra il violoncello a solo*, dated 1691, which, if unexceptional music, points up the unique and historic concentration of unaccompanied solos at the Este court.[27] But not all of the Este collection draws our attention toward virtuosic or unusual instrumental techniques

---

27 A detailed study of Galli's life and career at the Este court is Don Harrán, "Domenico Galli e gli eroici esordi della musica per violoncello solo non accompagnato," *Rivista italiana di musicologia* 34 (1999): 231–99.

and solo genres suited to exhibiting them: the largest share of the manuscripts comprises dances and dance-like binary forms. While similar pieces make up a little over half of printed instrumental music, dances and similarly tuneful but simple binary forms account for the majority of instrumental pieces in the manuscripts. On the basis of the virtuosic sonatas, chaconnes and *trombe*, the etude-like toccatas and simplified versions of some of the sonatas, and, now, these binary-form pieces, the Este manuscripts appear to have served several functions at Francesco's court: concert performance of rare and unpublished compositions fit for an important ducal court—the Duke's instrumental *musica segreta*; materials studied and performed by the music-loving Duke himself; and music to accompany social functions at court that were no doubt similar if not more extravagant than some of those described in the previous chapter.[28]

German influence at the Este Court

The virtuoso string music of the Este court comprises such a departure from anything else in Italian violin music that it is difficult to account for its existence in Italy at all. Peter Allsop has weighed the significance of the manuscripts for the history of violin playing, arguing for a revised view of Italian contributions as compared with the better-known virtuoso repertory of the German and south-German violinists Heinrich Biber, Johann Jakob Walther, and Johann Paul von Westhoff.[29] On the basis of the Este repertory and later, unpublished sonatas by Carlo Ambrogio Lonati, Allsop hypothesizes the existence of a continuous but unrecorded tradition of Italian virtuoso playing throughout the seventeenth century that rivaled and may even have surpassed that of violinists from north of the Alps.[30]

The Este manuscripts, however, furnish evidence of another possibility, that Italian violinists were directly inspired by their ultramontane counterparts. Although Allsop did not know it, the Modenese collection contains at least one example of German virtuoso music for the violin, unidentified until now.[31] The piece, a sonata for violin and continuo by Westhoff, is one of several in a set under the call-number Mus.E.282 in the Biblioteca Estense. The complete set comprises seven pieces for the solo violin: four sonatas (or sinfonias) for violin and continuo without attribution and three single-movement works by Colombi for unaccompanied violin (scordatura, chiaconna, and tromba). Westhoff's sonata is the first of the set, identifiable because that same piece appears in the *Mercure galant* of December, 1682, accompanied by the following report on its author and his appearance before Louis XIV:

---

28 The anonymous author of *A Discourse of the Dukedom of Modena* (London: Crook, 1674), 26, describes the Este dukes as "in the number of the seven great Princes of *Italy*, according to the ancient Division, which are, the Pope, King of *Spain*, Duke of *Savoy*, *Toscany* [sic], *Modena*, *Parma*, and *Montoa* [sic]."

29 Peter Allsop, "Violinistic Virtuosity in the Seventeenth Century: Italian Supremacy or Austro-German Hegemony?," *Il saggiatore musicale* 3 (1996): 233–58.

30 Ibid., 257–8.

31 Others may exist among the several unidentified sonatas in the Este manuscripts.

having made visits to many courts, he was passing here while coming back from London and had the honor of playing before the King and the entire court. His Majesty himself gave the name *la Guerre* to one of his airs, which [the King] made him repeat many times. Since he has received tokens of the King's generosity, this is proof that his airs pleased the great monarch. He was set to pass again through Italy, but having received orders from his highness the Elector of Saxony, he is obliged to return to him.[32]

According to the *Mercure* entry, Westhoff had already visited Italy. If so, he may have followed in the footsteps of Johann Jakob Walther, who spent the early 1670s in Florence and, in 1676, published his formidable *Scherzi da violino solo* with a dedication to Cosimo III de Medici.[33] Equally likely, however, is that Westhoff's sonata came to Modena by means of the *Mercure* article because the French King's descriptive subtitle for the third movement appears, in Italian, in the Modenese manuscript, inserted just beneath the first measure (see Figure 3.2).[34]

---

32 *Mercure galant* (December, 1682): 386–7, "l'ayant fait souhaiter dans plusieurs Cours, il a passé icy en revenant de Londres, & il a eu l'honneur de joüer du Violon devant le Roy, & devant toute la Cour. Sa Majesté a mesme donné le nom de *la Guerre* à un de ses Airs, qu'Elle luy a fait repéter plusieurs fois. Comme il a reçeu des marques de la libéralité du Roy, c'est une preuve que ses Airs ont plû à ce grand Monarque. Il avoit desse a de repasser en Italie, mais ayant reçeu des ordres de Son Altesse Electorale de Saxe, il est obligé de retourner aupres d'Elle."

33 Johann Jakob Walther, *Scherzi da violino solo con il basso continuo per l'organo ò cimbalo, accompagnabile anche con una viola ò leuto*, no opus (Leipzig and Frankfurt: n.p., 1676). In addition to techniques already discussed here, Walther uses ondeggiando and arpeggiando bowings in combination with higher left-hand positions. In his dedication to Cosimo III, Walther attributes the origins of his *Scherzi* to his time at the Medici court.

34 The inscription in the version that appears in the *Mercure galant* is "La guerra Cosi nominata di sua Maesta." That version lacks the *allegro* tempo designation and is notated in 4/4 meter, not 2/2.

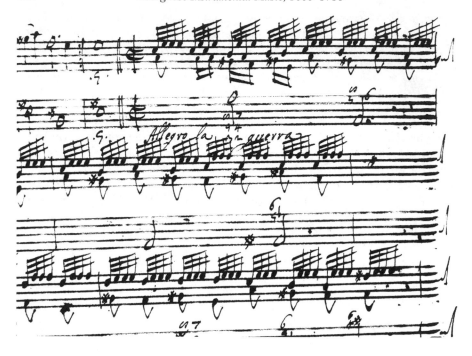

Figure 3.2   J. P. von Westhoff, Sonata a violino solo col suo basso continuo, "Allegro la guerra." Biblioteca Estense Universitaria, Modena (I-MOe)

The connections between the Modenese and French courts are well known to specialists in this period,[35] and Westhoff's sonata is one more indication of their close rapport. The significance of Westhoff's music in this context lies in its potential influence on Italian violin playing. A few techniques in his sonata are familiar to us already: rapid passagework that requires higher positions on the violin and extended double-stop tremolos. By contrast, the chords and bariolage in "La guerra"

---

35 The francophile leanings of the Modenese court were the result of a mid-century shift of allegiance from Spain to France on the part of Duke Francesco I. One consequence of this was the marriage of his son, the eventual Duke Alfonso IV, to Laura Martinozzi, the niece of Cardinal Jules Mazarin. Their son and Colombi's patron would rule as Francesco II. All of this is chronicled by the anonymous author of *A Discourse of the Dukedom of Modena*, 28, who also sheds light on Modenese contact with French culture: "[the Modenese dukes] kept close to the *Spaniard*, till their Interest of late wrought a change upon their inclinations. For Duke *Francis* [grandfather of Francesco II] was in the late *Italian* Wars made General of the French; and *Mazarine*'s Neece is married to Prince *Almerigo* [recte Alfonso] his son, who hath left a young son [Francesco II] to succeed him. All things at present are managed by the advice of Cardinal [Rinaldo] *d'Esté*, Protector of the French Interest at Rome, and the sole Promoter of the late Union of his House to the French Crown.... He is a zealot in the French Cause; by whose friendship his Family is enriched and well moneyed, by reason of the late Generalship, as also the Country: for the Souldiers took up their Winter-quarters in *Modena*; which occasioned a great resort of the chief Officers, as well as inferiour persons."

(Example 3.16a) amount to a cutting-edge combination of left-hand and bowing techniques beyond anything we have yet seen. His use of ondeggiando bowing—signaled by the wavy slurs in Example 3.16b—in a tempo marked *Vivace* adds yet a further virtuoso technique to those mentioned in Colombi's works. In short, Westhoff's sonata is arguably the most difficult violin music to be found among the Este manuscripts and, therefore, anywhere in Italy.

Allsop has argued that Colombi's and, later, Lonati's manuscript works prove that a level of violin technique existed in Italy that was comparable to that of the

Example 3.16a   J. P. von Westhoff, Sonata a violino solo e suo basso continuo, MS, I-MOe, Mus.E.282, No. 1

Example 3.16b   J. P. von Westhoff, Sonata a violino solo e suo basso continuo, MS, I-MOe, Mus.E.282, No. 1

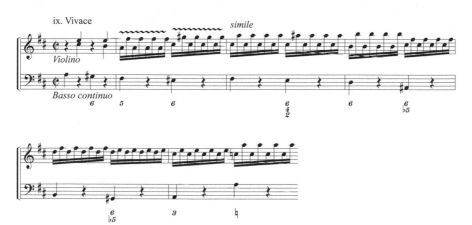

renowned German violinists. There is, however, nothing to say that these Italians weren't influenced and inspired by German violinists and violin music that was circulating in Italy in the 1670s and 80s. We can at least surmise that Colombi knew Westhoff's music from the early 1680s and that he may have known Walther's even earlier. Because none of the Este manuscripts is dated, no priority can be asserted— for example, first German music in Italy, then Colombi's unique contributions— from which we might hypothesize an influence. However, German influence does explain Colombi's extraordinary music, which has no known precedent in the Italian repertory for the violin. The most likely Italian influence on Colombi would have been that of Marco Uccellini, who was Colombi's predecessor at Modena as head of the court instrumental ensemble and maestro di cappella of the cathedral. Uccellini, one of the foremost Italian violinists of the mid seventeenth century, published numerous solo violin sonatas during the 1640s and 50s that reflect a style distinct from that of Colombi. In Uccellini we see the continuing tradition of intricate melodic divisions among Renaissance and early Baroque instrumentalists, a virtuosity largely of passagework, as seen in excerpts from his violin sonatas of 1649 (Examples 3.17a–b).[36] In Colombi, by contrast, the elements of his virtuosic style include frequent and varied kinds of chordal playing, and arpeggiando and slurred staccato bowings. These are ingredients found in the playing of virtuosos north of the Alps.

---

36 Marco Uccellini, *Sonate over canzoni da farsi à violino solo, & basso continuo*, Op. 5 (Venice: Vincenti, 1649).

Example 3.17a   M. Uccellini, Op. 5, No. 2 (1649)

iv. Allegro (mm. 27-35)

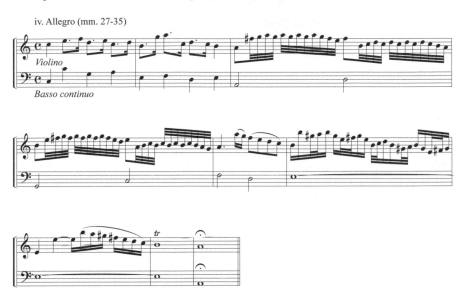

Example 3.17b   M. Uccellini, Op. 5, No. 7 (1649)

iii. (mm. 24-26)

Returning to the specific influence of Westhoff, the concentration of unaccompanied solos in the Este manuscripts may also reflect his impact. During the same visit to the court of Louis XIV in 1682, Westhoff also performed violin music without continuo, as recorded in the *Mercure* of January, 1683, which published a complete suite for unaccompanied violin by him. That piece is not found among the Este manuscripts, but it adds to the links between Westhoff, the French court, and Modena, building a case for his influence in Italy via Louis XIV and Francesco II.

Music Engraving in Bologna

The argument that German exemplars stimulated Italian violin virtuosity during the late seventeenth century is admittedly circumstantial, but it has the merit of explaining Colombi's extraordinary compositions, which are otherwise unanticipated in surviving mid-century Italian music. A remaining question concerns the limited dissemination of the virtuoso solos. Why, for example, did Colombi send the music shown in Example 3.1a to the presses, but not that of Example 3.1b? Allsop takes on this very question.[37] The answer, he contends, lies in the limitations of movable-type printing, which loom large in his estimation as a determinant of the style of music that Italians were capable of publishing. But for these limitations, he argues, Italian violinists might have published works just as dazzling as their German and south-German counterparts.

If, indeed, movable type had such an impact in the late *Seicento* as to suppress violin virtuosity in print, then a different form of print technology could have liberated it: copperplate engraving. Because it could replicate all of the details of handwritten music (including chords, which movable type could not), engraving could also represent Italian violin playing in as much detail as the manuscripts do. Actual music engravings that support this idea, however, are scarce. Before Corelli's Op. 5 violin sonatas (1700), Italian output was limited to that of a single craftsman, Carlo Antonio Buffagnotti, whose engraved prints of instrumental music are listed in Table 3.1.[38] Buffagnotti's rare set of talents—cellist, painter of theatrical scenery, and engraver—enabled him to create a handful of extraordinary prints, probably beginning in the late 1680s and continuing through the early 1700s.[39]

---

37 Allsop, "Violinistic Virtuosity."

38 Two of the prints in Table 3.1 lack Buffagnotti's signature as engraver—the *Sonate a tre* and *Sonate a violino e violoncello*—but numerous details in the handwriting enable us to attribute them to him.

39 None of Buffagnotti's engraved prints bear a date, but two of them can be dated approximately because they bear opus numbers of composers whose other works are dated: Giuseppe Torelli, *Concertino per camera a violino e violoncello*, Op. 4, 1687 or 1688; and Jacchini, *Sonate a violino è violoncello, et à violoncello solo per camera*, Op. 1, sometime shortly before 1695. His sonata anthologies contain music by composers active over a number of decades during the late seventeenth and early eighteenth centuries, but among them are younger composers—Jacchini (1667–1727), Giuseppe Aldrovandini (1671–1707), and Antonio Montanari (1676–1737)—who were almost certainly not composing before the late 1680s. And Buffagnotti's growing involvement in the theater suggests a dating of his engravings before the early eighteenth century: after sporadic work in scenery painting, he began to collaborate regularly in 1703 with Ferdinando Bibiena in scene design. Therefore, his sonata engravings likely fall into a period beginning in the late 1680s and ending in the early 1700s. For an iconographic reading of the illustrations in Buffagnotti's *Sonate per camera a violino e violoncello*, see Valeria De Lucca, "Una silloge strumentale per Francesco II d'Este: analisi e iconografia," *Rivista italiana di musicologia* 36 (2001): 3–23.

Table 3.1   Instrumental music engraved by C. Buffagnotti

Single-author Prints

Carlo Buffagnotti, *Menuetti, sarabande, et varij capricci di Carlo Buffagnotti* (Bologna, 1690s?)

Giuseppe Jacchini, *Sonate a violino et a violoncello solo*, Op. 1 (Bologna, before 1695)

Giuseppe Torelli, *Concertino per camera a violino e violoncello*, Op. 4 (Bologna, 1687/88)

Multi-author Prints

Sonate a tre di vari autori (Bologna?, 1690s?): Giuseppe Aldrovandini; Alessandro Stradella; Giuseppe Torelli; Domenico Gabrielli; Giuseppe Jacchini

Sonate a violino e violoncello di vari autori (Bologna?, 1690s?): Arcangelo Corelli; Giuseppe Torelli; Antonio Montanari; Giacomo Predieri; Carlo Mazzolini; Giuseppe Jacchini; Clemente Rozzi

Sonate per camera a violino e violoncello di vari autori (Bologna?, 1690s?): Giacomo Antonio Perti; Giuseppe Aldrovandini [two sonatas]; Domenico Marcheselli; Giuseppe Jacchini; Bartolomeo Laurenti [two sonatas]; Carlo Mazzolini; Filippo Carlo Belisi; Bartolomeo Bernardi; Antonio Grimandi; Giuseppe Torelli

---

To judge from Torelli's Op. 4 (Example 2.7c), Buffagnotti was indeed printing a different kind of music, distinguished by the chordal writing in several of its movements. Other Buffagnotti prints also include that specific feature, which was almost entirely absent from the vast repertory printed with movable type. All of this would seem to support Allsop's hypothesis. And yet, the engravings do not emphasize virtuoso techniques in particular: the highest violin pitch is d^2, about the same as that in the rest of the printed repertory during the 1680s and 90s; and there are neither unusual bowing indications nor even many slurs. Moreover, movable type was hindered only with respect to representing chords, and not extremes of range, sophisticated bowings, or scordatura. And, however inelegantly, even chords could be represented in movable type. Keyboard music adopted the unwieldy but workable solution of producing the music on multiple staves,[40] and this is precisely what Monti did a few years later for G. M. Bononcini's violin dances in double-stops from his Op. 4 (1671).[41]

---

40 Two examples are: Luigi Battiferri, *Ricercari a quattro, a cinque, e a sei, con 1, 2, 3, 4 5, 6 soggetti sonabili*, Op. 3 (Bologna: Monti, 1669) and Fabritio Fontana, *Ricercari* (Rome: Mutij, 1677).

41 Later Bolognese music shows that printers were eventually able to represent chords on a single staff using movable type. Giuseppe Torelli's *Concerti grossi*, Op. 8 (Bologna: Silvani, 1709), for example, contains triple- and even quadruple-stops.

Movable type and engraving weren't distinguished so much by the kind of music they could represent as by the way in which they did so, and the appeal of Buffagnotti's engravings lay as much in their elegance of manuscript-like representation and decorative detail as in their superior capacity for representing music. All of his engravings were cut freehand, without the use of punches for the recurring symbols of music notation (Figure 3.3). And added to the music in several of these prints were not only ornate title pages (Figure 3.4), but also fantastical illustrations, almost obscuring the music in several cases (Figs. 3.5–3.6). But most significant is just how few music engravings were produced in late seventeenth-century Bologna. Buffagnotti produced only a handful, and he was alone in doing so. His labor-intensive prints thus had the character of rare collectibles. And while they did allow composers more easily to introduce chordal technique into published music, their impact was limited to a niche market for what were exotic and costly prints.[42] Rather than reveal a virtuoso repertory that movable type could not represent, Buffagnotti's engravings show us experiments—most of which may have been private commissions because they were never advertised for sale—of short duration and little influence.[43]

---

42 Oscar Mischiati, ed., *Indici, cataloghi e avvisi degli editori e librai musicali italiani dal 1591 al 1798* (Florence: Olschki, 1984), contains the music catalogs of Marino Silvani from the end of the seventeenth and beginning of the eighteenth centuries. Silvani's listings, which include the selling price, do not include Buffagnotti's engravings. They do, however, list Corelli's Op. 5 violin sonatas and later works that also used copperplate engraving, and these cost roughly twice as much as the next most expensive prints.

43 Only Torelli's Op. 4 title page bears the note "si vendono da Marino Silvani [sold by Marino Silvani]" (see Figure 3.4).

Figure 3.3   G. Torelli, *Concertino per camera a violino e violoncello*, Op. 4 (Bologna: Buffagnotti engraving, 1687/88), violin partbook, 1. Museo Internazionale e Biblioteca della Musica di Bologna (I-Bc)

Figure 3.4   G. Torelli, *Concertino per camera a violino e violoncello*, Op. 4
(Bologna: Buffagnotti engraving, 1687/88), title page. Museo
Internazionale e Biblioteca della Musica di Bologna (I-Bc)

Figure 3.5   C. Buffagnotti, *Menuetti, sarabande, et varij caprici* (Bologna: Buffagnotti engraving, 1690s?), Sarabanda (violoncello partbook). Museo Internazionale e Biblioteca della Musica di Bologna (I-Bc)

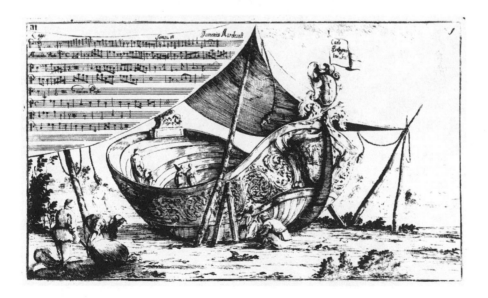

Figure 3.6   *Sonate per camera a violino e violoncello di vari autori* (Bologna: Buffagnotti engraving, 1690s?), sonata by D. Marcheselli (violoncello partbook). Museo Internazionale e Biblioteca della Musica di Bologna (I-Bc)

To return to the question of why the Este repertory and music like it was so little published, the principal factor involved was the market for instrumental prints and not printing technology. The virtuoso works of the Este court not only illustrate the little-known techniques of Italian virtuoso instrumentalists, but also shed light on the proper milieu for their performances: the courts of major princes. And by providing a repertory distinct from that which was published, these works also reveal the characteristics of the music that composers saw fit to print. This is not to argue for too neat a distinction in musical categories of dissemination, function, and style: manuscripts in no way preclude the distribution of repertory any more than prints insure its widest circulation; the Este manuscripts and Bolognese prints do overlap in the inclusion of a large number of accompanimental dances, which were just as useful at the Modenese court as anywhere else that dancing took place; and the published repertory begins to show evidence of performing virtuosity toward the end of the century. The larger distinctions between the Este manuscripts and the Bolognese prints, however, show complementary repertories of Italian instrumental music that differ along stylistic and functional lines. The diversional, accompanimental, and pedagogical uses of the dances surveyed in the previous chapter illustrate the broader market for the printed repertory, and the same can be said for the church sonatas. The Este manuscripts, by contrast, reveal the *riserva* collection of the best of Italian instrumentalists for solo display at a princely court.

Chapter Four

Da Chiesa and *Da Camera**

Since the early eighteenth century, when Sébastien de Brossard first described the two kinds of sonata commonly known to *les Italiens* as the sonata da chiesa and the sonata da camera,[1] historians have accepted these terms as representative of late-*Seicento* practice.[2] Referring to what Anglophone musicology has casually but consistently called the church sonata, Manfred Bukofzer asserted in his 1947 survey of Baroque music that "the very common term da chiesa of the title-pages … [affirms] the fact, now often forgotten, that the sonatas were church music."[3] Bukofzer's conclusion would seem inescapable, except for the fact that Italian composers used the term less predictably than he asserts.[4] Consequently, the sonata

---

* An earlier version of this chapter was published as "Sonata (da chiesa) Terminology and its Implications," in *Atti del XI Convegno Antiquae Musicae Italicae Studiosi—Como*, Alberto Colzani, Andrea Luppi, and Maurizio Padoan, eds. (A.M.I.S.—Como, 2006), 119–44.

1   The earliest definitions of the term *sonata* are summarized in William S. Newman, *The Sonata in the Baroque Era*, 4th ed. (New York: Norton, 1983), 22–8. Originally, these definitions appeared in non-Italian sources: Michael Praetorius, *Syntagma musicum*, vol. 2 (Wolfenbüttel, 1618–19); Athanasius Kircher, *Musurgia universalis* (Rome, 1650); Daniel Speer, *Vierfaches musicalisches Kleeblatt* (Ulm, 1697); Tomás Baltazar Janowka, *Clavis ad thesaurum* (Prague, 1701), Sébastien de Brossard, *Dictionnaire de musique* (Paris, 1703); Johann Mattheson, *Das neu-eröffnete Orchestre* (Hamburg, 1713). This exemplifies the historiographic problem at its most fundamental level: those responsible for the practice are not those describing it.

2   Newman, *Sonata*, 22: "Further light can be turned on the meaning of the word 'sonata' in the Baroque Era by consulting the dozen or so definitions written by the most renowned of the contemporary theorists … two general concepts come to the fore. One is that of the sonata as pure musical fantasy, subject only to the whims and good taste of the composer. The other concept, expressed after 1700, centers on the distinction between the *sonata da chiesa* and the *sonata da camera*."

3   Manfred Bukofzer, *Music in the Baroque Era* (New York: Norton, 1947), 54. The original, in less abbreviated form, reads: "The formal characteristics of the canzona held true in the solo and trio sonata only with some modifications. The sections of the trio sonata frequently coincided with the contrast of imitative and chordal textures, but in the solo sonata imitative texture was less prominent…. The initial fugal section was often preceded by a chordal introduction, a feature that became a fixture in the church sonata, but the very common term *da chiesa* of the title pages had, until about 1650, hardly a formal significance, merely affirming the fact, now often forgotten, that the sonatas were church music."

4   Peter Allsop, "Secular Influences in the Bolognese Sonata da Chiesa," *Proceedings of the Royal Association of Music* 104 (1977–78): 89–100; Allsop, "Sonata da Chiesa—A Case of Mistaken Identity?," *The Consort* 53 (1997): 4–14; Allsop, "The Italian Sonata and the Concept of the 'Churchly,'" *Barocco padano I: atti del IX Convegno Internazionale sulla*

da chiesa genre has undergone significant reevaluation in the work of Peter Allsop, who rightly points out that the term appears less frequently among the printed titles of *Seicento* composers than we have casually believed. This begs the question: if the term "sonata da chiesa" was not a standard genre term of the sonata repertory, why should we assume sonatas to have been church music? Allsop poses this very question and, headed for the opposite pole from Bukofzer, concludes that sonatas were not intended as church music by their authors, even if they were occasionally used as such. Rather, he argues, late-*Seicento* composers developed a style of sonata for all purposes—*da chiesa*, *da camera*, and so forth—which they simply termed "sonata."[5] Allsop, moreover, has proposed the term "free sonata" where Bukofzer and others assumed "sonata da chiesa," and seventeenth-century composers had simply but enigmatically used "sonata."[6]

The question of churchliness has far-reaching consequences for our understanding of instrumental music in Bologna, whose reputation is founded on (1) San Petronio trumpet sonatas, which it would seem are de facto *da chiesa*, and (2) a well-wrought contrapuntal style sometimes considered academic, but also ideally suited to the conservative decorum of the church. This chapter therefore takes up sonata designations, particularly those of "church sonata," and investigates whether Italian composers recognized a genre of sonata for the church and, if they did, what its churchliness entailed. The terminology used in the printed repertory between the years 1637 and around 1750 answers some of this, but this evidence is at once less straightforward and more revealing than Bukofzer and Allsop imply. This is particularly evident when we see how the terminology changed, decade by decade in the late seventeenth century, and how meanings hinted in the genre terms are amplified by the testimony of composers themselves. A final consideration here is how Bolognese publishers interpreted the genre terminology and disseminated their interpretations in inventory catalogs. As we shall see, the church sonata was no creation of sonata historiography. Rather, it loomed large in the imaginations of late-*Seicento* composers, their publishers, and patrons.

Musica Sacra nei Secoli XVII–XVIII, Como, 16–18 luglio 1999 (Como: Antiquae Musicae Italicae Studiosi, 2002), 239–47; and Allsop, *Arcangelo Corelli: "New Orpheus of Our Times"* (Oxford: Clarendon Press, and New York: Oxford University Press, 1999).

5   See Allsop, "Sonata da Chiesa," 14: "It was patently in Corelli's interest to develop a style which would be equally appropriate to secular and sacred settings"; and Allsop, "Italian Sonata," 247: "When in the letter of dedication of his *Concerti grossi*, Corelli issued a statement of mission to 'unite in these my *Concerti* one style which will serve both for the solemnity of the Church and for the sumptuous evening entertainments which are customarily enriched with the harmony of famous singers and the most renowned Professors of musical instruments', he was merely voicing intentions which had existed for over a century."

6   Allsop, "Sonata da Chiesa," 6: "Most sets of free sonatas, however, bear no designation and it remains to be proven whether the great majority of these were conceived primarily as church music by virtue of their content."

Sonata Terminology and Markedness Theory

Allsop's reservations and revisions appear well founded: Corelli, whom Brossard cited as a model, never used the term "sonata da chiesa"; nor did many of his contemporaries. Tables 4.1a–4.1c provide an overview of what Corelli and others did use by showing how genre terminology was applied to instrumental works with and without dance movements. The three tables list printed titles of sonata collections—those that are dance-based, on the one hand, and those that are not, on the other. Table 4.1a illustrates the distinction between the general title "sonata" (or "sinfonia")[7]—by which we may understand multi-movement works without dance titles—and titles that simply list individual dances. Table 4.1b shows a few instances in which the term "sonata" without further designation (i.e., non-dance) contrasts either with listings of individual dances or with the collective "sonata da camera"; and Table 4.1c furnishes instances in which "sonata" (or "sinfonia," or "concerto," but again without further designation) is used in contradistinction to "sonata" (or "concerto," or "concertino") designated *da camera*.[8]

Table 4.1a   "Sonata" vs. listings of individual dances in printed titles

Giovanni Battista Bassani

Op. 1: *Balletti, correnti, gighe, e sarabande à violino, e violone, overo spinetta* (Bologna, 1677)

Op. 5: *Sinfonie [Suonate* in table of contents] *a due, e trè instromenti, con il basso continuo per l'organo* (Bologna, 1683)

Pietro Degli Antonii

Op. 1: *Arie, gighe, balletti, correnti, allemande, e sarabande a violino, e violone, ò spinetta* (Bologna, 1670)

---

7   The picture is slightly muddled by the fact that composers sometimes used the terms "concerto," "concertino," or "sinfonia" interchangeably with "sonata." For instance, Angelo Berardi, *Miscellanea musicale* (Bologna: Monti, 1689; facsimile, Bologna: Forni, 1970), 45, describes the sonatas of Corelli as follows: "I concerti di Violino, e d'altri Strumenti si chiamano Sinfonie, & hoggi sono in preggio, e stima quelle del Sig. Arcangelo Corelli Violinista celebre, detto il Bolognese, nuovo Orfeo de nostri giorni." With a similar description of Corelli as a modern-day Orpheus, Francesco Gasparini, *L'armonico pratico al cimbalo* (Venice: Bortoli, 1708; facsimile, New York: Broude, 1967), 69, also refers to Corelli's sonatas as "le vaghissime Sinfonie del Sig. Arcangelo Corelli Virtuosissimo di Violino, vero Orfeo de' nostri tempi."

8   Corelli's *Sonate a tre composte per l'accademia del ... Cardinale Otthoboni* [sic], Op. 4 (Rome, 1694), deserves special mention as a collection of sonatas for the *accademia* patronized by Cardinal Pietro Ottoboni. When the Roman publisher of Corelli's Op. 4, Giovanni Giacomo Komareck, reprinted the work in 1695, he titled it *Sonate da camera*. Therefore, Corelli's Op. 4, specially designated as music for Ottoboni's *accademia*, comprised mostly dance movements that earned the more generic title of sonata da camera in the Komareck reprint. In the remaining reprints of Corelli's Op. 4 before 1700, the Amsterdam publisher Etienne Roger reverted to the earlier Italian usage of a detailed listing of dances while publishers in Bologna, Modena, and Venice kept the original printed title.

Op. 3: *Balletti, correnti, & arie diverse à violino, e violone per camera* (Bologna, 1671)

Op. 4: *Sonate a violino solo* (Bologna, 1676)

Op. 5: *Suonate a violino solo col basso continuo per l'organo* (Bologna, 1686)

Andrea Grossi

Op. 1: *Balletti, correnti, sarabande, e gighe a tre, due violini, e violone, overo spinetta* (Bologna, 1678)

Op. 2: *Balletti, correnti, sarabande, e gighe a trè, due violini, e violone, overo spinetta* (Bologna, 1679)

Op. 3: *Sonate a due, trè, quattro, e cinque instromenti* (Bologna, 1682)

Op. 4: *Sonate a trè, due violini, e violone, con il basso continuo per l'organo* (Bologna, 1685)

Gioseffo Placuzzi

Op. 1: *Suonate à duoi, à trè, à quattro, à cinque, & otto instromenti* (Bologna, 1667)

Op. 2: *Balletti, correnti, gighe, allemande, sarabande, e capricci a due violini, col suo basso per spinetta, ò violone* (Bologna, 1682)

Table 4.1b   "Sonata" vs. listings of individual dances or "sonata da camera" in printed titles

Pirro Albergati

Op. 1: *Balletti, correnti, sarabande, e gighe, à violino e violone* (Bologna, 1682)

Op. 2: *Suonate a due violini col suo basso continuo per l'organo* (Bologna, 1683)

Op. 5: *Pletro armonico composto di dieci sonate da camera à due violini, e basso* (Bologna, 1687)

Carlo Antonio Marino

Op. 1: *Sonate da camera a trè strumenti* (Bologna, 1687)

Op. 2: *Balletti, correnti, gighe, e minuetti diversi a trè, due violini, violoncello, ò spinetta* (Venice, 1692)

Op. 3: *Suonate a tre, et a cinque, doi, e tre violini, viola, et violoncello obligato, col basso per l'organo* (Amsterdam, 1697–98)

Op. 5: *Suonate alla francese a tre* (Amsterdam, 1700)

Table 4.1c   "Sonata" vs. "sonata da camera" in printed titles

Bartolomeo Bernardi

Op. 1: *Sonate da camera a trè, due violini, violoncello col violone ò cimbalo* (Bologna, 1692)

Op. 2: *Sonate à trè, due violini, e violoncello, con il basso per l'organo* (Bologna, 1696)

Giulio Taglietti

Op. 1: *Sonate da camera a trè: due violini, e violoncello, ò cembalo* (Bologna, 1695)

Op. 2: *Concerti e sinfonie a tre, due violini, violone, ò cembalo* (Venice, 1696)

Giuseppe Torelli

Op. 1: *Sonate à tre stromenti con il basso continuo* (Bologna, 1686)

Op. 2: *Concerto* [various dances listed in the table of contents] *da camera à due violini* (Bologna, 1686)

Op. 3: *Sinfonie* ["Sonate" in the table of contents] *à 2. 3. 4. istromenti* (Bologna, 1687)

Op. 4: *Concertino per camera* [various dances listed in the table of contents] *a violino e violoncello* (Bologna, 1687–88)

Antonio Veracini

Op. 1: *Sonate à tre, due violini, e violone, ò arcileuto, col basso per l'organo* (Florence, 1692)

Op. 2: *Sonate da camera a violino solo* (Modena, before 1696)

Op. 3: *Sonate da camera a due, violino, e violone, ò arcileuto, col basso per il cimbalo* (Modena, 1696)

Tomaso Antonio Vitali

Op. 1: *Sonate a trè, doi violini, e violoncello, col basso per l'organo* (Modena, 1693)

Op. 2: *Sonate à doi violini, col basso per l'organo* (Modena, 1693)

Op. 3: *Sonate da camera a trè due violini, e violone* (Modena, 1695)

Although hardly exhaustive, Tables 4.1a–4.1c sufficiently illustrate that rather than use two equal and opposed terms, "sonata da chiesa" and "sonata da camera," late-*Seicento* composers appear to have employed two unequal and opposed terms: "sonata" (an unmarked term) and "sonata da camera" (a marked term). By designating them unmarked and marked, I am drawing on terminology used to describe the phenomenon known in linguistics as markedness. Markedness refers to a pair of terms in which the unmarked term is broader or generic in meaning while the marked one is more restricted and precise. A non-musical pair of terms that furnishes a simple example from traditional written and spoken English is "man/ woman." "Man," a word sometimes used to mean all humankind, as well as the male of the human species, is the unmarked term. "Woman," the more restricted term, refers only to the female of the human species and is therefore the marked term. A second non-musical pair of terms—"nurse/male nurse"—reverses the gendering of markedness seen in "man/woman." The term "nurse" is unmarked and non-specific with respect to gender, but bears the presumption of a female subject because most nurses are women. By contrast, the marked term, "male nurse," specifies a male member of a female-dominated profession.[9]

This latter pair of terms, "nurse/male nurse," furnishes a close parallel to "sonata/ sonata da camera," not in terms of gender, but in terms of what an unmarked term may implicitly connote. Tables 4.1a–4.1c show us only that the unmarked term "sonata" excludes dances and little else,[10] but a look at further terminological evidence adds crucial information to our understanding of its implicit meaning. Table 4.2 provides a comprehensive overview of the use of the term *chiesa* in prints of instrumental music from a broad period of over a century, 1637–c.1750. It shows that the use of *da chiesa*, *per chiesa*, or *in chiesa*, occurs only rarely in isolation, that is, in single-genre prints, concentrated around the turn of the eighteenth century.[11] By contrast, *da chiesa* designations appear consistently throughout the period covered in Table 4.2 in combination with, or rather, in opposition to *da camera* designations. Indeed, from the 1630s through the beginning of the 1670s, *da chiesa* occurs exclusively in opposition to *da camera*. (I include Giovanni Pittoni's 1669 *Sonate da chiesa per tiorba sola* among those prints that use the *da chiesa* designation in opposition to *da camera* because Pittoni published his *Sonate da camera per tiorba sola* shortly afterward in that same year. In my interpretation, his use of *da chiesa* in opposition to *da camera* comprises two side-by-side publications.)[12]

---

9   My use of the "nurse/male nurse" opposition and, indeed, of markedness theory in general is a borrowing from Robert Hatten's stimulating book, *Musical Meaning in Beethoven: Markedness, Correlation, and Interpretation* (Bloomington & Indianapolis, IN: Indiana University Press, 1994), 34–9.

10   At the end of the *Seicento*, composers began to produce sonatas da camera without dance movements, but these are nonetheless stylistically distinct from the unmarked sonatas from that same time. See, for example, Antonio Veracini, *Sonate da camera a violino solo*, Op. 2 (Modena: Rosati, n.d.); and Veracini, *Sonate da camera a due, violino, e violone, ò arcileuto, col basso per il cimbalo*, Op. 3 (Modena: Rosati, 1696). Neither of these prints, designated *da camera*, contains dances, but both are stylistically distinct from Veracini's first publication, *Sonate à tre, due violini, e violone, ò arcileuto col basso per l'organo*, Op. 1 (Florence: Navesi, 1692).

11   Again (see n. 7), we are dealing with pieces that bear a range of genre designations; along with sonatas (spelled *sonate* or *suonate*), there are also sinfonias, concertos, concertini, capricci, divertimenti, and trattenimenti among the pieces listed in Table 4.2. In some cases, musicians used the terms "sinfonia," "canzon," "trattenimento," or, less commonly, "concerto" interchangeably with "sonata" (see Merula, 1637; and Bononcini, 1675). In other cases, especially collections of concertos, composers had in mind a genre distinct from the sonata. In all cases, however, the dichotomy of venue between church and chamber still applies. The fundamental applicability of this stylistic distinction is also borne out in the six published works of Corelli, which cover trio sonatas, solo sonatas, and concerti grossi. Throughout his oeuvre and across these genres, Corelli maintains the distinction between those works that include dance movements and those that do not.

12   Pittoni's prefatory notes illustrate how he had conceived of these two publications as a contrasting pair, and he introduces his Op. 2 *Sonate da camera per tiorba sola col basso per il clavicembalo* (Bologna: Monti, 1669; facsimile, Florence: Studio per Edizioni Scelte, 1980) with that idea in mind: "Ritorno forse à tediarti con le presenti mie Compositioni per

Table 4.2   Church designations in printed instrumental music, 1637–c.1750

Tarquinio Merula, *Canzoni, overo sonate concertate per chiesa, e camera a due et a tre*, Op. 12 (Venice, 1637).
Massimiliano Neri, *Sonate e canzone a quattro da sonarsi con diversi stromenti in chiesa & in camera con alcune correnti pure à quattro*, Op. 1 (Venice, 1644).
Marco Uccellini, *Sonate, correnti, et arie da farsi con diversi stromenti sì da camera, come da chiesa, à uno, à due, & à trè*, Op. 4 (Venice, 1645).
Biagio Marini, *Diversi generi di sonate, da chiesa, e da camera, à due, trè, & à quattro*, Op. 22 (Venice, 1655).
Giovanni Legrenzi, *Suonate dà chiesa, e dà camera, correnti, balletti, allemande, e sarabande à tre, doi violini, e violone, con il basso continuo*, Op. 4 (Venice, 1656).
Giovanni Antonio Pandolfi-Mealli, *Sonate à violino solo, per chiesa e camera*, Op. 3 (Innsbruck, 1660).
Giovanni Antonio Pandolfi-Mealli, *Sonate à violino solo, per chiesa e camera*, Op. 4 (Innsbruck, 1660).
Marco Uccellini, *Sinfonici concerti brievi e facili à uno, à due, à trè, & à quattro strumenti ... per chiesa, e per camera*, Op. 9 (Venice, 1667).
Maurizio Cazzati, *Varii, e diversi capricci per camera, e per chiesa ... a uno, due, e tre*, Op. 50 (Bologna, 1669).
Giovanni Pittoni, *Sonate da chiesa per tiorba sola col basso per l'organo*, Op. 1 (Bologna, 1669). Soon after in that same year Pittoni published his *Sonate da camera per tiorba sola col basso per il clavicemalo*, Op. 2 (Bologna, 1669).
Giovanni Maria Bononcini, *Sonate da chiesa a due violini*, Op. 6 (Venice, 1672).
Agostino Guerrieri, *Sonate di violino a 1. 2. 3. 4. per chiesa, & anco aggionta per camera*, Op. 1 (Venice, 1673).
Giovanni Maria Bononcini, *Trattenimenti musicali à trè, & à quattro stromenti* [*Suonate da chiesa à trè istromenti* and *Suonate da camera à trè istromenti* are listed in the table of contents], Op. 9 (Bologna, 1675).
Giovanni Buonaventura Viviani, *Capricci armonici da chiesa, e da camera à violino solo*, Op. 4 (Innsbruck, 1678).
Giovanni Battista Vitali, *Sonate da chiesa à due violini*, Op. 9 (Amsterdam, 1684).
Giovanni Bononcini, *Sinfonie da chiesa a quattro, cioè due violini, alto viola, e violoncello obligato*, Op. 5 (Bologna, 1687).

---

la Tiorba: Mà dovendo questo servire per Camera, & essendo perciò elleno condotte con stile diverse dall'altre c'havrai vedute nella mia Prim'Opera, hò voluto che gusti insieme e dell'uno, e dell'altro modo, facendomi à credere, che se non il Primo, il Secondo almeno sia per dilettarti [I return perhaps to annoy you with my present compositions for the theorbo, these, however, serving for the chamber and for this being carried out in a different style than you will have seen in my first work. I wanted you to try together first one and then the other type, convincing myself that if not the first then at least the second will delight you]."

Domenico Zanatta, *Suonate da chiesa à 3 strumenti, due violini e violoncello, col basso per l'organo*, Op. 1 (Bologna, 1689).

Giovanni Battista Gigli, *Sonate da chiesa e da camera à 3 strumenti, col basso continuo per l'organo*, Op. 1 (Bologna, 1690).

Benedetto Vinaccesi, *Sfere armoniche overo sonate da chiesa à due violini, con violoncello, è parte per l'organo*, Op. 2 (Venice, 1692).

Giovanni Maria Ruggieri, *Suonate da chiesa a due violini, e violone, ò tiorba con il suo basso continuo per l'organo*, Op. 3 (Venice, 1693).

Domenico Zanatta, *Concertini da camera e sonate da chiesa a trè, due violini, e violoncello, col basso continuo*, Op. 3 (Venice, 1696).

Bernardo Tonini, *Suonate da chiesa a tre, due violini & organo, con violoncello ad libitum*, Op. 2 (Venice, 1697).

Giovanni Maria Ruggieri, *Suonate da chiesa a due violini, e violoncello col suo basso continuo per l'organo*, Op. 4 (Venice, 1697).

Andrea Fiorè, *Sinfonie da chiesa à trè, cioè due violini, e violoncello con il suo basso continuo per l'organo*, Op. 1 (Modena, 1699).

Francesco Antonio Urio, *Sonate per chiesa à 5, due violini, e violone, col basso per l'organo, & una pastorale per il SS. Natale*, Op. 3 (Bologna, c.1700)—not extant, but listed in Giuseppe Antonio Silvani's catalog.

Giovanni Bianchi, *Sei concerti di chiesa a quattro, due violini, viola & violoncello col basso per l'organo, e sei sonate a tre, due violini, violoncello e basso per l'organo…*, Op. 2 (Amsterdam, 1703).

Domenico Dalla Bella, *Suonate da chiesa à tre, due violini, e violoncello obligato col basso per l'organo*, Op. 1 (Venice, 1704).

Louis Le Quoynte, *XVI Suonate da chiesa sopra sedici diversi tuoni a doi violini col basso per l'organo e viola da braccio con violoncello se piace*, Op. 4 (Amsterdam?, before 1704)—not extant, but listed in the music library from the estate of the Amsterdam music collector Nicolas Selhof, 1759.

Giuseppe Bergonzi, *Sinfonie da chiesa, e concerti a quattro a due violini concertati, e due ripieni con l'alto viola obbligata, col basso per l'organo*, Op. 2 (Bologna, 1708).

Tomaso Albinoni, *Sonate da chiesa a violino solo e violoncello o basso continuo*, Op. 4 (Amsterdam, c.1709).

Francesco Onofrio Manfredini, *Sinfonie da chiesa à due violini, col basso per l'organo & una viola à beneplacito, con una pastorale per il Santissimo Natale*, Op. 2 (Bologna, 1709).

Evaristo Felice Dall'Abaco, *Concerti a quattro da chiesa cioè due violini, alto viola, violoncello, e basso continuo*, Op. 2 (Amsterdam, 1712).

Evaristo Felice Dall'Abaco, *Sonate da chiesa e da camera* a tre cioè due violini, *violoncello e basso continuo*, Op. 3 (Amsterdam, 1712).

Giuseppe Matteo Alberti, *Concerti per chiesa, e per camera ad uso dell'accademia, eretta nella sala del sig. co. Orazio Leonardo Bargellini*, Op. 1 (Bologna, 1713).

Cesare Monteventi, *Sonate per chiesa a tre, due violini, e violone, o tiorba col basso continovo per l'organo*, Op. 1 (Bologna, 1718).

Domenico Patrizio Borghi, *Sonate per chiesa e per camera*, Op. 1 (Bologna, 1720).

Andrea Zani, *Sei sinfonie di camera e altretanti concerti da chiesa: à quattro stromenti*, Op. 2 (Casalmaggiore, 1729).

Paolo Bellinzani, *Dodici sonate da chiesa a 3 con due violini e basso ad imitazione di quelle di Corelli* (MS, c.1720–30).

Lorenzo Gaetano Zavateri, *Concerti da chiesa, e da camera*, Op. 1 (Bologna?, 1735).

Carlo Tessarini, *Sonate da camera e chiesa con pastoralle*, Op. 9 (Paris, c.1747).

Pier Luigi (Pietro Antonio?) Locatelli, *XII Sonate per chiesa e per camera*, no opus (Amsterdam? before 1759)—not extant, but listed in the music library from the estate of the Amsterdam music collector Nicolas Selhof, 1759.

Sources: Claudio Sartori, *Bibliografia della musica strumentale italiana stampata in Italia fino al 1700*, 2 vols (Florence: Olschki, 1952–68); Oscar Mischiati, ed., *Indici, cataloghi e avvisi degli editori e librai musicali italiani dal 1591 al 1798* (Florence: Olschki, 1984); *Indice delle opere di musica degli editori Bolognesi: M. Cazzati, G. Monti, M. Silvani, G.A. Silvani, eredi di G.A. Silvani* (Bologna: Forni, 1978); François Lesure, *Bibliographie des éditions musicales publiées par Estienne Roger et Michel-Charles Le Cène (Amsterdam, 1696–1743)* (Paris: Société Française de Musicologie, 1969); *Catalogue of the Music Library, Instruments and other Property of Nicolas Selhof, Sold in The Hague, 1759* (Amsterdam: Frits Knuf, 1973).

The significance of this usage emerges in the context of markedness. Referring again to the non-musical example of "nurse/male nurse," the term "female nurse" rarely occurs independently, because it is redundant. However, when describing a gathering of male and female nurses, a context in which we may want to specify a group that includes both genders, the designation "female" in proximity with "nurse" is made necessary. Similarly, the use of terms seen in Table 4.2 suggests the implicitness of church music in the unmarked term "sonata." Within the entire sonata repertory of the late seventeenth century, the independent use of the term "sonata da chiesa" occurs relatively infrequently (see Tables 4.1a–4.1c) because the sonata's churchliness is understood. "Sonata da chiesa" becomes the term of choice in opposition to "sonata da camera" within a title that includes both genres of sonata.

Sonata per Chiesa e per Camera

The nature of this terminological opposition merits further comment because it bears an ambiguity not illustrated in the analogy with male and female nurses. Seventeenth-century collections designated *da chiesa e da camera* refer to one of two things:

(1) a collection of works suitable for both church and chamber; or (2) a collection of works that comprises some for church and others for chamber. A look at individual titles and the specific contents that those titles describe clarifies which of these two possibilities applies. Those cases, however, change tellingly over time. Tables 4.3a–4.3c illustrate the first of the two possible meanings of titles that mix church and chamber designations in which the contents—sonatas or canzonas—are deemed suitable for both venues. Each of these collections includes dances, which we may presume were not appropriate for use in church, but the sonatas and canzonas are explicitly described as works for both church and chamber.

Table 4.3a   T. Merula, *Canzoni, overo sonate concertate per chiesa, e camera a due et a tre*, Op. 12 (Venice, 1637)

a due	a tre
La Gallina Canzon à 2 Violini	Ruggiero à doi Violini, & à 3, col Basso
La Pedrina Canzon à 2 Violini	Ballo detto Eccardo à doi Violini, & à 3, col Basso
La Treccha Canzon à 2 Violini	Chiacona à doi Violini, & à 3, col Basso
La Pollachina Canzon à 2 Violini	L'Ara Canzona à 3. doi Violini, col Basso
La Loda Canzon à 2 Violini	La Strada Canzon à 3. doi Violini, & Basso
La Pochetina Canzon à 2 Violini	Ballo detto Gennaro à 3. doi Violini, & Basso
La Bellina Canzon à 2 Violini	Ballo detto Pollicio à 3. doi Violini, & Basso
La Chisa Canzon à 2 Violini	
La Cattarina Canzon à 2 Violini	
La Bianca Canzon à 2 Violini	
La Ruggiera Canzon à 2 Violini	
La Maruta Canzon à 2 Violini	
La Merula Canzon à 2 Violini	
L'Arisia Canzon à 2 Violini	
La Dada Canzon à 2 Violini	
La Pighetta Canzon à 2 Violini	

Table 4.3b   M. Neri, *Sonate e canzone a quattro da sonarsi con diversi stromenti in chiesa & in camera con alcune correnti pure à quattro*, Op. 1 (Venice, 1644)

Canzone Prima à 3	Canzone Prima à 4	Corrente Prima
Canzone Seconda à 3	Canzone Seconda à 4	Corrente Seconda
Canzone Terza à 3	Sonata Prima à 4	Corrente Terza
Canzone Quarta à 3	Sonata Seconda à 4	Corrente Quarta
		Corrente Quinta
		Corrente Sesta

Table 4.3c   G. Legrenzi, *Suonate dà chiesa, e dà camera, correnti, balletti, allemande, e sarabande à tre, doi violini, e violone, con il basso continuo*, Op. 4 (Venice, 1656)

[Sonata] "La Brembata"	Corrente Prima	Sarabanda Prima
[Sonata] "La Secca Soarda"	Corrente Seconda	Alemana Prima "La Pozzi"
[Sonata] "La Benaglia"	Corrente Terza	Sarabanda Seconda
[Sonata] "La Tassa"	Corrente Quarta	Alemana Seconda "La Sanfiora"
[Sonata] "La Fini"	Corrente Quinta	Sarabanda Terza
[Sonata] "La Pezzoli"	Corrente Sesta	Alemana Terza "La Polini"
[Sonata] "La Calcagni"	Balletto Primo	
[Sonata] "La Biffi"	Balletto Secondo	
[Sonata] "La Terzi"	Balletto Terzo	
[Sonata] "La Strozzi"	Balletto Quarto	
[Sonata] "La Forni"	Balletto Quinto	
[Sonata] "La Tognini"	Balletto Sesto	

By contrast, Tables 4.4a–4.4d list sonata collections whose titles refer to church and chamber and whose individual pieces belong either to one or the other. This distinction in performing venue, moreover, becomes more and more explicit over time: Biagio Marini's Op. 22 collection (Table 4.4a) is ambiguous, but the sinfonias and sonatas stand apart from the dances as likely *da chiesa* pieces, and this is bolstered in the case of the sinfonias by their church-tone labels; Agostino Guerrieri's Op. 1 (Table 4.4b) offers a clearer case in which church sonatas are set apart from the dances and the Ruggiero variations in both the title and the table of contents; and Giovanni Battista Gigli's Op. 1 and Domenico Zanatta's Op. 3 (Tables 4.4c and 4.4d) instance collections in which the contents are divided unambiguously between church and chamber.

Table 4.4a   B. Marini, *Diversi generi di sonate, da chiesa, e da camera, a due, trè, & a quattro*, Op. 22 (Venice, 1655)

Balletto primo	Sinfonia primo tuono	Passacaglia a quattro & a trè, tralasciando la viola
Balletto secondo	Sinfonia secondo tuono	
Balletto terzo	Sinfonia terzo tuono	
Balletto quarto, Alemano	Sinfonia quarto tuono	
	Sinfonia quinto tuono	
Zarabanda prima	Sinfonia sesto tuono	
Zarabanda seconda		
Zarabanda terza		
Zarabanda quarta	Sonata per due violini ò cornetti	
	Sonata per violino e basso	
	Sonata prima à trè	
Corrente prima	Sonata seconda à trè	
Corrente seconda	Sonata terza, trè violini	
Corrente terza	Sonata quarta à quattro	
Corrente quarta		

Table 4.4b　　A. Guerrieri, *Sonate di violino a 1. 2. 3. 4. per chiesa, & anco aggionta per camera*, Op. 1 (Venice, 1673)

Sonata malinconica à solo	La Balbi, Sonata à 3	Balletto primo per camera
La Rotini, Sonata à solo	La Ravarina, à 3 violini	Balletto secondo
La Sevaschina, à solo	La Gotella, à 3 violini	Partite sopra Ruggiero
La Tità, à solo	La Pietra, à 3, due violini & teorba	
	La Viviani, à 3, due violini & teorba	
La Rezonicha, à 2 violini		
La Brignoli, à 2 violini	La Sevasca, à 4	
La Spinola, à 2 violini	La Rovetta, à 4	
La Benedetta, à 2 violini		
La Marchetta, à 2 violini		
La Rosciana, à 2 violini		
La Galeazza, à 2 violini		
La Pinella, à 2 violini		
La Lucina, à 2 violini,		
arpa over teorba		

Table 4.4c　　G. B. Gigli, *Sonate da chiesa, e da camera à 3 strumenti, col basso continuo per l'organo*, Op. 1 (Bologna, 1690)

Sonata Prima da Chiesa	Sonata Prima da Camera
Sonata Seconda da Chiesa	Sonata Seconda da Camera
Sonata Terza da Chiesa	Sonata Terza da Camera
Sonata Quarta da Chiesa	Sonata Quarta da Camera
Sonata Quinta da Chiesa	Sonata Quinta da Camera
Sonata Sesta da Chicsa	Sonata Sesta da Camera

Table 4.4d　　D. Zanatta, *Concertini da camera e sonate da chiesa a trè, due violini, e violoncello, col basso continuo*, Op. 3 (Venice, 1696)

Concertino Primo	Sonata Primo
Concertino Secondo	Sonata Secondo
Concertino Terzo	Sonata Terzo
Concertino Quarto	Sonata Quarto
Concertino Quinto	
Concertino Sesto	

The trend toward more explicit designations and toward the independence of the sonata da chiesa genre within mixed collections parallels the greater concentration of prints entirely devoted to sonatas da chiesa in the final decades of the seventeenth century. And yet, if I am correct in my earlier assertion that sonata used by itself connotes churchly music, we might wonder how the term "sonata da chiesa" came to be used as an independent designation at all. Allsop considers its occurrence within Italian sources to be anomalous, and he attributes its dissemination instead to misrepresentations by northern Europeans, starting with Brossard.[13] I would argue, on the contrary, that its use came about as part of a terminological reform on the part of Italians themselves—in particular, Bolognese music publishers. The post hoc revision of titles claimed by Allsop in fact occurs prior to Brossard in the catalogs of the Bolognese music seller and publisher, Marino Silvani. Tables 4.5a–4.5c illustrate the renaming of the works of Andrea Grossi (4.5a), Giovanni Battista Bassani (4.5b), and Giovanni Battista Vitali (4.5c) between the inventory catalogs of Giacomo Monti (1682) and Marino Silvani (1698–99), in which the unmarked designation "sonata" is changed to "sonata da chiesa." Simultaneously, listings of individual dances are replaced by the collective title "sonata da camera" in Tables 4.5b and 4.5c—a change in terminology already seen in Tables 4.1a–4.1c.

Table 4.5a   A. Grossi, Opp. 3 and 4: from "sonata" to "sonata da chiesa"

Opus (year)	(1) original title	(2) Giacomo Monti, 1682	(3) Marino Silvani, 169899
Op. 3 (1682)	*Sonate a due, trè, quattro, e cinque instromenti*	*Suonate a 2. 3. 4, e 5. instromenti, con alcune per tromba*	*Sonate da chiesa a 2. 3. 4. e 5. strumenti, con alcune per tromba*
Op. 4 (1685)	*Sonate a trè, due violini, e violone con il basso continuo per l'organo*	—	*Sonate da chiesa a 3. strumenti*

---

13 Allsop, "Italian Sonata," 239: "The expression 'sonata da chiesa' was rarely used in Italy before the last decade of the seventeenth century, and its later application to an earlier repertory must therefore rely to some extent on *post hoc* criteria. It seems that in this respect northern Europeans were privileged with a special insight which invested them with the right to change the titles of Italian publications if they did not comply with their preconceptions."

Table 4.5b   G. B. Bassani, Opp. 1 and 5: from "sonata" to "sonata da chiesa" and from individual dances to "sonata da camera" in catalog listings

Opus (year)	(1) Original title	(2) G. Monti, 1682 catalog	(3) M. Silvani, 1698–99 catalog	(4) *Catalogo* n.d.
Op. 1 (1677)	*Balletti, correnti, gighe, e sarabande à violino, e violone, overo spinetta, con il secondo violino à beneplacito*	*Balletti, gighe, correnti, e sarabande a violino, e violone, con il secondo violino se piace*	*Sonate da camera a 3 strumenti*	*Suonate da camera a 3 strumenti*
Op. 5 (1683)	*Sinfonie ["Suonate" in the table of contents] a due, e trè instromenti, con il basso continuo per l'organo*	—	*Sonate da chiesa a 3 strumenti*	*Suonate da chiesa a 2 e 3 strumenti col basso per l'organo*

Table 4.5c   G. B. Vitali, Opp. 1–5: from "sonata" to "sonata da chiesa" and from individual dances to "sonata da camera" in catalog listings

Opus (Year)	(1) Original Title	(2) G. Monti, 1682 catalog	(3) M. Silvani, 1698–99 catalog	(4) *Catalogo*, n.d.
Op. 1 (1666)	*Correnti, e balletti da camera a due violini, col suo basso continuo per spinetta, ò violone*	*Correnti, e balletti a 3, due violini, e violone*	*Sonate da camera a 3. strumenti*	*Suonate da camera a due violini, e violone*
Op. 2 (1667)	*Sonate a due violini, col suo basso continuo per l'organo*	*Suonate a due violini, col basso per l'organo*	—	—

Op. 3 (1667)	*Balletti, correnti alla francese, gagliarde, e brando per ballare. Balletti, correnti, e sinfonie da camera à quattro stromenti*	*Correnti, balletti, e gagliarde per ballare, correnti, Balletti, e sinfonie da camera a quattro instromenti*	*Sonate da camera a 4. strumenti*	*Sonate da camera a 4. strumenti*
Op. 4 (1668)	*Balletti, correnti, gighe, allemande, e sarabande à violino, e violone, ò spinetta, con il secondo violino a beneplacito*	*Correnti, balletti, gighe, allemande, e sarabande a violino, e violone, con il secondo violino a beneplacito*	*Sonate da camera a violino, e violone, col secondo violino a beneplacito*	*Suonate da camera a violino, e violone, col secondo violino a beneplacito*
Op. 5 (1669)	*Sonate a due, trè, quattro, e cinque stromenti*	*Suonate a 2. 3. 4. e 5. instrumenti*	*Sonate da chiesa a 2. 3. 4. e 5. strumenti*	*Suonate da chiesa a 2. 3. 4. 5. strumenti*

Sources: (1) Claudio Sartori, *Bibliografia della musica strumentale italiana stampata in Italia fino al 1700* (Florence: Olschki, 1952–68); (2) *Indice dell'opere di musica sin'hora stampate da Giacomo Monti in Bologna* (Bologna, 1682); (3) *Indice dell'opere di musica sin'hora stampate in Bologna. Si vendono da Marino Silvani …* (Bologna, 1698–99); (4) Giovanni Battista Martini, attrib., *Catalogo degli aggregati della Accademia Filarmonica di Bologna*, MS, I-Baf., n.d..

Specifically, Table 4.5a shows Monti's preservation of Grossi's Op. 3 title and Silvani's alteration of the Opp. 3 and 4 titles from the original "sonata" to "sonata da chiesa." Included in Tables 4.5b and 4.5c are listings from a further source, the *Catalogo degli Aggregati della Accademia Filarmonica* attributed to Giovanni Battista Martini;[14] and these tables show, again, closely similar listings for the original publications and Monti's 1682 catalog. Silvani, by contrast, is shown to have altered the titles of individual dances to "sonata da camera" and the unmarked

---

14 In recent decades, there has been some disagreement over whether Martini wrote this *Catalogo*. Sergio Durante, "Note su un Manoscritto 'Martiniano'," in *Padre Martini: musica e cultura nel Settecento europeo*, ed. Angelo Pompilio (Florence: Olschki, 1987), 123–33, dates the manuscript to around 1736 and attributes it to Olivo Penna with additions made by Martini. More recent arguments in favor of Martini's authorship, however, are advanced by Laura Callegari-Hill, "I primi storici dell'Accademia Filarmonica," in *Studi in onore di Guiseppe Vecchi*, ed. Italo Cavallini (Modena: Mucchi, 1989), 53–65, and Giuseppe Vecchi, "Per una storia dell'Accademia Filarmonica di Bologna, I. premessa: l'Accademia Filarmonica e le sue fonti storiche: Padre G. B. Martini," *Quadrivium* 2/1 (1991): 111–23.

"sonata" to "sonata da chiesa."[15] Also noteworthy are the similarities between Martini's listings and Silvani's. This latter information suggests a likely next step in the dissemination of the revised terminology: publisher's titles were copied by music historians and lexicographers who consulted such catalogs in their research. Giuseppe Ottavio Pitoni, for example, relied heavily on publishers' catalogs in the compilation of musical biographies for his *Notitia de' contrapuntisti e compositori di musica*, written around 1725.[16]

This is not to suggest that the newer terminology originated with one publisher in the 1690s. Rather, Silvani codified and disseminated that which was occurring already in the printed repertory during the 1670s, 80s, and 90s, as illustrated in Table 4.2. Furthermore, this trend is evidenced not only in Bolognese prints, but also in those from Modena and Venice.

Genre and Ethos; Context and Style

While this clarifies the use of sonata terminology, more remains to be said about its meaning and the motivation for the terminological changes described above. Composers and publishers designated sonatas (or at least thought of them) in terms of church and chamber venues because there was a tradition of classifying music in such terms, as seen in the taxonomies of Marco Scacchi, Angelo Berardi, and others.[17] This manner of categorizing musical genres could also be applied to voice types and, on occasion, to instruments. In these cases, the venue designation reflects the projecting qualities of the voice or instrument—loud, strong, or full being associated with the larger space of the church; soft or intimate, with the smaller chamber.[18] As discussed in the Introduction in connection with instrumental ensembles, unmarked sonatas

---

15 Marino Silvani's listing of unmarked sonatas as sonatas da chiesa may also be seen in the mini-catalogs of specific composers that he sometimes included in individual prints of their music. For instance, Silvani's *Indice delle opere del Bonporti* included in Bonporti's Op. 10 *Inventioni da camera* (Bologna, 1712), lists Bonporti's Op. 1 *Sonate à 3* as *Sonate da chiesa à 3*. Silvani's listing of *Opere sin ora date in luce da Giuseppe Valentini* in Valentini's Op. 7 *Concerti grossi* (Bologna, 1710), similarly alters Valentini's Op. 1 *Sinfonie à 3* to *Sinfonie per chiesa à 3*.

16 For example, see Pitoni, *Notitia de' contrapuntisti e compositori di musica*, MS, c.1725; modern ed. by Cesarino Ruini (Florence: Olschki, 1988), 232: "Biagio Marini. Musico e sonatore di violino del serenissimo di Parma.... *L'Indice* di musica del Vincenti porta le composizioni varie ... l'*Indice* del Franzini li madrigali, balletti e sinfonie a 1, 2, 3, 4."

17 For a discussion of this tradition of genre classification, which has roots in the Artusi–Monteverdi polemic and continues through Johann Mattheson's *Der vollkommene Capellmeister* (1739), see Claude Palisca, "The Genesis of Mattheson's Style Classification," in *New Mattheson Studies*, ed. George J. Buelow and Hans Joachim Marx (Cambridge: Cambridge University Press, 1983), 409–23.

18 See David Fallows, "The Performing Ensembles in Josquin's Sacred Music," *Tijdschrift van de Vereniging voor Nederlandse Muziekgeschiedenis* 35 (1985): 32–64, p. 54, n. 86. Fallows draws upon remarks by Vicentino, Zarlino, Zacconi, and others in support of his assertion that from the sixteenth century "church music was sung at a considerably higher dynamic level than court music."

and sonatas da chiesa almost always call for the organ as the continuo instrument, and sonatas da camera, the spinet or harpsichord. Some composers ensure a further distinction in sound volume between church and chamber sonatas by calling for organ in addition to the violone or violoncello in the former, as opposed to spinet or harpsichord in place of the bass string instrument in the latter.[19]

Beyond this eminently practical distinction, the testimony of sonata composers themselves both strengthens our understanding of the unmarked sonata as a genre conceived for a sacred context and sheds light on what may be described as its sacred ethos.[20] The Roman composer Giovanni Antonio Leoni, in the dedication of his sonatas for violin and continuo to Cardinal G. B. Pallotta, begins with a paean to the liturgical uses of music:

> The favorable patronage that Your Eminence holds for music (and for its professors) is already noted by the world, not availing yourself of it in a profane use to obtain delightful uplift from your gravest concerns, but employing it wholly in the divine service and cult. And who does not know that you have created for the virtuoso musicians in this city the venerable Chiesa della Lauretana Vergine [Santa Casa di Loreto], a sacred Parnassus, at which your noble talents are gathered innumerable times during the year to make devout pomp, now with sweetest *concenti* of divine praise and now with harmonious sinfonias, the very imitators of those angelic melodics that already have accompanied the Santa Casa when, with inaudible flight roaming over the seas on the paths toward heaven, they happily reached the Picene shores in order to enrich you with celestial treasures?[21]

---

19 Corelli is the most famous example. His *Sonate a trè*, Op. 1 (1681) and *Sonate à tre*, Op. 3 (1689) use "violone ò arcileuto col basso per l'organo"; by contrast, his *Sonate da camera a trè*, Op. 2 (1685) and *Sonate à tre*, Op. 4 (1694) call only for "violone ò cimbalo." This distinction of scoring in printed music between organ for sacred works and harpsichord or spinet for secular works is remarkably consistent throughout the seventeenth and early eighteenth centuries, and can be traced back to the beginning of the seventeenth in the scoring of two well known works: Lodovico da Viadana's *Cento concerti ecclesiastici*, which calls for organ accompaniment, and Claudio Monteverdi's fifth book of madrigals for five voices, which calls for "clavicembano, chittarone od altro simile istromento." See the Introduction (pp. 42–9) for a survey of instrumental ensembles in the Bolognese repertory.

20 Here we may note that the price in Silvani's catalogs of both unmarked sonatas and sonatas da chiesa were consistently higher in comparison with sonatas da camera or dances, and we may speculate that Silvani had a higher price in mind for the weightier genre.

21 Giovanni Antonio Leoni, *Sonate di violino a voce sola*, Op. 3 (Rome: Mascardi, 1652), dedication: "E' già notata al mondo la favorevol protettione che l'Eminenza Vostra tiene hoggidì della Musica, e de' professori di essa, non servendosene già ad uso profano per dilettevole sollevamento delle sue più gravi cure, mà impiegandola tutta al servitio, e culto divino. E chi non sà che ella à i Virtuosi Musici hà costituito in questa Città, la Venerabil Chiesa della Lauretana Vergine, come un sacro Parnaso, ove innumerabil volte trà l'anno si ragunano à far devota pompa de suoi nobil talenti, hor con dolcissimi concenti delle divine lodi, hor con armoniose Sinfonie, imitatrici apunto di quell'Angeliche melodie, che già accompagnarono la Santa Casa quando con volo inaudito peregrinando sovra i mari, per le vie del Cielo, felicemente giunse[ro] alle Picene spiagge per arricchirle di celesti tesori?"

Leoni then goes on to make it clear that his sinfonias, played in church in the presence of His Eminence, could fulfill that role, as Leoni says, "wholly in the divine service and cult":

> I avail myself of the belief that [my violin sonatas] can reasonably hope to merit in some part the favor of so worthy and noble protection, there being many of them composed by me expressly for the Church of the Santa Casa, mentioned above, and played there in the presence of Your Eminence.[22]

The Florentine violinist-composer Antonio Veracini makes the same distinction as does Leoni between mere sensual delight and a more profound, spiritual experience of the music. In the dedication of his Op. 1 *Sonate à tre* (1692) to the Grand Duchess of Tuscany, Veracini praises her deeper understanding of his sonatas:

> That the human soul is none other than a harmony was the view of Aristoxenus, *musico* and philosopher of antiquity. This opinion is born out in the great soul of your most serene highness, in which resounds a wondrous tuning of all of the virtues. So it is that you are nourished by the spirit of our music, which consists of fleeting sounds and songs. Yet your delight is solid when it is served by this [music], not for the simple titillation of the ears, but to return the soul to contemplation of the immortal and heavenly, then passing to the consideration of the divine.[23]

Equally informative is the 1685 dedication written by the Modenese composer Giovanni Bononcini to his teacher in Bologna, Giovanni Paolo Colonna, expressing his personal and professional debt:

> This is not otherwise a simple letter of unofficial dedication, but a confessional instrument of a most binding debt. I would have recorded this in the first of my efforts that I had taken to the presses had I not deemed this third one a more solid foundation for my intentions, wherein I undertake to perform for the church while in my first and second it served for me not to risk more than to jest for the chamber.[24]

---

22 Ibid., "mi giova credere, che possano ragionevolmente sperare di meritare in qualche parte il favore di sì degna, e nobil protettione, essendo molte di esse da mè composte à posta, e sonate nella sudetta Chiesa della Santa Casa alla presenza di Vostra Eminenza."

23 Veracini, Op. 1, dedication: "Che l'Anima umana, altro non fosse, che una Armonia, fu parere d'Aristosseno antico Musico, e Filosofo. Questa opinione si verifica nella grand'Anima di V. A. S. nella quale un mirabile accordamento di tutte le virtù perfettamente risuona. Quindi è, che ella pasce lo Spirito di questa nostra Musica, che in Suoni, e Canti passeggieri consiste; ma è solido il suo diletto, mentre si serve di quella, non per sollecicamento semplice dell'orecchio, ma per rimetter l'Anima nella contemplazione della Immortale, e Celeste; e quindi passare alla considerazione della Divina."

24 Giovanni Bononcini, *Sinfonie a 5. 6. 7. e 8. instrumenti, con alcune à una e due trombe, servendo ancora per violini*, Op. 3 (Bologna: Monti, 1685), dedication: "Questa non è altrimente una semplice lettera d'ufficiosa Dedica, mà un'instromento confessionale di strettissimo debito. Havrei dovuto registrarlo nel primo de gli ardimenti, che mi son preso con le Stampe, se non havessi stimato più sodo fondamento alla mia intentione questo terzo, dove imprendo ad operare per Chiesa, quando nel primo, e nel secondo convenne non m'arrischiassi à più, che à scherzare per Camera."

Significantly, Bononcini's third "effort" conceived as church music and dedicated to a church musician, bears the unmarked title of *Sinfonie*, in which *da chiesa* is understood. His testimony also underscores the elevated status of the church genres over the chamber, which we may analogize with the spiritual over the physical on the basis of Leoni's and Veracini's dedications. In the preface to his sonatas da chiesa, the Brescian composer Benedetto Vinaccesi testifies to this same distinction in prestige associated with the churchly venue, writing that

> when these [sonatas] are heard in church, they invite you to a place where errors are more readily pardoned and where a virtuous spirit extends its mantle of protection more easily over such defects that can be discovered by modern Aristarchuses of this genre, on whose small heads are Ears of Syracuse larger than a mountain.[25]

The association made between sacred venue, spiritual function, and more refined, if demanding, music is thus made clear.[26] Vinaccesi's modest attitude, however, raises another issue that has consequences for our sense of genre within the sonata repertory: one of function, or practical use, and its independence from style as indicated by designations of venue. As sonatas da chiesa, Vinaccesi's compositions are appropriate for performance in church, but there is nothing to say that they

---

25 Benedetto Vinaccesi, *Sfere armoniche overo sonate da chiesa à due violini, con violoncello, e parte per l'organo*, Op. 2 (Venice: Sala, 1692), preface to the *dilettante amorevole*: "facendosi essi sentir nella Chiesa, t'invitano in un Luogo dove più facilmente si perdonano gli errori, e dove l'Animo Virtuoso distende con più agevolezza il manto della sua Prottezione sù quei difetti, che ponno venir scoperti da moderni Aristarchi di questo Genere, nel piccol Capo de quali vi sono Orecchie di Siracusa più grandi d'un Monte." Two of Vinaccesi's metaphors merit explanation. Aristarchus (c.217–145 BC) was a celebrated philologist and librarian from Samothrace. Because of his severe revisions of Homer's poetry, stern critics after him came to be known as *Aristarchi*. "Orecchie di Siracusa" (ears of Syracuse) refers to a cave near the Sicilian city whose opening is shaped like a pointed ear. Its proper name is the Ear of Dionysius, named for Dionysius the Elder (c.430–367 BC), tyrant of Syracuse, who eavesdropped on the conversations of the prisoners he kept there. According to legend the acoustics within the cave enabled Dionysius to hear even the softest whispers of the conspiring prisoners.

26 Gioseffo Placuzzi, *Il numero sonoro, lodolato in modo armonici et aritmetici di balletti, correnti, gighe, allemande, sarabande, e capricci*, Op. 2 (Bologna: Monti, 1682), a fancifully titled collection of courtly dances, draws upon the same distinction in propriety between the secular and the sacred in its dedication to Ippolito Venetico, canon at the cathedral of Ferrara, but with reference to the dedicatee's social standing as a cleric rather than to any specific performing context. The dedication begins as follows: "Molt'Illustre e Reverendissimo Signore. Presento al Merito di V. S. Reverendissima questo mio debolissimo Parto, in segno di contributione in qualche parte di quanto devo alla sua bontà; e se bene sò non essere il dono proportionato, per essere questi miei trattenimenti per Camera più adatati à Secolari che a persona Ecclesiastica, nulla di meno, per genio, che lei ha alla Musica, mi persuado saranno grati alla sua benignità [Most Illustrious and Reverend Signore, I present to the merit of your Most Reverend Lordship this poorest offspring as a sign of contribution toward some part of that which I owe to your generosity. And, even though I know that the gift is not proportional (these entertainments of mine for the chamber being more suited to secular persons than to a cleric), I am nonetheless persuaded that they will be pleasing to your kindliness]."

are destined exclusively for it. In this case, Vinaccesi's tentativeness leads him to prefer that his church sonatas be tried out in a more forgiving context than a church service.

Two prints from the early eighteenth century give us more explicit information on the connections among genre designations, musical style, and probable performing contexts. The setting in both cases is neither church nor chamber, but instead the *accademia*, that is, a performance usually in a *sala* (hall) or theater within an aristocrat's home. Musical style, however, continues to be conceived according to the familiar dichotomy between church and chamber. The title of Giuseppe Matteo Alberti's Op. 1 (Bologna, 1713) makes this clear: *Concerti per chiesa, e per camera ad uso dell'accademia, eretta nella sala del sig. conte Orazio Leonardo Bargellini* [Church and chamber concertos for use of the *accademia* held in the hall of the Signor Count Orazio Leonardo Bargellini]. The *Concertini accademici à quattro*, Op. 4 (Bologna, 1708), by an author who refers to himself as Accademico Formato (probably Francesco Giuseppe De Castro), furnishes a more detailed description of its contents with respect to style and performing venue.[27] In an introductory note, the Accademico Formato summarizes the several musical styles of his concertos:

> Intention of the author ... he has entitled these sonatas "Concerti accademici";[28] however, if we consider the style that he has maintained, these are not to be called sonatas da camera because of the number of instruments that is required according to the intention of this same author [multiple strings per part are called for in order to balance the trumpet or oboe that is called for in several concertos]. Nor are they for the church because, aside from the fourth concerto, the others seem to him more for the *accademia*, or for the theater.[29]

---

27 The styling "Accademico Formato," although used by De Castro in his *Trattenimenti armonici*, Op. 1 (1695) means only that the author of the *Concerti accademici* was, like De Castro, a member of the Accademia de Formati that was founded within the Jesuit Collegio de' Nobili of Brescia. For further information on De Castro and the instrumental repertory associated with the Brescian Collegio, see Marco Bizzarini, "Diffusione della sonata a tre nella Brescia di fine Seicento: il ruolo del Collegio de' Nobili," in *Barocco padano I: atti del IX Convegno Internazionale sulla Musica Sacra nei Secoli XVII–XVIII*, ed. Alberto Colzani, Andrea Luppi, and Maurizio Padoan (Como: Antiquae Musicae Italicae Studiosi, 2002), 279–309. On the authorship of the *Concerti accademici*, see Bizzarini, 301, n. 56.

28 Although it may seem otherwise, there is neither ambiguity nor confusion in this reference to sonatas as concertos and vice versa. See Chapter 7, pp. 333–6 for an explication of concerto terminology that demystifies juxtapositions of this kind.

29 Accademico Formato [Francesco Giuseppe De Castro?], *Concerti accademici à quattro, cioè un' oboè, due violini, e violone, con la parte per il cembalo*, Op. 4 (Bologna: Peri, 1708): "Intenzione dell'autore ... Hà posto in fronte à queste Sonate il titolo di Concerti Accademici; imperochè, se si considerii lo stile, che hà tenuto, non sono da dirsi Sonate da Camera, attesa la moltiplicità di Strumenti, che secondo l'intenzione del medemo Autore, vi si richiede: non sono ne meno da Chiesa; perchè, toltone il Concerto Quarto, gl'altri tutti sembrano à lui più tosto da Accademia, ò da Teatro." De Castro's comments point out that, as mentioned above, the ensemble itself (or rather, its size and the volume of sound it could produce) was a significant criterion in how music was classified according to venue.

In seeking to put a finer point on venue-based style categories, the Accademico Formato begins by ruling out the traditional church and chamber venues for his concertos. His concertos are instead stylistically appropriate for the *accademia* and the theater, excepting the fourth, which he singles out as suitable for the church. In sum, Alberti and the Accademico Formato detail in the early eighteenth century what is left unclear in testimony from the late seventeenth: churchly style and performance in church were by no means the same thing. Therefore, neither the actual performing contexts nor patronage by a secular person belies churchly style. Rather, it was the norm to create and perform instrumental ensemble music—often bearing the unmarked designation of "sonata"—in theaters, in aristocratic academies, or elsewhere, while simultaneously conceiving such works as churchly in stylistic terms.

* * *

A final point concerns chronology: the use of the term "sonata da chiesa" independently is limited to the decades around the turn of the eighteenth century—that is, it appears among northern Italian prints starting with Bononcini's Op. 6 (Venice, 1672) and continues on until the decline of Italian music publishing in the 1720s. This decline supplies a clear reason for the disappearance of "sonata da chiesa" as a genre designation, which was rarely found in publications of Italian music by Amsterdam, London, and Parisian printers. By contrast, the performance of sonatas in church may be traced at least to the beginning of the seventeenth century. As before, the evidence is found in prints, but not those devoted solely to instrumental music. It is instead in mixed collections of vocal and instrumental genres that we may perceive the "discovery" of ensemble sonatas as church music. To judge from a decade-by-decade listing of such prints (Tables 4.6a–4.6c), composers began to add the instrumental canzona (and related sonata and sinfonia) to prints of masses, motets, and spiritual madrigals with increased frequency between the 1590s and the 1610s. Simultaneously, these same instrumental genres are less and less frequently represented in "secular" prints containing madrigals and canzonette. In short, printed collections from around the turn of the seventeenth century document the rising popularity of instrumental ensemble music as a complement to sacred vocal genres in worship. In practice, the church sonata begins here, and the terminology specific to this development would follow later in the century.

Table 4.6a   Printed collections of mixed genres, vocal and instrumental—1590–99

Sacred			Secular		
Year	**Author, Title**	**Contents**	**Year**	**Author, Title**	**Contents**
1595	Adriano Banchieri, *Concerti ecclesiastici*	motets; *canzoni francesi*	1590	Orazio Scaletta, *Amorosi pensieri, il secondo libro de madrigaletti*	*madrigaletti a cinque voci con una canzone francese à 4*

Sacred			Secular		
Year	**Author, Title**	**Contents**	**Year**	**Author, Title**	**Contents**
1597	Alessandro Marino, *Il primo libro di madrigali spirituali con una canzone a dodeci nel fine*	Spiritual madrigals; canzone a 12	1590	Lodovico Viadana, Canzonette a quatro voci	*canzonette* [songs] *& un'aria di canzon francese per sonare*
1597	Giovanni Gabrieli, *Sacrae symphoniae*	motets; canzonas; sonatas	1590	Various authors, *Dialoghi musicali*	*dialoghi* [madrigals] *con ... battaglie a otto voci, per sonar*
1599	Lodovico Bellandà, *Canzonette spirituali*	*canzoni spirituali* [songs]; *canzone a 3 da sonare*; *canzone a 4 da sonare*	1591	Various authors, *Intermedii et concerti ... nelle nozze del Serenissimo Don Ferdinando Medici*	Florentine intermedii, including sinfonias
			1592	Valerio Buona, *Il secondo libro delle canzonette*	*dodeci tercetti a note sole* [instrumental]
			1597	Giovanni Cavaccio, *Musica ... ove si contengono due fantasie, che dan principio e fine all'opera, canzoni alla franzese, pavana co'l saltarello, madrigali, & un proverbio*	*canzoni alla franzese, pavana co 'l saltarello, madrigali*
			1597	*Fiori del giardino di diversi eccelentissimi autori*	madrigals & canzonette, canzonas

Source: Claudio Sartori, *Bibliografia della musica strumentale italiana stampata in Italia fino al 1700* (Florence: Olschki, 1952–68).

Table 4.6b   Printed collections of mixed genres, vocal and instrumental—1600–09

Sacred			Secular		
Year	Author, Title	Contents	Year	Author, Title	Contents
1601	Gabriele Fattorini, *Il secondo libro de mottetti a otto voci*	motets, *canzona francese a 4*	1600 or 1601	Orazio Vecchi, *Canzonette a quattro*	canzonette [songs], saltarello, fantasia
1602	Lodovico Viadana, *Cento Concerti ecclesiastici*	*concerti* [concerted motets], *canzona francese*	1603	Francesco Stivorio, *Madrigali et canzoni a otto voci*	madrigals, canzonas
1603	Costantio Antegnati, *Missa Borromea, mottecta, cantionesque gallicae*	mass, motets, *canzoni francesi*			
1604	Giacomo Moro Viadana, *Concerti ecclesiastici*	motets, Magnificat, canzonas			
1606	Aloisio [Luigi] Balbi, *Concerti ecclesiastici ... con una canzone a quattro*	motets, canzona			
1607	Giulio Radino, Padovano, *Concerti per sonare et cantare ... cioè canzone, & ricercari à quattro, & otto, mottetti, messe, salmi, & Magnificat ...*	motets, masses, psalms, Magnificat, *canzoni francesi a 4*			

Sacred			Secular		
Year	Author, Title	Contents	Year	Author, Title	Contents
1607	Adriano Banchieri, *Ecclesiastiche sinfonie dette canzoni in aria francese a quattro voci, per sonare, et cantare*	motet-canzonas			
1608	Agostino Soderino, *Canzoni à 4 e 8 voci*	motets, canzonas			
1609	Hercole Porta, *Giardino di spirituali concerti*	motets, *sinfonia per sonare a 2*			
1609	Caterina Assandra, *Motetti*	motets, *canzone à 4. accomodata à suonare à duoi chori*			

Table 4.6c   Printed collections of mixed genres, vocal and instrumental—1610–15

Sacred			Secular		
Year	Author, Title	Contents	Year	Author, Title	Contents
1610	Claudio Monteverdi, *Sanctissimae Virgini Missa senis vocibus, ac vesperae pluribus*	mass, vespers, Magnificats, Ave maris stella, *Sonata sopra Sancta Maria a 8*	1611	Marc'Antonio Negri, *Affetti amorosi*	secular songs, sinfonias, sonatas

Sacred			Secular		
Year	Author, Title	Contents	Year	Author, Title	Contents
1610	Giovanni Paolo Cima, *Concerti ecclesiastici ... messa, e doi Magnificat, & falsi bordoni à 4, & sei sonate per instrumenti à due, tre, e quattro*	mass, motets, Magnificats, capriccios, *falsi bordoni,* sonatas			
1610	Antonio Mortaro, *Secondo libro delle messe, salmi, Magnificat, canzoni da suonare*	masses, psalms, Magnificat, falsi bordoni, canzonas			
1611	Amante Franzoni, *Concerti ecclesiastici*	motets, psalms, *canzoni francesi*			
1612	Adriano Banchieri, *Canzoni alla francese*	canzonas, fantasias, Magnificat			
1612	Antonio Cangiasi, *Melodia sacra quatuor, et quinque vocibus. Cum duobus motectis ad modum dialogi, & uno cum canzon francese*	motets, *canzona francese*			
1612	Giovanni Battista Riccio, *Il primo libro delle divine lodi ...*	motets, canzonas			

Sacred			Secular		
Year	**Author, Title**	**Contents**	**Year**	**Author, Title**	**Contents**
1613	Giulio Belli, *Concerti ecclesiastici a due et a tre voci*	motets, canzonas			
1613	Stefano Bernardi, *Motetti in cantilena a quattro voci con alcune canzoni per sonare*	motets, sonatas			
1613	Serafino Patta, *Sacrorum canticorum ...*	motets, canzonas *da sonare*			
1613	Giovanni Ghizzolo, *Messe, motetti, Magnificat, canzoni francese*	masses, motets, Magnificat, *falsi bordoni*, canzonas			
1613	Alessandro Grandi, *Il secondo libro de mottetti*	motets, sinfonia			
1614	Giovanni Battista Riccio, *Messa, & Magnificat a due voci, motetti a una, due, tre, & quattro, con alcune canzoni da sonare, a duoi & a quattro stromenti*	mass, motets, Magnificat, canzonas, sonata			
1614	Pietro Lappi, *Sacrae melodiae*	motets, sinfonias			

Sacred			Secular		
Year	**Author, Title**	**Contents**	**Year**	**Author, Title**	**Contents**
1614	Francesco Usper, *Messa, e Salmi da concertarsi nel'organo et anco con diversi stromenti ... et insieme sinfonie, et motetti*	mass, motets, sinfonias			
1614	Antonio Coma da Cento, *Sacrae cantiones*	motets, instrumental pieces *a 4*			
1615	Archangelo Borsaro, *Concerti diversi*	motets, *capriccio da sonare*			

At this juncture, two main points bear reiterating. First, during the late seventeenth century "sonata" and "sonata da chiesa" are generically equivalent designations. Second, while the term *da chiesa* connotes a more serious and learned style than does *da camera*, it does not impose restrictions on the use of the music it describes. Rather, "sonata da chiesa" implies appropriateness for the given venue by virtue of musical style; simultaneously, the genre may be considered a stylistically distinctive and functionally multi-purpose.

Example 4.1, an instrumental work in four parts composed by Tomaso Antonio Vitali in 1706, illustrates these main points in exceptional detail.[30] Vitali composed it for the purpose of attaining the rank of *compositore* in the Bolognese Accademia Filarmonica. As later recorded in the *Catalogo degli aggregati della Accademia Filarmonica* mentioned earlier, Vitali's application was successful.[31] The *Catalogo* also records that in the same year Vitali was selected by the *principe* of the Accademia to provide a sinfonia for the Mass given in the annual celebration of the feast of St Anthony of Padua, patron saint of the Accademia Filarmonica.[32] The chronological proximity of Vitali's promotion (July 8) and the annual celebration of the feast of St Anthony (July 13)[33] suggests that the same sinfonia that Vitali had presented to the Accademia for promotion was used during its festive Mass. If, however, the sinfonias of July 8 and July 13 are two different compositions, we may surmise at the very least that they were generically equivalent compositions, both called "sinfonia" used at the two different venues, musical *accademia* and sacred ceremony.

---

30 The original manuscript of Vitali's composition, which bears neither a title nor an indication of instrumentation, is found in the archives of the Accademia Filarmonica di Bologna (I-Baf) under the shelf-mark capsa II, n. 36.

31 *Catalogo degli aggregati della Accademia Filarmonica di Bologna*, MS, c.1736, facsimile with foreword by Anne Schnoebelen (Bologna: n.p., 1973), n. 402: "a 8 Luglio 1706 passò nell'ordine dei Compositori, avendo a tal'effetto presentato all'Accademia una sua Sinfonia a 4° egregiamente composta, qual si conserva con molte altre nella scanzia di nostra Residenza [on July 8, 1706 he attained the rank of composer, having presented to the Accademia for that purpose an extremely well composed sinfonia *a 4*, which is kept with many others in the bookcase of our residence]."

32 Ibid., "L'anno 1706 in occasione di celebrarsi dalla nostra Università la festa di S. Antonio di Padova Prottetore compose e suonò la Sinfonia universalmente applaudita [In the year 1706 on the occasion of the celebration in our university of the feast of St. Anthony of Padua, he composed and played the sinfonia, which was universally applauded]."

33 Osvaldo Gambassi, *L'Accademia Filarmonica di Bologna* (Florence: Olschki, 1992), 282–94, records that between the years 1667 and 1762, the Festa di S. Antonio was usually celebrated within the four or five weeks after St Anthony's feast day of June 13.

Example 4.1   T. A. Vitali, Sinfonia à 4 (1706), MS, I-Baf, capsa II, No. 36

Example 4.1   cont'd

Example 4.1   cont'd

iii. Grave

iv. Allegro assai

The Vitali sinfonia is, therefore, an example of an unmarked genre of instrumental music, stylistically appropriate for the church, but used in both sacred and secular contexts. In terms of the richly informative circumstances of this composition, no better model for a sonata da chiesa could exist. We should note, however, that Vitali's composition is neither called sonata nor designated *da chiesa*. And with that, we may begin to appreciate the intricacies of genre terminology and performing venue in Bolognese instrumental music.

Chapter Five

Sacred Music, Musical *Topoi*, and the Sonata in Church*

In S. Peter's Church [in Cento, Emilia], we saw a Picture of S. Francis and S. Bernard in an Ecstasy; an Angel in the Clouds is playing on the Violin; and the Harmony overpowers the Saints. This Subject is pretty frequent in Italy.[1]

If a close look at late-*Seicento* sonata terminology validates the idea of a "churchly" sonata among Italian composers and publishers, then we might expect the stylistic profiles of church and chamber sonatas—especially those published in Bologna—to bear out the terminology. The practice, however, was not so simple. Precisely in the period of terminological change that culminates in Sébastien de Brossard's clear-cut distinction between church and chamber sonatas, the two genres show evidence of a stylistic confluence.[2] Nor do taxonomies of style found in Italian theory shed much light on the matter: neither Marco Scacchi nor his student Angelo Berardi deal with instrumental music in their otherwise revealing categorizations of musical genres.[3]

---

*   An earlier version of this chapter appears as "Church Music, Musical *Topoi*, and the Ethos of the Sonata da chiesa," in *Atti del Sesto Congresso Internazionale di Studi Corelliani*, 2 vols, Gregory Barnett, Antonella D'Ovidio, and Stefano La Via, eds. (Florence: Olschki, 2007), 529–72.

1   Edward Wright, Esq., *Some Observations Made in Travelling through France, Italy, &c. in the Years 1720, 1721, and 1722*. 2 vols (London: Ward and Wicksteed, 1730), 107.

2   Sébastien de Brossard, *Dictionnaire de musique*, 3rd ed. (Amsterdam: Roger, c.1708; facsimile, Geneva: Minkoff, 1992), "Suonata" (pp. 139–40), English trans. based on Albion Gruber: "Il y en a pour ainsi dire, d'une infinité de manieres, mais les Italiens les reduisent ordinairement sous deux genres. Le premier comprend, les Sonates *da Chiesa*, c'est a dire, propres pour l'Eglise, qui commencent ordinairement par un mouvement *grave* & *majesteux*, proportionné à la dignité & sainteté du lieu; ensuite duquel on prend quelque Fugue gaye & animée, &c. Ce sont-là proprement ce qu'on apelle *Sonates*. Le second genre comprend les *Sonates* qu'ils apellent *da Camera*, c'est à dire, propres pour la Chambre. Ce sont proprement des suites de plusieurs petites pieces propres à faire danser, & composees sur le même Mode ou Ton [One could say that there is an infinity of styles, but the Italians reduce them ordinarily to two types. The first comprises the sonatas *da chiesa*—which is to say proper to the church— that begin usually with a *grave* and *majestic* movement, suited to the dignity and sanctity of the place; after which comes some sort of gay and animated fugue, etc. These are what one properly calls *sonatas*. The second type comprises the *sonatas* called *da camera*—which is to say, proper to the chamber. These are actually suites of several little pieces suitable for dancing and composed in the same mode or key]."

3   Angelo Berardi, *Miscellanea musicale* (Bologna: Monti, 1689; facsimile, Bologna: Forni, 1970), 40–41. See also Claude Palisca, "The Genesis of Mattheson's Style Classification,"

Given the complexities of genre terminology and the seeming confluence of church and chamber styles of sonata, recent scholars have tended to minimize or even dismiss distinctions between the two kinds of sonata.[4] Although such views hardly accord with the testimony and terminological usage surveyed in the previous chapter, it is difficult to argue otherwise when the testimony of composers and other writers typically omits any discussion of musical detail in favor of vague (if interesting) references to churchly affect and decorum. But rather than rely on our own assessments of musical style, let us instead take Bolognese sonata composers and publishers at their word and ask how the church sonata could have been perceived as churchly. Or, to frame the question in more specific terms, if sonatas da camera evoke all things courtly through their succession of courtly dance types (allemanda, corrente, sarabanda, giga, and so forth), what are the movement types in sonatas da chiesa that composers and their audiences recognized as distinctively churchly?

---

in *New Mattheson Studies*, ed. G. Buelow and H. J. Marx (Cambridge: Cambridge University Press, 1983), 409–23, which surveys late sixteenth- and seventeenth-century classifications of style, particularly that of Scacchi. See also Palisca, "Scacchi's Defense of Modern Music," *Words and Music: The Scholar's View*, ed. L. Berman (Cambridge, MA: Department of Music, Harvard University, 1972), 189–235.

4   Michael Talbot, "Arcangelo Corelli," *The New Grove Dictionary of Music and Musicians*, 2nd ed., ed. S. Sadie and J. Tyrrell, 29 vols (London: Macmillan Publishers Inc., and New York: Grove's Dictionaries Inc., 2001), vol. 6, 460: "In formal matters, Corelli is often credited with the clearest exposition of the difference between the 'church' and 'chamber' varieties of sonata, and the establishment of four movements as the norm in both. These generalizations require much qualification. As early as opp.1 and 2 the first signs of convergence of the two varieties are apparent. All but three of the op. 2 works have preludes (Corelli's term was taken up by many other composers) modelled on the opening slow movement of his typical church sonata, and nos. 3 and 4 contain additional 'abstract' movements. In op. 3 the church idiom comes closer to the chamber idiom in harbouring a greater proportion of movements in quick tempo and binary form, while the representation of abstract movements in the op. 4 chamber sonatas shows a slight increase over op. 2." Peter Allsop, "The Italian Sonata and the Concept of the 'Churchly,'" *Barocco padano I: atti del IX Convegno Internazionale sulla Musica Sacra nei Secoli XVII–XVIII*, ed. A. Colzani, A. Luppi, and M. Padoan (Como: Antiquae Musicae Italicae Studiosi, 2002), 239–47, p. 246: "behests that music in the liturgy should be 'churchly, grave, and devout', were not prescriptive but little more than pious exhortations. Ensemble sonatas may have been used in church but they were not intrisincally 'church music', not ritual instrumental music but instrumental music used ritualistically." Allsop, *The Italian "Trio" Sonata: From its Origins until Corelli* (Oxford: Clarendon Press, and New York: Oxford University Press, 1992), 66: "The various papal legislations … concern instrumental as much as vocal music, and the former was particularly susceptible to the influence of such profane melodies as dances and battaglie. As this was particularly true of Rome itself … they may have been mainly concerned with the removal of local abuses. The term 'da chiesa' never occurs in the context of Roman instrumental ensemble music since there was no church style easily recognizable by its grave and sober character. This may not accord with long-standing beliefs about the nature of church music at this period, but if composers could have agreed on a fixed and acceptable concept of a 'churchly' style in the seventeenth century, this would have relieved them of much unpleasantness, if not to say persecution, from the papal authorities."

This question is underscored by terms used today to describe (or replace) "sonata da chiesa" that are, in essence, negative descriptors: "abstract," "free," or (from my own previous work) "non-dance."[5] Such terms indicate only that which is absent; therefore, the aim of this chapter is to fill this void by tracing the stylistic influences that link instrumental ensemble music to a range of sacred genres. Composers of sonatas and concertos drew on *topoi* of seventeenth-century sacred music that were commonly heard and recognized as part of the Catholic liturgy.[6] In this way, the church sonata itself evoked for its listeners the solemnity of the church and affects of devotion. To put it literatim, musical *topoi* drawn from the church marked the sonata as churchly.

* * *

We may begin this examination of musical style and its expressive implications by considering what composers regarded as churchly in music for instrumental ensemble. An example at hand, the fourth concerto from the Accademico Formato's *Concerti accademici*, is the piece that its composer considered the churchly exception within his collection of "academic" concertos (see Chapter 4, pp. 182–3). The piece includes a fugal finale on a subject and countersubject (Example 5.1). Although the finale is an unremarkable fugue, it does give the impression of greater contrapuntal intricacy when compared with an allegro from any of the other concertos more properly considered *accademico*. For instance, the second movement from his first concerto (Example 5.2) features merely *concitato* dash within a simple textural and harmonic framework. For the Accademico Formato churchly propriety thus entails a degree of contrapuntal learning and perhaps less theatricality. This accords with what we saw in Tomaso Antonio Vitali's sinfonia, introduced at the end of the previous chapter (Example 4.1): the second-movement fugue of that piece, for example, features invertible counterpoint. One of its two subjects, moreover, fits the profile of a *stile antico* point of imitation, a *topos* that we will examine more closely further on in this chapter.

---

5   Gregory Barnett, "Musical Issues of the Late *Seicento*: Style, Social Function, and Theory in Emilian Instrumental Music," Ph.D. dissertation, Princeton University, 1997.

6   Leonard Ratner, *Classic Music: Expression, Form, and Style* (New York: Schirmer, 1980), is the seminal work on topics and musical expression of the Classical era. His single chapter on topics (pp. 9–30) presents a lexicon of them and the evidence for their basis in eighteenth-century musical thought. A more recent contribution to musical topic theory is that of Raymond Monelle, *The Sense of Music* (Princeton, NJ: Princeton University Press, 2000). His second and third chapters, "The Search for Topics" and "Topic and Leitmotiv," furnish thoughtful and wide-ranging treatments of the subject.

Example 5.1   Accademico Formato, Op. 4, No. 4 (1708)

Example 5.2   Accademico Formato, Op. 4, No. 1 (1708)

Ricercar Cromatico

The idea of a more learned or severe style in instrumental music recalls Brossard's recommendation that the sonatas for the church be "suited to the dignity and sanctity of the place," which is itself a distillation of ideas already expressed among the composers quoted in the previous chapter.[7] Such broad conceits of churchly dignity and sanctity, however, furnish only a starting point for analyzing the musical style of sonatas. In order to do better than vaguely associate good counterpoint with the church and dances with the chamber, we must turn to music solidly connected to the church for comparison with sonatas. The richest repertory in this respect is that written for the organ, and the most informative sources of this music are treatises on playing the organ in church, compendia of organ music for the church year, and published masses that include instrumental genres to accompany portions of the

---

7   See n. 1 in this chapter for Brossard's definition of church and chamber sonatas.

liturgy.[8] These are the sources that Stephen Bonta investigated in order to detail the liturgical contexts for instrumental music in his path-breaking article, "The Uses of the Sonata da Chiesa."[9] We return to them here to search out musical *topoi* common to the sacred repertory for organ and for the church sonata.

Two examples (Examples 5.3a and 5.3b) that offer a more detailed perspective of fugal style within the sonata repertory are drawn from works by Giovanni Bononcini and Arcangelo Corelli. Both excerpts illustrate an important *topos* among sonatas: the *ricercar cromatico*, an imitative work on a chromatic subject usually for keyboard. The genre is also characterized by strict contrapuntal techniques, such as subject inversion and invertible counterpoint.[10] By the latter part of the seventeenth century, the keyboard ricercar was considered a highly esteemed, if antiquated, genre. In the introduction to his Op. 3 *Ricercari* for organ (1669), the composer and organist Luigi Battiferri refers to it as "nearly extinct" and as a genre made famous by great keyboardists of the past: Luzzasco Luzzaschi, Ercole Pasquini, and, not least, Girolamo Frescobaldi. Battiferri also describes the ricercar as "the most learned of genres for playing, like the *cappella* genre of composing."[11] By the late *Seicento* the ricercar thus bears a distinguishing mark of erudition and long-standing tradition.

---

8   Adriano Banchieri, *L'organo suonarino*, Op. 13 (Venice: Amadino, 1605; facsimile, Bologna: Forni, 1969); Amante Franzoni, *Apparato musicale di messa, sinfonie, canzoni, motetti, & letanie della Beata Vergine a otto voci, con la partitura de bassi*, Op. 5 (Venice: Amadino, 1613); Bernardino Bottazzi, *Choro et organo, primo libro in cui con facil modo s'apprende in poco tempo un sicuro methodo di sonar sú 'l organo messe, antifone, & hinni* (Venice: Vincenti, 1614; facsimile, Bologna: Forni, 1980); Stefano Bernardi, *Concerti ecclesiastici* (Venice: Vincenti, 1616); Giovanni Battista Milanuzzi, *Armonia sacra* (Venice: Vincenti, 1622); Girolamo Frescobaldi, *Fiori musicali di diversi compositioni, toccate, kirie, canzoni, capricci, e ricercari*, Op. 12 (Venice: Vincenti, 1635; facsimile with an introduction by Luigi Ferdinando Tagliavini, Bologna: Forni, 2000); Giovanni Salvatore, *Ricercari a quattro voci, canzoni francesi, toccate, et versi per rispondere nelle messe con l'organo al choro* (Naples: Beltrano, 1641); Antonio Croci, *Frutti musicali di messe tre ecclesiastiche per rispondere alternatamente al choro ... con cinque canzoni & un ricercaro cromaticho*, Op. 4 (Venice: Vincenti, 1642); Giovanni Battista Fasolo, *Annuale che contiene tutto quello, che deve far un organista, per risponder al choro tutto l'anno*, Op. 8 (Venice: Vincenti, 1645); Giulio Cesare Arresti, *Messe a tre voci con sinfonie, e ripieni à placito, accompagnate da motetti, e concerti*, Op. 2 (Venice: Magni, 1663).

9   *Journal of the American Musicological Society* 22 (1969): 54–84. The repertory considered by Bonta is almost exclusively that written for the organ, which, he rightly surmises, has fundamental implications for instrumental ensembles.

10   The focus here is as much on contrapuntal technique as on the chromatic subject itself. However, the motif of a descending chromatic fourth is a widely used *topos* in its own right within various keyboard genres, opera, the madrigal, and motet during the seventeenth and eighteenth centuries. An entire volume devoted to that subject is Peter Williams, *The Chromatic Fourth during Four Centuries of Music* (Oxford: Clarendon Press, 1997).

11   Luigi Battiferri, *Ricercari a quattro, a cinque, e a sei*, Op. 3 (Bologna: Monti, 1669), preface: "essendo nel genere di suonare il più dotto, sicome nel genere di comporre è tale quello à Capella."

Example 5.3a   G. Bononcini, Op. 4, No. 4 (1686)

Example 5.3a   cont'd

(mm. 24-34)

Example 5.3b   A. Corelli, Op. 1, No. 11 (1681)

The chromatic subject adds a further defining element. The specific connection between the *ricercar cromatico* and the church lies in its heavy representation among the instrumental pieces recommended for use during the Mass in seventeenth-century manuals for organists.[12] The repertory of organ music from such sources is significant here, first, because it shows instrumental compositions that were specifically designated for liturgical use and, second, because we find among such pieces a number of movement types that match those from the sonata repertory. Examples 5.4a and 5.4b show the chromatic ricercars included by Bernardino Bottazzi and Antonio Croci in their anthologies of organ versets and other instrumental pieces designed for liturgical use. Neither Bottazzi nor Croci specifies the precise use of the *ricercar cromatico* within the liturgy of the Mass, but Frescobaldi employed this genre for use during the Offertory (*post il Credo*) among the organ masses in his 1635 *Fiori musicali* (Example 5.4c), seeing a fitting accompaniment to the solemn preparation of the Eucharistic elements in this severe style of music.[13] To be clear, sonata fugues

12 Croci, *Frutti musicali*, includes four chromatic ricercars, but does not specify their use for any one point in the liturgy of the Mass. Bottazzi, *Choro et organo*, includes a *ricercar cromatico* as the only free instrumental piece in his collection of masses for the organ. Banchieri, *L'organo suonarino*, contains the *Sonata quarta, fuga cromatica* (pp. 28–9), but does not specify its position in the Mass.

13 Frescobaldi, *Fiori musicali*, contains three ricercars labeled "dopo il Credo," that is, during the Offertory. Only the second of these is specifically marked as chromatic, but all three feature subjects with chromatic motion. See also *Girolamo Frescobaldi: Fiori musicali,*

trace their roots to the lively imitative sections within the canzona, and not to ricercars. Our interest, however, lies not in the origins of sonata fugues, but in how they took on the characteristics of genres that were used liturgically—in this case, the *ricercar cromatico*. With this in mind, the use of chromatic fugues in ensemble sonatas is suggestive. Certainly, this style of music implied a degree of solemnity by virtue of the contrapuntal techniques employed, and to listeners familiar with organ music used in church, an air of the sacred could only be more evident.

Example 5.4a   B. Bottazzi, *Choro et organo* (1614), Ricercar cromatico sopra il terzo tuono

ed. A. Macinati and F. Tasini (Bologna: Ut Orpheus Edizioni, 2001). Macinati and Tasini's informative preface illustrates in table form (p. XIII) which genres are associated with which moments of the Mass.

Example 5.4b   A. Croci, *Frutti musicali*, Op. 4 (1642), Ricercaro cromatico primo

Example 5.4c   G. Frescobaldi, *Fiori musicali*, Op. 12 (1635), Recercar cromaticho

Toccata Types: *Durezze e Ligature* and *Intonatione*

This is equally true of non-imitative movements in the sonata that cultivate diverse styles of organ toccata, one slow and suffused with an air of mystery, the other virtuosic and exhortative. Both types have an established place in liturgical organ music. The slow, awe-inducing genre of organ toccata that is also heard in the sonata belongs to a type of keyboard composition often designated *durezze e ligature* (dissonances and suspensions) for its agreeably pungent harmonies. Its connection to the church lies in its use as an accompaniment to the Elevation of the Host, (see Examples 5.5a and 5.5b). The effect of the music played at this most important moment of the Mass is to induce wonder and devotion, as attested early in the seventeenth century by Adriano Banchieri in his widely published *L'organo suonarino* (1605). According to Banchieri, "one plays at the Elevation, but softly and something *grave* that inspires devotion."[14]

---

14 Banchieri, *L'organo suonarino*, 39, "si suona alla Levatione, ma piano & cosa grave che muovi alla devotione."

Example 5.5a   G. Frescobaldi, *Fiori musicali*, Op. 12 (1635), Toccata cromatica
per l'elevatione

Example 5.5b   G. B. Fasolo, *Annuale* (1645), Benedictus et elevatio

Largo assai facendo godere le ligature, e durezze

The style is marked by chromatic harmonies, a continuous or nearly continuous series of dissonant suspensions, and piquant cross-relations—all performed in a slow tempo. Thus Giovanni Battista Fasolo instructs organists to play his Elevation piece "very slowly in order to relish the suspensions and dissonances [largo assai facendo godere le ligature, e durezze]" (see Example 5.5b). The far-reaching implications of these slow pieces for sacred music lie in the sense of mystery and wonder they inspired in listeners throughout the seventeenth and eighteenth centuries. This connection between the specific harmonic style and religious ardor is found in what the eighteenth-century theorist Giuseppe Paolucci described as the *pieno legato moderno*.[15] Paolucci's example, written by Giacomo Antonio Perti (Example 5.6), is a movement from a Magnificat setting that aspires to the same harmonic and affective intensity as the Elevation pieces.[16] In it we again see a *grave* movement and the now familiar harmonically piquant style, such that, in Paolucci's words, "not a note is sounded (apart from the cadences) that does not either make or receive a dissonance."[17] The effect of this music on the listener is its most striking characteristic in Paolucci's description: "apart from producing a most beautiful listening experience when done well, it also has the capacity to move the affections of the listener to devotion, which is the reason that music was introduced into churches."[18] Writing in 1765, Paolucci cannot be considered a late-*Seicento* source; however, his testimony corroborates and further details what is found in earlier sources on both this *topos* of sacred music and the affects it inspired.

---

15 Giuseppe Paolucci, *Arte pratica di contrapunto dimostrata con esempj di varj autori e con osservazioni*, vol. 1 (Venice: De Castro, 1765), 218–25.

16 The text, Luke I, 50, reads: "Et misericordia eius in progenies et progenies timentibus eum [And his mercy extends to those who fear him, from generation to generation]." This is a section of the Magnificat; however, Paolucci names only the author of this example, the long-lived Perti (1661–1756), so that its date of composition could fall anywhere between the late 1680s and the mid 1750s.

17 Ibid., 221, "non vi sia Nota (se si eccetuino le Cadenze) che non faccia, o non riceva Dissonanza."

18 Ibid., 225, "oltre a produrre un bellissimo sentire, quando sia ben fatto, è capace ancora a muovere gli affetti degli Ascoltanti a divozione, che è il fine per cui è stata introdotta la Musica nelle Chiese."

Example 5.6   G. A. Perti, pieno legato moderno

Such music is well represented among sonatas. Two movements, by T. A. Vitali and Corelli, draw upon the same slow tempo and harmonic style as the *durezze e ligature* and the *pieno legato moderno* (Examples 5.7a and 5.7b) in 9-8 and 7-6 suspensions, 6/5 clashes over the bass, cross-relations between major and minor harmonies, and other sometimes unexpected twists of the harmony.[19] It is precisely this kind of music that Giovanni Battista Martini, writing around 1750 and recalling the *grave* movements by Vitali, describes as having the power "to move the souls of the hearers to a most singular veneration" during the benediction of the sacrament.[20]

---

19 See Cesare Corsi, "Gli 'affetti del patetico italiano' negli 'squisiti gravi' corelliani: analisi del primo movimento della sonata opera III n. 9," in *Studi corelliani* V, ed. Stefano La Via (Florence: Olschki, 1996), 211–28, on the harmonic conventions of the Corellian grave.

20 Martini, "Scrittori di musica," Museo Internazionale e Biblioteca della Musica di Bologna, H.63, fol. 142 recto. This passage is quoted in Anne Schnoebelen, "The Concerted

Example 5.7a   T. A. Vitali, Op. 1, No. 5 (1693)

Mass at San Petronio in Bologna, ca. 1660–1730: A Documentary and Analytical Study," Ph.D. dissertation, University of Illinois, 1966, 34. The complete passage in Schnoebelen's translation reads as follows: "Among the distinguished properties of music, the movement of the affections is to be singled out. The Modenese have had among their citizens some manifest proofs of this. On occasion of the Benediction of the Most Holy Sacrament, it is customary for the string players to make heard certain Gravi which move the souls of the hearers toward a most singular veneration of the Most Holy Sacrament … because they are of a style which is grave and serious, but at the same time tender, which draws tears from the eyes, and the author of these is the celebrated Professor of Violin, Tommaso Vitali [Musica, fra le sue distinte proprietà, è singolare la mozione degli affetti. I Modonesi ne anno avuto fra i suoi Concitadini delle prove manifeste. In occasione della Benedizione del SS.mo Sagram.to sono soliti i suonatori da Arco di far sentire certi Gravi, che muovano l'Animo degli Ascoltanti a una Venerazione singolarissima verso il SS.mo Sagram.to, e di questo ve ne sono tra di voi tanti testimonj di queste Composizioni chiamate da Professori Gravi, perche in fatti sono di uno stile non solo grave, e serio, ma nell'istesso tempo tenero, che cava le lagrime dagli occhi, e l'Autore di essi è il celebre Professore di Violino Tommaso Vitali]."

Example 5.7b   A. Corelli, Op. 3, No. 9 (1689)

i. Grave

The virtuosic type of toccata is seen in Example 5.8a, which shows the *Toccata del primo tuono per l'Introito* from Croci's treatise for church organists. It is this style of toccata that furnishes the model for numerous introductory movements in the sonata repertory. Apart from virtuoso display, its features of rapid *passaggi* over pedal points or slowly changing harmonies have the practical function of establishing the pitch for a choir in sacred psalmody—the first psalm tone in the case of Example 5.8a. Croci's toccata belongs to a genre of organ composition known specifically as the *intonatione* in the exemplars of Andrea Gabrieli, published in 1593 by his nephew Giovanni (Example 5.8b),[21] which themselves may also reflect an earlier origin in ceremonial fanfares dating to the Middle Ages.[22] Maurizio Cazzati's use of triads over a held bass note for the opening of his solo motet "Intonate victoriam" (1666), Example 5.8c, furnishes a more fanfare-like example of this *topos*, along with the playful madrigalism on the genre title itself. The *intonatione* that begins Isabella Leonarda's motet "Veni Amor veni Jesu" (1690) (Example 5.8d) furnishes another example of the *topos* with its setting of a call to love.

---

21   Murray Bradshaw, *The Origin of the Toccata*, Musicological Studies and Documents, 28, ed. Armen Carapetyan (Rome: American Institute of Musicology, 1972), 16–17, discusses the close relationship of the toccata and the *intonatione*.

22   Otto Gombosi, "Zur Vorgeschichte der Tokkate," *Acta musicologica* 6/2 (1934): 49–53. Gombosi (p. 52), which is cited in Bradshaw, 13, draws a plausible connection between the toccata that begins Monteverdi's *Orfeo* and a genre of festive trumpet fanfare mentioned in a Spanish source dating to 1393.

Example 5.8a   A. Croci, *Frutti musicali*, Op. 4 (1642), Toccata del primo tuono per l'Introito

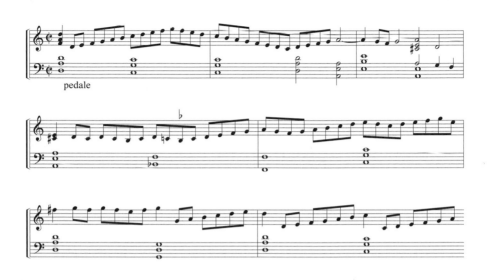

Example 5.8b   A. Gabrieli, *Intonationi d'organo* (pubd. 1593), Intonatione del primo tuono

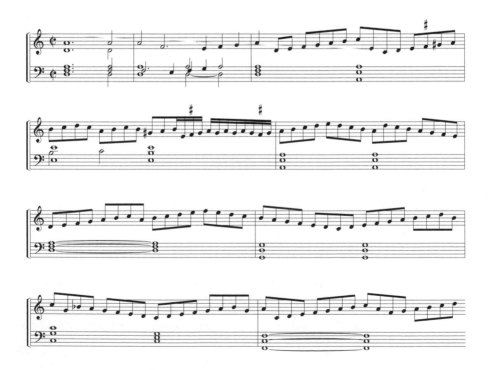

Example 5.8c   M. Cazzati, Op. 39, "Intonate victoriam" (1666)

Example 5.8d   I. Leonarda, Op. 15, "Veni Amor veni Jesu" (1690)

This is, then, a *topos* commonly found in sacred organ music—elaborately setting the pitch for a choir—that also bears the expressive connotations of an exhortative opening gesture, as seen in the two motet examples. In the sonata, the two senses of this music are easily compatible: whether the music was heard as a ritual intonation or as a fanfare-like exhortation, the effect recalls Brossard's sense of the dignified and majestic in the church sonata. The *Toccata à due violini* (Example 5.8e) from the Venetian composer Giovanni Buonaventura Viviani's Op. 1 (1673) shows the same type of music, but now scored for instrumental ensemble. Numerous similar but unlabeled examples occur throughout the sonata repertory, and Examples 5.9a–5.9c illustrate those of Corelli (in a *trombetta* style of fanfare-like arpeggios), T. A. Vitali, and Giuseppe Torelli.

Example 5.8e   G. B. Viviani, Op. 1, No. 9 (1673)

i. Toccata à due violini

Example 5.9a   A. Corelli, Op. 3, No. 12 (1689)

Example 5.9b   T. A. Vitali, Op. 1, No. 12 (1693)

Example 5.9c   G. Torelli, Op. 3, No. 12 (1687)

Kyrie Eleison

Corelli's example, in fact, offers up more than one *topos*, presenting a distinctive motto just before the toccata-style intonation that recalls settings of the Mass Ordinary. This motto from the very beginning of Corelli's sonata—a homorhythmic long–short–long rhythm—occurs frequently as an opening musical gesture in the late-*Seicento* sonata.[23] The same homorhythmic tutti (usually a dotted half note, quarter, and whole, or the same rhythm in durations half as long) that sets the syllables "Ky-ri-e" is a stereotype of seventeenth-century masses. The examples shown here by Lorenzo Penna, Giovanni Paolo Colonna, and Giovanni Battista Bassani (Examples 5.10a–5.10c) furnish typical settings. In all three, "Kyrie" is proclaimed *a tutti* and homorhythmically, and the immediately following "eleison" is treated more flexibly, sometimes with a brief flourish on its second syllable.

---

23 I am grateful to Anne Schnoebelen for bringing this *topos* of seventeenth-century masses to my attention. Her own remarks concerning the "stereotypical" Kyrie may be found in *Masses by Domenico Scorpione, Lorenzo Penna, Giovanni Paolo Colonna*, ed. Anne Schnoebelen, Seventeenth-Century Italian Sacred Music, Masses, 9 (New York: Garland, 1999), xv.

Example 5.10a   L. Penna, Op. 10 (1678), Messa detta l'Infiammata

Example 5.10b   G. P. Colonna, Op. 5 (1684), Messa terza

Example 5.10c   G. B. Bassani, Op. 18 (1698), Messa prima

The different ways in which this Kyrie *topos* occurs in the sonata shows the different degrees of exactness in adapting it to the instrumental medium. In Giovanni Bononcini's sinfonia (Example 5.11a), we can easily fit iterations of "Kyrie" to any of the musical lines (in the example, the text is placed under the first violin line). In sonatas by Andrea Grossi and Giovanni Maria Bononcini (Examples 5.11b and 5.11c), all of "Kyrie eleison" may be underlaid, allowing for embellishments of "eleison" on its second syllable. Example 5.11d shows the Kyrie *topos* in a sonata by Gioseffo Maria Placuzzi that illustrates the added affinity to concerted masses of the period in its polychoral scoring. (The Adagio from Cazzati's Sonata *a 8* "La Brembata," which appears in Chapter 7 as Example 7.3a, offers another example.) Placuzzi's sonata, moreover, recalls Corelli's in its combination of two musical *topoi*

associated with beginnings: the forceful, proclamatory Kyrie and the fanfare-like toccata. In both cases, the listener is treated to a sequence of gestures that announce beginnings and do so by drawing on distinct *topoi* of church music that are themselves initiators in a liturgical context.

Example 5.11a   G. Bononcini, Op. 4, No. 7 (1686)

Example 5.11b   A. Grossi, Op. 3, No. 12 (1682)

Example 5.11c   G. M. Bononcini, Op. 6, No. 3 (1672)

Example 5.11d   G. M. Placuzzi, Op. 1, No. 10 "La Malvasia" (1667)

Example 5.11d   cont'd

A Cappella Fugues

The impact of churchly musical style in the sonata da chiesa is nowhere better demonstrated than in its fugal movements marked *a cappella*. This particular *topos* of the sacred is associated, not with any specific genre, but rather with Counter-Reformation polyphony in general. The *stile da cappella* is the vocal polyphonic style of sacred music that is also enshrined as the *stile Palestrina* and the *stile antico*. The extraordinary dissemination of this *topos*—seen in J. S. Bach's "motet-style" fugues with his setting of the "Credo in unum Deum" from the B-minor Mass and even in Mozart's "learned style" (for example, the finale to the "Jupiter" Symphony)—similarly touches the sonata repertory of the late *Seicento* and early *Settecento*.[24] Here, the *topos* is sometimes made explicit in *a cappella* or *alla breve*

---

24 Scholarship on the *stile antico* in J. S. Bach and W. A. Mozart illustrate different uses of the *topos* in eighteenth-century music. See Christoph Wolff, "Bach and the Tradition of the Palestrina Style," in *Bach: Essays on his Life and Music* (Cambridge, MA: Harvard University Press, 1991), 84–104; and Elaine Sisman, *Mozart: The "Jupiter" Symphony* (Cambridge: Cambridge University Press, 1993), 68–79, in which she discusses the finale to Mozart's symphony and its "rhetoric of the learned style."

designations at the head of a particular style of fugue, but numerous other examples evidence the *cappella* style without any specific designation.

In his treatise *Arcani musicali* (1690), the theorist Angelo Berardi describes the musical features of the *cappella* style generally as "taken from the norms of Palestrina, unique in this sort of composition."[25] The specific features observed by Berardi include a fast tempo in binary meter (cut time); the avoidance of small note-values (i.e., less than a quarter note); stepwise motion in the individual parts; and the use of diatonic pitches.[26] Two sonata fugues (Examples 5.12a–5.12b) that bear the designation *a cappella* feature imitation in cut time on a subject in mainly half- and whole notes. That subject, moreover, covers a limited melodic range relative to much violin music of the period and proceeds in predominantly conjunct motion. (For the sake of contrast, I have included two fugue subjects that are more idiomatic to the violin from Corelli's oeuvre with Example 5.12a.) Example 5.12c furnishes a third instance of the *cappella topos*, but one that bears the label *alla breve* instead of *a cappella* and eighth-note embellishing figures added to the vocal-style theme.

---

25 Angelo Berardi, *Arcani musicali* (Bologna: Monti, 1690), 22: "Le Messe à Cappella vanno considerate dal compositore sotto uno stile grave divoto, & anco vivace, come se ne piglia la norma del Palestrina unico in questa sorte di cantilene."

26 Ibid.: "(1) Che le figure, e le pause per il più siano osservate sotto il tempo binario. (3) Non si devono usare le tirate di crome. (5) Che le parti della cantilena vadino trà di loro più di grado sia possibile. (6) Che le parti della cantilena modulino nelle loro corde naturali."

Example 5.12a   A. Fiorè, Op. 1, No. 8 (1699)

Example 5.12a   cont'd, Corellian fugue subjects from Op. 1, No. 4 (1681) and Op. 3,
               No. 7 (1689)

Example 5.12b   F. Manfredini, Op. 2, No. 5 (1709)

Example 5.12c   F. Manfredini, Op. 2, No. 11 (1709)

A further example attests the cultivation of the *cappella* style in movements that bear only tempo designations, but otherwise preserve the same musical features of the labeled pieces. In this case, the Allegro from Corelli's Op. 6, No. 5 (Example 5.12d), a concerto grosso, features cut time and the "white-note" themes, but intermingled with expositions reminiscent of this vocal polyphonic style (cf. mm. 1–9) are sequential episodes whose writing is more idiomatic to instruments (cf. mm. 9–12). In still other cases (Examples 5.13a and 5.13b), the *cappella* style appears even further removed from the Palestrinian idiom and more consciously adapted to late-*Seicento* violin technique. Nonetheless, these examples illustrate a typical and now familiar type of subject in long note-values spanning a small range of diatonic pitches.

Example 5.12d   A. Corelli, Op. 6, No. 5 (1714)

Example 5.13a   G. Torelli, Op. 5, Sinfonia No. 1 (1692)

Example 5.13b   T. A. Vitali, Op. 1, No. 8 (1693)

Dance *Topoi* and Churchly Decorum

While all of these examples convincingly link the sonata to sacred music, there remains the nagging problem of the courtly dance *topoi* that were used as sonata finales. By any measure, these would seem to stand out as glaring secularisms within an otherwise sacred stylistic profile. Nor are the ramifications here merely aesthetic. In official circles of the seventeenth century, any music that might be considered ill-suited to the decorum of the church was strongly discouraged as a hindrance to worship. We know this from the forceful opening of the *Piae sollicitudinis* (1657) of Pope Alexander VII:

> We are impelled by the fervor of pious solicitude, out of Our earnest desire to promote the observance of decorum and reverence in the churches of Rome, whence examples of good works go forth into all parts of the world, to banish from them vain introductions of whatever kind, and especially musical harmonies and symphonies in which is introduced anything that is indecorous or not in accord with ecclesiastical ritual, nor free from offense of the Divine Majesty, scandal to the faithful, and hindrance of devotion and elevation of hearts to things that are above.[27]

Pope Alexander, although never mentioning sonatas, does go on to specify that "music which imitates dance music and profane rather than ecclesiastical melody must be excluded, and must be banished from the churches."[28]

Sonata finales by Bartolomeo Bernardi and Giovanni Bononcini illustrate likely cases for banishment: Examples 5.14a and 5.14b show, respectively, a movement from Bernardi's Op. 2 church sonatas and a courtly dance, the gavotte, from his Op. 1 chamber sonatas. Similarities between the two are numerous: beyond the shared binary form, cut-time notation, and tempo designation of presto, the dance-like finale and actual dance use closely similar rhythms and thematic material. Example 5.14c adds a gavotte-styled finale from Bononcini's Op. 5 church sonatas. Examples 5.15a and 5.15b show a church sonata finale and a chamber sonata sarabanda by T. A. Vitali. Common to the courtly dance (Example 5.15b) and the dance-like finale (Example 5.15a) are four-measure phrases that frequently end with either a metrically unaccented cadence on the third beat of the measure or a downbeat cadence following a two-bar hemiola. They are, in light of churchly decorum, uncomfortably similiar.

---

27 This passage is taken from Robert Hayburn, *Papal Legislation on Sacred Music, 95 A.D. to 1977 A.D.* (Collegeville, MN: The Liturgical Press, 1979), 76.

28 Ibid., 77.

Example 5.14a   B. Bernardi, Op. 2, No. 6 (1696)

Example 5.14b   B. Bernardi, Op. 1, No. 8 (1692)

Example 5.14c   G. Bononcini, Op. 5, No. 1 (1687)

iv. Presto

Example 5.15a   T. A. Vitali, Op. 2, No. 2 (1693)

Example 5.15b   T. A. Vitali, Sonata No. 5 (MS, I-MOe, Mus.E.246)

Apart from such examples, which are by no means rare, further instances differ only in their explicitness as music meant for the church. In this regard, we may consider Example 5.16, which comprises excerpts from the final movement, marked *Aria*, of a sonata *a 2* written by Giulio Cesare Arresti, longtime organist at S. Petronio in Bologna. This sonata is included as music for liturgical use in his *Messe a tre voci*, Op. 2 (1663), most likely as a substitute for the Gradual during lesser feasts (*Missa de communi omnium festorum*).[29] Arresti, a career church musician, showed no hesitation in concluding his liturgical sonata with a lilting triple meter and repeated sections of regular and clear-cut phrases in a mostly homophonic texture.[30] In sum, this movement has many of the same dance-like characteristics as the sonata finales seen in Examples 5.14 and 5.15, and its *aria* designation is one typically found in collections of sonatas da camera. Probing further, we find a striking case of labeled dance movements within sonatas da chiesa in a Venetian print of 1673, Agostino Guerrieri's *Sonate di violino ... per chiesa*, Op. 1, dedicated to the Virgin Mary and, secondarily, to a mortal patron, Giovanni Domenico Spinola. As seen in Table 5.1, the complete title describes a collection of sonatas da chiesa, to which are added a few sonatas da camera. Table 5.1 also shows the contents of Guerrieri's printed collection, which comprise church sonatas in two, three, and four parts, plus the chamber sonatas—that is, two balletti (each followed by a corrente and sarabanda that are not listed in the table of contents) and variations on the Ruggiero (followed by a corrente, also not listed). Despite the clear distinction between church and chamber sonatas in the title and layout of the print, two of the sonatas da chiesa within ("La Tità" and "La Benedetta") conclude with movements that bear the label of "corrente." As far as I know, Guerrieri's Op. 1 presents a unique case in which one finds dance movements within sonatas explicitly designated as *da chiesa*; but we may also find a finale marked "giga" in Corelli's Op. 5, No. 5, one of the sonatas from the apparently *da chiesa* first part of his collection of solo violin sonatas.

---

29 Bonta, "The Uses of the Sonata da Chiesa," 63, n. 31.

30 Arresti does the same throughout his *Sonate a 2, & a tre, con la parte del violoncello a beneplacido,* Op. 4 (Venice: Magni, 1665).

Example 5.16   G. C. Arresti, *Messe a tre voci*, Op. 2 (1663)

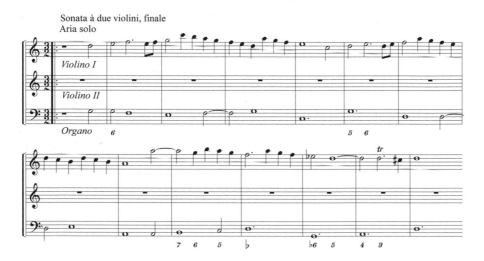

Example 5.16   cont'd

Table 5.1   A. Guerrieri, *Sonate di violino a 1. 2. 3. 4. per chiesa, & anco aggionta per camera*, Op. 1 (Venice, 1673)

Sonata malinconica, [sonata] à solo	La Balbi, sonata à 3
La Rotini, Sonata à solo	La Ravarina, à 3 violini
La Sevaschina, [Sonata] à solo	La Gotella, à 3 violini
La Tità, [Sonata] à solo [with corrente]	La Pietra, à 3, due violini & teorba
	La Viviani, à 3, due violini & teorba
La Rezonicha, à 2 violini	
La Brignoli, à 2 violini	La Sevasca, à 4
La Spinola, à 2 violini	La Rovetta, à 4
La Benedetta, à 2 violini [with corrente]	
La Marchetta, à 2 violini	Balletto primo per camera
La Rosciana, à 2 violini	Balletto secondo
La Galeazza, à 2 violini	Partite sopra Ruggiero
La Pinella, à 2 violini	
La Lucina, à 2 violini, arpa over teorba	

It is precisely such examples—apparent improprieties introduced into the sanctified sphere of the church—that cause us, first, to wonder what was motivating sonata composers to draw upon dance *topoi*, despite the legislations of the *Piae sollicitudinis*, and, second, to treat the genre distinctions of church and chamber sonata with caution. If we look at church music outside the sonata repertory, however, we begin to understand the liturgical role even of dance *topoi*. Returning to motets, there is similar music connoting, not unseemly affects of courtly diversion, but those of pious jubilation—that is, alleluias. In particular, the repeated four-bar phrases, larger sections articulated by fermatas, and tuneful homophony of the alleluia from G. B. Bassani's "Angelice voces" (1692) (Example 5.17a) are reminiscent of the sarabanda; Example 5.17b, from Angelo Domenico Legnani's "In dolore afflicta" offers a less symmetrically constructed, gigue-like alleluia; and Example 5.17c, from Cazzati's "Ave sacratissima Maria" (1661), bears notable similarities to the corrente.[31] We may therefore interpret such alleluias (and instrumental alleluia *topoi*), after the manner of late-*Seicento* composers and their listeners, as expressions of joy in worship.[32]

---

31 The sources of these motets are: Bassani, *Motetti a voce sola*, Op. 12 (Venice: Sala, 1692); Legnani, from *Sacre armonie a voce sola di diversi celebri autori* (Milan: Vigoni, 1692); Maurizio Cazzati, *Il quarto libro de motetti*, Op. 25 (Bologna: Pisarri, 1661). I am grateful to Margaret Murata for pointing me in the direction of alleluia settings during my search for dance *topoi* in sacred music.

32 Michael Talbot, *The Finale in Western Instrumental Music* (New York: Oxford University Press, 2001), finds the general affects of "joy, monumentality, and rest" (p. 37) as moods that characterize both culminating moments of the Mass and finales of instrumental music. He goes on to describe the joyful finale, what he calls the "relaxant type" (his other

Example 5.17a   G. B. Bassani, Op. 12 (1692), "Angelice voces"

types are "valedictory" and "summative"), in the fourth chapter (pp. 52–80). Although Talbot is wary of attaching dance labels where none originally existed, the affective connotations of his relaxant finale resonate with the "alleluia" *topos* discussed here.

Example 5.17b   A. D. Legnani, from *Sacre armonie ... di diversi celebri autori* (1692), "In dolore afflicta"

Example 5.17c   M. Cazzati, Op. 25 (1661), "Ave sacratissima Maria"

These and similar dance-like finales neatly underscore the liturgical position and function of the sonata as it was used during Mass and Vespers. In his work on the sources that detail the use of instrumental music in the liturgy, Stephen Bonta has shown that most place a complete sonata or canzona after the reading from the Epistles, that is, in place of the chanted Gradual or during its sotto-voce recitation.[33] Other possibilities for the performance of a sonata similarly place it just after significant moments in the liturgy: during the post-Communion;[34] at the conclusion of Mass or Vespers, that is, during the Deo Gratias; or in place of the reprised antiphon after a psalm during Vespers. In each of these ritual contexts, the sonata constitutes the sounded response to a prominent event of the liturgy or at the end of the service itself, and that response culminates in felicitous, exuberant, and clearly dance-like music. To view such finales in the church sonata simply as evidence of the influence of chamber sonatas overlooks seventeenth-century sacred musical style. Where we might be inclined to identify secular influences in comparing sonatas, church with chamber, all but the most dogmatic listeners of the period heard jubilant *topoi* of sacred alleluias.

The Para-Liturgical Sonata

Looming behind this survey of *topoi* and their sacred import lies the question of the liturgical use of the sonatas themselves. On the basis of organ treatises, Bonta has shown where sonatas could have been used during the Mass and Vespers. He has also speculated that this might have been done piecemeal, suggesting a neat distribution of a four-movement sonata plan (slow–fast–slow–fast) across the likeliest points of the Mass.[35] The sonata *topoi* seen here—with their origins in motets, masses, and liturgical organ genres—strengthen and add detail to his theory that sonatas were used movement by movement, and Table 5.2 gives likely uses during Mass of the movement-*topoi* set forth in this chapter based on the best affective fit between a *topos*, on the one hand, and a given moment in the liturgy, on the other.

---

33 See Bonta, "The Uses of the Sonata da Chiesa," Table IV (pp. 72–4) for a summary of instrumental pieces used in the Mass, and Table V (p. 81) for a summary of instrumental pieces used in Vespers.

34 Two instances of this are Milanuzzi (1622), *Canzon per il post communio*; and Frescobaldi (1635), *Canzon per il post comune*. There are further albeit less common possibilities. Franzoni, *Apparato musicale* (1613), includes brief sinfonias in four parts for the organ as introductions to the Sanctus and Agnus Dei.

35 Bonta, "The Uses of the Sonata da Chiesa," 78–9.

Table 5.2   Sonata movements and the liturgy

Sonata *topos*	Liturgy of the Mass
toccata d'intonatione	prelude (before the Introit or in place of it)
"Kyrie" *topos*	Kyrie (during recitation or as a verset)
a cappella fugues	Gradual
ricercar cromatico	Offertory
durezze e ligature	Elevation
dance *topoi*	Communion or Deo Gratias (i.e., postlude)

Because individual sonatas differ considerably in length and comprise varying numbers of movements, it is unlikely that any uniform scheme existed of integrating them into the liturgy of the Mass. A sonata might have anywhere from three to six movements in various arrangements of slow and fast tempos or of fugal, dance-like, grave, and other movement types. And yet, if there was no single plan for incorporating instrumental music into the liturgy, both printed and manuscript settings of the Mass—typically just items of the Ordinary and of these often only the Kyrie, Gloria, and Credo—allow for considerable leeway for doing so. A good picture of the practice is furnished by Bonta's survey of the treatises written for church organists, which offer diverse possibilities on what might be played or sung and at what point during the liturgy. According to his study, there are as many as seven distinct points within the Mass during which instrumental music may function as accompaniment to an action or as a substitute for plainchant—that is, before the service (prelude), Introit, Gradual, Offertory, Elevation, Communion, and Deo Gratias (postlude)—to which we may add two others suggested in sources discussed by Anne Schnoebelen in her dissertation and later work on Bolognese concerted masses (Sanctus and Agnus Dei)[36] and one more suggested by the Kyrie *topos* discussed here (although this movement type could also have functioned as a prelude).

In short, sonata movements could have been heard at as many as ten different points during the Mass, substituting for both Ordinary and Proper chants, and possibly comprising all of the music that was not otherwise chanted, so that we might speak of a "sonata mass" as we do of the organ mass. Vespers also offers a range of choices for the use of instrumental music as prelude, postlude, and antiphon substitute (psalm or Magnificat); but, as before, there is no reason to believe that

---

36 Schnoebelen, "The Concerted Mass at S. Petronio in Bologna," 196. See also, Schnoebelen, "The Role of the Violin in the Resurgence of the Mass in the 17th Century," *Early Music* 18 (1990): 537–42, p. 541. Some caution is necessary here. The frequent absence of Sanctus and Agnus Dei settings in published and manuscript masses of the mid and late seventeenth century certainly invites non-liturgical substitutes, but these may have been vocal or instrumental compositions. Schnoebelen argues for instrumental substitutes here on the basis of a description of a Mass celebrated by members of the Accademia Filarmonica in Bologna. In that description the Sanctus and Agnus Dei are described as "a braccio," which Schnoebelen interprets as "played by stringed instruments of the violin family," but more likely meant only "improvised."

sonatas or sonata movements were used consistently for any one or all of these. Printed sonata collections thus offer, not a specific blueprint, but a range of options for liturgical use, in which each sonata furnishes a selection of tonally related movement types expressing differing affects for dispersal across the whole of the liturgy. In choosing a sonata for liturgical performance, a maestro di cappella might instruct his instrumentalists to repeat, truncate, or even omit certain movements. The sonata offers, at the least, a flexible range of possibilities, and a printed collection of sonatas offers these possibilities in a variety of tonalities.[37]

Nor is a movement-by-movement use of sonatas the only choice. Larger churches or important feasts might call for a complete sonata to be played at a single moment during the liturgy, most likely the Gradual. The celebrations held by the Accademia Filarmonica on the feast day of its patron saint, St Anthony of Padua, called for a sinfonia at that point, and examples that might have been heard on that occasion would include any of Giuseppe Torelli's sinfonias (Op. 5), sonatas (Opp. 1 and 3), or even concertos (Opp. 5, 6, and 8) because he was a frequent contributor of the Accademia's feast-day sinfonia. Arresti, we may recall, uses a complete (three-movement) sonata of his Op. 2 *Messe a tre* (1663) probably as a substitute for the Gradual in his *Missa de communi omnium festorum*, which may reflect the practice of a large church, such as S. Petronio.

* * *

Throughout this chapter, musical *topoi* have proved crucial to our understanding of the sacred style and function of the sonata da chiesa. This line of enquiry, moreover, affords us insight into the early reception of late-*Seicento* and early-*Settecento* instrumental music, in which the sonata da chiesa not only evokes various genres of sacred music, but also inspires the devotional affects of their churchly contexts. A secular counterpart and precedent to this mode of expression in instrumental music might be seen in the *stile moderno* sonata, which not only introduced an unprecedented level of virtuosity into violin music in the 1620s, but also drew upon the expressive innovations of the *seconda prattica*.[38] To judge by seventeenth-century religious iconography, however, the violin and violin music were themselves symbols of the Divine. In paintings of St Francis's spiritual ecstasy or consolation by Giuseppe Cesari, Carlo Saraceni, and Gioacchino Assereto, for example, it is the violin that represents the sound of the divine presence.[39] Further appearances of the

---

37 See Chapter 6 on the interpretation of sonata tonalities as "church keys" (*tuoni ecclesiastici*), which were used liturgically throughout the *Seicento*.

38 See Andrew Dell'Antonio, *Syntax, Form and Genre in Sonatas and Canzonas: 1621–1635* (Lucca: Libreria Musicale Italiana, 1997), which investigates not only form and syntax, but also *seconda prattica* rhetoric in the canzonas and sonatas of Dario Castello, Giovanni Picchi, Giuseppe Scarani, and Girolamo Frescobaldi.

39 Andrew Dell'Antonio, "Construction of Desire in Early Baroque Instrumental Music," in *Gender, Sexuality, and Early Music*, ed. Todd M. Borgerding (New York and London: Routledge, 2002), 199–226, p. 201, points out the frequent connection between violin-playing and spiritual ecstasy in seventeenth-century iconography. Cesari's *S. Francesco*

violin in the representation of celestial music may be seen in depictions of the Holy Family.[40] If sonatas and concertos for violins could inspire affects of devotion and rapture, it must have been in part because the listener's imagination was prepared to experience violin music in that role.

The mention of iconographic evidence hints at further possibilities in the search for musical *topoi* and the interpretation of sonatas. Indeed, this investigation represents only a partial account because a host of other factors must also have been involved in the interpretation of this music. In closing, we might well speculate on two: performing venue and manner of performance. As demonstrated by the finales studied here, venue must also have had an impact, so that the interpretation of sacred ethos depends not only on the perception of sacred musical *topoi*, but also on the fact of hearing this music in a particular—in this case liturgical—context. Given a change from one venue to another, listeners might easily have interpreted the same music as either a gigue or an alleluia. A comparable example is the toccata that begins Monteverdi's *Orfeo* and serves equally well as the opening *responsorium* of his monumental Vespers.

The manner of performance could also have had an impact on the interpretation of musical *topoi*. J. J. Quantz, for example, advises performers on how they could mitigate the more "bold and bizarre" ideas of a composition for performance in church:

> a composition for the church requires more majesty and seriousness than one for the theater, which allows greater freedom. If in a work for the church the composer has inserted some bold and bizarre ideas that are inappropriate to the place, the accompanists, and the violinists in particular, must endeavor to mitigate, subdue, and soften them as much as possible by a modest execution.[41]

Similar performance-practice considerations may well have applied to Italian musicians a half-century earlier, and the danger of these further criteria for churchly performance is that they run the risk of introducing circularity into the arguments

---

consolato is dated to the 1590s, Saraceni's *Estasi di S. Francesco*, to 1620, and Assereto's *Estasi di S. Francesco*, to the mid 1630s. Another depiction of religious ecstasy, Marcantonio Franceschini's *L'estasi della Maddalena* (1688), includes two singing cherubs accompanied by a violin and a lute, an ensemble suited, say, to a motet *a 2* with obbligato violin and continuo.

40 Orazio Borgianni, *Sacra familia* (c.1610), and Lorenzo Pasinelli, *S. Caterina adora il Bambino* (1687).

41 J. J. Quantz, *On Playing the Flute*, trans. and introduction by Edward R. Reilly, 2nd ed. (Boston: Northeastern University Press, 2001), 271. I am indebted to Neal Zaslaw for bringing Quantz's comments to my attention. The original German from the *Versuch einer Anweisung, die Flöte traversiere zu spielen* (Berlin: Voss, 1752), 245, reads: "eine Kirchenmusik erfodert mehr Pracht und Ernsthaftigkeit, als eine theatralische, welche mehr Frenheit zuläßt. Wenn in einer Kirchenmusik, von dem Componisten, einige freche und bizarre Gedanken, so sich in die Kirche nicht wohl schicken, mit sollten senn eingeflochten worden: so müssen die Accompagnisten, besonders aber die Violinisten, dahin trachten, daß solche durch einen bescheidenen Vortrag, so viel möglich, vermäntelt, gezähmet, und sanfter gemacht werden mögen."

pursued here: music is deemed churchly simply because it is heard in church or is played in solemn and reverential manner. If, in texted music, the distinction between an erotic love song and a hymn to the Virgin Mary is in some cases merely a matter of words, what limits are there for instrumental genres? Nonetheless, if these possibilities raise questions about the interpretation of musical *topoi* in the late-*Seicento* sonata, they also explain the seeming paradox of how we, on the one hand, perceive commonalities between church and chamber sonatas, while musicians of the period, on the other, maintained clear distinctions between them.

Outside of these speculations, we may easily appreciate how the study of musical *topoi* connects the sonata repertory to sacred genres of organ music, the mass, the motet, and the broader *stile antico*. This, in turn, deepens our understanding of churchly style in the sonata da chiesa well beyond the generalities of Brossard's dictionary entry, and it reconnects us to the late-*Seicento* experience of this repertory as inspiring and uplifting.

Chapter Six

Tonal Style, Modal Theory, and Church Tradition*

For as comfortably tonal as late-*Seicento* instrumental music may seem, the evidence for an earlier harmonic language or tonal dialect of the era stares out at us in the details of the Bolognese sonata. In particular, the so-called "incomplete" key signatures found in nearly every print and manuscript, illustrate a consistent practice of the seventeenth and early eighteenth centuries—one seen even in the music of J. S. Bach[1]—that defies the precepts of our tonal system. The tonality resembling A major, for example, is commonly notated with two sharps, not three; G minor almost always occurs with only a single flat; D minor occurs with no flats or sharps; and so forth.

Example 6.1a, taken from the final measures of Maurizio Cazzati's sonata "La Ghisigliera," from his Op. 35 (1665), illustrates another "anomaly" of late-*Seicento* tonal style. Here, an authentic cadence in A minor is followed by a brief finale that concludes the sonata with a Phrygian cadence on an E-major chord. Nor does this tonal curiosity occur only in Cazzati: several sonata composers of the late seventeenth century produced similar concluding passages that modern tonal theory would classify as A-minor compositions that end on their dominants. Example 6.1b shows another of these from Corelli's Op. 1, No. 4 (1681). In this movement, Corelli adds, to use modern terminology, a concluding half cadence in mm. 37–9 to the authentic cadence of m. 36, thereby ending what appears to be a sonata in A minor with an E-major chord. The brief final movement of Giovanni Legrenzi's sonata *a 3* "La Valvasona," shown in Example 6.1c, furnishes a third example of the same tonal characteristic. Although the opening sonority occurs on E, the subject of the movement (see violin 1, mm. 1–2, and violone, mm. 5–7) centers on A, and the authentic cadences in mm. 12 and 16 reinforce this tonal orientation. The final cadence, however, occurs on E, which is approached from A in the violone and basso continuo (mm. 17–19). A brief excerpt from the opening movement of the same sonata (Example 6.1d) manifests the same characteristic: a clear focus on A in mm. 29–31 ultimately leads to E.

---

*   An earlier version of this chapter appears as "Modal Theory, Church Keys, and the Sonata at the End of the Seventeenth Century," *Journal of the American Musicological Society* 51 (1998): 245–81.

    1   A well-known example is Bach's "Dorian" toccata and fugue, BWV 538, which uses a key signature of no flats or sharps, but has the pitch D for a tonic.

Example 6.1a   M. Cazzati, Op. 35, No. 4 "La Ghisigliera" (1665)

iii. Allegro (mm. 124-end)

Finale

Example 6.1b   A. Corelli, Op. 1, No. 4 (1681)

Example 6.1b   cont'd

Example 6.1c   G. Legrenzi, Op. 2, Sonata a 3, "La Valvasona" (1655)

Example 6.1d   G. Legrenzi, Op. 2, Sonata a 3, "La Valvasona" (1655)

i. (conclusion)

This chapter presents the rationale behind such examples by setting forth the collection of tonalities within which late-*Seicento* sonata composers conceived their music. This collection of tonalities, some of which defy the norms of major-minor tonality, comprises a core set of eight primary tonalities found throughout seventeenth-century treatises from which composers derived others by means of transpositions. The path toward explicating this earlier system lies in the existence of a persistent ordering of finals and key signatures that appears in collections of sonatas throughout the latter half of the century.

Traditional modal theory of the time supplies crucial information toward an understanding of late-*Seicento* tonal style because composers and theorists—for want of any other existing theory—continued to explain their practice in terms of modes. Two prints of sonatas within the Bolognese orbit that use specific modal designations for their contents form the cornerstone of this topic: Giovanni Maria Bononcini's *Sonate da chiesa*, Op. 6 (1672) and Giulio Cesare Arresti's *Sonate*, Op. 4 (1665).[2] Bononcini's and Arresti's ideas, as reflected in their modal designations, intersect with a widespread practice among composers of instrumental music and demonstrate a broadly disseminated conception of tonal organization of the late seventeenth century. In short, the purpose here is to outline the tonal system recognized by musicians of the late *Seicento*, one that furnishes a vital link between the theory and practice of the period and lays bare the roots of tonal style in the instrumental repertory.

Tonality, Mode, and Church Key

Theorists of the *Seicento* most often relied on the single term *tuono* (or *tono*) to describe several distinct ideas, all of which relate to some notion of tonal organization. As a consequence, three terms appear in this chapter that refer to one or another

---

2   Giulio Cesare Arresti, *Sonate a 2, et a tre*, Op. 4 (Venice: Magni, 1665); and Giovanni Maria Bononcini, *Sonate da chiesa a due violini*, Op. 6 (Venice: Magni, 1672; facsimile, Bologna: Forni, 1970). For a study of compositional style in Bononcini's Op. 6 see Angela Chiu-Wah Yeung, "A Study of Late Seventeenth-Century Compositional Practice: The Sonate da Chiesa (Opus 6) of G.M. Bononcini," Ph.D. dissertation, Columbia University, 1994.

meaning of *tuono;* these are tonality, mode, and church key. Tonality, such as E-tonality or G-tonality, is the term used here to describe a tonal center, or final, and a collection of related pitches as indicated by a key signature. It largely coincides with our term key, except that it connotes something broader: key, used by itself, implies one of the 24 major-minor keys, whereas tonality signifies an organization of pitches and tonal procedure not necessarily pertaining to the modern tonal system.

Mode refers to the theoretical system of eight or twelve modes—or, more specifically, to any one of these eight or twelve modes—as defined by medieval and Renaissance theorists in terms of specific *ambitus* and final. Table 6.1a shows the eight modes of medieval theory—four pairs of authentic and plagal modes on the finals D, E, F, and G—as summarized by Zaccaria Tevo in his treatise *Il musico testore* (1706).[3] Table 6.1b shows the late-Renaissance expansion of the eight-mode system summarized, again, by Tevo: authentic and plagal modes on two additional finals, A and C, bring the total to twelve.[4] Common to both eight- and twelve-mode systems is the arrangement of authentic and plagal *ambitus* with respect to a number of modal finals. The authentic *ambitus* ranges an octave above its final; the plagal, a fourth below and a fifth above it.

Table 6.1a   Z. Tevo, *Il musico testore* (Venice, 1706), 263: "li Modi, ò Tuoni delli Latini"

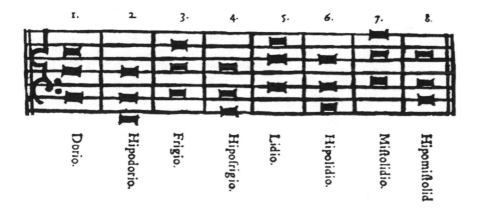

---

3   Zaccaria Tevo, *Il musico testore* (Venice: Bortoli, 1706; facsimile, Bologna: Forni, 1969), 262–3.

4   Ibid., 264–5.

Table 6.1b   Z. Tevo, *Il musico testore* (Venice, 1706), 265: "quattro furono aggiunti da [Henrico] Glareano"

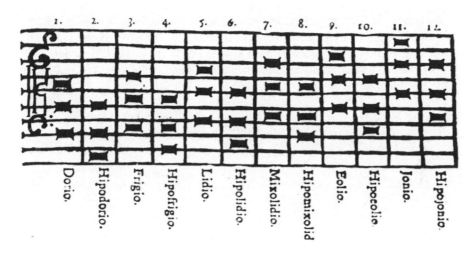

The church keys, or *tuoni ecclesiastici*, comprise a particular collection of tonalities—that is, a set of tonal centers plus key signatures used by composers—that were enumerated in Italian treatises throughout the seventeenth and early eighteenth centuries.[5] Table 6.1c shows a listing of the *tuoni ecclesiastici* or simply *tuoni* from Tevo's treatise—included are the several cadences he lists (*fondamentale*, *regolare*, and *media*) and key signature for each *tuono*.[6] Although church keys, like the modes, were known as *tuoni* by seventeenth-century theorists, they are not the same as modes: the church keys do not conform to the array of modal finals with authentic and plagal *ambitus*; they are always eight in number, never twelve; and they do not adhere to other rules of modal theory, such as the use of proper species

---

5   The use of the term "church key" originates with Joel Lester, "The Recognition of Major and Minor Keys in German Theory: 1680–1730," *Journal of Music Theory* 22 (1978): 65–103. That article and Lester, "Major-Minor Concepts and Modal Theory in Germany: 1592–1680," *Journal of the American Musicological Society* 30 (1977): 208–53, were later combined and expanded as *Between Modes and Keys: German Theory 1592–1802* (Stuyvesant, NY: Pendragon Press, 1989), in which he explains (pp. 78–9) that the term is a translation of Adriano Banchieri's "Otto Tuoni spettanti al canto fermo ecclesiastico" (*Cartella musicale*, 1614). These, in turn, refer to the eight psalm tones of sacred psalmody. For a thorough study of these tonalities, their origins in seventeenth-century ecclesiastical performance practice, and the treatises that discuss them, see Michael R. Dodds, "The Baroque Church Tones in Theory and Practice," Ph.D. dissertation, University of Rochester, 1999.

6   Tevo, 268–9, gives only the bass notes of six cadences for each *tuono* of the eight, which he terms *tuoni delli moderni* (p. 292) and *modi alla moderna* (p. 268). The first three of Tevo's six cadences for each *tuono* are shown in Table 6.1c: *fondamentale*, *regolare*, *media*. (Those not given in Table 6.1c are the two *irregolari* and the *finale*.) Most of the cadences listed show resolution in the bass from the fourth below or the fifth above. In each case, the *cadenza finale* concludes on the same pitch as the *cadenza fondamentale*, but the *finale* approaches that pitch from the fourth above or fifth below in Tones 1, 3, 4, and 5.

of perfect fourth and fifth within each modal *ambitus*. Instead, the church keys arose as tonalities adapted to the responsorial setting of the psalm tones, a practice that became more and more prevalent throughout the seventeenth century in the Divine Offices, particularly in lavish Vespers settings.[7] Drawing on the only available theory that described tonal organization, many *Seicento* theorists did attempt to describe the church keys in modal terms, but we must keep the distinction between modal theory and psalmodic practice firmly in mind when considering the tonal practice of the instrumental repertory.

Table 6.1c   Z. Tevo, *Il musico testore* (Venice, 1706), 268–9: "li Moderni, e Novissimi Maestri Musici d'hoggidì si servino solo di otto Modi, ò Tuoni"

Tuono, ò Modo	Cadenze: Fondamentale;	Regolare;	Media	Key Signature
1	d	a	f	—
2	g	d	b♭	♭
3	a	e	c	—
4	e	e	a	—
5	c	g	e	—
6	f	c	a	♭
7	e	b	g	♭
8	g	d	c	—

Late-*Seicento* Modal Theory

Modal theory is prevalent in writings on music throughout the seventeenth century, but a reader has only to open a treatise from this period to know that the modes presented difficulties. In his 1673 treatise *Musico prattico*, Giovanni Maria Bononcini introduces the subject cautiously, stating that "[t]he discussion of the *Tuoni*, or *Modi*, is a very difficult matter because of the diversity of opinions as to both their number

---

7   Michael R. Dodds, "Tonal Types and Modal Equivalence in Two Keyboard Cycles by Murschhauser," in *Tonal Structures in Early Music*, ed. Cristle Collins Judd (New York: Garland, 1998), 341–72, provides a clear and succint explanation of how the church keys came to assume their standardized form in the early seventeenth century (p. 342): "The church keys originated in the *alternatim* performance of psalms and canticles in Catholic offices, especially the office of Vespers. In this performance tradition, the psalm or canticle, preceded by an antiphon and followed by an antiphon or antiphon substitute, was performed in verse-by-verse alternation between two contrasting performance styles. These could be plainchant (with or without accompaniment); polyphonic organ versets; and monodic versets for one or more soloists. In order to bring the psalm tones into a comfortable tessitura for the choir, musicians over time developed more or less standard transpositions for certain of them. In addition, they generally treated the psalm tones' last pitch as the final—a pitch class different, in some cases, from the final of the corresponding mode."

and their name."[8] Some years later, in his *Miscellanea musicale* of 1689, the theorist Angelo Berardi seconds Bononcini's opinion: "One should not wonder that these modes have been called different things, have been considered in different ways, and have been reversed from low to high and vice versa."[9] While neither of these writers inspires much confidence in the intelligibility or usefulness of modal theory during the latter half of the seventeenth century, composers and theorists alike continually returned to its tenets when discussing their music. We must therefore assess late-*Seicento* perspectives on tonal practice through the theoretical language of the modes.

Like much twelve-mode theorizing, Bononcini's writings closely parallel those found in Gioseffo Zarlino's *Le istitutioni harmoniche* of 1558.[10] That work, in turn, draws heavily on the original twelve-mode theory of Heinrich Glarean's *Dodecachordon* of 1547.[11] Table 6.2a illustrates this by showing each of the twelve

---

8 Giovanni Maria Bononcini, *Musico prattico*, Op. 8 (Bologna: Monti, 1673; facsimile, Hildesheim: Georg Olms Verlag, 1969), 121: "Il trattare de i Tuoni, ò Modi è materia assai difficile per la diversità dell'opinioni, tanto nel numero loro, quanto nel nome." Noting Bononcini's use of the terms "modo" and "tuono," it is well to point out that late-*Seicento* theorists used them interchangeably. Under the heading *Nomi diversi di tuoni; ò modi* (diverse names of the *tuoni* or *modi*), Angelo Berardi, *Miscellanea musicale* (Bologna: Monti, 1689), 174, explains the diverse names given to the modes: "Altri l'hanno chiamati Armonie, alcuni Tropi, e diversi l'hanno nominati Sistemati [Others have called them *Armonie*, others *Tropi*, and others have designated them *Sistemati*]." Lorenzo Penna, *Li primi albori musicali* (Bologna: Giacomo Monti, 1672; facsimile of 1684 ed., Bologna: Forni, 1969), 128–32, does not use the term "modo," but refers to the same theory of modal categories by using the term "tuono": "Questi Tuoni sono chiamati Armoniali, formati di un Diapente, cioè di una quinta, e di un Diatesseron, cioè di una quarta, quali insieme formano un Diapason, cioè un ottava.... Questi Tuoni dunque Armoniali, prima furono quattro; poi otto; e finalemente sono stati ampliati al numero di dodici [These *Tuoni* are called *Armoniali*, being formed by a *Diapente*, that is, a fifth, and by a *Diatesseron*, that is, a fourth, which together form a *Diapason*, that is, an octave.... These *Tuoni* or *Armoniali* were originally four, then eight, and then were finally amplified to twelve]."

9 Berardi, *Miscellanea musicale*, 174, "Non bisogna maravigliarsi, se detti modi furono chiamati diversamente, mentre sono stati differentemente considerati, e rivoltati dal grave all'acuto, & e contra."

10 Ibid., 176–94; and Bononcini, *Musico prattico*, 121–37, give explanations of the twelve-mode system based mostly on those found in Gioseffo Zarlino, *Le istitutioni harmoniche*, Parte IV (Venice: n.p. [Pietro da Fino], 1558; facsimile, New York, Broude Bros., 1965). An English trans. of the fourth part of Zarlino's treatise is *On the Modes: Part Four of* Le istitutioni harmoniche, *1558*; trans. Vered Cohen, ed. Claude Palisca (New Haven: Yale University Press, 1983). A summary of Zarlino's theory may be found in Harold S. Powers and Frans Wiering, "Mode," part III, "Modal Theories and Polyphonic Music," in *The New Grove Dictionary of Music and Musicians*, 2nd ed., ed. Stanley Sadie and John Tyrrell, 29 vols (London: Macmillan Publishers Inc., and New York: Grove's Dictionaries Inc., 2001), vol. 16, 812–14.

11 Heinrich Glarean, *Dodecachordon* (Basel: Petri, 1547; facsimile, Hildesheim: Olms Verlag, 1969; and New York: Broude Bros., 1967); English trans. by Clement Miller, 2 vols, Musicological Studies and Documents, 6 (American Institute of Musicology, 1965). The writings of this theorist are outlined in Powers and Wiering, "Mode," 808–12.

modes, its composition, and final as explained in Bononcini's *Musico prattico*. Like his Renaissance precursors, Bononcini identified the species of perfect fourth and fifth and the particular arrangement of these interval species with respect to the modal final as the defining criteria for each mode.

Table 6.2a   G. M. Bononcini, *Musico prattico*, Op. 8 (Bologna, 1673)

Mode	Interval species[†] (pp. 122–3)	Final[††] and modal octave (pp. 122–34)
1	1st 5th + 1st 4th	D e f g a b c d
2	1st 4th + 1st 5th	a b c D e f g a
3	2nd 5th + 2nd 4th	E f g a b c d e
4	2nd 4th + 2nd 5th	b c d E f g a b
5	3rd 5th + 3rd 4th	F g a b c d e f
6	3rd 4th + 3rd 5th	c d e F g a b c
7	4th 5th + 1st 4th	G a b c d e f g
8	1st 4th + 4th 5th	d e f G a b c d
9	1st 5th + 2nd 4th	A b c d e f g a
10	2nd 4th + 1st 5th	e f g A b c d e
11	4th 5th + 3rd 4th	C d e f g a b c
12	3rd 4th + 4th 5th	g a b C d e f g

[†]Interval species:

Species	Fifths	Fourths
1st	d e f g a (*or* a b c d e)	a b c d (*or* d e f g)
2nd	e f g a b	b c d e (*or* e f g a)
3rd	f g a b c	c d e f (*or* g a b c)
4th	g a b c d (*or* c d e f g)	

[††]Modal finals are capitalized.

Beyond this foundation in Renaissance theory, late-*Seicento* theorists also recognized, as had Zarlino,[12] the use of key signatures beyond the single flat of *cantus mollis* as a useful means of transposing the modes to different pitch levels. Example 6.2, from Berardi's *Il perche musicale*, illustrates how a change of key signature effects the transposition of a single excerpt to various pitch levels—some resulting in a change of mode as well.[13]

---

12 Zarlino, *Istitutioni harmoniche*, part IV, ch. 17, 319–20 (pp. 52–3 in Cohen's English trans., *On the Modes*).

13 Berardi's demonstration of Mode 1 transposed down a minor third results in a B-final and three sharps. This combination of final and key signature does not occur, so far as I know, in any Italian instrumental composition of the late seventeenth century.

Example 6.2   Modal transpositions: A. Berardi, *Il perche musicale* (Bologna, 1693), 54

primo tuono
nelle sue corde
naturali

[primo tuono]
un tuono più basso

[primo tuono]
alla terza bassa

settimo tuono
una quarta più
basso

undecimo tuono
un tuono più alto

The first of the five brief examples given by Berardi bears no key signature, and he designates its mode as Mode 1 untransposed (*primo tuono nelle sue corde naturali*). The second and third examples feature the same music transposed down a whole-step and down a minor third, respectively. The mode of these second and third examples is unchanged; these are also Mode 1 examples, but transposed to different pitch-levels. The last two passages, still the same music, show transpositions of other modes, Mode 7 down a fourth and Mode 11 up a whole-step. Modal transposition provided an important line of reasoning to theorists who had to account for the various key signatures found in seventeenth-century music—anything up to three sharps or flats—in terms of the modes.

Bononcini's Op. 6 (1672) and Arresti's Op. 4 (1665)

Turning now to the sonatas of Bononcini's Op. 6, Table 6.2b shows the modal designation (*tuono*), final, key signature, and transposition of all twelve of these sonatas and lists them in the order in which they appear in the print. Two particulars in this arrangement stand out: only seven of the twelve modes appear (in no specific order), and nine of the sonatas use transposing key signatures. The significance of both details emerges in Bononcini's discussion of the modes in his treatise *Musico prattico*, in which he asserts that composers of his day used only seven modes— the same as those found in his Op. 6 sonatas.[14] Specifically, Bononcini taught that certain modes of the traditional twelve had fallen out of use in late-*Seicento* practice. Furthermore, the surviving seven modes sufficed because some of these could be used by means of transposition to replace those no longer in use.

Table 6.2b   G. M. Bononcini, *Sonate da chiesa*, Op. 6 (Venice, 1672)

Sonata	*Tuono*	Final	Key Signature	Transposition
1	11	C*	—	—
2	12	F	♭	↓P5
3	11	B♭	♭♭	↓M2
4	11	D	♯♯	↑M2
5	8	A	♯♯	↑M2
6	10	E	♯	↓P4
7	9	B	♯♯	↑M2
8	8	G	—	—
9	1	D	—	—

Sonata	*Tuono*	Final	Key Signature	Transposition
10	1	C	♭♭	↓M2
11	2	G	♭	↑P4
12	12	E♭	♭♭	↑m3

*Finals in uppercase letters signify major-third tonalities; finals in lowercase letters signify minor-third tonalities.

---

14 Bononcini, *Musico prattico*, 137–8. On p. 137, the chapter is entitled "Quali de sopradetti Tuoni vengano ordinariamente pratticati da Compositori [Which of the above-named modes are ordinarily used by composers]." He begins forthrightly: "I Tuoni ordinariamente pratticati da Compositori sono sette [Seven modes are ordinarily used by composers]." The remainder of that chapter simply lists what is shown here in Table 6.2c.

Table 6.2c shows the final, key signature, and transposition of each of the seven practicable modes presented in Bononcini's treatise and illustrates his explanation of them in terms of Renaissance twelve-mode theory. The numbering of these modes (*tuoni*) in the left-most column shows that Bononcini followed the traditional twelve-mode numbering, but reordered individual modes according to how he saw some of them as replacing others. He describes the seven modes as follows: Modes 1 and 2 remain in contemporary practice (however, Mode 2 is transposed up a fourth from d to g); Modes 3 and 4 are both replaced by the transposed Mode 10; Modes 5 and 6 are replaced by Modes 11 and 12, both transposed down a fifth; Mode 7 is replaced by transposed Mode 9, also transposed down a fifth; and Mode 8 is untransposed. Tables 6.2b and 6.2c thus illustrate the unity of Bononcini's theory and practice: Table 6.2c shows the theoretical rationale for the seven tonalities that he used in his Op. 6 sonatas (themselves summarized in Table 6.2b).

Table 6.2c   G. M. Bononcini, *Musico prattico*, Op. 8 (Bologna, 1673), 137–8

Tuono	Final	Key Signature	Transposition
1	d		—
2	g	♭	↑P4
10 (replaces modes 3 and 4)	a	—	—
11 (replaces mode 5)	C	—	—
12 (replaces mode 6)	F	♭	↓P5
9 (replaces mode 7)	d	♭	↓P5
8	G	—	—

With Bononcini's theory-in-practice close at hand, we may compare the views of his contemporary Giulio Cesare Arresti by examining Arresti's Op. 4, the second of the two prints of sonatas mentioned earlier that use modal designations. Table 6.3a lists the designations (*tono*), finals, and key signatures of all twelve sonatas in Arresti's Op. 4; Table 6.3b shows the modes of traditional dodecachordal theory, those taught by Bononcini, arranged as tonalities (finals and key signatures only). A comparison of Tables 6.3a and 6.3b reveals the considerable differences between Arresti's and Bononcini's dodecachordal systems. While it would seem that Arresti meant to present Modes 1–12 in numerical order in his print of sonatas, these twelve modes in no way correspond with Bononcini's. In Bononcini's theory, the unaltered twelve modes have no key signatures (to use one is to indicate a transposition), and they form six authentic–plagal pairs with finals on D, E, F, G, A, and C (see Table 6.2a). Arresti's twelve sonatas (Table 6.3a), by contrast, deviate from Bononcini's theory and practice in the following ways: (1) he indicates no transpositions even though several sonatas do bear key signatures; (2) pairs of consecutive modes do not share a final; and (3) Arresti composed in every one of the twelve modes, and not just seven.

Table 6.3a   G. C. Arresti, *Sonate*, Op. 4 (Venice, 1665)

Sonata	*Tono*	Final	Key signature
1	1	d	—
2	2	g	♭
3	3	a	—
4	4	e	—
5	5	C	—
6	6	F	♭
7	7	D	♯
8	8	G	—
9	9	d	♭
10	10	A	♯♯
11	11	E	♯♯♯
12	12	c	♭♭

Table 6.3b   The modes of dodecachordal theory represented as tonalities

Mode	Final	Key signature
1	d	—
2	d	—
3	e	—
4	e	—
5	F	—
6	F	—
7	G	—
8	G	—
9	a	—
10	a	—
11	C	—
12	C	—

Without recourse to a treatise by Arresti, we are hard-pressed to uncover the rationale behind the tonalities of his twelve sonatas. Nonetheless, the comparison between Arresti's sonatas and Bononcini's theory turns up a vital similarity: Arresti's representations of Modes 1–8 and Bononcini's list of the seven practicable modes comprise nearly identical sets of finals and key signatures (cf. Tables 6.2c and 6.3a). Disregarding Arresti's and Bononcini's differing modal categorizations, the two lists of tonalities (Arresti's 1–8 and Bononcini's 1–7) correspond closely, except for Bononcini's consolidation of Modes 3 and 4.[15]

This similarity between the two lists is no coincidence: orderings of tonalities from numerous sonata prints and theoretical schemes conform to identical or similar arrangements when compared to the finals and key signatures of Arresti's first eight modes and Bononcini's practicable seven. Table 6.4a, listings of the church keys, shows the tonalities (finals and key signatures) of eight-fold systems in five treatises that span the seventeenth and early eighteenth centuries.[16] The treatises listed here provide a representative selection covering nearly a century of octonary listings of *tuono*, all of which instance the set of tonalities seen in Arresti's and Bononcini's sonatas.

Nor do Arresti's and Bononcini's prints stand alone in their use of designations for the same ordering of tonalities. Table 6.4b shows the tonalities of three more prints of sinfonias with their designations of *tuono*. Moreover, numerous prints and manuscripts of instrumental music that do not use designations of *tuono* nonetheless order their sonatas according to the same scheme of tonalities as seen in Table 6.4c. All of the collections of instrumental music represented in Tables 6.4b and 6.4c adhere to identical or similar arrangements of finals and key signatures.

---

15 In contrast with Bononcini's use of a minor-third tonality for Mode 7, Arresti used a major-third tonality. This particular difference between the two composers reflects the unusually diverse set of tonal criteria used by *Seicento* theorists and composers to represent Mode 7. See Tables 6.4a–c, for example, which show seven different representations of Mode (or *Tuono*) 7.

16 Adriano Banchieri, *Cartella musicale* (Venice: Giacomo Vincenti, 1614; facsimile, Bologna: Forni, 1968); Penna, *Li primi albori*; Bartolomeo Bismantova, *Compendio musicale*, MS, Ferrara, 1677–94 (facsimile, Florence: Studio per Edizioni Scelte, 1978); Anonymous, *Regole del contrappunto*, MS, early 1700s, I-Bc, P.120, n. 5; and Tevo, *Musico testore*.

Table 6.4a   The church keys in treatises (finals and key signatures)

A. Banchieri (1614): "gl'Otto Tuoni Ecclesiastici"			L. Penna (1672): "li Tuoni armoniali"			B. Bismantova (1677–94): "del Tuono"			Anonymous (early 1700s): "li Toni"			Z. Tevo (1706): "gli otto Tuoni delli Moderni"		
Tuono	Final	Key Sig.	*Tuono*	Final	Key Sig.	*Tuono*	Final	Key Sig.	*Tuono*	Final	Key Sig.	*Tuono*	Final	Key Sig.
1	d	—	1	d	—	1	d	—	1	d	—	1	d	—
2	g	♭	2	g	♭	2	g	♭	2	g	♭	2	g	♭
3	a	—	3	a	—	3	a	—	3	a	—	3	a	—
4	e	—	4	e	—	4	e	—	4	e	—	4	e	—
5	C	—	5	C	—	5	C	—	5	C	—	5	C	—
6	F	♭	6	F	♭	6	F	♭	6	F	♭	6	F	♭
7	d	♭	*7	d / D / e	♭ / ♯ / ♯	7	d	♭	7	e	♯	7	e	♯
8	G	—	8	G	—	8	G	—	8	G	—	8	G	—

* Penna lists three tonalities in the category of *settimo tuono.*

Sources: Adriano Banchieri, *Cartella musicale* (Venice: Vincenti, 1614), 70–72; Lorenzo Penna, *Li primi albori musicali* (Bologna: Monti, 1672), 128–32; Bartolomeo Bismantova, *Compendio musicale*, MS, 1677–94; Anonymous, *Regole del contrappunto*, MS, early 18th century; Zaccaria Tevo, *Il musico testore* (Venice: Bortoli, 1706), 327–32.

Table 6.4b   Tonal cycles in Merula, Leoni, and Marini

Tarquinio Merula, Op. 17 (1651): Sinfonie di tutti gli Tuoni				Gio. Ant. Leoni, Op. 3 (1652): Sonate di violino a voce sola				Biagio Marini, Op. 22 (1655): Sinfonia 1° Tuono … 6° Tuono			
Sinfonia	*Tuono*	**Final**	**Key Sig.**	*Sonatas*	*Tono*	**Final**	**Key Sig.**	*Sinfonia*	*Tuono*	**Final**	**Key Sig.**
Prima	1	d	—	Nos. 1–4	1	d	—	*Prima*	1	d	—
Seconda	2	g	♭	Nos. 5–10	2	g	♭	*Seconda*	2	g	♭
Terza	3	a	—	Nos. 11–15	3	a	—	*Terza*	3	a	—
Quarta	4	e	—	Nos. 16–20	4	e	—	*Quarta*	4	e	—
Quinta	5	C	—		—			*Quinta*	5	C	—
Sesta	6	F	♭	Nos. 21–24	6	F	♭	*Sesta*	6	F	♭
Settima	7	d	♭			—				—	
Ottava	8	G	—	Nos. 25–28	8	G	—			—	

Sources: Tarquinio Merula, *Il quarto libro delle canzoni da suonare a doi & a tre*, Op. 17 (Venice: Vincenti, 1651); Giovanni Antonio Leoni, *Sonate di violino a voce sola*, Op. 3 (Rome: Mascardi, 1652); and Biagio Marini, *Per ogni sorte d'stromento [sic] musicale, diversi generi di sonate da chiesa e da camera*, Op. 22 (Venice: Magni, 1655).

Table 6.4c   Tonal schemes followed in works for instrumental ensemble (finals and key signatures)

Tuono	G. Legrenzi, Op. 2 (1655): sonatas a 2			G. Legrenzi, Op. 2 (1655): sonatas a 3			G. M. Placuzzi, Op. 1 (1667)			P. Degli Antonii, Op. 4 (1676)		
	Suonata	Final	Key Sig.	*Suonata*	Final	Key Sig.	*Suonata.*	Final	Key Sig.	*Sonata*	Final	Key Sig.
1	*1* "La Cornara"	d	—	*1* "La Zabarella"	d	—	*1*	d	—	*1*	d	—
2	*2* "La Spilimberga"	g	♭	*2* "La Mont'Albana"	g	♭	*2*	g	♭	*2*	g	♭
3	*3* "La Frangipana"	a	—	*3* "La Porcia"	a	—	*3*	a	—	*3*	a	—
4		—		*4* "La Valvasona"	e	—	*4*	e	—	*4*	e	#
5	*4* "La Strasolda"	C	—	*5* "La Querini"	C	—	*5*	C	—	*5*	C	—
6		—			—		*6*	F	♭	*6*	F	♭
7	*5* "La Col'Alta"	D	#	*6* "La Torriana"	c	♭	*7*	D	##	*7*	D	##
8	*6* "La Raspona"	G	—	*7* "La Justiniana"	G	—	*8*	G	—	*8*	G	—
—							*9*	D	##	*9*	B♭	♭
—							*10*	C	—	*10*	A	##
—								—		*11*	c	♭♭
—										*12*	E♭	♭♭

Sources: Giovanni Legrenzi, *Sonate a due, e tre*, Op. 2 (Venice: Magni, 1655); Gioseffo Maria Placuzzi, *Suonate à duoi, à trè, à quattro*, Op. 1 (Bologna: Monti, 1667); Pietro Degli Antonii, *Sonate a violino solo*, Op. 4 (Bologna: Monti, 1676).

Table 6.4c   cont'd

Tuono	G. B. Degli Antonii, Op. 5 (1689)			Gio. Legrenzi, Op. 16 (1691)			Domenico Galli, MS (1691)			Bernardo Tonini, Op. 2 (1697)		
	Ricercata	Final	Key Sig.	*Balletto*	Final	Key Sig.	*Trattenimento*	Final	Key Sig.	*Sonata*	Final	Key Sig.
1	*1*	d	—	*1*	d	—	*1*	d	—	*1*	d	—
2	*2*	g	♭	*2*	g	♭	*2*	g	♭	*2*	g	♭
3	*3*	a	—	*3*	a	—	*3*	a	—	*3*	a	—
4	*4*	e	—	*4*	e	—	*4*	e	—	*4*	e	♯
5	*5*	C	—	*5*	C	—	*5*	c	♭♭	*5*	C	—
6	*6*	F	♭	*6*	F	♭	*6*	F	♭	*6*	F	♭
7	*7**	E	♯♯	*7*	D	♯	*7*	d	♭	*7*	B♭	♭
8	*8*	G	—	*8*	G / e	— / ♯	*8*	C	—	*8*	G	—
—	*9*	E♭	♭♭	*9*	B♭ / B♭	♭ / ♭♭	*9*	d	—	*9*	c	♭♭
—	*10*	b	♯♯				*10*	B♭	♭♭	*10*	A	♯♯
—		—						—		*11*	D	♯♯
—		—						—		*12*	b	♯♯

* G♯ is not in the key signature, but is written throughout the piece.

Sources: Giovanni Battista Degli Antonii, *Ricercate à violino, e violoncello ò clavicembalo*, Op. 5 (Bologna: Monti, 1689); Giovanni Legrenzi, *Balletti e correnti a cinque stromenti, con il basso continuo per il cembalo*, Op. 16 (Venice: Sala, 1691); Domenico Galli, *Trattenimento musicale sopra il violoncello*, no opus, MS, 1691, I-MOe, shelf-number MUS. C. 81; Bernardo Tonini, *Suonate da chiesa a tre, due violini & organo, con violoncello ad libitum*, Op. 2 (Venice: Sala, 1697).

The Church Keys and their Transpositions

Although incompatible with traditional dodecachordal theory, the finals and key signatures of Arresti's sonatas in their particular order point up a widespread practice among his contemporaries. On this broader level, the agreement among the eight tonalities of those prints that have eight, or the first eight of those that have ten or twelve (like Arresti's Op. 4), testifies to a common idea among late-*Seicento* sonata composers of tonal space as embodied in this set of finals and key signatures. To judge from his formulation of a similar set of seven tonalities, Bononcini was certainly aware of this tonal scheme, but his connection of it to the dodecachordal theory of Glarean and Zarlino contradicts the orderings of every other print. The eight-fold scheme of tonalities seen in the various prints reveals a recurrent organizing principle in Italian instrumental music, but it is not compatible with Zarlinian modal theory. Bononcini, by asserting an equivalence between these eight finals and key signatures (reduced to seven in his treatise) and the modes, aims to simplify a complex set of affairs. However, none of the tonalities in 6.4a through 6.4c are modal, transposed or otherwise. Instead, they originate in *alternatim* psalmody and, as a collection of tonalities, comprise the church keys or *tuoni ecclesiastici* described earlier. Despite their origins in psalmody, these *tuoni* were widely used by composers for various instrumental genres, both secular and sacred.[17]

In separate studies that treat these church keys, Joel Lester and Harold Powers have traced paths laid out by French, German, and Italian treatises back to Pietro Pontio's *Raggionamento di musica* (1588) and Adriano Banchieri's *Cartella musicale* (1614).[18] As Powers noted, Pontio first demonstrated the distinction between modes and psalm tones, and Banchieri first set the psalm tones down schematically as finals and key signatures, the form in which they were transmitted throughout the seventeenth century. Banchieri's *tuoni ecclesiastici*, according to Powers, take their finals from the last note of specific psalm tone *differentiae*, and they derive their key signatures from a system of transpositions designed to reduce the range of the different reciting tones of each psalm tone.[19]

In short, the eight tonalities that permeate the sonata repertory were first detailed by Banchieri as those used for the polyphonic setting of the psalm tones.[20]

---

17 See n. 7 above, in which their original function is described in Dodds, "Tonal Types."

18 Harold S. Powers, "From Psalmody to Tonality," in *Tonal Structures in Early Music*, ed. Cristle Collins Judd (New York: Garland, 1998), 275–340; and Lester, *Between Modes and Keys*, 77–82. Powers's article is devoted to the history of the psalm tone tonalities, otherwise known as psalm tone keys or church keys. See also Powers and Wiering, "Mode," 814–19.

19 Powers, "From Psalmody to Tonality," 291, 296, and Table 4. Other studies of seventeenth-century psalmody and the church keys cited by Powers in his article are Almonte C. Howell, Jr., "French Baroque Organ Music and the Eight Church Tones," *Journal of the American Musicological Society* 11 (1958): 106–18; Robert Frederick Bates, "From Mode to Key: A Study of Seventeenth-Century French Liturgical Organ Music and Music Theory," Ph.D. dissertation, Stanford University, 1986; and Walter Atcherson, "Key and Mode in Seventeenth-Century Music Theory Books," *Journal of Music Theory* 17 (1973): 204–33.

20 Ibid.; and Powers and Wiering, "Mode," 817, ex. 23.

Bononcini's set of seven finals and key signatures originates in these tonalities and not in the modes.[21] His rationalization of them in terms of modal theory, however, does follow the lead of a number of theorists (including Banchieri himself) who sought to reconcile psalmodic practices and modal theory.[22]

Despite the complexities of Bononcini's detailed modal theory and its prehistory, his collection of seven tonalities stands at the center of *Seicento* instrumental practice. Furthermore, as both Bononcini and Berardi attest, transposition by means of key signatures represents a crucial part of the musical practice from the late seventeenth century.[23] A particularly clear demonstration of both the core set of tonalities and transpositions of this set comes from Giovanni Battista Degli Antonii's *Versetti per tutti li tuoni*, Op. 2 (1687), whose table of contents is shown in Table 6.5a. The title of the print indicates both "natural" and transposed *tuoni* among the versets; the table of contents further specifies untransposed versions and whole-step transpositions (both downward and upward) for each of eight tonalities—except for the fourth and seventh, which occur only in untransposed form. Degli Antonii's eight *tuoni*, untransposed, employ the same set as those in the octonary schemes in treatises by Banchieri, Penna, etc. (see Table 6.4a); the various instrumental works listed in Tables 6.4b and 6.4c; Arresti's *toni* 1–8 (Table 6.3a); and Bononcini's seven (Table 6.2c). Degli Antonii further expands these eight tonalities into a larger set of 16 through upward and downward transpositions of a whole-step (see Table 6.5b).

---

21 See especially Table 5 of Powers, "From Psalmody to Tonality."

22 Powers and Wiering, "Mode," 816. An early example of this kind of reconciliation may be found in Banchieri, *Cartella musicale*, 112–36, in which he describes each of the twelve modes in terms of the eight *tuoni ecclesiastici*. Bononcini goes about the same procedure, but in the reverse order: he explains his seven practicable "modes" in terms of the dodecachordal system.

23 Writings from this period that are relevant to transposition are Angelo Berardi, *Il perche musicale* (Bologna: Monti, 1693), 53–4; Berardi, *Miscellanea musicale*, 176–8; and Bononcini, *Musico prattico*, 137–47 and 154–5. Unlike Berardi, who presents various modal transpositions without comment, Bononcini discusses transpositions either in the context of the seven practicable modes (and how these relate to the modes of the dodecachordal system) or in the context of how one might recognize the mode of a composition. Bononcini (p. 146) also mentions an expressive impact of transpositions, but does not relate this to his seven practicable modes. He writes: "Per rendere il Canto più allegro, ò più mesto li trasportano tutti ordinariamente una voce più alta, ò più bassa per mezo di questi segni *b♯* … senza variar luogo alle Chiavi, le quali non si trasportano [In order to make the song happier or sadder, it is transposed usually up or down a whole-step by means of these *b♯* … without changing the position of the clefs, which are not transposed]."

Table 6.5a   G. B. Degli Antonii, V*ersetti per tutti li tuoni tanto naturali, come trasportati per l'organo*, Op. 2 (Bologna, 1687)[†]

Contents:	
Versetti del Primo Tuono naturale.	Page 8
Versetti del Primo Tuono, una voce più alta.	15
Versetti del Primo Tuono, una voce più bassa.	21
Versetti del Secondo Tuono naturale.	26
Versetti del Secondo Tuono, una voce più alta.	31
Versetti del Secondo Tuono, una voce più bassa.	36
Versetti del Terzo Tuono naturale.	42
Versetti del Terzo Tuono, una voce più alta.	48
Versetti del Terzo Tuono, una voce più bassa.	54
Versetti del Quarto Tuono.	59
Versetti del Quinto Tuono naturale.	64
Versetti del Quinto Tuono, una voce più alta.	70
Versetti del Quinto Tuono, una voce più bassa.	76
Versetti del Sesto Tuono naturale.	82
Versetti del Sesto Tuono, una voce più alta.	88
Versetti del Sesto Tuono, una voce più bassa.	94
Versetti del Settimo Tuono.	100
Versetti del Ottavo Tuono naturale.	106
Versetti del Ottavo Tuono, una voce più alta.	112
Versetti del Ottavo Tuono, una voce più bassa.	118

[†]   In English translation, the title reads: "Versets in all of the *tuoni*, both natural and transposed, for the organ."

Table 6.5b   The *tuoni* of G. B. Degli Antonii, *Versetti*

Tuono	naturale (untransposed)		una voce più alta ($\uparrow$M2)		una voce più bassa ($\downarrow$M2)	
	Final	Key Signature	Final	Key Signature	Final	Key Signature
1	d	—	*e	♯	c	♭♭
2	g	♭	*a	—	f	♭♭♭
3	a	—	b	♯♯	*g	♭
4	e	—	None included		None included	
5	C	—	D	♯♯	B♭	♭♭

6	F	♭	*G	—	*E♭	♭♭
7	d	♭	None included		None included	
8	G	—	A	♯♯	*F	♭

*   Irregular key signature for the transposition indicated.

Thus, Bononcini's explication of a fundamental set of tonalities, and its expansion into a more comprehensive system by means of transposing key signatures, provides an invaluable source for our understanding of late-*Seicento* tonalities. A blueprint for seventeenth-century tonal practice, his Op. 6 sonatas augment the seven practicable "modes," the core set of tonalities, to a greater number by transposing several of the original seven to various pitch levels. The ramifications of this discovery would be that the finals and key signatures of all compositions ought to agree either with what may be considered the "primary" or core set of tonalities—the church keys or their rough equivalent in Bononcini's seven commonly used "modes"—or with transpositions of them.

In order to explore the applicability of these primary tonalities and their transpositions to a broader sample of instrumental prints, I have combined Bononcini's practicable modes and the octonary sets of church keys into a composite set of tonalities which may then be tested against a representative selection from the late-*Seicento* sonata repertory, that is, the sonatas of Bononcini, Corelli, and Giuseppe Torelli. Tables 6.6a through 6.6c list the tonalities of Bononcini's Op. 6 (Table 6.6a) and those used by Arcangelo Corelli (Table 6.6b) and Giuseppe Torelli (Table 6.6c) arranged, or rearranged in Bononcini's case, according to the composite set of tonalities and their transpositions. Bononcini's rearranged Op. 6 furnishes a useful start, showing his practice uncoupled from his theory. Corelli and Torelli, two of the best-known composers of instrumental music from the late *Seicento*, are taken here as models of the compositional practice of the period.[24]

Table 6.6a   The tonalities of G. M. Bononcini, Op. 6

Tuono	Primary tonality (untransposed)		Transposed ↓P4 or ↑P5 and ↓ P5 or ↑P4		Transposed ↓M2 and ↑M2	
	Final	Key Signature	Final	Key Signature	Final	Key Signature
1	d	—			c	♭♭
2	g	♭				
3 and 4	[a	—]*	e	♯	b	♯♯
5	C	—			B♭	♭♭
6	F	♭			E♭	♭♭

---

24   Both composers have attained positions of note in the history of music, Torelli as an important and early contributor to the concerto, and Corelli as the unparalleled master of the trio sonata, the concerto grosso, and the solo violin sonata.

7	D	♯♯			A	♯♯
8	G	—				
Tonus Peregrinus	[d	♭]*				

* Tonalities in brackets do not occur in Bononcini's Op. 6 sonatas, but are listed among the seven practicable modes explained in his treatise, *Musico prattico*.

Table 6.6b   The tonalities of A. Corelli, Opp. 1–6

Tuono	Primary tonality (untransposed)		Transposed ↓P4 or ↑P5 and ↓P5 or ↑P4		Transposed ↓M2 and ↑M2		Transposed ↓m3 and ↑m3	
	Final	Key Sig.	Final	Key Sig.	Final	Key Sig.	Final	Key Sig.
1	d	— (5)†			c	♭♭ (3)	f	♭♭(1)**
2	g	♭ (6)						
3 and 4	a	— (3)	e	♯ (4)	b	♯♯(4)	f♯	♯♯♯ (1)
5	C	— (6)						
6	F	♭ (10)	B♭	♭ (7)	E♭	♭♭ (1)		
7	D	♯♯ (8)						
8	G	— (4)			A	♯♯ (5)	E	♯♯♯ (3)
Tonus Peregrinus	d	♭ (1)						

** Corelli writes in the flat for cach A♭—as well as for each D♭—of this piece.
† Numbers in parentheses indicate the number of times that tonality occurs in the composer's complete published oeuvre.

Table 6.6c   The tonalities of G. Torelli, Opp. 1–6

Tuono	Primary tonality (no transposition)		Transposed ↓P4 or ↑P5 and ↓P5 or ↑P4		Transposed ↓M2 and ↑M2	
	Final	Key Sig.	Final	Key Sig.	Final	Key Sig.
1	d	— (6)†			c	♭♭ (5)
2	g	♭ (7)				
3 and 4	a	— (7)	e	♯ (6)	b	♯♯ (3)
5	C	— (5)			B♭	♭♭ (1)
6	F	♭ (6)	B♭	♭ (2)		
7	D	♯♯ (8)				
8	G	— (6)			A	♯♯ (8)

My composite set and the tonalities to which its categories apply are shown in the two left-hand columns of Tables 6.6a through 6.6c under "Tuono" and "Primary tonality." On the one hand, the categories used in the composite set follow Bononcini's plan by combining Modes 3 and 4 into a single category; on the other, they alter his scheme by substituting a D-tonality with two sharps for the D-tonality with one flat that he used. (Bononcini's scheme may be compared with mine by referring back to Table 6.2c.) The basis for this substitution lies in the precedent set by Arresti and others who use a D-tonality with two sharps to represent the seventh *tuono*.[25] The D-tonality with two sharps also occurs far more frequently in the sonata literature, whereas the D-tonality with one flat occurs only infrequently.[26] Theorists sometimes characterized the latter tonality as a ninth tone, the *tonus peregrinus*, a designation I have adopted in Tables 6.6a and 6.6b for a ninth *tuono*.[27]

By arranging the finals and key signatures used by these composers according to the primary tonalities and their transpositions, Tables 6.6a through 6.6c account for the majority of sonata tonalities from this period, not only those that agree with modern tonal practice in terms of key signature, but also those that do not—that is, key signatures known as "incomplete." The categorization of tonalities in Tables 6.6a through 6.6c according to families related by transpositions is predicated, not only on Bononcini's (Table 6.2b), Berardi's (Example 6.2), and Degli Antonii's examples (Table 6.5b) of transposed *tuoni*, but also on the use of related tonalities within a single composition. Composers regularly cast the inner movements of their sonatas in a tonality a fifth away from that of the opening and closing movements. While some effect this change between movements without a change in key signature, others mark the related tonality of the inner movement with a new signature. Torelli, for example, uses the following pairs of tonalities between different movements within a composition: A, no signature, and E, one sharp; E, one sharp, and B, two sharps; A, two sharps, and E, three sharps.[28] The first two pairs of these finals and key signatures can be explained in terms of major-minor tonality as A minor, E minor, and B minor; but the third pair—A major with only two sharps and E major with

---

25 The D-tonality with B♭ originated as the tonality for the polyphonic setting of the seventh psalm tone transposed down a fifth into *cantus mollis*, while the more common D-tonality in *cantus durus* (no flat in its key signature) was that used for the first psalm tone. For an account of the replacement of the D-tonality with one flat by the D-tonality with two sharps, first attested and illustrated in French organ music and accompanying theory, see Powers, "From Psalmody to Tonality," 305–12. Tone 7, in fact, has the most variants of all the church keys, including an E-tonality with one sharp (see Table 6.1c for Tevo's listing of Tone 7).

26 Tables 6.6b and 6.6c show that Corelli uses a D-tonality with a single flat only once and that Torelli never uses it. Nor does Bononcini use this tonality in his Op. 6, even though he presents it as one of the seven modes in common use.

27 Penna, *Li primi albori*, 123. Note that Arresti uses a D-tonality with one flat for the ninth sonata of his Op. 4 (see Table 6.3a).

28 Giuseppe Torelli, *Sonate à tre stromenti*, Op. 1 (Bologna: Micheletti, 1686), *Sonata terza* contains movements whose tonalities are E with one sharp and B with two sharps. His *Sonata settima* contains both A with no signature and E with one sharp. Torelli, *Concerti grossi*, Op. 8 (Bologna: Silvani, 1709), *Concerto terzo* contains E with three sharps and A with two sharps.

only three—defies categorization according to the modern system of major-minor keys. This facet of the earlier practice exemplifies how simultaneously familiar and foreign seventeenth-century "keys" seem according to a modern perspective: the tonalities used in the late *Seicento* largely accord with those used in later centuries, but the apparent idiosyncrasies of the earlier practice reveal a system distinct from that of major-minor tonality.

Two Cases: The "Phrygian" E-Tonality and the "Plagal" G-Tonality

If Tables 6.6a through 6.6c clarify the system of primary versus transposed tonalities in effect during the seventeenth century, they cannot furnish better than provisional outlines in the matter of categorizing transposed tonalities because composers' transposition schemes were not consistent. B♭ tonalities, for example, used one or two flats in their key signature—sometimes in the practice of a single composer (see Table 6.6c). Similarly, G. B. Degli Antonii's scheme of transposed tonalities shown in Table 6.5b reveals a striking number of anomalies when transposed tonalities are compared with their untransposed correlatives.[29] In short, we cannot be sure of the transposition or of the psalm tone category for some tonalities solely on the basis of a final and key signature. Largely identical tonalities of this period do not necessarily use the same key signature, and transpositions were sometimes effected with irregular key signatures by modern standards.

As a further step in establishing the psalm tone origins of seventeenth-century tonalities, however, we can make specific determinations of a composition's affinity with one or another psalm tone on the basis of cadence points and other details in the course of the composition. Tonalities relating to two of the eight psalm tones, the fourth and the eighth, afford particularly illuminating examples.

---

29 Even Bononcini's carefully rationalized Op. 6 sonatas include an anomalous key signature. The last sonata of the print, No. 12, although described as an instance of Mode 12 transposed up a minor third, uses a key signature of two flats and not three (see Table 6.2b). From his writings, moreover, we know that Bononcini himself considered such examples to be anomalies. In *Musico prattico*, 154–5, he lists a number of exceptions that defy the rules of transposition set out immediately beforehand: Mode 1 transposed up a major second = E with one sharp (not two); Mode 8 transposed down a minor third = E with two sharps (not three); Mode 11 transposed down a major second = B♭ with one flat (not two); and Mode 12 transposed up a minor third = E♭ with two flats (not three), as in his Op. 6, No. 12. Although Bononcini provides no explanation for the missing accidentals of certain key signatures, he does give advice for determining the transposition (and thus the mode) of a composition in such cases: "i detti segni si ritrovano poi collocati trà la Composizione nelle corde, ove doverebbero essere posti nel principio; per il che si deve ancora riguardare alle cadenze regolari, mediante le quali non si potrà errare [the above-mentioned signs are to be found among the notes of the composition, instead of placed at the beginning as they should be; for which reason one must still look to the regular cadences, by means of which one cannot err]."

Tone 4

Perhaps more than any other tonality in late-*Seicento* instrumental music, the E-tonality that is derived from Tone 4 of the eight psalm tones produces examples that defy analysis in terms of major-minor tonality. Referring to Table 6.7a, taken from Banchieri's *Cartella musicale*, we see that his scheme for composing polyphony on Tone 4 uses E as the final, which is taken from the last note of the psalm tone's *differentia* or *fine*. While Banchieri gives no principal degrees for Tone 4, the points of imitation he gives use the final, E, and the fourth degree above the final, A. The emphasis on the fourth degree reflects the prominence of the psalm tone's reciting tone, which is A. Banchieri's duo in Tone 4 (Example 6.3a) provides a case in point: the main subject outlines an A-minor triad, and the occasional use of G♯ (mm. 4 and 17) intensifies this sense of A as the tonic. Cadences on E, the actual tonic of this short piece (m. 14 and mm. 18–19), typify the Phrygian cadence wherein E is approached from F♮, a half-step above. An earlier example in four voices occurs in a Tone 4 verset from an anonymous collection, *Intavolatura d'organo*, published in 1598 (see Example 6.3b):[30] G♯s strengthen the cadences on A (see mm. 7, 9, and 18), but the movement itself ends on E where that pitch is approached from F♮ in the top voice and from A in the bass.

---

30 The full title of this collection of versets (Venice: Vincenti, 1598; facsimile, Bologna: Forni, 1970) reads: *Intavolatura d'organo facilissima: accommodata in versetti sopra gli otto tuoni ecclesiastici, con la quale si può giustamente risponder à messe, à salmi, & à tutto quello che è necessario al choro* [Very easy organ tablature: organized in versets on the eight *tuoni ecclesiastici*, with which one can correctly respond to the choir for masses, psalms, and everything necessary for the choir].

Table 6.7   A. Banchieri, *Cartella musicale*, 3rd ed. (Venice, 1614)

(a) Tone 4 in plainchant and in polyphony

Intonation, reciting tone, and principal differentia, p. 71

Polyphonic composition on the psalmtone (tenor voice only), p. 85

(b) Tone 8 in plainchant and polyphony

Intonation, reciting tone, and principal differentia, p. 71

Polyphonic composition on the psalmtone (tenor voice only), p. 87

Example 6.3a   A. Banchieri, *Cartella musicale* (Venice, 1614), Duo del quarto
tuono ecclesiastico

Example 6.3b Anonymous, *Intavolatura d'organo* (Venice, 1598), Primo [versetto] del quarto tuono

The tonality descended from the fourth psalm tone, neither major nor minor, instead evinces Phrygian characteristics in the Tone 4 compositions by Banchieri and the anonymous author of the 1598 *Intavolatura*. This same tonality occurs frequently in the sonata repertory. Example 6.4 furnishes excerpts from the first movement of Cazzati's, Op. 55, No. 4, "La Cagnola." From a modern tonal perspective, A functions as the tonic and E as the dominant. Yet E, the seeming dominant articulated through the Phrygian cadence, is the most frequent and final point of arrival in the movement and the sonata. The characteristics of this example recall Examples 6.1a– 6.1d from the opening of this chapter; there, too, seeming A-minor compositions feature endings on E. All of these pieces (Examples 6.1a–6.1d and Example 6.4) demonstrate the tonality—distinct from the later and more familiar E minor and A minor—that is derived from polyphonic settings of Tone 4.

Example 6.4　　　M. Cazzati, Op. 55, No. 4 "La Cagnola" (1670)

Example 6.4   cont'd

(mm. 21-end)

Half a century after Banchieri's time, such Phrygian pieces presented an enigma to the theorist-composer Bononcini, who attempted to de-emphasize the unique features of the Phrygian E-tonality by merging it with Tone 3, a minor-third A-tonality (see Table 6.2c). Although he rationalizes all of the *tuoni ecclesiastici* in terms of modal categories, Bononcini's consolidation of Tones 3 and 4 reveals a crucial aspect of his thinking that brings his perspective closer to our own: since dominant harmonic relationships were becoming the determinants of a tonal center in Italian music, Phrygian pieces that ended on E, as approached from either A or F, were heard by Bononcini as A-tonalities that ended on their dominants (and not as distinct E-tonalities). The E-tonality that Bononcini himself used includes an F♯ in its key signature, so he could interpret it only as a transposed A-tonality and not as a separate E-tonality.[31] By subsuming what appeared to be two similar variants of an A-tonality under a single category, Bononcini the modal theorist-practitioner offered a relatively modern interpretation. Well into the eighteenth century, theorists continued to argue that newer theories based on two modes, major and minor, amounted to an oversimplification precisely because of the Phrygian tonality.[32] The distinction between E Phrygian and A minor in the examples shown here underscores both the subtleties and the critical consequence of seventeenth-century tonal style.

Bononcini never used the Phrygian tonality in his sonatas, but neither did he ignore its existence altogether. Examples 6.5a and 6.5b show his duos in "Mode 10" that replace "Modes 3 and 4." True to his desire to merge what are actually Tones 3 and 4 of the *tuoni ecclesiastici* by representing them with one replacing A-tonality,

---

31 The E-tonality with one sharp that Bononcini uses for his Op. 6, No. 6 is, in fact, categorized by him as Mode 10 (the replacement for Modes 3 and 4) transposed down a perfect fourth (see Table 6.2b).

32 Lester, *Between Modes and Keys*, 124, reports Johann Kuhnau's reservations concerning Johann Mattheson's scheme of 24 major and minor keys. Kuhnau's doubts hinge, in part, on the question of Phrygian tonalities.

Bononcini used just one duo for both. He also included one feature to distinguish them: while the first duo (Example 6.5a), to use our terminology, conforms to A minor with a cadence on the tonic, the second (Example 6.5b) includes a cadence on E—the emblematic Phrygian cadence of Tone 4—added onto the end and marked *cadenza finale del quarto tuono*.[33] Remarkably, Corelli appears to have distinguished the finale of his Op. 1, No. 4 (Example 6.1a) as a Tone 4 composition in precisely the same way as Bononcini had done with his duo: Corelli's Presto contains nothing that would disturb an analysis in A minor until the final bars (mm. 36–9), which, enigmatically to our ears, end this sonata finale with a Phrygian cadence on E.

Example 6.5a   G. M. Bononcini, *Musico prattico* (Bologna, 1673), 140

Duo del decimo Tuono nelle sue proprie Corde
naturali, che serve in luogo del terzo

Example 6.5b   G. M. Bononcini, *Musico prattico* (Bologna, 1673), 140–41

Duo del decimo Tuono nelle sue proprie Corde
naturali, che serve in luogo del quarto

Cadenza finale del
quarto Tuono

33 Bononcini, *Musico prattico*, 140–41.

Tone 8

The seventeenth-century analog to G major provides another case of that era's distinctive tonal style—a G-tonality based on the eighth psalm tone that differs from common-practice major keys. The distinction lies in its use of C (along with or instead of D) as its secondary cadential point, hence my term "plagal" to describe it. In the eighth psalm tone, as explained by Banchieri (see Table 6.7b), the last note of the principal *differentia* is G, and this is taken by Banchieri and others as the final for polyphonic settings of that psalm tone. An additional detail of this tonality derives from the reciting tone of Tone 8, which is C. As seen in Table 6.7b, Banchieri includes C along with G and D as principal degrees of Tone 8. The importance of C in Tone 8 carries over to its derived G-tonality: two examples (Examples 6.6a and 6.6b), a duo by Banchieri himself and a four-part setting from the anonymous 1598 collection of versets, illustrate how C, not D, functions as a pitch center second only to G in polyphonic settings of Tone 8.[34] In Banchieri's duo (Example 6.6a) only one cadence occurs on D in m. 15, while cadences on C occur three times in mm. 5, 8, and 18. This last unison on C in m. 18 ultimately resolves by contrary motion to the final cadence of the piece on G. Similar to Banchieri's duo in Tone 8, both of the two Tone 8 versets from the 1598 *Intavolatura* favor C as a secondary degree behind the tonic G: the first of the two versets (shown here in Example 6.6b) presents a subject that pivots between G and C as the two melodic poles in the motif (mm. 1–4). As in Banchieri's duo, C acts here as a strong point of arrival, as seen particularly in mm. 9 and 11. Also noteworthy is the plagal cadence that ends this verset, reinforcing—to use modern terms—the tonic–subdominant polarity of the piece.

---

34 These are free polyphonic settings in that they do not incorporate the psalm tone as a cantus firmus. Instead, they assume only the tonal characteristics of the psalm tone.

Example 6.6a   A. Banchieri, *Cartella musicale* (Venice, 1614), Duo dell'ottavo tuono ecclesiastico

Example 6.6b   Anonymous, *Intavolatura d'organo* (Venice, 1598), Primo [versetto] dell'ottavo tuono

Examples taken from late-*Seicento* sonatas in this G-tonality illustrate various methods for giving prominence to C, which may be traced to the original psalm tone itself. Example 6.7a shows excerpts from Arresti's Op. 4, No. 8 (1665). This piece belongs to his print of sonatas ordered by *tono*, and Arresti includes the designation, *ottavo tono* at the beginning of this one. Here the second movement illustrates the prominence of C—making its mid-point cadence (marked by the double bar after m. 21) on that pitch—within this piece that begins and ends in G.

Example 6.7a   G. C. Arresti, Op. 4, No. 8 (1665)

ii. Ottavo Tono (mm. 1-8)

Example 6.7a   cont'd

(mm. 16-24)

Excerpts from Legrenzi's Op. 2 (1655) add further examples. In his edition of Legrenzi's Op. 2 sonatas, Stephen Bonta observes that Legrenzi organized his sonatas according to the *tuoni ecclesiastici*.[35] The first two columns in Table 6.4c, which is based on information given in Bonta's edition, shows Legrenzi's manner of doing so: his Op. 2 separates the sonatas *a 2* and *a 3*, and both subsets loosely follow the pattern of the *tuoni ecclesiastici*. As seen in Table 6.4c, however, there are omissions: Tone 6 occurs among neither the sonatas *a 2*, nor the sonatas *a 3*; and Tone 4 does not occur among the sonatas *a 2*. Despite these gaps, musical features of the individual sonatas beyond final and key signature illustrate the close connection between the tonal features of Legrenzi's sonatas and those of the *tuoni ecclesiastici*. As seen in Example 6.7b, the sonata "La Raspona" illustrates this trait in the successive entrances of the subject: the first two occur on G (mm. 1–3), but the next occurs on C in m. 5, just before an authentic cadence on that pitch in m. 6. Subsequent entries occur on D in m. 9 and again on C in m. 14, immediately before a cadence on that pitch. The end of the movement itself elides with the beginning of the following movement, which is articulated by a cadence on C, the tonic of the second movement. The last measures of the final movement reinforce the tonal polarity of "La Raspona" between G and C by means of a florid plagal cadence in G (Example 6.7c).

---

35 *The Instrumental Music of Giovanni Legrenzi: Sonate a due e tre, opus 2, 1655*, ed. Stephen Bonta (Cambridge, MA: Harvard University Press, 1984), xiv.

Example 6.7b   G. Legrenzi, Op. 2, Sonata a 2 "La Raspona" (1655)

Example 6.7c   G. Legrenzi, Sonata a 2, "La Raspona"

iv. (conclusion)

A similar propensity for emphasizing the fourth degree in Bolognese G-tonality sonatas occurs where there are neither modal designations nor any discernible arrangement of the sonatas within a print according to the church keys. Example 6.8a, taken from Giovanni Battista Vitali's Op. 2, No. 11 (1667), shows the brief fugue that initiates the sonata, in which the cadences made at the ending of the subject repeatedly stress the first (mm. 5, 9, and 13) and fourth scale degrees (mm. 3, 7, and 11). The final two movements of Giovanni Battista Bassani's Op. 5, No. 3 (1683) (Examples 6.8b and 6.8c) similarly treat C as the most prominent scale degree after G. In Bassani's Largo the beginning and ending cadences in G (mm. 1–3 and 6–8) are both prepared by a pronounced emphasis on C. In the subsequent movement (Allegro, allegro), the only strong cadences occur on G (mm. 3–4 and 16–17) and C (mm. 8–9 and 12–13). In all three cases (Examples 6.8a through 6.8c), the feature that marks these G-tonality pieces as derived from Tone 8 of the psalm tones likewise distinguishes them from compositions that we might otherwise analyze as G major.

Example 6.8a   G. B. Vitali, Op. 2, No. 11 (1667)

Example 6.8b   G. B. Bassani, Op. 5, No. 3 (1683)

iv. Largo (complete)

Example 6.8c   G. B. Bassani, Op. 5, No. 3 (1683)

* * *

Modern scholars have reacted in various ways to the tonal style of late-*Seicento* instrumental music, which has been taken to exemplify both modern keys and Renaissance modes. One of the greatest claims made for late-*Seicento* music is that modern tonal style coalesced within the repertory of its sonatas, particularly Corelli's. Manfred Bukofzer, for one, has asserted that "Arcangelo Corelli can take the credit for the full realization of tonality in the field of instrumental music."[36] Along similar lines of thinking, the works of composers immediately prior to Corelli have been described as incipiently tonal, bearing ever fewer traces of an earlier modal system as they progress forward in time.[37] One might be tempted to explain the first examples given in this chapter according to the same rationale: on the one hand, Examples 6.1a–d are related to one another as compositions in a tonality akin to A minor; on the other hand, Corelli's sonata, composed later in the century, is closest to the modern key with just a final cadence on E to distinguish it from A minor. (Cazzati's and Legrenzi's sonatas, by contrast, would stand at a greater distance from the realized modern tonal system.)

Recently, however, Corelli's music has been argued as evidence, not for emerging tonality in late seventeenth-century music, but for a long-standing modal conception of the period: the twelve-mode system that originates with Heinrich Glarean's *Dodecachordon* (1547).[38] Peter Allsop, Corelli's most recent biographer, observes that "throughout his career, Corelli shows a particular liking for the … less tonal cadence structures of Tone XII, which characteristically contrasts the tonic of C major with E minor as its *cadenza di mezzo*."[39] "Tone XII" or Mode 12, which is the plagal mode whose final is C, is here defined by its characteristic of making its

---

36 Manfred Bukofzer, *Music in the Baroque Era* (New York: Norton, 1947), 222. Dennis Libby, "Interrelationships in Corelli," *Journal of the American Musicological Association* 26 (1973): 263–87, seconds Bukofzer's opinion and goes into more detail (p. 267): "Very often one feels that the music is similar to something used elsewhere because it is the underlying harmonic progression and the way that it fits into the overall tonal format that really interests Corelli much more than the surface character of the music. Corelli's tendency to systematization and self-limitation in his tonal and harmonic procedures, as in others, helps to make this all very evident in the music. However, it was in this very systematization, while many of his contemporaries were casting about more experimentally in various directions, that Corelli created the basis of his later historical standing as one of the 'realizers' of tonality." To cite a more recent example, Richard Taruskin, *The Oxford History of Western Music*, 6 vols (Oxford and New York: Oxford University Press, 2005), vol. 2, *The Seventeenth and Eighteenth Centuries*, 181–92, similarly traces the origins of modern tonal style to late seventeenth-century Italian instrumental music in general and to Corelli in particular.

37 John Suess, "The Ensemble Sonatas of Maurizio Cazzati," *Analecta musicologica* 19 (1979): 146–85, finds a clear modal influence in Cazzati's earlier sonatas from the early 1640s. By contrast, Cazzati's later sonatas from the years 1665–70 illustrate, for Suess, a more tonal style.

38 Peter Allsop, *Arcangelo Corelli: "New Orpheus of Our Times"* (Oxford: Clarendon Press, and New York: Oxford University Press, 1999), 99–105 and 118–19, treats Corelli's tonal style and the twelve modes.

39 Ibid., 104.

secondary cadences in E minor, rather than the A minor that we might expect in a tonal piece in C.

The discovery of "modalisms" in Italian instrumental music has progressed even beyond Corelli to Vivaldi, whose harmonic practice in the concertos has been represented as "occupying a borderland between modality and tonality."[40] These more recent assertions share a crucial assumption with earlier scholarship: each of these assessments of tonal style view it within a modal–tonal dichotomy, and the resulting analytical method is to attribute modal practice to cases where some facet of the key or harmony defies tonal norms; works without such anomalies are deemed tonal. The evidence presented here resists such summaries of tonal practice. Moreover, it shifts the emphasis upon which our understanding is based from the more purely theoretical traditions to the composer's own perspective as determined by practical experience.

That practical experience was had in the church. As discussed in Chapter 1, Bolognese sonata composers most often worked in churches in the capacity of maestro di cappella, organist, or rank-and-file instrumentalist in an ensemble, so that their familiarity with the *tuoni ecclesiastici* was assured. Their musical training was also strongly grounded in church practice. This is shown by the fact that treatises of all kinds (see Table 6.4a)—from the scholarly to the practical and from those focused on the liturgy to those directed at a general audience of musicians—include the *tuoni ecclesiastici* as those used in polyphonic composition. Given this training and professional experience, sonata composers naturally transferred the tonal norms of church music to instrumental genres—even to dances, which were naturally intended for use outside the church (see Table 6.4c). In this way, tonalities that originated in psalmody could take on the broader role of "tonalities commonly used by composers today," as Bononcini described them.

A further practical argument for the use of the *tuoni ecclesiastici* in sonatas comes from the use of sonatas in the liturgy. In this system of tonalities and transpositions, a maestro di cappella seeking to integrate sonata movements with Mass items, psalms, motets, and organ versets into a unified tonal scheme could do so with ease. The tonal categories applied, for example, to Degli Antonii's organ versets also apply to sonatas. This investigation into tonal style in the sonata thus adds another criterion by which the instrumental repertory reveals its connections to church practice, even if it did not function exclusively as church music. If the Chapters 4 and 5 detail the impact of church practice on sonata terminology and musical style, this chapter illustrates its influence on tonal style.

No single tonal system can explain the thinking of all sonata composers or rationalize all of the seeming anomalies of late-*Seicento* practice. The *tuoni ecclesiastici* represent a broadly disseminated practice, but they do not explain everything. Three final examples (Examples 6.9a–6.9c) testify to the diversity of smaller currents within the larger stream of late seventeenth-century tonal practices. The first (Example 6.9a), Cazzati's *Capriccio sopra dodici note* from his

---

40 See the conclusion of Bella Brover-Lubovsky, "Between Modality and Tonality: Vivaldi's Harmony," *Informazioni e studi vivaldiani* 21 (2000): 111–33.

Op. 22 (1660), presents no trouble for modern tonal analysis: it is in B major. The puzzle lies in its notation of all of the sharps in the body of the piece. Assuming that Cazzati would not have understood the meaning of "B major," his notation provides no indication of how he would have explained the tonality of his capriccio. However, it does point up a revealing habit: no matter what tonality he chose, Cazzati almost invariably used a key signature of either no sharps and flats or one flat only.[41] These correspond to the two key signatures possible—*cantus durus* and *cantus mollis*— within the medieval gamut traditionally represented by Guido's hand. Cazzati's tonal gamut included keys ranging from E♭ major to B major, but his notation of them remains faithful to Guido.

Example 6.9a   M. Cazzati, Op. 22 (1660), Capriccio sopra dodici note

---

41   Cazzati's Op. 35 (1665) sonatas with trumpet that use two sharps are exceptional in this regard. That key signature may be connected with the trumpet itself, which for Cazzati played in only two "keys": C major when unmuted; D major when muted.

And Bononcini, despite his theoretical bent, furnishes a similar example in the *Sonata decima* from his Op. 1 (1666) (Example 6.9b). As in Cazzati's capriccio, the tonality is clear by modern standards. And yet, Bononcini, despite his later theory of transpositions, notates his sonata with a key signature of one flat so that the tonal center itself, Eb, requires the addition of a flat throughout the body of the piece. As notated, Bononcini's sonata thus evidences no mode that is compatible with his later theory: with its final of Eb whose flat is not included in the key signature, it cannot be a transposition of any mode recognized in his theory. At this earlier point in his career, seven years before he published his treatise, Bononcini seems to have followed Cazzati's example of notating his pieces in either *cantus durus* or *cantus mollis* irrespective of the tonal center or presumed transposition of the piece. Only later, during the drafting of his theoretical treatise, did he simultaneously codify and begin to practice a set of modally conceived rules that would supersede his earlier habits.[42]

Example 6.9b   G. M. Bononcini, Op. 1, No. 10 (1666)

---

42 Bononcini's treatise, *Musico prattico*, was published in 1673, seven years after his Op. 1 sonatas, but he refers to it as early as 1671.

The last example presented here dispenses with the theory of its time and instances the simple labeling of a tonal center. The unaccompanied dance melodies seen in Example 6.9c come from a Bolognese manuscript collection of the latter half of the seventeenth century. The manuscript itself appears to be suited to pedagogical and diversional uses, but there is no trace of traditional or rigorous theory in its pages.[43] Rather, the labeling of tonal centers simply according to pitch—for example, "in D, sol, re" or "in A la, mi, re"—evidences a more casual understanding of tonal coherence and the manner in which it is most conveniently conveyed.

Example 6.9c   MS, I-Bc, AA.360, fols. 154^{r-v}

All of the evidence presented here conveys a rich picture of tonal practice in the instrumental repertory and its complex relationship to the theory of the period. A sign of the times is found in the exhaustive treatise of Zaccaria Tevo from 1706 that is cited at the beginning of this chapter. Unlike his colleagues of a generation earlier, Tevo presents no single theory of tonal coherence, but rather, all of them: the eight modes of the medieval church; Glarean's twelve modes; the eight "tuoni delli moderni" (church keys); and the two *tuoni* of *certi novissimi* (major and minor keys). Regarding these, he writes,

> Certain most recent [writers] assert that the *tuoni* are only two in number, and that their foundation is considered according to the major and minor thirds that occur in them (not distinguishing between them apart from these), so that the minor third forms a *tuono* and the major third forms another, the octaves, fifths, and fourths being the same [for both].[44]

As Tevo attests, a plurality of theories existed, and each informs our understanding of late-*Seicento* practice in its own right, enabling us to better understand the nuances of the tonal style in the music of this time.

---

43 This manuscript is located in the Museo Internazionale e Biblioteca della Musica di Bologna under the shelf-mark AA.360.

44 Tevo, 269: "Vogliono certi novissimi, che li Tuoni siino solo due, & il fondamento loro è sopra la consideratione delle terze maggiori, e minori, che entrano in essi, non distinguendoli se non per queste, siche vogliono, che la terza minore formi un Tuono, e la maggiore un'altro, affirmando, che le ottave, quinte, e quarte sempre siino le stesse."

Chapter Seven

The Concerto Before the Concerto

It was said that the harpsichord does not complete the full expression of human sentiment. It was here that Giacomo Perti spoke, therefore, of string instruments united in a miraculous concerto, and he said that they could second the whole of the human heart.[1]

A pivotal moment in Bolognese instrumental music was 1692, when Giuseppe Torelli linked the term "concerto" in his Op. 5 to the practice of using multiple string players per part. In later publications he would add details of scoring that we recognize as defining characteristics of the Baroque concerto, such as solo/tutti designations in his Op. 6 (1698) and concertino/ripieno designations in his posthumously published Op. 8 (1709).[2] The famous sixth concerto of Torelli's Op. 8, in "the pastoral form for the most Holy Nativity,"[3] serves well to illustrate both the music and a typical use of the new genre. The scoring of Torelli's "Christmas Concerto" features two violin soloists, a four-part string ensemble (first and second violins, viola, violone or archlute), and basso continuo played on the organ.[4] Torelli recommends that the four-part ensemble use multiple players per part, and that the two "violini del concertino" play solo.[5] The sixth concerto and four others also use an *alto viola*

---

1   This is taken from Giovanni Maria Casini's recollection of a musical discussion hosted by prince Ferdinando de' Medici, transcribed in Mario Fabbri, *Alessandro Scarlatti e il Principe Ferdinando de' Medici* (Florence: Olschki, 1961), 107, "Si disse che il Cembalo non completa tutto l'esprimere di sentimento umano. Fu qui che Jacomo Perti parlò allora d'istrumenti a corda uniti in mirabil concerto, e disse che potevano secondare tutto l'humano cuore."

2   *Concerti grossi, con una Pastorale per il Santissimo Natale*, Op. 8 (Bologna: Silvani, 1709).

3   Torelli's designation reads, "in forma di Pastorale per il Santissimo Natale." The Pastorale is evoked in Torelli's second-movement Vivace by his use of a drone in fifths or octaves and of lilting triplets or compound meter in the two movements shown. Other concertos of the first half of the eighteenth century that include similar pastorale movements in commemoration of Christmas are Arcangelo Corelli, Op. 6, No. 8 (1714); Francesco Manfredini, Op. 3, No. 12 (1718); and Pietro Antonio Locatelli, Op. 1, No. 8 (1721).

4   There are seven partbooks to Torelli's Op. 8: violino primo del concertino; violino secondo del concertino; violino primo di rinforzo; violino secondo di rinforzo; alto viola; violone, ò arcileuto; organo. In this collection, concertos are scored for either one or two solo violins.

5   Torelli, Op. 8, preface: "Eccoti l'Ottava mia debol fatica data sin hora alle stampe, che fidato sù la speranza d'haver riportato un cortese compatimento nelle altre, non dispero di incontrar simil fortuna in questa. Avvertendoti, che i Violini del Concertino sijno soli, senza verun radopiamento, per evitar maggior confusione, che se poi vorrai moltiplicare gl'altri Stromenti di rinforzo, questa sí è veramente la mia intentione, e vivi felice [Here for you is

obbligato, that is, a contrapuntally essential viola part, as opposed to a non-essential viola *à beneplacito*.

The first allegro of the concerto (Example 7.1) is unified by a ritornello that coincides with tutti scoring and that appears four times (the first and last in the tonic, the second on the fifth scale degree in minor, and the third in the relative major).[6] The first two ritornellos, one in G and the other in D, occur with no break between them, as seen in the first excerpt of Example 7.1, which shows all of the first ritornello and the beginning of the second. The construction of the ritornellos is bipartite: the first section introduces its lilting melody in three-part imitation for violins and viola over a drone bass, and makes a half cadence in m. 6; the second section, which continues through m. 10, amounts to sequential extension. The third and fourth ritornellos of the movement vary this slightly: the third makes no half cadence, and the ritornello, instead of sequencing, ends the movement with a few measures of cadencing. The continuation of the movement in Example 7.1 (mm. 27–39) shows part of the third ritornello, the second of the two violin solos that separate the ritornellos, and the first measure of the fourth and final ritornello. Two short sections (mm. 18–22 and mm. 31–8) for the solo violins separate the second from the third and the third from the fourth ritornellos, and these sections are characterized by non-thematic, sequential material.

---

my eighth weak labor now given to the presses, in which, trusting in the hope based on having received a courteous forbearance with the others, I do not despair of meeting a similar fortune with this. Be advised that the violins of the *concertino* be *soli* without any duplication in order to avoid any confusion. Then, if you want to multiply the other instruments of the *rinforzo*, this is truly my intention; and *vivi felice*]."

6   For a survey of ritornello principles in the concerto before Vivaldi, see Michael Talbot, "The Concerto Allegro in the Early Eighteenth Century," *Music & Letters* 52 (1971): 8–18 and 159–72.

Example 7.1   G. Torelli, Op. 8, No.6 (1709)

ii. Vivace (mm. 1-12)

Example 7.1   cont'd

(mm. 27-39)

Example 7.1   cont'd

The movement illustrates most of the characteristics that define the eighteenth-century concerto familiar to modern listeners of Vivaldi, Bach, or Telemann: scoring that features contrasted forces within a larger ensemble (two solo violins versus a larger body of multiplied strings in this case); thematic differentiation between those forces; ritornello form; solo/tutti markings; and the use of the term "concerto" as genre designation. This particular concerto was likely used as part of the Nativity Mass, either as an introduction preceding the Introit, as a postlude after the Ite Missa Est, or possibly to accompany the ceremony during the Gradual or the Elevation of the Host. Concertos were thus the functional equivalents of sonatas, but used for the most auspicious occasions, such as major feasts, because of the extra forces required to perform them. Church services were not the only performing circumstances of either the sonata or concerto. Evidence of this is found in a later print of concertos mentioned in Chapter 4: Giuseppe Matteo Alberti's *Concerti per chiesa, e per camera ad uso dell'accademia eretta nella sala del sig. co. Orazio Leonardo Bargellini*, Op. 1 (1713). Alberti's concertos, written in a style he deemed as suited to both church and chamber, were composed for the musical performances held in the house of a Bolognese count.[7] In the large manuscript repertory of trumpet sinfonias preserved in the archives of S. Petronio, several bear the designations *per l'accademia*, *avanti l'opera*, *avanti l'oratorio* to suggest concert performance similar to Alberti's concertos and use with staged entertainments as overture music.[8] The designation *da morto ... con trombe sordine* is given to a trumpet sonata by Giuseppe Jacchini, composed in 1695, possibly for the funeral of Giovanni Paolo Colonna, maestro di cappella at S. Petronio.[9]

Much in this summary is well known; the question pursued here is how Torelli arrived at this point in his Op. 8, that is, how he came to create pieces with a ritornello design, calling them concertos. The broader scope of this enquiry also encompasses developments in Bolognese music in decades leading to Torelli's concerto publications of the 1690s and 1700s. This chapter covers developments in Bolognese instrumental music that led to the concerto, following a path of musical similarities that travels across differences of genre and instrumentation. That path

---

7   According to the early eighteenth-century diarist Antonio Barilli, *Zibaldone ossia Giornale ... di quanto è seguito in Bologna dal principio del anno 1707. per tutto l'anno 1716* (MS, I-Bu, ms. 225), I: 114 verso, these concertos "were played under the direction of Alberti in the usual *accademia* of the Count by a great number of instrumentalists with the attendance of many nobles, and they met with universal applause [furono sonati sotto la direzione del medesimo signor Alberti nell'Accademia solita dal detto signor conte, da gran numero di suonatori coll'intervento di molta nobiltà et incontrarono l'applauso universale]." Barilli's testimony is quoted in Corrado Ricci, *I teatri di Bologna nei secoli XVII e XVIII* (Bologna: Successori Monti, 1888; facsimile, Bologna: Forni, 1965), 248–9.

8   Franz Giegling, *Giuseppe Torelli: ein Beitrag zur Entwicklungsgeschichte des italienischen Konzerts* (Kassel and Basel: Bärenreiter, 1949), 79–88, contains a catalog of Torelli's works with annotations appended. That catalog forms the basis of the greatly expanded works-list that accompanies Anne Schnoebelen and Marc Vanscheeuwijck, "Torelli, Giuseppe," in *The New Grove Dictionary of Music and Musicians*, 2nd.ed., ed. Stanley Sadie and John Tyrrell, 29 vols (London: Macmillan Publishers Inc., and New York: Grove's Dictionaries Inc., 2001), vol. 25, 618–19. In that works-list are found Giuseppe Torelli, *Sinfonia avanti l'opera* (G.14), *Sinfonia con trombe, obue, e altri strumenti p[er] l'Accademia, 1707* (G. 29), *Sinfonia avanti l'opera dell'Astaralte* (not catalogued in Giegling); and *Sinfonia per l'Accademia, 1705* (incomplete; not catalogued in Giegling). A pair of sinfonias by Giacomo Antonio Perti, also from the S. Petronio archives, are designated *avanti l'oratorio*. For evidence of the use of sonatas (or sonata movements) in the theater, see Stephen Bonta, Introduction to *The Instrumental Music of Giovanni Legrenzi, Le Cetra Sonate a due, tre, e quattro stromenti, Libro Quattro, Op. 10, 1673* (Cambridge, MA: Harvard University Department of Music, 1992), xiv.

9   Jacchini, *Da morto, sonata con trombe sordine*. MS, I-Bsp, J.I.5. See Marc Vanscheeuwijck, Preface to Giuseppe Maria Jacchini, *Sonate a violino e violoncello e a violoncello solo per camera* (Bologna: Forni, 2001).

begins with the polychoral sonata of the 1650s, a prototype and point of departure, and ends with the fundamental contributions made by Torelli. The route between these points follow a collection of coalescing musical features—particulars of scoring, texture, and form. Where they appear, how they develop independently of one another, and how they come together in the single genre known as "concerto" comprise the present discussion. Because of the prominence of this genre in studies of eighteenth-century music—that of Vivaldi, J. S. Bach, Bach's sons, Telemann, and Mozart—this final chapter, perhaps more than any other in this book, illustrates the links between seventeenth- and eighteenth-century compositional practices.

The Polychoral Sonata

From Arnold Schering (*Geschichte des Instrumentalkonzerts*, 1905) onward, the so-called "Bologna School" has been put forward as an important contributor to the development of the concerto.[10] Historians have focused particularly on the Bolognese trumpet sonata as an early manifestation;[11] and, in addition to this, some have speculated about the possible relationship between polychoral sonatas, trumpet sonatas, and—ultimately—concertos.[12] Don L. Smithers, in his study of early trumpet music, made this connection with the simple observation that many of the Bolognese trumpet pieces are antiphonal in nature.[13]

Bolognese composers produced only a handful of pieces scored for double choirs of instruments between the 1650s and the 1680s, even though composition for multiple choirs had been popular in Venetian music, and composers since Giovanni Gabrieli had transferred this scoring practice to instruments. Bolognese sonata composers were no doubt tapping into a well-established tradition in sacred vocal music that had spread well beyond the Veneto during the seventeenth century. Whatever their inspiration, composers saw the polychoral sonata, not as a distinct genre, but simply as one for a greater number of voices than the more common trio sonata. Theorists' categories of counterpoint are similarly based on the number of voices in the texture: in his treatise *Li primi albori musicali*, Lorenzo Penna runs through the various categories of counterpoint beginning with two voices and

---

10 Arnold Schering, *Geschichte des Instrumentalkonzerts bis Ant. Vivaldi* (Leipzig: Breitkopf & Härtel, 1905; 2nd ed, 1927; reprint, Hildesheim: Olms, 1965). A book-length, English-language study of the genre is Arthur Hutchings, *The Baroque Concerto* (New York: W. W. Norton, 1961; rev. ed., New York: Scribner's, 1979). For a more recent and concise treatment of the early concerto, see Michael Talbot, "The Italian Concerto in the Late Seventeenth and Early Eighteenth Centuries," in *The Cambridge Companion to the Concerto*, ed. Simon P. Keefe (Cambridge and New York: Cambridge University Press, 2005), 35–52.

11 Sanford E. Watts, "The Stylistic Features of the Bolognese Concerto," Ph.D. dissertation, Indiana University, 1964, is devoted to pieces for one or more trumpets, strings, and continuo of the 1680s and 90s now found in the archives of the basilica of S. Petronio.

12 Artur Schlossberg, "Die italienische Sonata für mehrere Instrumente im 17. Jahrhundert," Ph.D. diss., University of Heidelberg, 1932, 88.

13 Don L. Smithers, *The Music and History of the Baroque Trumpet before 1721* (London: J. M. Dent, 1973), 96.

proceeding to two or more choirs of voices.[14] In similar fashion, many prints of instrumental music contain pieces for ensembles of different sizes, arranging them from small to large.[15] Polychoral sonatas were simply categorized as *a 8* (or *a 12*) in printed collections that contain them alongside sonatas *a 2*, *a 3*, and the like.

Having a sufficient number of voices to make up distinct choirs within the ensemble, however, created possibilities unavailable in smaller ensembles. Two pieces—both drawn from Maurizio Cazzati's *Correnti e balletti a cinque alla francese, e all'itagliana con alcune sonate à 5, 6, 7, 8* (1654)—illustrate the textural differences between a sonata and a polychoral sonata.[16] The introductory slow movement and fugal allegro, respectively, of Cazzati's Sonata *à 5*, "L'Alessandri," are typical of the mid-century instrumental repertory: the slow movement contains some counterpoint featuring suspensions and simple imitation (Example 7.2a); the fugal movement features more thorough-going imitation among the individual voices of the five-part ensemble, especially in the exposition shown in the example (Example 7.2b).

---

14 Lorenzo Penna, *Li primi albori musicali* (Bologna: Monti, 1672; facsimile of the 1684 edition, Bologna: Forni, 1969), 79–89.

15 A few of these from the latter half of the century are Maurizio Cazzati, *Sonate à due, trè, quattro, e cinque, con alcune per tromba*, Op. 35 (Bologna: Silvani, 1665); Gioseffo Placuzzi, *Suonate à duoi, à trè, à quattro, à cinque, & otto instromenti*, Op. 1 (Bologna: Monti, 1667); Giovanni Battista Vitali, *Sonate a due, trè, quattro, e cinque stromenti*, Op. 5 (Bologna: Monti, 1669); Giovanni Bononcini, *à 5. 6. 7. e 8. istromenti, con alcune à una e due trombe, servendo ancora per violini*, Op. 3 (Bologna: Monti, 1685). As mentioned in the text, all prints of this nature order their contents in terms of ensemble size from smallest to largest.

16 Cazzati's Op. 15 was first published by Alessandro Vincenti in Venice. In 1667, it was reprinted by Giacomo Monti in Bologna with a new dedication written by Marino Silvani.

Example 7.2a   M. Cazzati, Op. 15, "L'Alessandri" (1654)

i. (mm. 1-7)

Example 7.2b M. Cazzati, Op. 15, "L'Alessandri" (1654)

In the slow introduction of the polychoral sonata, the sonata *a 8*, "La Brembata" (Example 7.3a), the voices move homorhythmically, presenting blocks of strings rather than any contrapuntal textures. The allegro movement (Example 7.3b) is characterized by alternations between two choirs of homorhythmic voices whose repeated, clear-cut phrases are the antithesis of the web-like texture of the through-composed fugue seen in Example 7.2b. The interest in Cazzati's polychoral sonata lies in the sonority of the string choirs and in the spatial effect of their alternation, not in the play of individual lines against one another.

Example 7.3a   M. Cazzati, Op. 15, "La Brembata" (1654)

i. Adagio (mm. 1-6)

Violino primo choro

Alto viola primo choro

Tenore viola primo choro

Basso violone da brazzo primo choro

Violino secondo choro

Alto viola secondo choro

Tenore viola secondo choro

Basso violone da brazzo secondo choro

Basso continuo

Example 7.3b   M. Cazzati, Op. 15, "La Brembata" (1654)

Example 7.3b cont'd

Sonata con Tromba

Although Cazzati never again composed for opposed choirs of instruments, he did retain the antiphonal style in later instrumental works by adapting it to a new scoring. In his *Sonate à due, trè, quattro, e cinque, con alcune per tromba*, Op. 35 (1665), he scores the final three works for a single trumpet against a choir of strings. Despite the introduction of the trumpet in Cazzati's Op. 35, "La Caprara," (Example 7.4), the texture of this piece is identical to that of his sonata for two choirs: Cazzati has simply given the role of one of the choirs to the solo trumpet. The sonata *a 7* with two trumpets, composed in 1680 by the Bolognese cellist and composer Petronio Franceschini, adds a second trumpet, but otherwise pits contrasting brass and string sonorities against one another as had Cazzati more than a decade earlier.[17] The final movement, shown in Example 7.5, whose theme begins with the dactylic, repeated-note motto popular in the early-*Seicento* canzona, goes further to feature the trumpets over the accompanying strings: more florid and higher-ranging material is given to the trumpets in longer episodes while the strings intone the same theme throughout, imitatively or homophonically.

Example 7.4   M. Cazzati, Op. 35, "La Caprara" (1665)

---

17 Petronio Franceschini, *Suonata a 7 con due trombe* (MS, 1680, I-Bsp, D.XII.9). This sonata is available in modern edition with continuo realization as *Sonata in D for Two Solo Trumpets, Strings & Continuo*, ed. Edward Tarr (London: Musica Rara, 1968). Tarr's preface to his edition of this piece contains a detailed discussion of the greater technical demands made on the trumpeters as compared to those of Cazzati's sonatas.

Example 7.4   cont'd

Example 7.5   P. Franceschini, Suonata à 7, MS, I-Bsp D.XII.9 (1680)

Example 7.5   cont'd

(mm. 28-41)

These earliest trumpet sonatas of Cazzati and Franceschini offer adaptations of polychoral writing to the contrasting sonorities of strings and brass. The stylistic consequence of their concentration on sonorities, as in Cazzati's sonata *a 8* for strings, was a move away from intricate fugal writing. But not all composers handled the trumpet in this way. Andrea Grossi, whose *Sonate a due, trè, quattro, e cinque instromenti*, Op. 3 (1682), includes three sonatas *a 5* that use solo trumpet and strings but feature both antiphonal and fugal styles.[18] In the first movement of his Op. 3, No. 10 (Example 7.6) trumpet and strings trade similar and sometimes identical phrases and motifs until the final five bars of the movement (mm. 22–6), in which the opening material of the piece is sounded by trumpet and strings together. The final movement of his Op. 3, No. 11 (Example 7.7), however, treats the trumpet and strings as equals within a fugal texture, but employs a similar concluding gesture in which all of the voices are brought together on material that begins the piece. The combining of forces to create a strong conclusion has long roots in polychoral music, but Grossi's interest in rounding out a movement with its beginning idea is not seen in Cazzati's sonata *a 8* or his trumpet sonatas, and it introduces a modest recapitulatory procedure to the genre. The trumpet sonatas of Giovanni Bononcini's *Sinfonie*,[19] Op. 3 (1685), similarly employ either antiphonal or more contrapuntal textures. Recapitulatory conclusions occur here too, but they are clearest in the antiphonal treatments of trumpet and strings. Bononcini's contrapuntal example with trumpet, his Op. 3, No. 5 (Example 7.8), is less a fugue than an extended imitative treatment of a motif in different keys, in which the opening motif and key return at m. 36 to close the piece. The first and last movements of his Op. 3, No. 8 (Examples 7.9 and 7.10) offer more literal recapitulations of opening material that occur after a series of contrasting episodes (compare mm. 1–4 and 36–9 in Example 7.9, and mm. 1–4 and 44–8 in Example 7.10). Brief as they are, the concluding sections of Examples 7.8–7.10 introduce larger-scale gestures than were typically conceived in the more process-oriented fugal or imitative allegros of the instrumental repertory. In combination, antiphonal scoring and recapitulatory conclusions represent a novel procedure in the sonata, and they emphasize the contrast and then combination of sonorities in the new-fangled trumpet sonata.

---

18 Andrea Grossi, *Sonate a due, trè, quattro, e cinque instromenti*, Op. 3 (Bologna: Monti, 1682). Grossi, a violinist at the court of Mantua (*musico, e sonatore di violino dell'Altezza Serenissima di Mantova*), published all of his music in Bologna. This amounts to five collections of sonatas and dances printed between 1678 and 1696, the first four of which survive. The *Scielta delle suonate a due violini, con il basso continuo per l'organo* (Bologna: Monti, 1680), an anthology of sonatas by various composers, also includes one by Grossi.

19 The complete title is *Sinfonie a 5. 6. 7. e 8. istromenti, con alcune a una e due trombe, servendo ancora per violini* (Bologna: Monti, 1685).

Example 7.6   A. Grossi, Op. 3, No. 10 (1682)

i. Vivace (mm. 1-9)

Example 7.6　　　cont'd

(mm. 20-26)

Example 7.7   A. Grossi, Op. 3, No. 11 (1682)

iv. Allegro, e spiritoso (mm. 1-12)

Example 7.7   cont'd

(mm. 31-36)

Example 7.8   G. Bononcini, Op. 3, No. 5 (1685)

ii. Allegro (mm. 1-9)

Example 7.8   cont'd

Example 7.9   G. Bononcini, Op. 3, No. 8 (1685)

ii. Allegro (mm. 1-10)

Example 7.9   cont'd

(mm. 34-39)

Example 7.10   G. Bononcini, Op. 3, No. 8 (1685)

vi. Allegro, spiccato (mm. 1-11)

Example 7.10   cont'd

Giuseppe Torelli, Op. 5 (1692)

To modern ears, the Bolognese trumpet sonata also represents a point of arrival for the Baroque concerto, pitting a distinctive solo timbre against one of strings, which, during the important feasts at S. Petronio, would have represented a large group with several players per part. But by the early 1690s, innovations that presage the concerto turn away from trumpet pieces and toward works that actually use the term "concerto" and solo/tutti designations. Johann Joachim Quantz attributed the invention of the genre to the Italians in general and Torelli in particular.[20] Later in the century, John Hawkins pointed to Torelli's Op. 8 *Concerti grossi* (1709) as the earliest examples.[21] But Charles Burney speculated that other composers might have written concertos before Torelli without publishing them. Concerto origins, as we know, well predate Torelli, but he did make a singular contribution by using the term in conjunction with the specific practice of part-doubling in performance. His *Sinfonie à 3 e concerti à 4*, Op. 5 (1692), whose title page is shown as Figure 7.1, adopts this usage to distinguish the sinfonias from the concertos in a prefatory note to the reader (Figure 7.2):

> This fifth work of mine, which I now present to you, gentle reader, consists of six *Sinfonie à tre* and six *Concerti à quattro*. If it pleases you to perform these *Concerti*, it would not be ill-advised to multiply all of the instruments if you wish to discover my intention. Enjoy, and *vivi felice*.[22]

---

20 Quantz, *Versuch einer Anweisung, die Flöte traversiere zu spielen* (Berlin, 1752; in English trans. as *On Playing the Flute*, 2nd ed., trans. and ed. Edward Reilly, Boston: Northeastern University Press, 2001), 310: "The concerto owes its origins to the Italians. Torelli is supposed to have made the first."

21 John Hawkins, *A General History of the Science and Practice of Music* (1776; reprint, New York: Dover, 1963), vol. 2, 772, "the most considerable of his works is his eighth opera, published at Bologna by his brother Felice Torelli, after the death of the author, viz., in 1709.... He is said to be the inventor of that noble species of instrumental composition the Concerto grosso." Charles Burney, *A General History of Music, From the Earliest Ages to the Present Period (1789)* (1789; reprint, New York: Dover, 1957), vol. 2, 434, "Concertos, merely instrumental, either for the church of chamber, seem to have had no existence, till about the time of Corelli. The honour of the invention has been assigned to Torelli, his contemporary, but from no good authority." Hawkins's informant in this is unknown, but may have been Quantz. Neither Giovanni Battista Martini, *Serie cronologica de' principi dell'Accademia Filarmonica di Bologna* (Bologna, 1776; facsimile, Bologna: Forni, 1970), nor the *Catalogo degli aggregati della Accademia Filarmonica di Bologna*, MS, c.1736, attributed to G. B. Martini, facsimile with foreword by Anne Schnoebelen (Bologna: n.p., 1973), nor Giuseppe Ottavio Pitoni, *Notitia de' contrapuntisti e compositori di musica*, MS, c.1725, modern ed. by Cesarino Ruini (Florence: Olschki, 1988) credit him in such fashion.

22 The original Italian reads: "Avertimento a chi legge. Questa mia quint'Opera, che ora ti presento ò Cortese Lettore consiste in sei Sinfonie à trè, e sei Concerti à Quattro: Se ti compiaci suonare questi Concerti non ti sia discaro moltiplicare tutti gl'Instromenti, se vuoi scoprire la mia intentione. Compatisci, e vivi felice."

VIOLINO PRIMO

SINFONIE A' TRE
E CONCERTI A'QVATTRO
CONSECRATI
Alla Serenifsima Altezza Elettorale
DI
GIOVANNI GVGLIELMO
Per la gratia di Dio Conte Palatino del Rheno, Arciteforiere,
& Elettore del Sacro Rom. Imperio, Duca di Bauiera,
Giuliers, Cleues, e Berghes, Co. di Veldents,
Sponheim, della Marca, Rauensberg, &
Moers, Signore di Rauenfteim, &c.

DA GIVSEPPE TORELLI VERONESE
ACCADEMICO FILARMONICO,

OPERA QVINTA.

IN BOLOGNA   M.DC.LCXII.

Per Gioleffo Micheletti.   Con licenza de' Superiori,

Figure 7.1   G. Torelli, *Sinfonie à tre e concerti à quattro*, Op. 5 (Bologna:
Micheletti, 1692), violino primo, title page. Museo Internazionale e
Biblioteca della Musica di Bologna (I-Bc)

Violino Primo.

AVERTIMENTO
A CHI LEGGE.

Vesta mia quint' Opera, che ora ti presento ò Cortese Lettore consiste in sei Sinfonie à trè, e sei Concerti à Quattro: Se ti compiaci suonare questi Concerti non ti sia discaro moltiplicare tutti gl' Instromenti, se vuoi scoprire là mia intentione. Compatisci, e vivi felice.

Figure 7.2   G. Torelli, *Sinfonie à tre e concerti à quattro*, Op. 5 (Bologna: Micheletti, 1692), violino primo, 1. Museo Internazionale e Biblioteca della Musica di Bologna (I-Bc)

Many composers for instrumental ensemble, Torelli included, had used the term "concerto" (or "concertino") as a genre designation, but never with a performance practice or any specific genre characteristics in mind. From this point on, however, Torelli would use the term in conjunction with multiplying players on a part.

If the instructions of his preface are clear, his reasons for using "concerto" are less so for the modern reader expecting one or more soloists in the scoring. The concertos of his Op. 5 have no solos, and Torelli would not consistently link solo/tutti contrasts with the concerto until his Op. 8. Noting this, past historians have rationalized Torelli's Op. 5 concertos, perhaps implausibly, as compositions that feature a virtuosic first violin part versus accompanimental second violin, viola, and bass.[23] Others have equated Torelli's Op. 5 concertos with the so-called "orchestral concerto" of the early eighteenth century.[24] A useful starting point for investigating Torelli's conception of the genre is to see precisely how these concertos differ from the sinfonias of the same print, in addition to the distinction of part-doubling. The six sinfonias of Torelli's Op. 5 feature movement types that are typical of the late-*Seicento* sonata: the cycle of movements consists of one or more introductory movements, a fugal allegro, an adagio or largo, and an imitative finale in compound or triple meter. The fugal movements in these sinfonias are considerably longer than any that Torelli had composed in his earlier publications. The *Sinfonia prima*, for example, contains a fugue of over 67 measures whereas those in his Opp. 1 and 3 are 25–35 measures on the average. The sinfonia fugues, moreover, are contrapuntally dense compositions. While composers often allowed themselves the luxury of episodic digressions, Torelli was careful to weave the principal subject into the texture almost continuously in the fugues of his Op. 5 sinfonias.

The Op. 5 concertos, by contrast, furnish something different, starting with a more homophonic texture whose sonority is increased not only by the massed strings that Torelli recommends but also by the addition of a viola part. And all of the slow movements of the Op. 5 concertos are reduced more or less to cadential passages, several as short as two or three measures in length, that provide a brief introduction or interlude to the fast movements that dominate the works. Among these fast movements, there is some degree of formal recapitulation that recalls those of the Bolognese trumpet sonata. The three excerpts given in Examples 7.11–7.13 show a few variations of the same basic procedure of returning to the opening material at the end of a movement. The profusion of dotted rhythms in the first allegro of the *Concerto primo* (Example 7.11), for example, illustrates an Italian's perhaps too literal rendition of French *notes inégales* performance. As seen in the excerpts, the movement begins and ends with the same material (mm. 1–6 and mm. 38–43), a similar reprise to those seen in the trumpet sonatas of Grossi and Bononcini. Between these beginning and ending periods, the movement is sustained with new phrases and harmonic sequencing. Throughout, the texture features melody-and-accompaniment homophony or dialog between treble and bass instruments in which the viola is allied with either the violins or the basses.

---

23 See Schering, *Geschichte des Instrumentalkonzerts*, 31; and Hutchings, *Baroque Concerto*, 92.

24 Richard E. Norton, "The Chamber Music of Giuseppe Torelli," Ph.D. dissertation, Northwestern University, 1967, 126–7.

Example 7.11   G. Torelli, Op. 5, Concerto No. 1 alla Francese (1692)

Example 7.11   cont'd

(mm. 35-49)

Example 7.11   cont'd

In other examples, Torelli incorporates medial reprises of the movement's opening motto and a degree of imitation into the texture. The final movement of his *Concerto terzo* uses a canonic motto of five measures that occurs five times, touching on the dominant and relative minor keys in addition to the tonic. Tonic and dominant ritornellos without break between them begin the movement (Example 7.12) and give way to a short sequential episode that leads to an internal statement in the tonic. One further example from Torelli's Op. 5 shows the range of possibilities within this new type of movement. The segments of this movement, both recurring motto-sections and episodes, are brief throughout, and the breadth of utterances is comparable to the short exchanges between forces in the polychoral or trumpet sonatas. The incipient ritornello principles he adopts in conjunction with such brief periods, however, threaten to introduce repetitiveness with so little time between statements of the motto. Torelli seems to have been aware of that danger, working in a more expansive episode in some instances. The opening allegro of his *Concerto quinto* (Example 7.13) uses a tonally closed, bipartite ritornello (mm. 1–4), repeated after just a brief transition at the fifth degree (mm. 5–8), and sets the first violin line apart for the long episode (mm. 8–23) that separates the opening and closing mottos. That episode offers something to seize upon in the search for solos in the Op. 5 concertos, but it is an exception in its length and not particularly virtuosic. Rather, Torelli's conception of the genre lay in its assembly of reinforced parts, and in textures and experiments with form that would best complement the ensemble's sonority.

Example 7.12   G. Torelli, Op. 5, Concerto No. 3 (1692)

Example 7.12   cont'd

Example 7.13   G. Torelli, Op. 5, Concerto No. 5 (1692)

i. Allegro (mm. 1-25)

Example 7.13   cont'd

Example 7.13   cont'd

The makeup of Torelli's ritornellos varies considerably from one example to the next: it could be a tonally open or closed musical period; its internal structure could be through-composed or bipartite, homophonic or canonic. Nonetheless, the common traits in Torelli's Op. 5 concertos of part-doubling, proto-ritornello-form allegros, and, not least, the "concerto" designation, define a new genre of instrumental music distinct from the sinfonias. Most significant in the differences between Torelli's Op. 5 concertos and sinfonias is that they recall the two stylistic paths followed in the trumpet sonata, which themselves evolved from precedents laid out in the polychoral sonata and the sonata for small ensemble. Torelli's Op. 5 concertos thus fit into a continuum of genres, beginning with the polychoral sonata and continuing with the trumpet sonata, that experiment with scoring and formal procedures with an enlarged ensemble and turn away from the sonata's characteristic fugal allegro. Torelli's specific contribution to this development is his application of the term "concerto" to it and the specification of orchestral performance.

His next publication, the *Concerti musicali*, Op. 6 (1698),[25] devoted entirely to concertos, also contains a note to the reader, similar to that of his Op. 5, but with two details of performance practice not seen in the previous collection:

> Here is the sixth print of my unworthy labors—five have passed through the presses of the illustrious city of Bologna, which was my residence—and this sixth I endeavor to present to you in the famous city of Augsburg. I would point out that in some of the concertos you will find written "solo," in which case [they] must be played by only one violin. For the remainder, duplicate each of the parts using three or four instruments per part so that you may discover my intention. *Vivi felice.*[26]

---

25   Torelli, *Concerti musicali*, Op. 6 (Augsburg: Wagner, 1698).

26   "*Cortese Lettore.* Eccoti la sesta impressione delle mie deboli fatiche: cinque sono passate sotto il torchio nell'Inclita Città di Bologna (già fu mia stanza) è questa ardisco

The opposition between solo and tutti passages is now, in 1698, part of his concept of the concerto genre.[27] Moreover, the tutti passages correspond to recapitulated sections that separate solos of an episodic nature. A contrast between soloist and ensemble, however, was by no means firm in Torelli's conception of the concerto at this point: only three of the Op. 6 concertos follow this procedure of distinguishing passages for solo violin; the others resemble his Op. 5 concertos.[28] Nor was ritornello form the only movement type in his Op. 6 allegros. Rather, Torelli included fugal and non-recapitulatory allegros as well. The term "concerto," however, had now come to dominate in Torelli's published output, and with it came the practice of part-doubling.[29] Like his Op. 6, his next and last publication, the *Concerti grossi*, Op. 8, would also be devoted solely to concertos bearing the recommendation to multiply parts.[30]

The Uncontentious Concerto

Prior to his Op. 5, Torelli published two collections of dance suites—for trio ensemble and for unaccompanied violin and cello—that he respectively entitled *Concerto da camera*, Op. 2 (1686) and *Concertino da camera*, Op. 4 (1687-88). Most of his published music therefore bore the term "concerto" (five of seven known opuses including the Op. 4 *Concertino*), but it is difficult to say what the word meant to him because it comprehended such a diversity of pieces. The history and meaning of the word "concerto" have been parsed on different occasions by music historians because of this sort of enigma.[31] During the sixteenth and seventeenth centuries, the

---

di fartela comparire nella famosa Città di Augusta. Ti avverto, che se in qualche concerto troverai scritto solo, dovrà esser suonato da un solo Violino; Il Rimanente poi fà duplicare le parti etiamdio trè ò quattro per stromento, che cosi scoprirai la mia intenzione, e vivi felice."

27 For a detailed study and critical edition of Torelli's Op. 6, see Giuseppe Torelli, *Concerti musicali: Op. 6*, ed. and introduction by John Suess (Middleton,WI: A-R Editions, 2002).

28 Five movements in Op. 6 bear solo/tutti designations for the first violin: the first and third movements of concerto No. 6, both allegro; the opening adagio of concerto No. 10, and the first and third movements of concerto No. 12, both allegro.

29 A recent study, Richard Maunder, *The Scoring of Baroque Concertos* (Rochester: Boydell Press, 2004), examines an unprecedented number of Baroque-era concertos in order to prove the specific point that Baroque concertos were performed with one player per part (see his Introduction, especially pp. 1–2). Maunder's chapter on Bologna begins his survey of repertory with a much softer stance and very tentative findings. His conclusions for Torelli's Op. 5 (pp. 18–19), based on the number of partbooks of manuscript copies that survive at S. Petronio, are that actual performances of the Op. 5 concertos used from one to three performers per part. This assumes that each player had a partbook, which remains unproven. In his summary (p. 36) he writes that Torelli expected as many as four players per part, "although manuscript sources suggest that he would nevertheless have accepted single strings."

30 An Op. 7 by Torelli is not known to exist. It is possible that the publishers who issued Torelli's posthumous Op. 8 mistakenly thought that there had been one.

31 David D. Boyden, "When is a Concerto Not a Concerto?," *The Musical Quarterly* 43 (1957): 220–32; John A. Meyer, "The Idea of Conflict in the Concerto," *Studies in Musicology* 8

term appears as the title of an even greater assortment of musical genres: antiphons, psalms, and motets, as well as diverse pieces for instrumental ensemble. As David Boyden has pointed out, "concerto"—derived from *concertare*, which to sixteenth-century Italians meant "to join or bind together"—described a musical ensemble.[32] Late-Renaissance musicians, however, discovered that the Latin verb *concertare* had an almost antithetical meaning to that one: to dispute or contend. This generated at least some discussion among Italian theorists because Ercole Bottrigari, in his *Desiderio* (1594), suggested that musicians allow "concerto" to revert to its Latin meaning and use *concento* to mean a harmonious joining together. He neatly distinguished the two in a statement asserting that instruments using mismatched temperaments would "produce a real concerto, or battle, of instruments, instead of a *concento*, a union and concord of diverse voices and sounds."[33]

If Bottrigari sought to resolve an apparent contradiction in the meaning of one term by introducing another, Alfred Einstein, writing from the vantage point of the mid twentieth century, supplied a satisfying rationale for preserving the two musical connotations of "concerto."[34] According to Einstein, "concerto" in its sense of dispute and contest signified something in music that Bottrigari could not yet have known at the end of the sixteenth century, before the advent of the *seconda prattica*. With that stylistic sea-change, however, voices contended with one another for pre-eminence in sometimes dissonant opposition. The new style of music thus bore out the proper Latin meaning of rivalry in "concerto," which musicians embraced; and the essence of older equal-voice polyphony, too, was captured by the word. Boyden followed Einstein's reasoning and applied it to instrumental repertory in his well-known survey of concerto etymology.[35] Since that time, seventeenth-century applications of the term have been interpreted by musicologists to reflect either concordance or contention in music.

In the context of instrumental concertos, that idea of struggle is interpreted on the basis of soloistic parts that break out of the overall texture, or of contrasted groups that vie for our attention.[36] But Torelli's Op. 5 concertos hardly suggest struggle,

---

(1974): 38–52; Franco Piperno, "'Concerto' e 'concertato' nella musica strumentale italiana del secolo decimo settimo," in *Deutsch-italienische Musikbeziehungen: Deutsche und italienische Instrumentalmusik 1600–1750*, ed. Wulf Konold (Munich and Salzburg: Musikverlag Emil Katzbichler, 1996), 129–55.

32 Boyden, "Concerto," 221.

33 Bottrigari, *Il desiderio overo, de' concerti di varij strumenti musicali* (Venice: Amadino, 1594; facsimile, Bologna: Forni, 1969), 12: "produrre quel vero concerto, ò battaglia de strumenti in vece di concento; la qual importa unione."

34 Alfred Einstein, *The Italian Madrigal*, 3 vols (Princeton, NJ: Princeton University Press, 1949), vol. 2, 821. Claude Palisca, *Baroque Music*, 3rd ed. (Englewood Cliffs, NJ: Prentice-Hall, 1991), 66–9, takes issue with the idea that Renaissance musicians had any idea of opposition in mind when using "concerto," pointing out that Bottrigari meant only to delight his readers in some word-play in his treatment of the subject. However, he goes on to say that the word did develop the added sense of contention around the middle of the seventeenth century.

35 Boyden, "Concerto."

36 Ibid., 229–30.

competition, or even contrasted forces. Rather, he appears to have had in mind a consistent, long-standing, and very basic idea of the term to mean ensemble or corps. As mentioned at the outset of this chapter, Torelli is the musician who united "concerto" with a specific set of features, but to understand his historic usage we would do better to peel away the interpretations of rivalry and contention emphasized in modern scholarship. To take examples that were relatively close to Torelli's sphere of activity, G. M. Bononcini's position as head of Francesco II d'Este's *concerto degli strumenti* meant that he led the instrumental ensemble at court (Torelli held a similar position as *maestro di concerto* at the Ansbach court of the Margrave of Brandenburg in the late 1690s); the Concerto Palatino della Signoria di Bologna was a civic instrumental ensemble used for a multitude of official, ceremonial purposes; and the Concerto de' Putti, led by the Bolognese cleric Giorgio Buoni, was a group of young performers and composers whose sonatas were gathered into three publications in 1693. In the same vein, if more abstract, is the theorist Angelo Berardi's brief encomium, written in 1689, to Corelli's music: "The *concerti* of violins and of other instruments are called *sinfonie*, and are held in high regard nowadays—particularly those of Signor Arcangelo Corelli, a celebrated violinist called Il Bolognese, the new Orpheus of our times."[37] Berardi uses the word "concerto" not in the modern, genre-based sense, but in its older meaning referring to a group of instruments working "in concert," that is, together. He then uses "sinfonia" for that which Corelli himself had named "sonata," preferring the more learned Greek-derived term to the plainer past participle of the Italian *sonare* (to sound).[38]

In Torelli's usage, the titles of his Opp. 2 and 4, where "concerto" and "concertino" are used in the collective singular form and qualified with *da camera*, both signify "chamber concert" in the sense of a collection of dances.[39] His Op. 5, however, uses the term in a different fashion in order to describe a musical innovation: here Torelli uses "concerto" to describe not the complete print, but individual works within it that are to be performed with multiple players per part. In sum, when Torelli came to use the word to distinguish pieces that used part-doubling, the ancient and Renaissance etymologies explored by Einstein and Boyden were probably far from his mind. Rather, the effects of the scoring are the point: rich, homophonic textures, allegros that feature less intricate textures and articulate larger gestures of reprises, and brief slow movements that amount to no more than imposing cadences constitute the musical style suited to the sound of multiplied strings. The defining feature, the instrument for which these effects were written, is the reinforced corps of strings.

---

37 *Miscellanea musicale* (Bologna: Giacomo Monti, 1689; facsimile, Bologna: Forni, 1970), 45: "I concerti di Violino, e d'altri Strumenti si chiamano Sinfonie, & hoggi sono in preggio, e stima quelle del Sig. Arcangelo Corelli Violinista celebre, detto il Bolognese, nuovo Orfeo de nostri giorni."

38 Berardi, who was maestro di cappella at S. Maria in Trastevere in Rome toward the end of his life, follows the usage of the Roman composers, such as Alessandro Stradella (*sinfonia*) and Lelio Colista (*simfonia*), in titling ensemble music for violins.

39 The individual dances within these prints are not to be considered as belonging to the same genre as his later works. Maunder, 36, implies this in his summary of late seventeenth-century Bologna, which covers all instrumental music associated with the term "concerto": "Some of the concertos discussed in this chapter, are for small 'chamber' groups, playing one-to-a-part."

His Opp. 6 and 8 concertos would add contrast through solo violin parts, but the concerto idea in this initial formulation by Torelli reflects the harmonious aggregate, the ensemble itself.

Giuseppe Jacchini

Between the publication of Torelli's Opp. 6 and 8 (1698 and 1709), another instrumentalist in the *cappella musicale* of S. Petronio, Giuseppe Jacchini, contributed his own experiments with form and scoring in his *Concerti per camera*, Op. 4 (1701) and *Trattenimenti per camera*, Op. 5 (1703).[40] Throughout his five published works, all for ensembles of instruments, Jacchini sought to elevate the profile of his instrument, the violoncello, which he played to acclaim, as both accompanist and soloist.[41] In everything he published, the violoncello is given contrapuntally essential material, as either an equal partner in a string duo or an obbligato with solos to rival the music he gave to violins (or in his Op. 5 *Trattenimenti*, to trumpets). Jacchini's compositions are otherwise relatively simple pieces, texturally and harmonically, and he classified all of them as music for the chamber, perhaps because of their lighter style. The specific milieu of these pieces, beyond secular performing spaces in general, is hinted in a few of his dedications, which refer to his patrons' delight in performing instrumental music as a diversion from other cares:

> Having had the honor of serving Your most Illustrious Lordship—when, in hours less occupied by matters more serious, You practiced the recreation of playing, ennobling such a delicate virtue with your talent—I doubted not at all to whom I should dedicate these compositions of mine, foreseeing an authoritative protector for them.[42]

---

40 Giuseppe Jacchini, *Concerti per camera a 3 e 4 strumenti, con violoncello obligato*, Op. 4 (Bologna: Silvani, 1701); and *Trattenimenti per camera a 3. 4. 5. e 6. strumenti con alcune a una, e due trombe*, Op. 5 (Bologna: Silvani, 1703).

41 See Vanscheeuwijck, Preface to *Sonate a violino e violoncello*, which reproduces the praises of Jacchini's cello playing by G. B. Martini and J. F. A. von Uffenbach.

42 Jacchini, *Trattenimenti per camera*, dedication to Cornelio Malvasia: "Avendo io l' onore di servire V. S. Illustrissima, quando nell' ore men' occupate per le applicazioni più serie Ella s' essercita nel divertimento del Suono nobilitando col suo genio una così delicata Virtù, non hò punto dubbitato à chi dovessi dedicare questi miei Componimenti provedendoli d' un auttorevole Protettore."

One further peforming circumstance was Jacchini's position in Bolognese *collegi*—schools for the nobility—as a cello teacher.[43] Jacchini, having performed with his patron, possibly as his teacher in the Collegio de' Nobili, likely conceived his showy but also accessible chamber music for *esercizii* in the school or for *accademie* of aristocratic households.[44] An early example of his particular style (Example 7.14) is almost idiosyncratic in its focus on the cello. The last movement of the *Sonata prima à 4, con violoncello obligato*, from his Op. 2 (1695), features a running line for the solo cello underscored by solo/tutti markings and punctuated at cadences by the full ensemble.[45] The cello's moment in the spotlight is brief, but it creates an eccentric little movement whose first half is quasi cello concerto and second half, typical dance-like finale. Jacchini's next published collection, the *Concerti per camera*, Op. 3 (1697), comprises dance suites for violin and cello duet, similar in content and scoring to his Op. 1 (before 1695). His Opp. 4 and 5, written for larger ensembles of up to six parts plus continuo, demonstrate the further steps he took toward creating concert repertory for the cello. In these prints the solo versus tutti scoring that was infrequent in Torelli's Op. 6 and in Jacchini's own Op. 2 becomes standard: there are solo episodes for the cello in all of Jacchini's Opp. 4 and 5 compositions, some of which also feature passages for solo violin and, in his Op. 5, for one or two trumpets.

---

43 Two sources convey this information: (1) The biographical entry for Jacchini in the *Catalogo degli aggregati della Accademia Filarmonica di Bologna*: "Fù M[aest]ro ne Collegi Nobili, e S. Luigi"; and (2) published librettos of year-end performances given by the students that list the *maestri* of instruments and dancing. See Claudio Sartori, *I libretti italiani a stampa dalle origini al 1800*, 7 vols (Cuneo: Bertola and Locatelli, 1990–94), No. 4623, No. 17562, and No. 22323.

44 See Chapter 2 for discussions of these two performing contexts.

45 Jacchini, *Sonate da camera a trè, e quattro stromenti, col violoncello obligato*, Op. 2 (Bologna: Monti, 1695).

Example 7.14   G. Jacchini, Op. 2, No. 1 (1695)

iii. Aria allegro, e spicco (mm. 1-32)

Example 7.14   cont'd

In comparison with Torelli, Jacchini's approach to harmony and texture in these later prints is simpler by far: harmonies rarely range away from tonic and dominant, and tutti passages are often homophonic blocks of quarter-note motion. In addition to solo/tutti contrasts, Jacchini relies on rounded, or recapitulatory allegros, and within that framework he explores several choices for coordinating form and scoring. The opening movement of his Op. 4, No. 9 (Example 7.15) presents an unusual formulation of recapitulatory procedure in a concerto movement. In this case, the recapitulated section encompasses both solo and tutti material (mm. 1–5 and mm. 44–51). Those sections, however, do not account for the entirety of ritornello material in the piece: the ensuing solo in m. 6 is also repeated, occurring in dialogue between violoncello and violin (mm. 9–11), again with the order of entry reversed (mm. 15–16), and yet again for cello followed by violin (mm. 28–30). The result is a piecemeal ritornello form, fanfare-like in its insistent reliance on tonic and dominant harmonies, in which the first twelve measures furnish all of the material that will punctuate the cello's passagework and repeated-note figures.

Example 7.15   G. Jacchini, Op. 4, No. 9 (1701)

Example 7.15 cont'd

Example 7.15   cont'd

Example 7.15   cont'd

Another movement taken from Jacchini's Op. 5, No. 6 (see Example 7.16), shows a similar but more organized procedure in which tutti and solo passages are cleanly distinguished. The opening tutti (mm. 1–10) is identical to that which closes the movement beginning in m. 30, and it furnishes a motto (see mm. 20–21) that appears in different keys to separate the cello solos. In sum, Jacchini uses a ritornello-form movement in which tutti ritornellos alternate with the solo cello—the basic ingredients of a Baroque concerto. And yet, Jacchini called it a sonata within a collection entitled *Trattenimenti*. For him, "concerto" furnished an apt metaphor rather than the genre concept as we understand it. Only in Torelli do musical characteristics and genre designation come together consistently.

Example 7.16   G. Jacchini, Op. 5, No. 6 (1703)

Example 7.16   cont'd

Sonatas Writ Large

The last set of examples of this chapter returns to Torelli's *Concerti grossi*, Op. 8, showing them in the light of prior developments in Bolognese music of the late seventeenth century. The scoring and form of Torelli's Op. 8 offer significant expansions upon the procedures analyzed in his earlier concertos: the later pieces consistently include one or more internal ritornellos, and they make use of separate partbooks for the first and second violins *di concertino* rather than rely on solo/tutti indications. This use of separate partbooks for the violin soloists reflects Torelli's incorporation of virtuoso technique into the concerto in the form of frequent double-stops, a range of pitches up to f³, and, as shown in Examples 7.17a and 7.17b, *arpeggio battuto* and *ondeggiando* bowings.[46]

Example 7.17a   G. Torelli, Op. 8, No. 4 (1709)

violino primo del concertino

arpeggio battuto

Example 7.17b   G. Torelli, Op. 8, No. 5 (1709)

ondeggiando

violino primo del concertino

---

46 *Battuto* here means to play the arpeggios using separate bow-strokes for each note. *Ondeggiando*, by contrast, signifies slurred articulation.

Torelli's final publication thus combines the ingredients of the concerto for soloist(s) and orchestra as it crystallized in the eighteenth century: (1) scoring that features contrasted groups within a larger ensemble, (2) thematic differentiation, (3) virtuosity, (4) ritornello form, and (5) the use of the term "concerto" and solo/tutti markings in the music. And yet, if Torelli's concertos mark the arrival of the genre as we recognize it, they also reveal his continued experiments with form and scoring. In comparison with the first example of this chapter, excerpts from another of Torelli's Op. 8 concertos, No. 2 (Example 7.18), reveal a different approach toward the arrangement of solo and tutti passages within the framework of a ritornello movement. We may recall that the first allegro from Torelli's "Christmas Concerto" (Op. 8, No. 6) coordinates tutti scoring with ritornello statements in different keys. Tutti and solo portions of the movement are thus cleanly differentiated and coordinated with ritornellos and non-thematic episodes. The second concerto offers an ingenious variation (Example 7.18): Torelli uses a ritornello of similar construction, motto plus sequencing, but divides it between solo violins (motto) and tutti (sequencing), to create a solo-plus-tutti ritornello akin to that in Jacchini's Op. 4, No. 9 (Example 7.15). In this design, moreover, there are no episodes between ritornellos, but rather within them. The second excerpt of Example 7.18, begins with a later ritornello (m. 23), which, although it begins with the same canonic motto in the two solo violins, is expanded from its previous length of five measures to nine, at which point (m. 32) the tutti portion of the ritornello is sounded, this time on the fourth degree of the tonality instead of the fifth. This portion of the ritornello, too, is expanded, but more radically, first through added sequencing, and then in a lengthy toccata-like flourish that lasts through m. 46 (shown through m. 42 in the example).

Example 7.18   G. Torelli, Op. 8, No. 2 (1709)

i. Allegro (mm. 1-10)

Example 7.18   cont'd

(mm. 23-42)

Example 7.18   cont'd

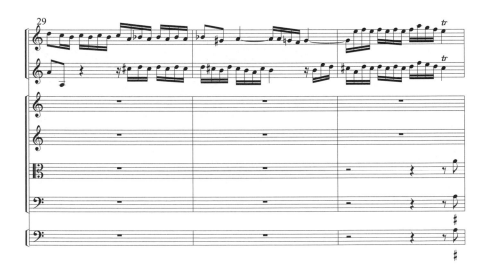

Example 7.18   cont'd

Example 7.18   cont'd

Torelli, or perhaps his publisher, Marino Silvani, entitled this posthumous publication *Concerti grossi*, a designation laden with meaning in Baroque music because of its association with scoring practices by composers mainly in Rome. That tradition was made famous in the final publication of Arcangelo Corelli, his Op. 6 (1714), also entitled *Concerti grossi* and published after the composer's death. Perhaps because of the priority of Torelli's Op. 8, Hawkins credited him with having invented the genre, but Corelli's efforts in this vein date back to the early 1680s, as reported by the south German composer Georg Muffat, who based his *Armonico tributo* (1682) on Corelli's concertos.[47] Corelli, in turn, was inspired by Roman practices of the 1660s and 70s that used contrasted concertino and concerto grosso scoring.[48] Working in that tradition, Corelli created a genre of aggrandized trio sonata whose alternation of concertino and tutti passages created chiaroscuro-like effects of texture, sometimes but certainly not always heightened by concertante writing in the solo passages. By reproducing a passage favored by Corelli—violins in thirds over a running bass—that he used in a church sonata (Op. 1, No. 11), a chamber sonata (Op. 4, No. 8), and a concerto grosso (Op. 6, No. 3), Examples 7.19a–7.19c illustrate this kind of scoring, and the close relationship between trio sonata and concerto grosso in the Roman tradition. The Corellian concerto grosso, while it presumes a specific scoring, does not coordinate its effects with any particular form. Ritornello principles play no more part here than in the Corellian trio sonata. By contrast, the concerto grosso of Torelli, defined by ritornello principles, represents a tradition with roots in Bolognese trumpet sonatas and his own earlier concerto scorings for massed strings. In short, the Bolognese and Roman performance traditions yielded distinct forms of concerto that happen to share the same name in Torelli's and Corelli's valedictory publications.[49]

---

47 The first collection of published works to bear the title of *Concerti Grossi* is Lorenzo Gregori's Op. 2 (1698). Gregori's approach to scoring is similar to that seen in Torelli's Op. 6 of the same year, whereby solo and tutti passages are marked in a single part of music (in one concerto, the fourth, Gregori supplies a separate part for the tutti first violins). Gregori's concertos, however, tend to distinguish the most active passages with solo designations, and his scoring is unconnected with ritornello form.

48 See Owen Jander, "Concerto Grosso Instrumentation in Rome in the 1660's and 1670's," *Journal of the American Musicological Society* 21 (1968): 168–80. One of the earlier pieces in concerto grosso scoring is found in the collection originally belonging to Duke Francesco II d'Este in Modena, now in the Biblioteca Estense Universitaria. It is Alessandro Stradella's explicitly titled *Sinfonia a violini e bassi a concertino e concerto grosso distinti*, MS, I-MOe Mus.F.1129, No. 2.

49 Further confusion is engendered by the distinction in modern usage between the solo concerto and the concerto grosso—the former having just one soloist, the latter having more than one. According to that distinction, Torelli's Op. 8 contains both solo concertos (one violin soloist) and concerti grossi (two violin soloists). Torelli, however, did not make that distinction in terminology.

Example 7.19a   A. Corelli, Op. 1, No. 11 (1681)

Example 7.19b   A. Corelli, Op. 4, No. 8 (1694)

Example 7.19c   A. Corelli, Op. 6, No. 3 (1713)

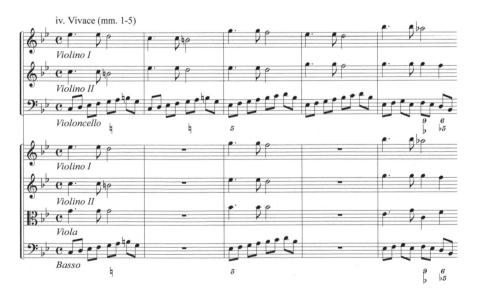

Although not clear-cut enlargements of trio sonatas, Torelli's Op. 8, too, may be interpreted as expansions upon earlier tendencies in his sonatas. In Chapter 2, the ballo from Torelli's Op. 4 (Example 2.8a) demonstrated his early fondness for more challenging violin parts, and the allemanda from his Op. 2 (Example 2.7b) introduced one of several binary ritornello-form movements that Torelli conceived for that dance type. Ritornello principles and soloistic passages for the violin occur together in his earlier work in a manner to suggest that his last concertos were to some degree sonatas writ large. The opening two movements of his sonata *a 4*, Op. 3, No. 11 (1686) (Examples 7.20a–b), offer what are concerto movements that lack only solo/tutti designations (added here in brackets). The opening composite of three sections divides into slow cadential tutti passages that sandwich the toccata-like solos of the two violins. The second movement (Example 7.20b) seems a fugue in its first measures, but instead amounts to a ritornello form, whose motto is presented imitatively in the opening and closing sections of the piece (the closing is not shown) and in a single voice with accompaniment in the medial statement (viola, mm. 16–17). Between the opening imitative ritornello and its condensed homophonic form is a solo flourish for the two violins (mm. 11–15). With the mere addition of ripieno scoring in the tutti sections hypothesized here, the piece stands as a concerto for two violins and obbligato viola akin to any in the Op. 8 collection.[50]

---

50 Something close to this—called *Sonata à 4*, however—exists in manuscript form in the S. Petronio archives. Giegling, *Torelli*, 67, has identified this piece, catalogued as TV 57: "Sie ist mit der elften Sonate des op. 3 (1687) identisch und stellt in den schnellen Sätzen dem Tutti ein Concertino von zwei Violinen, Viola und Violoncello gegenüber." Oddly, as he goes on to mention, the ripieno and concertino parts of the manuscript version play identical material.

Example 7.20a   G. Torelli, Op. 3, Sinfonia No. 11 (1687)

Example 7.20b   G. Torelli, Op. 3, Sinfonia No. 11 (1687)

Example 7.20b   cont'd

As Michael Talbot has recently discovered, Torelli made just such a conversion from a sonata for two violins and continuo, probably written in the mid-to-late 1690s, to a concerto for two violins with the addition of ripieno strings, including a non-obbligato viola.[51] In the concerto version, the piece is stylistically identical to the Op. 8 concertos for two violins, and it may well be that Torelli's Op. 8 represents a retrospective collection of pieces originally scored as sonatas and never published

---

51 Giuseppe Torelli, *Sinfonia (Sonata) in A major (TV 50)*, Michael Talbot, ed. and preface (Oxon, UK: Edition HH Ltd, 2006). As Talbot details in his introduction, the concerto (actually termed sinfonia), for two violins, ripieno strings and continuo, exists in manuscript in the S. Petronio archives, catalogued by Franz Giegling (*Torelli*, 82) as TV 50 and dated between 1696 and 1708. The sonata, for two violins and continuo (also called a sinfonia and uncatalogued by Giegling), is found in a manuscript in the British Library, and its various contents comprise works either written by the Berlin composer J. C. Pepusch or collected by him. The piece, as Talbot points out (p. x), is written on Italian-style paper by Torelli, but in handwriting of his later period. On that basis, the sonata is a work composed around the time Torelli left Italy in 1696 that he had with him during his time in Germany. With a few minor exceptions, the concerto version differs only in terms of scoring and reflects a straightforward conversion from the one genre to the other.

that were converted to concertos—either through use at S. Petronio or for the projected Op. 8. However they came about, Torelli's later concertos represent an amalgamation of techniques he accumulated over the whole of his career, writing, first, sonatas and dances for smaller ensembles, and later, concertos for larger ones. They also reinforce an idea of the Baroque concerto, not as a distinct or even well-defined genre, but as a convergence of principles applied to instrumental music—scoring for a larger ensemble and later part-doubling, contrasted groups and later thematic differentiation within that ensemble, formal recapitulation and later ritornello form—associated with a term already in musical use that appropriately draws attention to a corps of performers and its inner dynamics.[52] To recapitulate, the ingredients that make up the Torellian concerto of the early eighteenth century are a scoring of contrasted forces, thematic differentiation between them, reinforced tutti, soloistic virtuosity, ritornello form, the use of the term "concerto," and solo/tutti markings in the music. The polychoral sonata offers the point of departure with its antiphonal scoring for larger-than-normal ensemble. Then, the coalescing of concerto characteristics steadily increases from the trumpet pieces discussed above of the 1660s and 80s through the concertos of the 1690s and early 1700s, but the manner in which these ingredients were combined and coordinated never ceased to be an avenue of exploration. Torelli's most distinctive contribution was not simply that he had explored these possibilities of coordinated scoring and form, but that he was the first to have explicitly and consistently associated them with the concerto.

* * *

Torelli's death in 1709 concludes not only the early history of the concerto, but also the period of Bolognese musical ascendancy surveyed in this book. From this point, Bologna quickly recedes in importance in the history of instrumental music, in part because the driving force behind the flourishing instrumental repertory, music publishing in Bologna and then in Modena, was in steep decline by this time. Around the turn of the century, northern European publishers, mainly Estienne Roger in Amsterdam and John Walsh in London, began to make incursions into the market for Italian music by producing much neater and more legible prints from engraved copper plates. All of Italian music publishing suffered because of this new and formidable competition, but the decline in Bologna was surely hastened by the death in 1711 of Marino Silvani. Silvani, who had worked in Bologna since at least the mid 1660s as a music seller and publisher, frequently took the initiative to collect repertory for publication, persuading the composer and finding a patron to back the costs. Indeed, the era of thriving Bolognese music publishing covered here is nearly

---

52 Piperno, "'Concerto' e 'concertato'," posits concerto and concertato as compositional principles of opposition between contrasting timbres, dynamic levels, and styles that may be found in every kind of instrumental ensemble. Thus, passages of dialog between two violins or of contrast between diverse movement types offer instances of this broader concept of the concerto in seventeenth-century instrumental music. The principles studied here that converge in the eventual genre thus comprise only a subset of actual concerto techniques exploited.

contemporaneous with his decades-long tenure in the business. His passing surely altered the musical landscape of the city.

Compositional innovation, like printing, also declined in Bologna from the second decade of the eighteenth century. The next set of concertos published there after Torelli's Op. 8, those of Giuseppe Matteo Alberti, Op. 1 (1713), is symptomatic: the concertos are plainly, if expertly, Vivaldian. Stylistic innovation had moved elsewhere, and yet, the performing traditions that had begun in Bologna during the late seventeenth century endured throughout the eighteenth. During his visit in the summer of 1770, Charles Burney attended the annual performance of a Mass and Vespers at S. Giovanni in Monte by members of the Accademia Filarmonica, who formed an ensemble of "near a hundred voices and instruments."[53] One of the highlights of the ceremony came at the end of the Mass, which

> was finished by a symphony, with solo parts, by Signor Gioanni Piantanida, principal violin of Bologna, who really astonished me. This performer is upwards of sixty years of age [he was just past 64], and yet has all the fire of youth, with a good tone, and modern taste; and, upon the whole, seemed to me, though his bow-hand has a clumsy and aukward look, more powerful upon his instrument than any one I had, as yet, heard in Italy.[54]

The bulk of Burney's remarks, however, focused on other matters. Eighteenth-century Bologna had become known, largely through the efforts and reputation of G. B. Martini, as a preserver of music history, and Burney's main interest lay in visiting with Martini and with Farinelli, one a theorist-historian and the other, by that time, a living historical figure. Only at Martini's insistence, had Burney prolonged his Bolognese sojourn to witness the ceremony of the Accademia Filarmonica. And of the music he heard, only Piantanida's performance and a *Dixit* by Giancalisto Zanotti really impressed him. For the rest, Burney had particularly damning remarks for the works of Antonio Caroli, the current maestro di cappella at S. Petronio and thus a central figure in Bolognese musical life. Caroli had contributed a Graduale to the ceremony, and Burney dismissed it harshly as music written in a "dry and uninteresting stile ... which would have been thought trite and dull sixty years ago." Bologna, the *cappella musicale* of S. Petronio, and the Accademia Filarmonica had indeed all persisted and would continue to do so, but their moment in history had passed.

---

53 Charles Burney, *The Present State of Music in France and Italy* (London, 1773; facsimile, New York, Broude, 1969), 230–31.

54 Burney, *Present State*, 232.

Appendix A
Printed Instrumental Music in the Bolognese Orbit

Accademico Formato [Francesco Giuseppe De Castro?], Op. 4, *Concerti accademici à quattro, cioè un'oboè, due violini, e violone, con la parte per il cembalo* (Bologna: Peri, 1708 [RISM A 222]).

Albergati, Pirro, Op. 1, *Balletti, correnti, sarabande, e gighe à violino e violone, con il secondo violino à beneplacito* (Bologna: Giacomo Monti, 1682 [RISM A 601]).

——, Op. 2, *Suonate a due violini col suo basso continuo per l'organo, & un'altro à beneplacito per tiorba, ò violoncello* (Bologna: Giacomo Monti, 1683 [RISM A 603]).

——, Op. 5, *Pletro armonico composto di dieci sonate da camera à due violini, e basso con violoncello obligato* (Bologna: Giacomo Monti, 1687 [RISM A 606]).

——, Op. 8, *Concerti varii da camera, a trè, quattro, e cinque* (Modena: Fortuniano Rosati, 1702 [RISM A 609]).

Alberti, Giuseppe Matteo, Op. 1, *Concerti per chiesa, e per camera ad uso dell'accademia eretta nella sala del sig. co. Orazio Leonardo Bargellini, nobile patrizio Bolognese* (Bologna: Fratelli Silvani, 1713 [RISM A 665]).

Aldrovandini, Giuseppe, Op. 4, *Concerti à due, violino, e violoncello, ò tiorba* (Bologna: Marino Silvani, 1703 [RISM A 818]).

——, Op. 5, *Sonate a 3, due violini, e violoncello, col basso per l'organo* (Bologna: Marino Silvani, 1706 [RISM A 819]).

Alghisi, Paris Francesco, Op. 1, *Sonate da camera a trè, due violini, e violoncello, ò cembalo* (Modena: Christoforo Canobi, 1693 [RISM A 851]).

Allevi, Giuseppe, *Terzo libro delle compositioni sacre a due, trè, e quattro voci, accompagnata parte da violini, con sonate à trè, e le letanie della Beatissima Vergine à quattro voci con il basso continuo* (Bologna: Giacomo Monti, 1668 [RISM A 866]).

Ariosti, Attilio, *Divertimenti da camera à violino, e violoncello* (Bologna: Carlo Maria Fagnani, 1695 [RISM A 1421]).

Arresti, Giulio Cesare, Op. 2, *Messe a tre voci, con sinfonie, e ripieni à placito, accompagnate da motetti, e concerti* (Venice: Francesco Magni, 1663 [RISM A 2484]).

——, Op. 4, *Sonate a 2, & a tre, con la parte del violoncello a beneplacido* (Venice: Francesco Magni, 1665 [RISM A 2486]).

Bassani, Giovanni Battista, Op. 1, *Balletti, correnti, gighe, e sarabande à violino, e violone, overo spinetta, con il secondo violino à beneplacito* (Bologna: Giacomo Monti, 1677 [RISM B 1161]).

——, Op. 5, *Sinfonie a due, e trè instromenti, con il basso continuo per l'organo* (Bologna: Giacomo Monti, 1683 [RISM B 1171]).

Belisi, Filippo Carlo, Op. 1, *Balletti, correnti, gighe, e sarabande da camera à due violini, e violoncello, con il suo basso continuo* (Bologna: Gioseffo Micheletti, 1691 [RISM B 1698]).

Berardi, Angelo, Op. 7, *Sinfonie a violino solo* (Bologna: Giacomo Monti, 1670 [RISM B 1974]).

Bergonzi, Giuseppe, Op. 1, *Divertimenti da camera a tre, due violini ò* [recte *e*] *arcileuto* (Bologna: Marino Silvani, 1705 [RISM B 2024]).

——, Op. 2, *Sinfonie da chiesa, e concerti a quattro a due violini concertati, e due ripieni con l'alto viola obbligata, col basso per l'organo* (Bologna: Peri, 1708 [RISM B 2025]).

Bernardi, Bartolomeo, Op. 1, *Sonate da camera a trè, due violini, e violoncello col violone, ò cimbalo* (Bologna: Pier-Maria Monti, 1692 [RISM B 2039]).

——, Op. 2, *Sonate à trè, due violini, e violoncello, con il basso per l'organo* (Bologna: Carlo Maria Fagnani, 1696 [RISM B 2040]).

——, Op. 3, *Sonate a violino solo col basso continuo* (Amsterdam: Estienne Roger, n.d. [1706] [RISM B 2042]).

Bianchi, Giovanni, Op. 1, *Sonate à trè, due violini, e violoncello, col basso per l'organo* (Modena: Fortuniano Rosati, 1697 [RISM B 2586]).

Bissone, Giovanni Ambrogio, Op. 1, *Divertimenti armonici per camera à 3. strumenti* (Bologna: Pier-Maria Monti, 1694 [RISM B 2754]).

Bononcini, Giovanni, Op. 1, *Trattenimenti da camera a trè, due violini, e violone, con il basso continuo per il cembalo* (Bologna: Giacomo Monti, 1685 [RISM B 3604]).

——, Op. 2, *Concerti da camera a trè, due violini, e violone, con il basso continuo per il cembalo* (Bologna: Giacomo Monti, 1685 [RISM B 3605]).

——, Op. 3, *Sinfonie a 5. 6. 7. e 8. istromenti, con alcune à una e due trombe, servendo ancora per violini* (Bologna: Giacomo Monti, 1685 [RISM B 3607]).

——, Op. 4, *Sinfonie a trè istromenti, col basso per l'organo* (Bologna: Giacomo Monti, 1686 [RISM B 3608]).

——, Op. 5, *Sinfonie da chiesa a quattro, cioè due violini, alto viola, e violoncello obligato* (Bologna: Giacomo Monti, 1687 [RISM B 3609]).

——, Op. 6, *Sinfonie a due strumenti, violino, e violoncello, col basso continuo per l'organo* (Bologna: Giacomo Monti, 1687 [RISM B 3611]).

Bononcini, Giovanni Maria, Op. 1, *Primi frutti del giardino musicale a due violini* (Venice: Francesco Magni, 1666 [RISM B 3652]; facsimile, Bologna: Il Fabbro Armonioso, 1979).

——, Op. 2, *Sonate da camera, e da ballo a 1. 2. 3. è 4* (Venice: Francesco Magni, 1667 [RISM B 3626]; facsimile, Bologna: Antiquae Musicae Italicae Studiosi, 1971).

——, Op. 3, *Varii fiori del giardino musicale, overo sonate da camera a 2. 3. e 4. col suo basso continuo* (Bologna: Giacomo Monti, 1669 [RISM B 3627], facsimile, Bologna: Forni, 1983).

——, Op. 4, *Arie, correnti, sarabande, gighe, & allemande a violino, e violone, over spinetta, con alcune intavolate per diverse accordature* (Bologna: Giacomo Monti, 1671 [RISM B 3628]).

——, Op. 5, *Sinfonia, allemande, correnti, e sarabande a 5. e 6. col suo basso continuo; et aggiunta d'una sinfonia à quattro, che si può suonare ancora al contrario rivoltando le parti* (Bologna: Giacomo Monti, 1671 [RISM B 3630]).

——, Op. 6, *Sonate da chiesa a due violini* (Venice: Francesco Magni, 1672 [RISM B 3631] ; facsimile, Bologna: Forni, 1970).

——, Op. 7, *Ariette, correnti, gighe, allemande, e sarabande; le quali ponno suonarsi a violino solo; a due, violino e violone; a trè, due violini e violone; et a quattro, due violini, viola, e violone* (Bologna: Giacomo Monti, 1673 [RISM B 3634]).

——, Op. 9, *Trattenimenti musicali à trè, & à quattro stromenti* (Bologna: Giacomo Monti, 1675 [RISM B 3637]).

——, Op. 12, *Arie, e correnti a trè, due violini, e violone* (Bologna: Giacomo Monti, 1678 [RISM B 3641]).

Bonporti, Francesco Antonio, Op. 10, *Invenzioni da camera a violino solo con l'accompagnamento d'un violoncello, e cembalo, o liuto* (Bologna: Giuseppe Antonio Silvani, 1712 [RISM B 3659]).

Borri, Giovanni Battista, Op. 1, *Sinfonie a trè, due violini, e violoncello con il basso per l'organo* (Bologna: Gioseffo Micheletti, 1688 [RISM B 3769]).

Brasolini, Domenico, Op. 1, *Suonate da camera à trè, due violini e clavicembalo, o violoncello* (Bologna: Pier-Maria Monti, 1689 [RISM B 4266]).

Brevi, Giovanni Battista, Op. 3, *Bizzarie armoniche overo sonate da camera a trè strumenti col suo basso continuo* (Bologna: Pier-Maria Monti, 1693 [RISM B 4424]).

Buffagnotti, Carlo, *Menuetti, sarabande, et varij caprici* (Bologna?, engraved by Buffagnotti, n.d. [RISM BB 4927 I, 1]).

Buoni, Giorgio, Op. 1, *Divertimenti per camera a due violini, e violoncello* (Bologna: Pier-Maria Monti, 1693 [RISM B 4948]).

——, Op. 2, *Suonate a due violini, e violoncello, col basso per l'organo* (Bologna: Pier-Maria Monti, 1693 [RISM B 4949]).

——, Op. 3, *Allettamenti per camera a due violini, e basso* (Bologna: Pier-Maria Monti, 1693 [RISM B 4950]).

Cattaneo, Giacomo, Op. 1, *Trattenimenti armonici da camera a trè istromenti, due violini e violoncello, ò cembalo, con due brevi cantate à soprano solo, & una sonata per violoncello* (Modena: Fortuniano Rosati, 1700 [RISM C 1524]).

Cazzati, Maurizio, Op. 2, *Canzoni da sonare a tre, due violini, è violone, con il suo basso continuo, e nel fine un Confitebor, & un Laetatus à 3. voci* (Venice: Bartolomeo Magni, 1642 [RISM C 1578]; reprint, Bologna: Heredi di Evangelista Dozza, 1663 [RISM C 1579]).

——, Op. 15, *Correnti e balletti a cinque alla francese, et all'italiana con alcune sonate à 5. 6. 7. 8* (Venice: Alessandro Vincenti, 1654 [RISM C 1596]; reprint, Bologna: Giacomo Monti, 1667 [RISM C 1597]).

——, Op. 18, *Suonate a due violini col suo basso continuo per l'organo, & un altro à beneplacito per tiorba, ò violone* (Venice: Francesco Magni, 1656 [RISM C

1602]; reprints, Bologna: L'Eredi del Benacci, 1659 [RISM C 1604] and Bologna: Giacomo Monti, 1679 [RISM C 1606]).

——, Op. 22, *Trattenimenti per camera d'arie, correnti, e balletti, à due violini, e violone, se piace, con passacaglio, ciaccona, & un capriccio sopra 12 note* (Bologna: Antonio Pisarri, 1660 [RISM C 1613]; facsimile, Bologna: Antiquae Musicae Italicae Studiosi, 1971).

——, Op. 30, *Correnti, e balletti per sonare nella spinetta, leuto, ò tiorba; overo violino, e violone, col secondo violino à beneplacito* (Bologna: Antonio Pisarri, 1662 [RISM C 1624]; reprint, Bologna: Evangelista Dozza, 1663 [RISM C 1625]).

——, Op. 35, *Sonate à due, trè, quattro, e cinque, con alcune per tromba* (Bologna: Marino Silvani, 1665 [RISM C 1631]).

——, Op. 50, *Varii, e diversi capricci per camera, e per chiesa, da sonare con diversi instromenti, a uno, due, e tre* (Bologna: n.p., 1669 [RISM C 1650]).

——, Op. 55, *Sonate a due istromenti, cioè violino, e violone* (Bologna: n.p., 1670 [RISM C 1656]).

Colombi, Giuseppe, Op. 1, *Sinfonie da camera, brandi, e corrente alla francese ... à due, à trè, & à quattro* (Bologna: n.p., 1668 [RISM C 3435]).

——, Op. 2, *La lira armonica, sinfonie à due violini, col suo basso continuo* (Bologna: Giacomo Monti, 1673 [RISM C 3436]).

——, Op. 3, *Balletti, correnti, gighe, sarabande a due violini, e violone, ò spinetta* (Bologna: Giacomo Monti, 1674 [RISM C 3437]).

——, Op. 4, *Sonate a due violini con un bassetto viola se piace* (Bologna: Giacomo Monti, 1676 [RISM C 3438]).

——, Op. 5, *Sonate da camera a tre strumenti, due violini, e violone, ò cimbalo* (Bologna: Pier-Maria Monti, 1689 [RISM C 3439]).

De Castro, Francesco Giuseppe, Op. 1, *Trattenimenti armonici da camera a trè, due violini, violoncello, ò cembalo* (Bologna: Pier-Maria Monti, 1695 [RISM A 221]).

Degli Antonii, Giovanni Battista, Op. 1, *Ricercate sopra il violoncello ò clavicembalo* (Bologna: Gioseffo Micheletti, 1687 [RISM D 1336]; facsimile, Wyton, Huntington, UK: King's Music, 1998).

——, Op. 3, *Balletti, correnti, gighe, e sarabande da camera à violino, e clavicembalo ò violoncello* (Bologna: Marino Silvani, 1677 [*recte* 1687?] [RISM D 1339]; reprint, Bologna: Gioseffo Micheletti, 1688 [RISM D 1340]).

——, Op. 4, *Balletti, correnti, gighe, e sarabande à trè, due violini e clavicembalo ò violoncello* (Bologna: Gioseffo Micheletti, n.d. [1688–89] [RISM D 1341]).

——, Op. 5, *Ricercate à violino, e violoncello, ò clavicembalo* (Bologna: Gioseffo Micheletti, 1689 [no listing in RISM); reprint, Bologna: Gioseffo Micheletti, 1690 [RISM D 1342]).

——, Op. 6, *Balletti a violino, e violoncello, ò clavicembalo* (Bologna: Gioseffo Micheletti, 1690 [RISM D 1343]).

Degli Antonii, Pietro, Op. 1, *Arie, gighe, balletti, correnti, allemande, e sarabande a violino, e violone, ò spinetta con il secondo violino à beneplacito* (Bologna: Giacomo Monti, 1670 [RISM D 1346]).

——, Op. 3, *Balletti, correnti, & arie diverse à violino, e violone per camera, & anco per suonare nella spinetta, & altri instromenti* (Bologna: Giacomo Monti, 1671 [RISM D 1348]).

——, Op. 4, *Sonate a violino solo* (Bologna: Giacomo Monti, 1676 [RISM D 1349]).

——, Op. 5, *Suonate a violino solo col basso continuo per l'organo* (Bologna: Giacomo Monti, 1686 [RISM D 1350]).

Fiorè, Andrea, Op. 1, *Sinfonie da chiesa à trè, cioè due violini, e violoncello con il suo basso continuo per l'organo* (Modena: Fortuniano Rosati, 1699 [RISM F 868]).

Gabrielli, Domenico, Op. 1, *Balletti, gighe, correnti, alemande, e sarabande à violino, e violone, con il secondo violino à beneplacito* (Bologna: Giacomo Monti, 1684 [RISM G 91]).

Gaspardini, Gasparo, Op. 1, *Sonate a trè, due violini, e violoncino con il basso per l'organo* (Bologna: Gioseffo Micheletti, 1683 [RISM G 452]).

Gigli, Giovanni Battista, Op. 1, *Sonate da chiesa, e da camera à 3 strumenti, col basso continuo per l'organo* (Bologna: Pier-Maria Monti, 1690 [RISM G 2025]).

Granata, Giovanni Battista, Op. 5, *Novi capricci armonici musicali in varj toni per la chitarra spagnola, violino, e viola concertati, et altre sonate per la chitarra sola* (Bologna: Giacomo Monti, 1674 [RISM G 3394]; facsimile, Bologna: Forni, 1999).

——, Op. 6, *Nuovi souavi concenti di sonate musicali in varij toni per la chittara spagnola, & altre sonate concertate à due violini, e basso* (Bologna: Giacomo Monti, 1680 [RISM G 3395]).

——, Op. 7, *Armoniosi toni di varie suonate musicali concertate a due violini, e basso, con la chitarra spagnola* (Bologna: Giacomo Monti, 1684 [RISM G 3396]).

Grossi, Andrea, Op. 1, *Balletti, correnti, sarabande, e gighe a tre, due violini, e violone, overo spinetta* (Bologna: Giacomo Monti, 1678 [RISM G 4724]).

——, Op. 2, *Balletti, correnti, sarabande, e gighe a trè, due violini, e violone, overo spinetta* (Bologna: Giacomo Monti, 1679 [RISM G 4725]).

——, Op. 3, *Sonate a due, trè, quattro, e cinque instromenti* (Bologna: Giacomo Monti, 1682 [RISM G 4726]).

——, Op. 4, *Sonate a trè, due violini, e violone, con il basso continuo per l'organo* (Bologna: Giacomo Monti, 1685 [RISM G 4727]).

Jacchini, Giuseppe, Op. 1, *Sonate à violino è violoncello, et à violoncello solo per camera* (Bologna?, engraved by Buffagnotti, n.d. [RISM J 1]; facsimile with preface by Marc Vanscheeuwijck, Bologna: Forni, 2001).

——, Op. 2, *Sonate da camera trè, e quattro stromenti, col violoncello obligato* (Bologna: Pier-Maria Monti, 1695 [RISM J 2]).

——, Op. 3, *Concerti per camera à violino, e violoncello solo, e nel fine due sonate à violoncello solo col basso* (Modena: Fortuniano Rosati, 1697 [RISM J 3]).

——, Op. 4, *Concerti per camera à 3. e 4. strumenti, con violoncello obligato* (Bologna: Marino Silvani, 1701 [RISM J 4]).

——, Op. 5, *Trattenimenti per camera a 3. 4. 5. e 6. strumenti, con alcune à una, e due trombe* (Bologna: Marino Silvani, 1703 [RISM J 5]).

Laurenti, Bartolomeo Girolamo, Op. 1, *Suonate per camera à violino, e violoncello* (Bologna: Pier-Maria Monti, 1691 [RISM L 1091]).

Laurenti, Girolamo Nicolò, Op. 1, *VI concerti a tre violini, alto viola, violoncello e basso continuo* (Amsterdam: Michel Charles Le Cène, n.d. [RISM L 1092]).

Legrenzi, Giovanni, Op. 8, *Sonate a due, trè, cinque, e sei stromenti* (Venice: Francesco Magni, 1663 [RISM L 1619]; reprint, Bologna: Giacomo Monti, 1671 [RISM L 1621]).

Leonarda, Isabella, Op. 16, *Sonate à 1. 2. 3. e 4. istromenti* (Bologna: Pier-Maria Monti, 1693 [RISM I 103]).

Manfredini, Francesco, Op. 1, *Concertini per camera a violino, e violoncello, o tiorba* (Bologna: Marino Silvani, 1704 [RISM M 338]).

——, Op. 2, *Sinfonie da chiesa à due violini, col basso per l'organo & una viola à beneplacito, con una pastorale per il Santissimo Natale* (Bologna: Marino Silvani, 1709 [RISM M 339]).

Marino, Carlo Antonio, Op. 1, *Sonate da camera a trè strumenti* (Bologna: Giacomo Monti, 1687 [RISM M 687]).

Marotti, Ippolito, *Sonate per camera a violino, e violone, ò cembalo* (Bologna: Peri, 1710 [RISM M 715]).

Mazzaferrata, Giovanni Battista, Op. 5, *Il primo libro delle sonate a due violini con un bassetto viola se piace* (Bologna: Giacomo Monti, 1674 [RISM M 1514]).

Mazzolini, Carlo Andrea, Op. 1, *Sonate per camera à trè, due violini, e clavicembalo ò tiorba* (Bologna: Gioseffo Micheletti, 1687 [RISM M 1682]).

Monari, Clemente, Op. 1, *Balletti, e correnti da camera a due violini con il suo basso continuo* (Bologna: Gioseffo Micheletti, 1686 [RISM M 3004]).

——, Op. 2, *Sonate da camera à trè, due violini, e violone, ò cembalo* (Modena: Fortuniano Rosati, n.d. [RISM M 3005]).

Motta, Artemio, Op. 1, *Concerti a cinque* (Modena: Fortuniano Rosati, 1701 [RISM M 3822]).

Pegolotti, Tomaso, Op. 1, *Trattenimenti armonici da camera à violino solo, e violoncello* (Modena: Fortuniano Rosati, 1698 [RISM P 1142]).

Penna, Lorenzo, Op. 7, *Correnti francesi a quattro, cioè due violini, violetta, e violone, con il basso continuo per il clavicembalo, ò tiorba* (Bologna: Giacomo Monti, 1673 [RISM P 1192]).

Piazzi, Carlo, Op. 2, *Balletti, correnti, gighe, e sarabande à trè, due violini, e violone* (Bologna: Giacomo Monti, 1681 [RISM P 2040]).

Pistocchi, Francesco Antonio, Op. 1, *Capricci puerili variamente composti, e passeggiati in 40. modi sopra un basso d'un balletto ... per suonarsi nel clavicembalo, arpa, violino, et altri stromenti* (Bologna: Giacomo Monti, 1667 [RISM P 2456]).

Pittoni, Giovanni, Op. 1, *Sonate da chiesa per tiorba sola col basso per l'organo* (Bologna: Giacomo Monti, 1669 [RISM P 2482]; facsimile of Opp. 1 and 2, Florence: Studio per Edizioni Scelte, 1980).

——, Op. 2, *Sonate da camera per tiorba sola col basso per il clavicembalo* (Bologna: Giacomo Monti, 1669 [RISM P 2483]; facsimile of Opp. 1 and 2, Florence: Studio per Edizioni Scelte, 1980).

Pizzoni, Elzeario, Op. 1, *Balletti, correnti, gighe, e sarrabande* [sic] *per camera a due violini, e violone col suo basso continuo per spinetta, ò tiorba* (Bologna: Antonio Caldani, 1669 [RISM P 2491]).

Placuzzi, Gioseffo Maria, Op. 1, *Suonate à duoi, à trè, à quattro, à cinque, & otto instromenti* (Bologna: Giacomo Monti, 1667 [RISM P 2504]).

——, Op. 2, *Il numero sonoro, lodolato in modo armonici et aritmetici di balletti, correnti, gighe, allemande, sarabande, e capricci a due violini, col suo basso per spinetta, ò violone* (Bologna: Giacomo Monti, 1682 [RISM P 2505]).

Polaroli, Oratio, Op. 1, *Correnti, balletti, gighe, allemande, arie ... overo suonate da camera à trè* (Bologna: Giacomo Monti, 1673 [RISM P 5010]).

Prattichista, Francesco, Op. 1, *Concerti armonici di correnti, e balletti a tre, cioè due violini, e basso* (Bologna: Giacomo Monti, 1666 [RISM P 5411]).

Taglietti, Giulio, [Op. 1], *Sonate da camera a trè: due violini, e violoncello, ò cembalo* (Bologna: Carlo Maria Fagnani, 1695 [RISM T 44]).

Taglietti, Luigi, Op. 1, *Suonate da camera à trè, due violini, e violoncello, con alcune aggiunte à violoncello solo* (Bologna: Marino Silvani, 1697 [RISM T 45]).

Torelli, Giuseppe, Op. 1, *Sonate à tre stromenti con il basso continuo* (Bologna: Gioseffo Micheletti, 1686 [RISM T 980]).

——, Op. 2, *Concerto da camera à due violini, e basso* (Bologna: Gioseffo Micheletti, 1686 [RISM T 982]).

——, Op. 3, *Sinfonie à 2. 3. e 4. istromenti* (Bologna: Gioseffo Micheletti, 1687 [RISM T 984]).

——, Op. 4, *Concertino per camera a violino e violoncello* (Bologna: Marino Silvani, engraved by Buffagnotti, 1687–88 [RISM T 986]).

——, Op. 5, *Sinfonie à tre e concerti à quattro* (Bologna: Gioseffo Micheletti, 1692 [RISM T 987]).

——, Op. 6, *Concerti musicali* (Augsburg: Johann Christoph Wagner, 1698 [RISM T 990]).

——, Op. 8, *Concerti grossi con una Pastorale per il Santissimo Natale* (Bologna: Silvani, 1709 [RISM T 993]).

Uccellini, Marco, Op. 4, *Sonate, correnti, et arie da farsi con diversi stromenti sì da camera, come da chiesa, à uno, à due, & à trè* (Venice: Alessandro Vincenti, 1645 [RISM U 15]; reprint, Antwerp: Héritiers de Pierre Phalèse, 1663 [RISM U 16]).

——, Op. 5, *Sonate over canzoni da farsi à violino solo, & basso continuo* (Venice: Alessandro Vincenti, 1649 [RISM U 17]).

——, Op. 7, *Ozio regio, compositioni armoniche sopra il violino e diversi altri strumenti ... a uno, due, tre, quattro, cinque, e sei* (Venice: Francesco Magni, 1660 [RISM U 19]).

——, Op. 8, *Sinfonie boscarecie, brandi, corrente, con diversi balli alla francese, e all'itagliana, conforme si costuma ballare nella corte del ... duca di Modena; ogni cos' à violino solo, e basso, con l'agiunta di due altri violini ad libitum, per poter sonare à due, à trè, è à quattro conforme piacerà* (Venice: Francesco Magni, 1660 [RISM U 22]).

——, Op. 9, *Sinfonici concerti, brievi, è facili, à uno, à due, à trè, & à quatro strumenti; ogni cosa, con il suo basso continuo, per chiesa, è per camera. Con brandi, è corenti alla francese, è balletti al italiana, giusta l'uso aprovatissimo della corte di Parma* (Venice: Francesco Magni, 1667 [RISM U 25]).

Valentini, Giuseppe, Op. 7, *Concerti grossi a quattro e sei strumenti, cioè a due, e quattro violini, alto viola, e violoncello, con due violini, e basso di ripieno* (Bologna: Marino Silvani, 1710 [RISM V 114]).

Vannini, Elia, Op. 1, *Sinfonie a tre, due violini, e violoncello col suo basso continuo, e la violetta ad libitum* (Bologna: Gioseffo Micheletti, 1691 [RISM V 975]).

Various authors [Arcangelo Corelli, Giuseppe Torelli, Antonio Montanari, Giacomo Predieri, Carlo Mazzolini, Giuseppe Jacchini, Clementi Rozzi], *Sonate a violino e violoncello di vari autori* (n.p., engraved by Buffagnotti, n.d. [no listing in RISM]; facsimile, Bologna: Forni, 1974).

Various authors [Giacomo Antonio Perti, Giuseppe Aldrovandini, Domenico Marcheselli, Giuseppe Jacchini, Bartolomeo Laurenti, Carlo Mazzolini, Filippo Carlo Belisi, Bartolomeo Bernardi, Antonio Grimandi, Giuseppe Torelli], *Sonate per camera a violino e violoncello di vari autori* (n.p., engraved by Buffagnotti, n.d. [RISM c.1695[16]]; facsimile, Bologna: Forni, 1974).

Various authors [Giovanni Andrea Alberti, Giuseppe Alberti, Giuseppe Prandi, Pietro Bettinozzi, Pietro Paolo Laurenti, Francesco Manfredini, Pietro Giuseppe Sandoni, Francesco Farnè, Tomaso Vitali, Carlo Andrea Mazzolini, Giuseppe Torelli, Girolamo Nicolò Laurenti], *Corona di dodici fiori armonici tessuta da altrettanti ingegni sonori a tre strumenti* (Bologna: Peri, 1706 [RISM B/II/146]; facsimile, Bologna: Forni, 1974).

Various authors [Giovanni Battista Bassani, Giovanni Francalanza, Petronio Franceschini, Andrea Grossi, Pietro Degli Antonii, Alessandro Stradella, Giovanni Maria Bononcini, Giovanni Appiano, unknown Roman, unknown Venetian, Giacinto Pestalozza], *Scielta delle suonate a due violini, con il basso continuo per l'organo, raccolte da diversi eccelenti autori* (Bologna: Giacomo Monti, 1680 [RISM 1680[7]]; facsimile, Bologna: Forni, 1974).

Various authors [Giuseppe Aldrovandini, Alessandro Stradella, Giuseppe Torelli, Domenico Gabrielli, Giuseppe Jacchini], *Sonate a tre di vari autori* (n.p., engraved by Buffagnotti? n.d. [RISM c.1700[7]]).

Veracini, Antonio, Op. 2, *Sonate da camera a violino solo* (Modena: Fortuniano Rosati, n.d. [RISM V 1200]).

Veracini, Antonio, Op. 3, *Sonate da camera a due, violino, e violone, ò arcileuto, col basso per il cimbalo* (Modena: Fortuniano Rosati, 1696 [RISM V 1201]).

Vitali, Giovanni Battista, Op. 1, *Correnti, e balletti da camera a due violini col suo basso continuo per spinetta, ò violone* (Bologna: Marino Silvani, 1666 [RISM V 2141]).

——, Op. 2, *Sonate a due violini col suo basso continuo per l'organo* (Bologna: Giacomo Monti, 1667 [RISM V 2146]).

——, Op. 3, *Balletti, correnti alla francese, gagliarde, e brando per ballare. Balletti, correnti e sinfonie da camera à quattro stromenti* (Bologna: Giacomo Monti, 1667 [RISM V 2151]).

——, Op. 4, *Balletti, correnti, gighe, allemande, e sarabande à violino, e violone, ò spinetta con il secondo violino a beneplacito* (Bologna: Giacomo Monti, 1668 [RISM V 2155]).

——, Op. 5, *Sonate a due, trè, quattro, e cinque stromenti* (Bologna: Giacomo Monti, 1669 [RISM V 2160]).

——, Op. 7, *Varie partite del passemezo, ciaccona, capricij, e passagalli à tre, due violini, e violone, o spinetta* (Modena: Gasparo Ferri, 1682 [RISM V 2163]).

——, Op. 8, *Balletti, correnti, e capricci per camera a due violini, e violone* (Modena: Gasparo Ferri, 1683 [RISM V 2164]).

——, Op. 9, *Sonate da chiesa à due violini* (Amsterdam: Johann Philipp Heus, 1684 [RISM V 2167]).

——, Op. 11, *Varie sonate alla francese, & all'itagliana à sei stromenti* (Modena: Gasparo Ferri, 1684 [RISM V 2170]).

——, Op. 12, *Balli in stile francese à cinque stromenti* (Modena: Antonio Vitaliani, 1685 [RISM V 2171]).

——, Op. 13, *Artificii musicali ne quali si contengono canoni in diverse maniere, contrapunti dopii, inventionj curiose, capritii, è sonate* (Modena: Eredi Cassiani, 1689 [RISM V 2173]).

—— , Op. 14, *Sonate da camera a trè, due violini, e violone* (Modena: Christoforo Canobi, 1692 [RISM V 2174]).

Vitali, Tomaso Antonio, [Op. 1], *Sonate a trè, doi violini, e violoncello, col basso per l'organo* (Modena: Antonio Ricci, 1693 [RISM V 2177]).

——, Op. 2, *Sonate à doi violini, col basso per l'organo* (Modena: Christoforo Canobi, 1693 [RISM V 2176]).

——, Op. 3, *Sonate da camera a trè, due violini, e violone* (Modena: Fortuniano Rosati, 1695 [RISM V 2178]).

——, Op. 4, *Concerto di sonate a violino, violoncello, e cembalo* (Modena: Fortuniano Rosati, 1701 [RISM V 2179]).

Zanatta, Domenico, Op. 1, *Suonate da chiesa à 3. strumenti, due violini, e violoncello, col basso per l'organo* (Bologna: Pier-Maria Monti, 1689 [RISM Z 18]).

Appendix B

Instrumental Music in Manuscript from the Modenese Court of Francesco II d'Este

Anonymous, Dances for chitarra spagnola, MS, I-MOe, Mus.E.323.

Anonymous, Dances for chitarra spagnola, MS, I-MOe, Mus.F.1528.

Anonymous, Sonata cornettino solo, "M.S.," August 1686; and Sonata solo fagotto di "M.S.," 1686, MS, I-MOe, Mus.E.316.

Anonymous, Sonata dà camera à 2, MS, I-MOe, Mus.E.313.

Anonymous, Suonata à 2, violino è violoncello, MS, I-MOe, Mus.E.305.

Anonymous, Suonata à duoi; violino è violoncello, MS, I-MOe, Mus.E.317.

Colombi, Giuseppe, Chiacona a basso solo, MS, I-MOe, Mus.E.350.

——, Libro 1° del Colombi [duos for treble and bass instruments], MS, I-MOe, Mus.E.34/1–2.

——, Libro 2° del Colombi [duos for treble and bass instruments], MS, I-MOe, Mus.F.272/1–2.

——, Libro 3° del Colombi [duos for treble and bass instruments], MS, I-MOe, Mus.F.273/1–2.

——, Libro 4° del Colombi [duos for treble and bass instruments], MS, I-MOe, Mus.F.274/1–2.

——, Libro 5° del Colombi [duos for treble and bass instruments], MS, I-MOe, Mus.F.275/1–2.

——, Libro 6° del Colombi [duos for treble and bass instruments], MS, I-MOe, Mus.F.276/1–2.

——, Libro 7° del Colombi [duos for treble and bass instruments], MS, I-MOe, Mus.F.277/1–2.

——, Libro 8° del Colombi [trios for two trebles and bass], MS, I-MOe, Mus.F.278/1–3.

——, Libro 9° del Colombi [trios for two trebles and bass], MS, I-MOe, Mus.F.279/1–3.

——, Libro 10°: (1) Sinfonia a violino solo; (2) [Sinfonia] a violino solo; (3) [Sinfonia] a violino solo; (4) [Sinfonia] a violino solo; (5) [Sinfonia] a violino solo; (6) Sonata a violino solo; (7) [Sonata] a violino solo; (8) Sonata a violino solo; (9) Chiacona à [violino] solo; (10) Chiacona à [violino] solo; (11) Corrente à 2 corde; (12) Tromba à violino solo; (13) Tromba à basso solo, MS, I-MOe, Mus.F.280.

——, Libro 11°: Dance movements for two trebles and bass, MS, I-MOe, Mus.G.60/1–3.

——, Libro 12°: (1) [6 sonate] a due violini, MS, I-MOe, Mus.F.281.

——, Libro 13°: Brandi [26, for violin and violone], MS, I-MOe, Mus.F.282.

——, Libro 14°: Varie partite di barabani, ruggieri, e scordature di Giuseppe Colombi: [Scordatura], [toccata], [tromba], [tromba], [duo], [duo], Ruggiero a violino solo, [tromba], [duo], [scordatura], [tromba], Barabano à violino, e violone, Barabano à 2 violini, Ruggiero à 2 violini, Ruggiero à violino, e violone, MS, I-MOe, Mus. F.283.

——, Libro 15°: Balletti [for unaccompanied violin], MS, I-MOe, Mus.F.284.

——, Libro 16°: Toccata da violino del Colombi [unaccompanied], MS, I-MOe, Mus.F.285.

——, Libro 17°: Toccata da violone del Colombi [unaccompanied & incomplete], MS, I-MOe, Mus.F.286.

——, Libro 18°: Sinfonie da camera [for unaccompanied violin or incomplete], MS, I-MOe, Mus.G.58.

——, Libro 19°: Dances for unaccompanied violin or incomplete, MS, I-MOe, Mus. G.59.

——, Libro 20°: Varie sonate, MS, I-MOe, Mus.G.57.

——, Libro 21°: Dances for unaccompanied bass instrument, MS, I-MOe, Mus. G.56.

——, Libro 22°: [Balli in four parts: treble, soprano, mezzo-soprano, and bass clefs] del Colombi: Mustarda nova, gagliarda nova, borea nova, corrente nova, Duchessa nova, brando novo, unnamed dance, gavotta, MS, I-MOe, Mus.F.287.

Degli Antonii, Giovanni Battista, Ricercate per il violino [12 a 2, treble and bass], MS, I-MOe, Mus.D.9.

——, Ricercate per il violino (2 a 2, treble and bass = Nos. 1 and 2 of Mus.D.9), MS, I-MOe, Mus.D.10.

Degli Antonii, Pietro, Sonata a tre, due violini, violoncello con organo, MS, I-MOe, Mus.D.11.

Fiorè, Angelo Maria, Sinfonie à violoncello solo, con il basso continuo (2), MS, I-MOe, Mus.F.384.

Gabrielli, Domenico, Ricercari per il violoncello solo, con un canone a due violoncelli e alcuni ricercari per v.llo e B.C, MS, I-MOe, Mus.G.79; facsimile ed. as *Ricercari per violoncello solo; Canone a due violoncelli; Sonate per violoncello e basso continuo*, preface by Marc Vanscheeuwijck (Bologna: Forni, 1998).

——, Sonate (2) à violoncello solo, con il basso continuo, MS, I-MOe, Mus. F.416; facsimile and modern ed. as *Ricercari per violoncello solo; Canone a due violoncelli; Sonate per violoncello e basso continuo*, ed. Marc Vanscheeuwijck (Bologna: Forni, 1998).

Galli, Domenico, *Trattenimento musicale sopra il violoncello a solo* [12 sonatas], MS, I-MOe, Mus.C.81, 1691.

Giannettini/Giannottini, Antonio, Balli e sonate a 2 violini e basso; a violino e basso; e a basso solo, con basso continuo, MS, I-MOe, Mus.G.87.

——, Correnti (3), MS, I-MOe, Mus.E.61.

Lonati, Carlo Ambrogio, Sonata à violino solo, MS, I-MOe, Mus.F.639.

Millanta, Evilmerodach, Trattenimenti da camera à due, violino e violone con il basso continuo per il cembalo, MS, I-MOe, Mus.F.745.

Pozzatti, Giuseppe, Balletti a 2 e a 4 stromenti (balletti, correnti, gighe, allemande, e sarabande a tre e a quattro), MS, I-MOe, Mus.G.166.

Stradella, Alessandro, Sinfonie à più violini [12] e violino solo [9], MS, I-MOe, Mus.F.1129.

——, Sinfonie a 2, ò a 3, MS, I-MOe, Mus.G.210.

Various authors [Johann Paul von Westhoff (1 sonata); Anonymous (3 sinfonie); Giuseppe Colombi (1 chaconne, 1 scordatura, 1 tromba)], Sinfonie a violino solo [with basso continuo], MS, I-MOe, Mus.E.282.

Various authors [Pietro Soresina/Sorosina (1 sonata); Giuseppe Pozzatti (2 sonatas); Giuseppe Colombi (2 sonatas)], Sonate a due violini, con basso ad organo, MS, I-MOe, Mus.F.1347.

Various authors [Pietro Sorosina/Soresina (6 sonatas); Giuseppe Pozzatti (1 sonata); Giuseppe Colombi (1 tromba, incomplete)], Sonate a due stromenti, MS, I-MOe, Mus.F.1352.

Various authors [Luigi Mancia/Manzia (1 sonata, "La Sassolesa"); Giuseppe Colombi (3 sonatas); Anonymous (2 sonatas)], Sonate a violino solo o a 2, con basso, MS, I-MOe, Mus.F.1386.

Vitali, Giovanni Battista, Partite sopra diverse sonate—per il violone; per il violino, MS, I-MOe, Mus.E.244.

——, Sonate [for violin and bass violin], MS, I-MOe, Mus.F.1250/1–2.

——, Sonate a violino e violoncello, MS, I-MOe, Mus.E.246.

Bibliography

Primary Sources

I. Music Manuals, Dictionaries, and Theoretical Treatises

Anonymous, *Regole del contrappunto*, MS, early 18th century, I-Bc, P.120, n. 5.

Banchieri, Adriano, *Cartella musicale nel canto figurato, fermo & contrapunto* (Venice: Giacomo Vincenti, 1614; facsimile, Bologna: Forni, 1968); English trans. with commentary by Clifford Alan Cranna as "Adriano Banchieri's Cartella musicale (1614): Translation and Commentary," Ph.D. dissertation, Stanford University, 1981.

Berardi, Angelo, *Arcani musicali* (Bologna: Pier-Maria Monti, 1690).

——, *Documenti armonici* (Bologna: Giacomo Monti, 1687; facsimile, Bologna: Forni, 1970).

——, *Miscellanea musicale* (Bologna: Giacomo Monti, 1689; facsimile, Bologna: Forni, 1970).

——, *Il perche musicale* (Bologna: Pier-Maria Monti, 1693).

Bismantova, Bartolomeo, *Compendio musicale*, MS, Ferrara, 1677; expanded, 1694; (facsimile Florence: Studio per Edizioni Scelte, 1978).

Bononcini, Giovanni Maria, *Musico prattico*, Op. 8 (Bologna: Giacomo Monti, 1673; facsimile, Hildesheim: Olms Verlag, 1969; and New York: Broude, 1969).

Brossard, Sébastien de, *Dictionnaire de musique* (Paris: Christophe Ballard, 1703); English trans. by Albion Gruber as Dictionary of Music (Henryville, PA: Institute of Mediæval Music, 1982).

——, *Dictionnaire de musique*, 3rd ed. (Amsterdam: Estienne Roger, c.1708; facsimile, Geneva: Minkoff, 1992).

Gasparini, Francesco, *L'armonico pratico al cimbalo* (Venice: Antonio Bortoli, 1708; facsimile, New York: Broude, 1967); English trans. by Frank Stillings, ed. David Burrows as *The Practical Harmonist at the Harpsichord* (New Haven, CT: Yale University Press, 1963; reprint, New York: Da Capo, 1980).

Glarean, Heinrich, *Dodecachordon* (Basel: Heinrich Petri, 1547; facsimile, Hildesheim: Olms Verlag, 1969; and New York: Broude Bros., 1967); English trans. by Clement Miller, 2 vols, Musicological Studies and Documents, 6 (American Institute of Musicology, 1965).

Paolucci, Giuseppe, *Arte pratica di contrapunto dimostrata con esempj di varj autori e con osservazioni*, 3 vols (Venice: Antonio De Castro, 1765–72).

Penna, Lorenzo, *Li primi albori musicali* (Bologna: Giacomo Monti, 1672; facsimile of 1684 ed., Bologna: Forni, 1969).

Tevo, Zaccaria, *Il musico testore* (Venice: Antonio Bortoli, 1706; facsimile, Bologna: Forni, 1969).

Zannetti, Gasparo, *Il scolaro per imparar a suonare di violino, et altri stromenti* (Milan: Carlo Camagno, 1645; facsimile, Florence: Studio per Edizioni Scelte, 1984).

Zarlino, Gioseffo, *Le istitutioni harmoniche*, Parte IV (Venice: n.p. [Pietro da Fino], 1558; facsimile, New York: Broude, 1965); English trans. by Vered Cohen, ed. Claude Palisca as *On the Modes: Part Four of Le istitutioni harmoniche, 1558* (New Haven: Yale University Press, 1983).

II. Dance Treatises

Caroso, Fabritio, *Nobiltà di dame* (Venice: il Muschio, 1600; 2nd ed., 1605; 3rd ed., as *Raccolta di varij balli*, Rome: Guglielmo Facciotti, 1630; facsimile of 1605 ed., Bologna: Forni, 1970); English trans. of 1600 ed. by Julia Sutton and F. Marian Walker (Oxford and New York: Oxford University Press, 1986).

Degli Alessandri, Felippo, *Discorso sopra il ballo et le buone creanze necessarie ad un gentil huomo e ad una gentildonna* (Terni: Tomasso Guerrieri, 1620).

Dufort, Giovanni Battista, *Trattato del ballo nobile* (Naples: Felice Mosca, 1728; facsimile, Westmead, Farnborough: Gregg Press, 1972).

Jacobilli, Ludovico, *Modo di ballare*, MS, c.1615–20, Biblioteca Jacobilli, Foligno, A.III.19.

Mancini, Giulio Cesare, *Del origin[e] et nobiltà del ballo*, MS, c.1620, I-Rvat, Barb. Lat. 4315.

Negri, Cesare, *Le gratie d'amore* (Milan: Pacifico Pontio & Giovanni Battista Piccaglia, 1602; 2nd ed., as *Nuove inventioni di balli*, Milan: Girolamo Bordone, 1604; facsimile of 1602 ed., New York: Broude, 1969; and Bologna: Forni, 1969).

Troili, Bolognese, detto il Paradosso, Gioseffo, *Modo facile di suonare il sistro nomato il timpano* (Bologna: li Peri, 1686; 2nd ed., 1695; 3rd ed., 1702; facsimile of 1695 ed., Milan: Bollettino Bibliografico Musicale, 1933).

Weaver, John, *An Essay towards an History of Dancing, in which the Whole Art and its Various Excellencies are in Some Measure Explain'd. Containing the several sorts of dancing, antique and modern, serious, scenical, grotesque, &c. with the use of it as an exercise, qualification, diversion, &c.* (London: Jacob Tonson, 1712).

III. Diaries, Histories, and Travelogues

Addison, Joseph, *Remarks on the Several Parts of Italy* (London: Jacob Tonson, 1705).

Barilli, Antonio, *Zibaldone ossia giornale ... di quanto è seguito in Bologna dal principio del anno 1707 per tutto l'anno 1716*, MS, 18th century, I-Bu, MS No. 225.

Breve racconto dell'arrivo in Bologna della Serenissima regina Christina di Svezia et de' trattenimenti, e partenza di S. Maestà (Bologna: Giovanni Battista Ferroni, 1655).

Bromley, William, *Remarks Made in Travels through France & Italy: with many publick inscriptions lately taken by a person of quality* (London: Thomas Bassett, 1692).

Burnet, Gilbert, *Some Letters, Containing an Account of what Seemed Most Remarkable in Traveling through Switzerland, Italy, Some Parts of Germany, &c. in the Years 1685 and 1686* (Amsterdam: n.p., 1686).

Catalogo dei maestri di cappella della Accademia della Morte dal 1594 al 1683 e catalogo dei musicanti d'essa accademia, MS, late 17th century, I-FEc, Collezione Antonelli, MS No. 22.

Ciriani, Gioan Andrea, *Cronaca di Ferrara dal 1651 al 1673*, MS, 17th century, I-FEc, Collezione Antonelli, MS No. 269; transcription with introduction by Dino Tebaldi, unpublished typescript, 1995, I-FEc.

A Discourse of the Dukedom of Modena: containing the origine, antiquity, government, manners and qualities of the people: as also the temperature of the climate, with the nature and fertility of the soil (London: William Crook, 1674).

Dolfi, Pompeo Scipione, *Cronologia delle famiglie nobili di Bologna, con le loro insegne, e nel fine i cimieri* (Bologna: Giovanni Battista Ferroni, 1670; facsimile, Bologna: Forni, 1990).

Giraldi, Giovanni Battista, *Diario delle cose più rimarcabili successe dall'anno 1689 per tutti li 21 nov. 1730*, MS, 18th century, I-Bu, MS No. 3851.

Insignia degli Anziani del commune, Archivio di Stato di Bologna (I-Bas), Archivio degli Anziani.

Lassels, Richard, *The Voyage of Italy* (London: John Strakey, 1670).

Martini, Giovanni Battista, attrib., *Catalogo degli aggregati della Accademia Filarmonica di Bologna*, MS, c. 1736; facsimile with foreword by Anne Schnoebelen (Bologna: Accademia Filarmonica, 1973).

——, *Serie cronologica de' principi dell'Accademia Filarmonica di Bologna* (Bologna: Lelio della Volpe, 1776; facsimile, Bologna: Forni, 1970).

——, *Scrittori di musica*, MS, 18th century, I-Bc, H.63.

Masini, Antonio di Paolo, *Bologna perlustrata*, 3rd ed. (Bologna: l'Erede di Vittorio Benacci, 1666; facsimile, Bologna: Forni, 1986).

Misson, Maximilien, *Nouveau voyage d'Italie* (The Hague: Henry van Bulderen, 1691); in English trans. as *A New Voyage to Italy*, 2 vols (London: R. Bently, 1695).

Pitoni, Giuseppe Ottavio. *Notitia de' contrapuntisti e compositori di musica*, MS, c.1725; modern ed. by Cesarino Ruini (Florence: Olschki, 1988).

Relatione della festa popolare fatta in Bologna in occasione della Festa della Porchetta. A gl'illustrissimi signori Confaloniere et Anziani del quarto bimestre dell'anno 1667 (Bologna: li Manolessi, 1667).

Relazione della fiera popolare della Porchetta fatta in Bologna l'anno 1697 (Bologna: li Manolessi, 1697).

Thompson, Charles, *The Travels of the Late Charles Thompson, Esq.* (Reading: J. Newberry and C. Micklewright, 1744).

Tioli, Giovanni, *Cronaca bolognese di D. Gio. Tioli che comincia l'anno 1642 per tutto li 23 luglio 1708 il giorno della sua morte*, MS, 17th/18th century, I-Bu, MS No. 3847.

IV. Instruction for the Nobility in the arti cavalleresche

Accademia degli Ardenti (Bologna), *Capitoli dell'Accademia degli Ardenti nuovamente riformati* (Bologna: Giacomo Monti, 1673).

Accademia degli Ardenti (Bologna), *Informazione de' requisiti per l'ingresso de' giovani nobili nell'Accademia de' Signori Ardenti di Bologna, sotto l'educazione de' Padri Somaschi* (Bologna: Costantino Pisarri, 1703).

Accademia degli Ardenti (Bologna), *Ordine accademico praticato da' Signori Ardenti del Porto regolati da' pp. Somaschi ne' loro esercitii litterarj, e cavalleareschi nel fine de' studj dell'anno 1698* (Bologna: Pier-Maria Monti, 1698).

Collegio de' Nobili di Bologna, *Informatione del gouerno, studio, conditioni e spesa de' conuittori del Collegio de Nobili di Bologna eretto sotto la protettione di S. Francesco Saverio* (Bologna: Giacomo Monti, 1648).

Collegio Ducale di Modena (detto San Carlo), *Notizie per chi vuol mettere i suoi figlioli nel Collegio de' Nobili di Modana gouernato da sacerdoti della congregazione della B.ta Vergine, e S. Carlo sotto li benignissimi auspicii del serenissimo signor duca Francesco 2. d'Este* (Modena: eredi Cassiani stampatori capitolari, 1691).

Faret, Nicolas, *L'honnête homme; ou, L'art de plaire à la cour* (Paris, 1630; modern ed. of 1636 ed., Paris: Les Presses Universitaires de France, 1925; reprint, Geneva: Slatkine Reprints, 1970); Italian trans. as *L'arte di piacere alla corte del signor di Faret tradotta dal francese nella lingua italiana dal conte Alberto Caprara, al marchese Enea Magnani senatore suo nipote* (Bologna: Giovanni Battista Ferroni, 1662).

V. Music and Liturgical Practice

Banchieri, Adriano, *L'organo suonarino*, Op. 13 (Venice: Ricciardo Amadino, 1605; facsimile, Bologna: Forni, 1969); English trans. with commentary by Donald Marcase as "Adriano Banchieri, L'organo suonarino," Ph.D. dissertation, Indiana University, 1970.

Bottazzi, Bernardino. *Choro et organo, primo libro in cui con facil modo s'apprende in poco tempo un sicuro methodo di sonar sú'l organo messe, antifone, & hinni sopra ogni maniera di canto fermo* (Venice: Giacomo Vincenti, 1614; facsimile, Bologna: Forni, 1980).

Croci, Antonio. *Frutti musicali di messe tre ecclesiastiche per rispondere alternatamente al choro ... con cinque canzoni & un ricercaro cromaticho*, Op. 4 (Venice: Alessandro Vincenti, 1642).

Fasolo, Giovanni Battista, *Annuale che contiene tutto quello, che deve far un organista, per risponder al choro tutto l'anno*, Op. 8 (Venice: Alessandro Vincenti, 1645).

Franzoni, Amante, *Apparato musicale di messa, sinfonie, canzoni, motetti, & letanie della Beata Vergine a otto voci, con la partitura de bassi*, Op. 5 (Venice: Ricciardo Amadino, 1613).

Frescobaldi, Girolamo, *Fiori musicali di diversi compositioni, toccate, kirie, canzoni, capricci, e ricercari*, Op. 12 (Venice: Alessandro Vincenti, 1635; facsimile with an introduction by Luigi Ferdinando Tagliavini, Bologna: Forni, 2000).

Milanuzzi, Giovanni Battista, *Armonia sacra* (Venice: Alessandro Vincenti, 1622).

Oblighi de signori mastro di capella, e musici dell'Accademia dello Spirito Santo di Ferrara, MS, 17th century, I-FEc, M.F.119/14.

Ordini per la musica dell'insigne Collegiata di S. Petronio, reformate d'ordine de gl'illustrissimi signori Presidente, e Fabbricieri della reverenda Fabbrica di essa. Bologna: n.p., 1658.

Ordini stabiliti per il buon governo dell'Accademia dello Spirito Santo di Ferrara (Ferrara: Gioseffo Gironi, 1636).

Ordini stabiliti per lo buon governo dell'Accademia della Compagnia della Morte in Ferrara (Ferrara: Gioseffo Gironi, 1648).

Salvatore, Giovanni, *Ricercari a quattro voci, canzoni francesi, toccate, et versi per rispondere nelle messe con l'organo al choro* (Naples: Ottavio Beltrano, 1641).

Secondary Sources

Allsop, Peter, *Arcangelo Corelli: "New Orpheus of Our Times"* (Oxford: Clarendon Press, and New York: Oxford University Press, 1999).

——, *"Da camera e da ballo—alla francese et all'italiana"*: Functional and National Distinctions in Corelli's *sonate da camera,"* *Early Music* 26 (1998): 87–96.

——, "Sonata da Chiesa—A Case of Mistaken Identity?," *The Consort* 53 (1997): 4–14.

——, "The Italian Sonata and the Concept of the 'Churchly,'" *Barocco padano I: atti del IX Convegno Internazionale sulla Musica Sacra nei Secoli XVII–XVIII, Como, 16–18 luglio 1999*, ed. Alberto Colzani, Andrea Luppi, and Maurizio Padoan (Como: Antiquae Musicae Italicae Studiosi, 2002), 239–47.

——, *The Italian "Trio" Sonata: From its Origins until Corelli* (Oxford: Clarendon Press, and New York: Oxford University Press, 1992).

——, "Un 'nuovo virtuosismo': la tecnica violinistica italiana del XVII secolo e l'ascesa tedesca," in *Relazioni musicali tra Italia e Germania nell'età barocca*, ed. Alberto Colzani, Norbert Dubowy, Andrea Luppi, and Maurizio Padoan (Como: Antiquae Musicae Italicae Studiosi and Centro italo-tedesco Villa Vigoni, 1997), 201–16.

——, "Violinistic Virtuosity in the Seventeenth Century: Italian Supremacy or Austro-German Hegemony?," *Il saggiatore musicale* 3 (1996): 233–58.

Alm, Irene, "Operatic Ballroom Scenes and the Arrival of French Social Dance in Venice," *Studi musicali* 25 (1996): 345–71.

Apel, Willi, *Italian Violin Music of the Seventeenth Century* (Bloomington: Indiana University Press, 1990).

Barnett, Gregory, "Form and Gesture: Canzona, Sonata and Concerto," in *The Cambridge History of Seventeenth-Century Music*, ed. Tim Carter and John Butt (Cambridge: Cambridge University Press, 2005), 799–889.

——, "L'organizzazione tonale nella musica italiana secentesca: le sinfonie e le sonate di Tarquinio Merula, Biagio Marini e Giovanni Legrenzi," in *Barocco padano I: atti del IX Convegno Internazionale sulla Musica Sacra nei Secoli XVII–XVIII*, ed. Alberto Colzani, Andrea Luppi, and Maurizio Padoan (Como: Antiquae Musicae Italicae Studiosi, 2002), 211–35.

——, "Modal Theory, Church Keys, and the Sonata at the End of the Seventeenth Century," *Journal of the American Musicological Society* 51 (1998): 245–81.

Baroncini, Rodolfo, "Organici e 'orchestre' in Italia e in Francia nel XVII secolo: differenze e omologie," *Studi musicali* 25 (1996): 373–408.

Baroni, Mario, "Legrenzi e l'armonia del XVII secolo," in *Giovanni Legrenzi e la cappella ducale di San Marco*, ed. Francesco Passadori and Franco Rossi (Florence: Olschki, 1994), 399–417.

Bernstein, Jane, *Print Culture and Music in Sixteenth-Century Venice* (Oxford and New York: Oxford University Press, 2001).

Bizzarini, Marco, "Diffusione della sonata a tre nella Brescia di fine Seicento: il ruolo del Collegio de' Nobili," in *Barocco padano I: atti del IX Convegno Internazionale sulla Musica Sacra nei Secoli XVII–XVIII*, ed. Alberto Colzani, Andrea Luppi, and Maurizio Padoan (Como: Antiquae Musicae Italicae Studiosi, 2002), 279–309.

Bonta, Stephen, "A Formal Convention in 17th-Century Italian Instrumental Music," in *International Musicological Society Report of the Eleventh Congress, Copenhagen 1972*, ed. Henrik Glahn, Søren Sørensen, and Peter Ryom (Copenhagen: Hansen, 1974), 288–95.

——, "From Violone to Violoncello: A Question of Strings?," *Journal of the American Musical Instrument Society* 3 (1977): 64–99.

——, "Terminology for the Bass Violin in Seventeenth-Century Italy," *Journal of the American Musical Instrument Society* 4 (1978): 5–43.

——, "The Instrumental Music of Giovanni Legrenzi: Style and Significance," in *Giovanni Legrenzi e la cappella ducale di San Marco*, ed. Francesco Passadori and Franco Rossi (Florence: Olschki, 1994), 325–49.

——, "The Use of Instruments in Sacred Music in Italy, 1560–1700," *Early Music* 18 (1990): 519–35.

——, "The Use of Instruments in the Ensemble Canzona and Sonata in Italy, 1580–1650," *Recercare* 4 (1992): 23–41.

——, "The Uses of the Sonata da Chiesa," *Journal of the American Musicological Society* 22 (1969): 54–84.

Borgir, Tharald, *The Performance of the Basso Continuo in Italian Baroque Music* (Ann Arbor: U.M.I., 1987).

Boyden, David D, *The History of Violin Playing from its Origins to 1761* (Oxford: Clarendon Press, 1965).

——, "When is a Concerto Not a Concerto?" *Musical Quarterly* 48 (1957): 220–32.

Bradshaw, Murray C, *The Origin of the Toccata*, Musicological Studies & Documents, 28, ed. Armen Carapetyan (Rome: American Institute of Musicology, 1972).

Brett, Ursula, *Music and Ideas in Seventeenth-Century Italy: The Cazzati–Arresti Polemic*, 2 vols (New York: Garland, 1989).

Brizzi, Gian Paolo, *La formazione della classe dirigente nel Sei–Settecento* (Bologna: Mulino, 1976).

Brover-Lubovsky, Bella, "Between Modality and Tonality: Vivaldi's Harmony," *Informazioni e studi vivaldiani* 21 (2000): 111–33.

Bukofzer, Manfred, *Music in the Baroque Era* (New York: Norton, 1947).

Callegari, Laura, Gabriella Sartini, and Gabriele Bersani Berselli, eds., *La librettistica bolognese nei secoli XVII e XVIII: catalogo ed indici* (Rome: Torre d'Orfeo, 1989).

Callegari-Hill, Laura, *L'Accademia Filarmonica di Bologna, 1666–1800* (Bologna: Antiquae Musicae Italicae Studiosi, 1991).

Calessi, Giovanni Pierluigi, *Ricerche sull'Accademia della Morte di Ferrara* (Bologna: Antiquae Musicae Italicae Studiosi, 1976).

Calore, Marina, *Bologna a teatro: vita di una città attraverso 1 suoi spettacoli, 1400–1800* (Bologna: Giudicini e Rosa, 1981).

Carpanetto, Dino, and Giuseppe Ricuperati, *Italy in the Age of Reason, 1685–1789*, trans. Caroline Higgitt (London: Longman, 1987).

Carter, Stewart, "The String Tremolo in the Seventeenth Century," *Early Music* 19 (1991): 43–59.

Cavicchi, Adriano, "Corelli e il violinismo Bolognese," in *Studi corelliani*, ed. Adriano Cavicchi, Oscar Mischiati, and Pierluigi Petrobelli (Florence: Olschki, 1972), 33–47.

——, "Prassi strumentale in emilia nell'ultimo quarto del Seicento: flauto italiano, cornetto, archi," *Studi musicali* 2 (1973): 111–43.

Corsi, Cesare, "Gli 'affetti del patetico italiano' negli 'squisiti gravi' corelliani: analisi del primo movimento della sonata opera III n. 9," in *Studi corelliani* V, ed. Stefano La Via (Florence: Olschki, 1996), 211–28.

Crocker, Eunice C, "An Introductory Study of the Italian Canzona for Instrumental Ensembles and its Influence upon the Baroque Sonata," Ph.D. dissertation, Radcliffe College, 1943.

Croll, Gerhard, "'S'Alza la tenda': annotazioni sulla 'Sinfonia avanti l'opera,'" in *Giovanni Legrenzi e la Cappella Ducale di San Marco*, ed. Francesco Passadore and Franco Rossi (Florence: Olschki, 1994), 269–74.

Crowther, Victor, "A Case-Study in the Power of the Purse: The Management of the Ducal Cappella in Modena in the Reign of Francesco II d'Este," *Journal of the Royal Musical Association* 115: 2 (1990): 207–19.

——, *The Oratorio in Bologna, 1650–1730* (Oxford and New York: Oxford University Press, 1999).

——, *The Oratorio in Modena* (Oxford: Clarendon Press, and New York: Oxford University Press, 1992).

Culley, Thomas D., SJ, *Jesuits and Music, I: A Study of the Musicians Connected with the German College in Rome during the 17th Century and of their Activities in Northern Europe* (Rome: Jesuit Historical Institute, 1970).

Damerini, Adelmo. "La sonata di G. B. Vitali," *Chigiana* 15 (1958): 61–9.

Daverio, John, "Formal Design and Terminology in the Pre-Corellian 'Sonata' and Related Instrumental Forms in the Printed Sources," Ph.D. dissertation, Boston University, 1983.

——, "In Search of the Sonata da Camera before Corelli," *Acta musicologica* 57 (1985): 195–214.

De Lucca, Valeria, "Una silloge strumentale per Francesco II d'Este: analisi e iconografia," *Rivista italiana di musicologia* 36 (2001): 3–23.

Dell'Antonio, Andrew, *Syntax, Form and Genre in Sonatas and Canzonas: 1621–1635* (Lucca: Libreria Musicale Italiana, 1997).

Dodds, Michael Robert, "The Baroque Church Tones in Theory and Practice," Ph.D. dissertation, University of Rochester, 1999.

Dubowy, Norbert, *Arie und Konzert: Zur Entwicklung der Ritornellanlage im 17. und frühen 18. Jahrhundert*, Studien zur Musik, 9 (Munich: Wilhelm Fink Verlag, 1991).

Ecorcheville, Jules, ed., *Vingt suites d'orchestre du XVIIe siècle français* (Paris and Berlin, 1906; facsimile, New York: Broude, 1970).

Enrico, Eugene, *The Orchestra at San Petronio in the Baroque Era* (Washington, DC: Smithsonian Institute Press, 1976).

Eynard, Marcello, "Il ruolo di Giovanni Maria Bononcini nella produzione di sonate da chiesa a due violini e basso continuo in ambito modenese," in *Marco Uccellini: Atti del Convegno "Marco Uccellini da Forlimpopoli e la sua musica" (Forlimpopoli, 26–7 ottobre 1996)*, ed. Maria Caraci Vela and Marina Toffetti (Lucca: Libreria Musicale Italiana, 1999), 99–139.

Fabbri, Paolo, "Politica editoriale e musica strumentale in Italia dal Cinque- al Settecento," in *Deutsch-italienische Musikbeziehungen: deutsche und italienische Instrumentalmusik 1600–1750*, ed. Wulf Konold (Munich and Salzburg: Musikverlag Emil Katzbichler, 1996), 25–37.

Fanelli, Jean Grundy "The Manfredini Family of Musicians of Pistoia, 1684–1803," *Studi musicali* 26 (1997): 187–232.

Fanti, Mario, ed., *Notizie e insegne delle accademie di Bologna da un manoscritto del Secolo XVIII* (Bologna: Rotary Club di Bologna, 1983).

Finscher, Ludwig, "Corelli als Klassiker der Triosonate," in *Nuovi studi corelliani*, ed. Giulia Giachin (Florence: Olschki, 1978), 23–31.

Fornari, Giacomo, "Del declino della musica strumentale in Italia nel Settecento," in *Intorno a Locatelli*. 2 vols, ed. Albert Dunning (Lucca: Libreria Musicale Italiana, 1995), vol. 1, 241–74.

Förster, Wolf Dietrich, "Corelli e Torelli: concerto grosso e sonata con tromba," in *Nuovissimi studi corelliani*, ed. Sergio Durante and Pierluigi Petrobelli (Florence: Olschki, 1982), 329–46.

Gambassi, Osvaldo, *L'Accademia Filarmonica di Bologna: fondazione, statuti e aggregazioni* (Florence: Olschki, 1992).

——, *La cappella musicale di S. Petronio: maestri, organisti, cantori, e strumentisti dal 1436 al 1920* (Florence: Olschki, 1987).

——, *Il Concerto Palatino della Signoria di Bologna: cinque secoli di vita musicale a corte (1250–1797)* (Florence: Olschki, 1984).

———, "Organici vocali e strumentali in S. Petronio nella seconda metà del '600," in *Tradizione e stile: atti del II convegno internazionale di studi sul tema la musica sacra in area lombardo-padana nella seconda metà del '600*, ed. Alberti Colzani, Andrea Luppi, and Maurizio Padoan (Como: Antiquae Musicae Italicae Studiosi, 1989), 73–84.

———, "Origine, statuti e ordinamenti del Concerto Palatino della Signoria di Bologna," *Nuova rivista musicale italiana* 18 (1984): 261–83 and 469–502.

Gaspari, Gaetano, *Catalogo della biblioteca del Liceo Musicale in Bologna*, 5 vols (Bologna, 1890–1905; facsimile, Bologna: Forni, 1961).

———, *Musica e musicisti a Bologna: ricerche, documenti e memorie riguardanti la storia dell'arte musicale in Bologna* (Bologna, 1867–68; facsimile, Bologna: Forni, 1969).

Giegling, Franz, *Giuseppe Torelli: ein Beitrag zur Entwicklungsgeschichte des italienischen Konzerts* (Kassel and Basel: Bärenreiter, 1949).

Göhler, Albert, *Verzeichnis der in den Frankfurter und Leipziger Messkatalogen der Jahre 1564 bis 1759 angezeigten Musikalien* (Leipzig, 1902; reprint, Hilversum: Knuf, 1965).

Harper, John, *The Forms and Orders of Western Liturgy from the Tenth to the Eighteenth Century* (Oxford: Clarendon Press: 1991).

Harrán, Don, "Domenico Galli e gli eroici esordi della musica per violoncello solo non accompagnato," *Rivista italiana di musicologia* 34 (1999): 231–99.

Hayburn, Robert, *Papal Legislation on Sacred Music, 95 A.D. to 1977 A.D.* (Collegeville, MN: The Liturgical Press, 1979).

Hilton, Wendy, "A Dance for Kings: The 17th-Century French *Courante*," *Early Music* 5 (1977): 161–72.

———, *Dance of Court & Theater: The French Noble Style, 1690–1725*, ed. Caroline Gaynor; labanotation by Mireille Backer (Princeton, NJ: Princeton Book Co., 1981).

Holler, Karl Heinz, *Giovanni Maria Bononcini's "Musico prattico" in seiner Bedeutung für die musikalische Satzlehre des 17. Jahrhunderts* (Strasbourg: P. H. Heitz, 1963).

Hudson, Richard, *The Allemande, the Balletto, and the Tanz*, 2 vols (Cambridge: Cambridge University Press, 1986).

Hutchings, Arthur, *The Baroque Concerto* (New York: Norton, 1961; rev. ed, New York: Scribner's, 1979).

Jander, Owen, "Concerto Grosso Instrumentation in Rome in the 1660's and 1670's," *Journal of the American Musicological Society* 21 (1968): 168–80.

Jensen, Niels Martin, "Solo Sonata, Duo Sonata, Trio Sonata: Some Problems of Terminology and Genre in 17th-Century Italian Instrumental Music," in *Festskrift Jens Peter Larsen*, ed. Nils Schiørring, Henrik Glahn, and Carsten E. Hatting (Copenhagen: Wilhelm Hansen, 1972), 83–101.

Judd, Robert, "Italy," in *Keyboard Music before 1700*, 2nd ed., ed. Alexander Silbiger (New York and London: Routledge, 2004), 235–311.

Klenz, William, *Giovanni Maria Bononcini of Modena: A Chapter in Baroque Instrumental Music* (Durham, NC: Duke University Press, 1962).

Kübler, Suzanne, "Contesto storico-stilistico e destinazioni d'uso delle sonate per tromba di Maurizio Cazzati," *Rivista italiana di musicologia* 29 (1994): 139–56.

Kunze, Stefan, "Die Entstehung des Concertoprinzips im Spätwerk Giovanni Gabrielis," *Archiv für Musikwissenschaft* 21 (1964): 81–110.

Latham, Mark, "Italian Seventeenth-Century Instrumental Music in Durham Cathedral Library: An Essay in Sources and Attribution with Particular Reference to the Works for Trumpet in the Bamburgh Collection Manuscript M175," master's thesis, University of Newcastle upon Tyne, 1997.

Lepore, Angela, "La sonata a tre in ambito corelliano," in *Intorno a Locatelli*. 2 vols, ed. Albert Dunning, vol. 1 (Lucca: Libreria Musicale Italiana, 1995), 527–99.

Lester, Joel, *Between Modes and Keys: German Theory 1592–1802* (Stuyvesant, NY: Pendragon Press, 1989).

Lesure, François, ed, *Bibliographie des éditions musicales publiées par Estienne Roger et Michel-Charles le Cène* (Amsterdam, 1696–1743) (Paris: Société Française de Musicologie, 1969).

Libby, Dennis, "Interrelationships in Corelli," *Journal of the American Musicological Society* 26 (1973): 263–87.

Linfield, Eva, "Formal & Tonal Organization in a 17th-Century Ritornello/Ripieno Structure," *Journal of Musicology* 9 (1991): 145–64.

Lorenzetti, Stefano, "La parte della musica nella costruzione del gentilhuomo: tendenze e programmi della pedagogia seicentesca tra Francia e Italia," *Studi musicali* 25 (1996): 17–40.

——, "'Per animare agli esercizi nobili': esperienza musicale e identità nobiliare nei collegi di educazione," *Quaderni storici* 95 (1997): 435–60.

Luin, Elisabetta, "Repertorio dei libri musicali di S. A. S. Francesco II d'Este nell'Archivio di Stato di Modena," *Bibliofilia* 38 (1936): 418–45.

McCrickard, Eleanor F., "Temporal and Tonal Aspects of Alessandro Stradella's Instrumental Music," *Analecta musicologica* 19 (1979): 186–243.

——, "The Roman Repertory for the Violin before the Time of Corelli," *Early Music* 18 (1990): 563–573.

McFarland, Thomas John, "Giuseppe Colombi: His Position in the 'Modenese School' during the Second Half of the Seventeenth Century," Ph.D. dissertation, Kent State University, 1987.

Mangsen, Sandra, "Ad libitum Procedures in Instrumental Duos and Trios," *Early Music* 19 (1991): 29–40.

——, "Instrumental Duos and Trios in Printed Italian Sources, 1600–1675," Ph.D. dissertation, Cornell University, 1989.

——, "The Dissemination of Pre-Corellian Duo and Trio Sonatas in Manuscript and Printed Sources: A Preliminary Report," in *The Dissemination of Music: Studies in the History of Music Publishing*, ed. Hans Lennenberg (New York: Gordon and Breach, 1994), 71–105.

——, "The 'Sonata da Camera' before Corelli: A Renewed Search," *Music & Letters* 76 (1995): 19–31.

——, "The Trio Sonata in Pre-Corellian Prints: When Does 3 = 4?," *Performance Practice Review* 3 (1990): 138–64.

Matteucci, Anna Maria, "La cultura dell'effimero a Bologna nel XVII secolo," in *Barocco romano e barocco italiano: il teatro, l'effimero, l'allegoria*, ed. Marcello Fagiolo and Maria Luisa Madonna (Rome: Gangemi Editore, 1985), 159–73.

Maule, Elita, "La 'Festa della Porchetta' a Bologna nel Seicento: indagine su una festa barocca," *Il carrobbio* 6 (1980): 251–62.

——, "Momenti di festa musicale sacra a Bologna nelle 'Insignia' degli Anziani (1666–1751)," *Il carrobbio* 13 (1987): 255–66.

Maunder, Richard, *The Scoring of Baroque Concertos* (Rochester: Boydell Press, 2004).

Maylender, Michele, *Storia delle accademie d'Italia*, 5 vols (Bologna: Capelli, 1926–30; facsimile, Bologna: Forni, 1976).

Medici, Michele, *Memorie storiche intorno le accademie scientifiche e letterarie della città di Bologna* (Bologna: Tipi Sassi nelle Spaderie, 1852).

Mele, Donato, *L'Accademia dello Spirito Santo: un istituzione musicale ferrarese del secolo XVII* (Ferrara: Liberty House, 1990).

Mischiati, Oscar, "Aspetti dei rapporti tra Corelli e la scuola bolognese," in *Studi corelliani*, ed. Adriano Cavicchi, Oscar Mischiati, and Pierluigi Petrobelli (Florence: Olschki, 1972), 23–32.

——, ed., *Indici, cataloghi e avvisi degli editori e librai musicali italiani dal 1591 al 1798* (Florence: Olschki, 1984).

Mishkin, Henry G., "The Italian Concerto before 1700," *Bulletin of the American Musicological Society* 7 (1943): 20–22.

——, "The Solo Violin Sonata of the Bologna School," *Musical Quarterly* 29 (1943): 92–112.

Monaldini, Sergio, ed., *L'Orto dell'Esperidi: musici, attori e artisti nel patrocinio della famiglia Bentivoglio (1646–1685)* (Lucca: Libreria Musicale Italiana, 2000).

Morini, Nestore, *La R. Accademia Filarmonica di Bologna: monografia storica* (Bologna: Cappelli, 1930; reprint, Bologna: Tamari, 1966).

Muffat, Georg, *Georg Muffat on Performance Practice: The Texts from* Florilegium Primum, Florilegium Secundum, *and* Auserlesene Instrumentalmusik, ed. and trans. David K. Wilson (Bloomington and Indianapolis: Indiana University Press, 2001).

Newman, William S., *The Sonata in the Baroque Era*, 4th ed. (New York: Norton, 1983).

North, Roger, *Roger North on Music*, ed. John Wilson (London: Novello, 1959).

Norton, Richard Edward, "The Chamber Music of Giuseppe Torelli," Ph.D. dissertation, Northwestern University, 1967.

Palisca, Claude, "The Genesis of Mattheson's Style Classification," in *New Mattheson Studies*, ed. George J. Buelow and Hans Joachim Marx (Cambridge: Cambridge University Press, 1983), 409–23.

Pelicelli, Nestore, "Musicisti in Parma nel secolo XVII," *Note d'archivio per la storia musicale* 10 (1933): 32–43, 116–26, 233–48, 314–25.

Pickard, Alexander L., Jr., "A Practical Edition of the Trumpet Sonatas of Giuseppe Jacchini," DMA dissertation, Eastman School of Music, 1974.

Pincherle, Marc, Corelli: *His Life, his Work*, trans., Hubert E. M. Russell (New York: W. W. Norton, 1956).

Piperno, Franco, "'Concerto' e 'concertato' nella musica strumentale italiana del secolo decimo settimo," in *Deutsch-italienische Musikbeziehungen: deutsche und italienische Instrumentalmusik 1600–1750*, ed. Wulf Konold (Munich and Salzburg: Musikverlag Emil Katzbichler, 1996), 129–55.

——, "Corelli e il 'concerto' Seicentesco: lettura e interpretazione dell'opera VI," in *Studi corelliani* IV, ed. Pierluigi Petrobelli and Gloria Staffieri (Florence: Olschki, 1990), 359–80.

——, "Le viole divise in due chori: policoralità e 'concerto' nella musica di Alessandro Stradella," *Chigiana* 39 (1982): 399–423.

Plessi, Giuseppe, ed. and introduction, *Le insignia degli anziani del comune dal 1530 al 1796: catalogo-inventario* (Rome: Ministero dell'Interno Pubblicazioni degli Archivi di Stato, 1954).

Powers, Harold S., "From Psalmody to Tonality," in *Tonal Structures in Early Music*, ed. Cristle Collins Judd (New York: Garland, 1998), 275–340.

—— and Frans Wiering, "Mode," part III, " Modal Theories and Polyphonic Music," in *The New Grove Dictionary of Music and Musicians*, 2nd ed., ed. Stanley Sadie and John Tyrrell, 29 vols (London: Macmillan Publishers Inc., and New York: Grove's Dictionaries Inc, 2001), vol. 16, 796–823.

Prizer, William F., "Some Bolognese Sonate con Tromba," 2 vols, master's thesis, Yale University, 1969.

Ricci, Corrado, *I teatri di Bologna nei secoli XVII e XVIII* (Bologna: Successori Monti, 1888; facsimile, Bologna: Forni, 1965).

Rinaldi, Mario, *Arcangelo Corelli* (Milan: Edizioni Curci, 1953).

Roncaglia, Gino, "Giuseppe Colombi e la vita musicale modenese durante il regno di Francesco II d'Este, " *Atti e memorie della Accademia di Scienze, Lettere e Arti di Modena*, 5th ser., 10 (1952): 47–52.

——, *La cappella musicale del duomo di Modena* (Florence: Olschki, 1957).

——, "La scuola strumentale modenese nel secolo XVII," *Chigiana* 13 (1956): 69–82.

Rönnau, Klaus, "Zur Genesis der Ritornellform im frühen Instrumentalkonzert," *Bericht über den Internationalen Musikwissenschaftlichen Kongress Berlin 1974*, ed. Hellmut Kühn and Peter Nitsche, (Kassel: Bärenreiter, 1980), 280–82.

Rostirolla, Giancarlo, "La professione di strumentista a Roma nel Sei e Settecento," *Studi musicali* 23 (1994): 87–174.

Sartori, Claudio. *Bibliografia della musica strumentale italiana stampata in Italia fino al 1700*, 2 vols (Florence: Olschki, 1952–68).

——, *I libretti italiani a stampa dalle origini al 1800*, 7 vols (Cuneo: Bertola and Locatelli, 1990–94).

Schenk, Erich, "Beobachtugen über die Modenesische Instrumentalmusikschule des 17. Jahrhunderts," *Studien zur Musikwissenschaft* 26 (1964): 25–46.

——, "Osservazioni sulla scuola istrumentale modenese nel Seicento," *Atti e memorie della Accademia di Scienze, Lettere e Arti di Modena*, 5th ser., 10 (1952): 1–30.

Schering, Arnold, *Geschichte des Instrumentalkonzerts bis Ant. Vivaldi* (Leipzig: Breitkopf & Härtel, 1905; 2nd ed., 1927; reprint, Hildesheim: Olms, 1965).

Schlossberg, Artur, "Die italienische Sonata für mehrere Instrumente im 17. Jahrhundert," Ph.D. dissertation, University of Heidelberg, 1932.

Schnoebelen, Anne, "Cazzati vs. Bologna 1657–1671," *Musical Quarterly* 57 (1971): 26–39.

——, "Performance Practices at S. Petronio in the Baroque," *Acta musicologica* 41 (1969): 37–55.

——, "The Concerted Mass at S. Petronio in Bologna, ca. 1660–1730: A Documentary and Analytical Study," Ph.D. dissertation, University of Illinois, 1966.

——, "The Role of the Violin in the Resurgence of the Mass in the 17th Century," *Early Music* 18 (1990): 537–42.

——, and Marc Vanscheeuwijck, "Torelli, Giuseppe," *The New Grove Dictionary of Music and Musicians*, 2nd ed., ed. Stanley Sadie and John Tyrrell, 29 vols (London: Macmillan Publishers Inc., and New York: Grove's Dictionaries Inc., 2001), vol. 25, 615–19.

Selfridge-Field, Eleanor, "Canzona & Sonata: Some Differences in Social Identity," *International Review of the Aesthetics and Sociology of Music* 9 (1978): 111–19.

——, "Instrumentation and Genre in Italian Music, 1600–1670," *Early Music* 19 (1991): 61–7.

——, *Venetian Instrumental Music from Gabrieli to Vivaldi*, 3rd ed., rev. (New York: Dover, 1994).

Senhal, Jiří, "Zur Differenzierung der Sonata da Chiesa und Sonata da Camera in der zweiten Hälfte des 17. Jahrhunderts," in *Colloquium musica cameralis, Brno, 1971*, ed. Rudolf Pecman (Brno: Mezinárodní Hudební Festival, 1977), 303–10.

Sirk, Chiara, "L'Accademia degli Ardenti, detta anche del Porto: l'educazione dei nobili tra teatro, musica e danza," *Il carrobbio* 18 (1992): 309–23.

Smithers, Don L., *The Music and History of the Baroque Trumpet before 1721* (London: J. M. Dent, 1973).

Sorbelli, Albano, *Storia della stampa in Bologna* (Bologna: Zanichelli, 1929; facsimile, Bologna: Forni, 2003).

Sparti, Barbara, "'Baroque or not Baroque—is that the Question?' or Dance in 17th-Century Italy," in *L'arte della danza ai tempi di Claudio Monteverdi: atti del Convegno Internazionale, Torino, 6–7 settembre 1993*, ed. Angelo Chiarle (Turin: Centro Stampa della Giunta Regionale, 1996), 73–93.

——, "La 'danza barocca' è soltanto francese?," *Studi musicali* 25 (1996): 283–302.

Spitzer, John, and Neal Zaslaw, *The Birth of the Orchestra: History of an Institution, 1650–1815* (Oxford and New York: Oxford University Press, 2004).

Staffieri, Gloria, "Arcangelo Corelli compositore di 'sinfonie'—nuovi documenti," in *Studi corelliani* IV, ed. Pierluigi Petrobelli and Gloria Staffieri (Florence: Olschki, 1990), 335–58.

Stefani, Gino, *Musica barocca: poetica e ideologia* (Milan: Bompiani, 1974).

Stevens, Denis, "Seventeenth-Century Italian Instrumental Music in the Bodleian Library," *Acta musicologica* 26 (1954): 67–74.

Suess, John G, "Giovanni Battista Vitali and the Sonata da Chiesa," Ph.D. dissertation, Yale University, 1963.

——, "Giovanni Battista Vitali e i suoi Artifici musicali Op. XIII (1689)," *Nuova rivista musicale italiana* 27 (1993): 623–31.

——, "Giuseppe Colombi's Dance Music for the Estense Court of Duke Francesco II of Modena," in *Marco Uccellini: atti del convegno "Marco Uccellini da Forlimpopoli e la sua musica" (Forlimpopoli, 26–7 ottobre 1996)*, ed. Maria Caraci Vela and Marina Toffetti (Lucca: Libreria Editrice Musicale, 1999), 141–62.

——, "Observations on the Accademia Filarmonica of Bologna in the Seventeenth Century and the Rise of a Local Tradition of Instrumental Music," *Quadrivium* 8 (1967): 51–62.

——, "The Ensemble Sonatas of Maurizio Cazzati," *Analecta musicologica* 19 (1979): 146–85.

——, "The Instrumental Music Manuscripts of Giuseppe Colombi of Modena: A Preliminary Report on the Non-Dance Music for Solo Violin or Violone," in *Seicento inesplorato: l'evento musicale tra prassi e stile—un modello di interdipendenza*, ed. Alberto Colzani, Andrea Luppi, and Maurizio Padoan (Como: Antiquae Musicae Italicae Studiosi, 1993), 387–409.

——, "The Rise of the Emilian School of Instrumental Music in Late 17th-Century Italy," in *La musique et le rite sacré et profane: actes du XIIIe Congrès Internationale de Musicologie, Strasbourg, 29 aout – 3 septembre, 1982*, ed. Marc Honegger, Christian Meyer, and Paul Prévost (Strasbourg: Association des Publications près les Universités de Strasbourg, 1986), 499–516.

Tagliavini, Luigi Ferdinando, "La scuola musicale bolognese," in *Musicisti della scuola emiliana per la XIII settimana musicale*, ed. Adelmo Damerini and Gino Roncaglia (Siena: Accademia Musicale Chigiana, 1956), 9–22.

Talbot, Michael, "A Thematic Catalogue of the Orchestral Works of Giuseppe Matteo Alberti (1685–1751)," *Royal Musical Association Research Chronicle* 13 (1976): 1–26.

——, *Benedetto Vinaccesi: A Musician in Brescia and Venice in the Age of Corelli* (Oxford: Clarendon Press, 1994).

——, *Preface to Giuseppe Torelli, Sinfonia (Sonata) in A major (TV 50)* (Oxon, UK: Edition HH, Ltd, 2006).

——, "The Concerto Allegro in the Early Eighteenth Century," *Music & Letters* 52 (1971): 8–18 and 159–72.

——, "The Italian Concerto in the Late Seventeenth and Early Eighteenth Centuries," in *The Cambridge Companion to the Concerto*, ed. Simon Keefe (Cambridge, UK, and New York: Cambridge University Press, 2005), 35–52.

——, "The Taiheg, the Pira and Other Curiosities of Benedetto Vinaccesi's 'Suonate da camera a tre', Op. I," *Music & Letters* 75 (1994): 344–64.

Thompson, Margaret, "For Dancing or Diversion: G. B. Vitali's Chamber Sonatas," in *Liber amicorum John Steele: A Musicological Tribute*, ed. Warren Drake Stuyvesant, NY: Pendragon Press, 1997), 337–55.

Tilmouth, Michael, "Music and British Travellers Abroad," in *Source Materials and the Interpretation of Music: A Memorial Volume to Thurston Dart*, ed. Ian Bent (London: Stainer & Bell, 1981), 357–82.

Torchi, Luigi, ed., *L'arte musicale in Italia*, 7 vols (Milan: Ricordi, 1897).

Vanscheeuwijck, Marc, "Musical Performance at San Petronio in Bologna: A Brief History," *Performance Practice Review* 8 (1995): 73–82.

——, Preface to *Domenico Gabrielli, Ricercari per violoncello solo, Canone a due violoncelli, Sonate per violoncello e basso continuo* (Bologna: Forni, 1998).

——, Preface to *Giuseppe Maria Jacchini, Sonate a violino e violoncello e a violoncello solo per camera* (Bologna: Forni, 2001).

——, *The Cappella Musicale of San Petronio in Bologna under Giovanni Paolo Colonna (1674–1695)* (Brussels and Rome: Institut Historique Belge de Rome, 2003).

Vatielli, Francesco, *Arte e vita musicale a Bologna* (Bologna: Zanichelli, 1927; facsimile, Bologna: Forni, 1969).

——, "Il Corelli e i maestri bolognesi del suo tempo," *Rivista musicologica italiana* 23 (1916): 173–200 and 390–412.

Vitali, Carlo, "Giovanni Battista Vitali editore di musica fra realizzazione artistica e insuccesso imprenditoriale," *Nuova rivista musicale italiana* 27 (1993): 359–74.

——, "Giovanni Paolo Colonna maestro di cappella dell'Oratorio Filippino in Bologna: contributi bio-bibliografici," *Rivista italiana di musicologia* 14 (1979): 128–54.

——, "L'opera III di Corelli nella diffusione manoscritta," in *Nuovissimi studi corelliani*, ed. Sergio Durante and Pierluigi Petrobelli (Florence: Olschki, 1982), 367–80.

Watts, Sanford E., "The Stylistic Features of the Bolognese Concerto," Ph.D. dissertation, Indiana University, 1964.

Zaslaw, Neal, "When is an Orchestra Not an Orchestra?," *Early Music* 16 (1988): 483–95.

Index